CHRISTIANITY AND NATURAL LAW

Historically, natural law has played a pivotal role in Christian approaches to the law and a contested role in legal philosophy generally. However, comparative study of natural law across global Christian traditions is largely neglected. This book provides not only the history of natural law ideas across mainstream Christian traditions worldwide but also an ecumenical comparison of the contemporary natural law positions of different traditions. Its focus is not solely theoretical: it tests the practical utility of natural law by exploring its use in the legal systems of the churches studied. Alongside analysis of the assumptions underlying the concept, it also proposes a jurisprudence of Christian law itself. With chapters written by distinguished lawyers and theologians across the world, this book is designed for those studying and teaching law or theology, those who practise and study ecumenism and those involved in the practice of church law.

Norman Doe is a professor and director of the LLM in Canon Law at Cardiff University Law School. He is also a visiting professor at Paris University and KU Leuven and Chancellor of the Diocese of Bangor. His books include *Fundamental Authority in Late Medieval English Law* (1990), *Canon Law in the Anglican Communion* (1998), *Law and Religion in Europe* (2011) and *Christian Law* (2013).

LAW AND CHRISTIANITY

The Law and Christianity series publishes cutting-edge work on Catholic, Protestant, and Orthodox Christian contributions to public, private, penal, and procedural law and legal theory. The series aims to promote deep Christian reflection by leading scholars on the fundamentals of law and politics, to build further ecumenical legal understanding across Christian denominations, and to link and amplify the diverse and sometimes isolated Christian legal voices and visions at work in the academy. Works collected by the series include groundbreaking monographs, historical and thematic anthologies, and translations by leading scholars around the globe.

Books in the Series

Calvin's Political Theology and the Public Engagement of the Church Matthew J. Tuininga
God and the Secular Legal System Rafael Domingo
How Marriage Became One of the Sacraments Philip Reynolds
Christianity and Freedom edited by Timothy Samuel Shah and Allen D. Hertzke
The Distinctiveness of Religion in American Law Kathleen A. Brady
Pope Benedict XVI's Legal Thought Marta Cartabia and Andrea Simoncini
The Western Case for Monogamy over Polygamy John Witte
Great Christian Jurists in English History R.H. Helmholz and Mark Hill QC
Agape, Justice, and Law Robert F. Cochran and Zachary R. Calo
Christianity and Natural Law: An Introduction edited by Norman Doe

Christianity and Natural Law

AN INTRODUCTION

EDITED BY
NORMAN DOE
Cardiff University

CAMBRIDGE
UNIVERSITY PRESS

CAMBRIDGE
UNIVERSITY PRESS

University Printing House, Cambridge CB2 8BS, United Kingdom

One Liberty Plaza, 20th Floor, New York, NY 10006, USA

477 Williamstown Road, Port Melbourne, VIC 3207, Australia

314-321, 3rd Floor, Plot 3, Splendor Forum, Jasola District Centre, New Delhi - 110025, India

79 Anson Road, #06-04/06, Singapore 079906

Cambridge University Press is part of the University of Cambridge.

It furthers the University's mission by disseminating knowledge in the pursuit of education, learning and research at the highest international levels of excellence.

www.cambridge.org
Information on this title: www.cambridge.org/9781107186446
DOI: 10.1017/9781316890615

First published 2017

A catalogue record for this publication is available from the British Library

ISBN 978-1-107-18644-6 Hardback
ISBN 978-1-316-63721-0 Paperback

Contents

Contributors

Will Adam is the Archbishop of Canterbury's Ecumenical Adviser, the editor of the *Ecclesiastical Law Journal* (published by Cambridge University Press) and the author of *Legal Flexibility and the Mission of the Church: Dispensation and Economy in Ecclesiastical Law* (Ashgate, 2011), a book based on his doctoral research in canon law. He is a research fellow at the Centre for Law and Religion at Cardiff University, and a fellow of the Royal Historical Society.

Owen Anderson is an associate professor of philosophy and religious studies at Arizona State University's New College. In 2013–2014, he was the William E. Simon research fellow in the James Madison Program at Princeton University and a visiting scholar at Princeton Seminary. He has published seven books including *The Declaration of Independence and God* (2015) and *The Natural Moral Law* (2013) with Cambridge University Press. His areas of research include epistemology, the ethics of belief, intellectual history and religious pluralism. A central focus of his research has been the clarity of God's existence. He regularly teaches philosophy of religion, introduction to philosophy, applied ethics, world religions, western religious traditions and religion in America.

Paul Babie holds a chair of law in the Adelaide Law School of the University of Adelaide. He is currently Associate Dean of Law (Research) of the Adelaide Law School, Associate Dean (Research) of the Faculty of the Professions and Director of the Research Unit for the Study of Society, Law and Religion. His primary research interests are legal theory (especially the nature and concept of property and the relationship between law and theology), and law and religion (especially the relationship between constitutions and religious freedom). He has published widely in both fields. He teaches property law, property theory, law and religion and Roman law. He is also a member of the editorial board of the Routledge Research Series in Law and Religion.

Helen Costigane, a member of the Society of the Holy Child Jesus, is the former vice-principal (academic) of Heythrop College, in the University of London, where she taught canon law, Christian ethics and pastoral theology, and is now Programme

Director, MA Theology, at St. Mary's University, Twickenham. She is a member of the Canon Law Societies of Great Britain and Ireland, America and Australia, as well as the Ecclesiastical Law Society. Being also a chartered accountant, she has a particular interest in the civil and canonical aspects of ecclesiastical goods, and the interface between Catholic canon law and civil law generally.

Norman Doe is a professor and director of the Centre for Law and Religion at Cardiff University Law School. A barrister, he studied at Cardiff, Cambridge and Oxford universities. His books include studies on medieval law, Anglican canon law, law and religion in Europe and Christian law. A visiting professor at Paris University and KU Leuven, he has acted as a consultant on canon law to the Anglican Communion, served on the Lambeth Commission (2003–2004), was a visiting scholar at Trinity College Oxford (2011) and Corpus Christi College Oxford (2015) and is Chancellor of the Diocese of Bangor in the Church in Wales.

Paul Goodliff is a Baptist minister, currently serving as the minister of Abingdon Baptist Church, Oxfordshire, and a theologian. He is a visiting lecturer at the University of Roehampton, Regent's Park College, in the University of Oxford and Bristol Baptist College, and he is also an associate research fellow at Spurgeon's College, London. He has published in the areas of pastoral theology and ecclesiology, and has served as both general superintendent of the Baptist Union of Great Britain's Central Area and as head of ministry for the same union.

John A. Harrod graduated from London University in sociology before reading theology at Cambridge University while preparing for the ministry of the Methodist church at Wesley House. He later gained a doctorate from Manchester University in moral philosophy. After some fifteen years in pastoral ministry he spent the rest of his working life in theological education, latterly as principal of Hartley Victoria College, the Methodist foundation within the ecumenical Partnership for Theological Education in Manchester. His principal publication is *Weaving the Tapestry of Moral Judgement: Christian Ethics in a Plural World* (Epworth, 2007). Now retired and living in Cornwall he is married with a grown-up son and daughter and five grandchildren.

Richard H. Helmholz is Ruth Wyatt Rosenson Distinguished Professor of Law at the University of Chicago, a fellow of the American Academy of Arts and Sciences and a corresponding fellow of the British Academy. His publications include *Roman Canon Law in Reformation England* (Cambridge University Press, 1990) and *The Canon and Ecclesiastical Jurisdiction from 597 to the 1640s* (Oxford University Press, 2004). He is a member of the editorial board of the Ecclesiastical Law Journal (Cambridge University Press).

Dr Leo J. Koffeman (1948) serves as an extraordinary professor in the Department of Church History and Church Polity of the University of Pretoria (South Africa). He is a minister of the Protestant Church in the Netherlands. In September 2015, he retired as professor of church polity and ecumenism at the Protestant Theological University (Amsterdam, The Netherlands). From 2007 to 2014, he was a member of the Faith and Order Commission of the World Council of Churches. His main publication so far is *In Order to Serve: An Ecumenical Introduction to Church Polity* (Zürich: LIT Verlag, 2014).

Antti Raunio is a professor of systematic theology at the School of Theology in the Philosophical Faculty at the University of Eastern Finland at Joensuu, Finland. He has published widely in the fields of Reformation theology and its Patristic and medieval background; Luther's theology and its interpretations; social ethics; the theology of spirituality; and ecumenical theology. He also has an interest in theological hermeneutics, and relations between theology and natural science. His hobbies include literature, music and European classic cars.

Russell Sandberg is Head of Law and Reader in Law in the School of Law and Politics at Cardiff University where he researches at the Centre for Law and Religion. He is the author of *Law and Religion* (Cambridge University Press, 2011) and *Religion, Law and Society* (Cambridge University Press, 2014). He is a co-author of *Religion and Law in the United Kingdom* (Kluwer Law International, 2nd edn, 2014) and editor of *Religion and Legal Pluralism* (Ashgate, 2015). He is also the managing editor of the International Consortium for Law and Religion Studies (ICLARS) Series on Law and Religion, published by Routledge.

Mary Anne Plaatjies Van Huffel is a professor who teaches ecclesiology and church polity at the University of Stellenbosch in South Africa. Her major publications deal with the empowerment of women in post-apartheid South Africa, a post-structural approach; the control, secession and vesting of rights with regard to ecclesiastical property; the institutionalization of Christian women's organizations, from docile recipients to agents of change; the Belhar Confession, a Christian statement of belief originally written in Afrikaans in 1982, during the struggle against apartheid, and adopted (after a slight adjustment) by the Dutch Reformed Mission Church in South Africa in 1986; a theological reflection on patriarchy as empire; and the relevance of the principles of church polity in the Reformed tradition.

Preface

Natural law thinking provides a valuable but much-contested conceptual framework within which to address questions fundamental to human well-being: What is good? Why is good important? How do we ascertain good? These questions have themselves stimulated diachronic and synchronic diversity within Christianity across its plurality of traditions. In point of fact, the return to first principles about the good in human and Christian life is increasingly important to the ecumenical movement today, as it seeks to achieve greater visible unity between the institutionally separated churches of the faith worldwide. The World Council of Churches, in a document which has taken twenty-five years to prepare, entitled *The Church: Towards a Common Vision* (2013), states: 'Ecumenical dialogue at the multilateral and bilateral levels has begun to sketch out some of the parameters of the significance of moral doctrine and practice for Christian unity'; moreover: 'If present and future ecumenical dialogue is to serve the mission and unity of the Church, it is important that this dialogue explicitly address the challenges to convergence represented by contemporary moral issues.'[1] However, natural law thinking has not traditionally been used by the ecumenical movement or in bilateral inter-church dialogues on moral issues. This book, therefore, is designed to explore the opportunities and challenges which natural law thinking presents for Christians, across the various denominational divides, in order for them to re-imagine together a conceptual framework for moral thought and practice. It seeks to add some colour to this 'sketch' in terms of denominational convergence and divergence in natural law thinking amongst selected Christian traditions across the world today, and so put natural law on the ecumenical agenda in the quest for unity around contemporary moral issues.

In January 2015, Professor John Witte, the distinguished editor-in-chief of the Cambridge University Press series *Christianity and Law*, invited me to serve as editor for the series of an introduction to Christianity and natural law. I have been

[1] World Council of Churches, *The Church: Towards a Common Vision*, Faith and Order Paper No. 214 (Geneva, 2013), paragraph 63.

honoured to do so. The series, with its international editorial board, is an ambitious one. No less so this volume, not least due to the fact that the concept of natural law, and natural law thinking in general, with its associated concepts such as divine law, justice and equity, have proved both an inspiration and a bone of contention in Christianity through the ages. This was the case in post-apostolic times and in the medieval period, persisted through and beyond the Reformation and the Enlightenment, and the concept of natural law continues to exercise contemporary Christianity in the modern world – as Christians, configured in their institutional churches across the great church traditions, face, reflect upon and grapple with so many fast-moving ethical, political and social issues today.

The term 'natural law' is used for a variety of doctrines which are often contested and differ in detail. In Christianity, natural law discourse concerns, at its core, the existence of God-given universal principles which God 'revealed' to humankind at creation. This original revelation has to do with what it means to be human and is related, therefore, to the social character of human nature and life. It may be contrasted with the 'special' revelation of God in Christ which is about our relation with God, the perfection of natural law and, ultimately, salvation. With natural law, a form of divine law, God implanted in the minds or hearts of every human the capacity to know right and wrong and thus to discern these universal principles, which are normative, which provide moral standards, or ethical constraints on human behaviour, and which determine what actions are right and wrong. These standards are applicable to all humans, discoverable through the use of reason and the exercise of conscience, and should be used as a source of and criterion to assess the legitimacy of action. Views of what natural law contains vary widely and often depend on prior ideas about 'nature', and perhaps the physical laws of cause and effect – natural law is its order or the sphere of rationality; and so natural law is rational law deducible from rational principles. As we shall see in this book, natural law theory is criticised for a host of reasons: that it proceeds from facts to normativity; how it may be seen as a species of divine law; and that its precepts of love for God and neighbour are too diffuse to be of practical value.

This volume consists of twelve chapters written by expert contributors with international reputations in the fields of law, theology and philosophy. The first chapter traces the concept of natural law in the development of canon law in the western church, focussing primarily on its use by the jurists in the medieval period, the pervasiveness of the concept and its deployment in technical juridical settings. Natural law was part of the staple diet of medieval jurists. Then follow seven chapters which are devoted to a study of natural law as it is and has been addressed in different Christian traditions or church families worldwide, namely: Catholic, Orthodox, Anglican, Lutheran, Methodist, Reformed and Baptist.[2] These traditions are

[2] The choice of these traditions does not imply any claim as to what is or is not 'orthodox' in Christianity. Nor does it seek to foreclose debate about natural law in other worldwide ecclesial families distinct from these particular denominational categories. This book is introductory; space does not allow an

selected for three reasons: they all have a global reach; they all have a strong tradition of theological reflection; and they all have a very distinctive juristic culture of positive ecclesial norms found in a multiplicity of juridical instruments the classification of which depends on the tradition in question – from canon law, through books of church order, to covenants of church polity, from the Episcopal model through to the Congregational model. This book, for the first time, offers a comparative approach to the incidence of natural law thinking in contemporary church legal instruments. Whilst there is much which these different Christian traditions share as between themselves, what also emerges is that there is at the same time diversity of opinion about natural law within each tradition – even within a tradition there are varieties of natural law thinking.

To prepare their studies for the volume, each contributor, from these church families, was encouraged to think freely about what or what not to include in their chapter. These scholars were also chosen as they represent a blend of disciplines, again, including theology and law. They all hold, or have held, academic positions. Yet at the same time several are directly familiar with the practice of institutional church life within their own tradition – particularly in ministry, and governance – and some have direct experience of ecumenical initiatives. A further consideration was to achieve as global a scholarly reach as possible: the contributors are drawn from Australia, England, Finland, Scotland, South Africa, The Netherlands, USA, and Wales.

Each contributor was asked to be guided by a number of core issues. First, there is the matter of how 'natural law' is defined within each tradition: what definitions exist, if any; where these definitions are to be found and who formulated them (for example, in church doctrine or law); and to what extent there is (dis)agreement or debate in the tradition about the definition of 'natural law'. Secondly, the contributors were asked to explore what if any the relationship might be in their own tradition between 'natural law' and the categories of 'divine law', or the 'law of God', and the 'moral law': whether natural law and these other categories are understood as the same, similar, or different entities, and the reasons for this; what is understood to be the purpose of natural law (and these other categories), its form (whether it is treated as prescriptive, with values, precepts, prohibitions, and permissions), and its subjects (those to whom it applies). Third, there are questions about the discovery of natural law and its content: where natural law is to be found; how it is ascertained (such as through revelation, reason, instinct, and ethics); and who has authority in the tradition to expound it. Fourthly, the contributors were asked to explore the role of scholarship on natural law thinking within the tradition: who were, and are, the leading thinkers; what methodology is employed; and what role the Bible plays in their approaches to natural law. Fifthly, there is the question of natural law in actual

exhaustive study. Indeed, it is hoped the book will encourage exploration of natural law thinking in global church families beyond those studied here.

Christian practice: how, in each tradition, natural law (and the associated categories of divine law, the law of God, and the moral law) is deployed (explicitly or implicitly) in the regulatory instruments of each institutional church (their systems of church law, church order, and church polity); whether it is used, as a determinant, by church legislators (in the legislative process and text), adjudicators (such as in the decisions of tribunals), and administrators; and how it is related to humanly-created norms of conduct – for example, whether it is understood to have an authority superior to positive law found in the books of church law, order and polity, such as to vitiate laws which are contrary to it, or the positive law of the State, and the implications of this for the enforceability of and obedience to law. Throughout, each contributor was asked to illustrate with examples of the use of natural law ideas in areas such as church governance and ministry, doctrine, worship, and rites, the administration of property, and relations with the State (whether each tradition teaches about respect for natural law by the State in its own exercise of power).

By way of contrast, there are three chapters on the concept of natural law as it is used beyond the individual traditions, and their institutional churches. One seeks to describe, explain, and evaluate the role of natural law thought and practice in the global ecumenical movement, particularly in bilateral and multilateral ecumenical initiatives involving two or more institutional churches from different Christian traditions, and in the work of the World Council of Churches. Another explores the role of natural law in Judaism and Islam as compared with Christianity – and the potential of natural law in inter-faith dialogue. The third explores philosophical presuppositions which underpin natural law discourse, how the framework provided by natural law enables us to engage in the most basic of questions about human social life, and what part natural law may have to play in the development of the conceptual foundations of law. The book ends with a chapter of reflection; it is an overview: which discusses how the Christian approaches studied compare with the treatment of natural law as it appears in contemporary secular legal theory and jurisprudence; which draws together commonalities and divergences in the approaches of the traditions with regard to the themes explored in each chapter; and which proposes an agenda for further collaborative research in this field around Christian jurisprudence. Throughout the book, being an Introduction to Christianity and Natural Law, the chapters are lightly footnoted, sign-posted with sub-headings, and, it is hoped, in their style, accessible.

In September 2015, a roundtable was held at Trinity College, Oxford. It was attended by the contributors who presented their draft chapters, engaged in discussion of the themes, and explored avenues for the further development of their individual contributions. We were very privileged also to have welcomed to the roundtable Professor Mark Hill QC, a leading scholar and practitioner in law and religion, and the Reverend James Campbell SJ, Vice-Principal and Tutor in Canon Law at Campion Hall at the University of Oxford. Both provided invaluable insights to the discussions ensuring that due respect was paid to the need to earth what otherwise might have proved an excessively abstract exercise, in the practical realities of daily life.

I am very grateful to John Witte for having arranged funding for this event. I am also deeply indebted to the President and Fellows of Trinity College, where I had the good fortune to be a visiting fellow in 2011, for hosting the meeting in such historical surroundings. Indeed, it was fitting that we should meet at Trinity. The college was founded in 1555 (during the time of the re-establishment of Roman Catholicism in England under Mary) and occupies the site of the medieval Durham College founded c. 1286 (and which at the Reformation was surrendered to the crown, in 1545) for Benedictine monks to whom the concept of natural law would have been so very familiar as they pursued their studies in theology and philosophy. John Henry (Cardinal) Newman (1801–1890) was also a student at Trinity; he too invoked the concept of natural law:

> I say, then, that the Supreme Being is of a certain character, which, expressed in human language, we call ethical. He has the attributes of justice, truth, wisdom, sanctity, benevolence and mercy, as eternal characteristics in His nature, the very Law of His being, identical with Himself; and next, when He became Creator, He implanted this Law, which is Himself, in the intelligence of all His rational creatures. The Divine Law, then, is the rule of ethical truth, the standard of right and wrong, a sovereign, irreversible, absolute authority in the presence of men and Angels.

Moreover, and in turn (citing Aquinas):

> The natural law . . . is an impression of the Divine Light in us, a participation of the eternal law in the rational creature. This law, as apprehended in the minds of individual men, is called 'conscience'; and though it may suffer refraction in passing into the intellectual medium of each, it is not therefore so affected as to lose its character of being the Divine Law, but still has, as such, the prerogative of commanding obedience.[3]

A key question posed by this introduction to Christianity and natural law, is what relevance views such as this – and those of the many historical and contemporary theologians, lawyers, and other scholars across the ecclesiastical traditions treated in this volume – about the meaning and value of natural law, and the use of natural law thinking in the practical world of church polity, have for Christians and their laws today. I am most grateful to each of the contributors, the insights they bring, and the hard work they have done, in enabling us to reflect on this important subject. Any editorial errors in this collection of studies are solely my responsibility.

3 John Henry Cardinal Newman, 'A Letter Addressed to the Duke of Norfolk on Occasion of Mr. Gladstone's Recent Expostulation [1874]', in *Certain Difficulties Felt by Anglicans in Catholic Teaching*, Vol. II (London: Longmans, Green, and Co., New Impression, 1900), 246–247.

1

Natural Law and Christianity

A Brief History

R.H. Helmholz

This introductory chapter assesses the extent to which history sheds any light on the character of Christianity's connection with natural law. Its conclusions are based on propositions drawn from the works of representative European jurists who lived and wrote between 1140 and 1650, particularly those jurists who dealt primarily with the canon law. Their treatises and judicial decisions provide repeated and telling examples of the ways in which Christian theology came into contact with natural law. Their understanding of the nature of the *ius divinum* also came into the picture. The chapter begins, however, with a brief exposition of two current but opposing theories about the relationship between Christianity and natural law.

THE RELATIONSHIP BETWEEN CHRISTIANITY AND NATURAL LAW

One theory which occupies a place in modern scholarship is that there is a necessary connection between natural law and traditional forms of the Christian religion. The other theory proposes that this is not the case. Both theories purport to find support in the historical record.

Arguments Pro: The Association of Natural Law with Christianity

It requires no prolonged effort to demonstrate that the prevailing view among scholars active today associates natural law with traditional forms of Christianity. Brian Bix's useful *Dictionary of Legal Theory*, for instance, links 'modern legal theorists identified (or self-identified) as natural law theorists' with 'the tradition established by the work of [St. Thomas] Aquinas'.[1] If Aquinas was indeed the leading light in formulating the tenets of natural law as they were understood and applied in European history, its essentially religious character follows almost as a matter of course.

Confirmation of the existence of a necessary connection between Christianity and natural law is not wanting in other evidence from today. Students of Catholic social

[1] Brian Bix, *Dictionary of Legal Theory* (Oxford: Oxford University Press, 2004), 144.

thought make a close connection between their subject and the teachings found within the natural law tradition, and again it is Thomas Aquinas, a thirteenth-century Christian theologian, who they take to have most authoritatively stated the tenets of natural law. More often than not, it is a conclusion found in Aquinas' work around which these modern formulations of natural law revolve.[2] Seeing a close tie between the tenets of natural law and the Christian religion described by St Thomas, as they do, therefore seems axiomatic. Not only is this view widely shared today, but Aquinas himself may be read as having endorsed it. He held that '[a]ll rational creatures share in and make their own the eternal reason through which they have a natural inclination to due acts and purposes, [and] this sharing is what we call natural law'.[3]

This historical connection between traditional Christianity and natural law seems even more firmly entrenched outside the realm of jurisprudential theory. Those among us who remember the efforts of Roman Catholic bishops to hold back the flood tide of contraception sixty years ago will also recall that their efforts were based in part upon dictates they derived from natural law. The close association they made between religion and natural law remains imprinted on the popular mind. It has surfaced again in more recent days as an argument against the introduction of same-sex marriage. Opponents say that it is not just the Bible that condemns the experiment. Natural law does too.

Furthermore, the association between natural law and the Christian religion has captured the minds of most modern jurists who deny the existence of natural law. They reject both, regarding them as something like equal partners. And here too, the historical record seems to support them. The connection between Christianity and natural law is something that lawyers who first discarded natural law in favour of legal positivism took for granted. Supreme Court Justice Oliver Wendell Holmes is the great American example. Disdaining any conception of law that appeared to him to be 'a brooding omnipresence in the sky', Holmes turned instead to a hard form of legal positivism. 'The jurists who believe in natural law,' he wrote, 'seem to me to be in that naïve state of mind that accepts what has been familiar and accepted by them and their neighbors as something that must be accepted by all men everywhere.'[4] For him, as for John Austin, the will of the sovereign expressed in statutes and judicial decisions fully defined the law's content. Legal theory was at best a prediction of what judges would do in fact, not an attempt to put natural law into practice. Rejection of natural law has thus gone hand in hand with rejection of anything specifically associated with the Christian religion as a factor in the law's

[2] E.g. Heinrich Rommen, *The Natural Law: A Study in Legal and Social History and Philosophy*, T.R. Hanley, trans. (Indianapolis, IN: Liberty Fund, 1999), 108. They do not end there, of course.

[3] *Summa theologiae*, I.II.91.2.

[4] O.W. Holmes, 'Natural Law', in *Collected Legal Papers* (New York: Harcourt, Brace and Howe, 1920, repr. 1952), 312. See also John Chipman Gray, *The Nature and Sources of the Law*, 2nd edn (Cambridge, MA: Harvard University Press, 1921), 309: natural law is described as 'this exploded superstition'.

present development. As a working assumption, this position can be said to govern mainstream legal thought today. In it, a close tie between natural law and traditional religion appears both self-evident and pernicious.

Arguments Con: The Disjunction of Natural Law and Christianity

But it is not as simple as this. Were he alive today, Thomas Aquinas himself might have begun by an opening sentence endorsing the modern opinion, something like 'It seems that natural law finds its origins in the Christian religion.' He might even have quoted some of the evidence just stated. But take note. He would not have stopped there. His very next sentence would have undermined this initial conclusion. It would have shown its falsity. He might have added: 'But to the contrary, a gloss on the text of St. Paul's letter to the Romans asserts that the Gentiles, who know not the true God, nevertheless act according to natural law.'[5] In other words, Aquinas himself would have gone on to add his own conclusion, one that showed the opening conclusion to be false. It could not be correct upon fuller consideration, precisely because all men and women, not just Christians, were governed by natural law.

And this, as I take it, has always been the most widely accepted view among writers about natural law. To them, there is no required connection between natural law and the Christian religion. That conclusion actually follows from what Aquinas himself taught. If all rational creatures have a natural inclination to shape their conduct according to rules drawn from natural law, it must follow that acceptance of the tenets of the Christian religion is not a necessary part of understanding the import of natural law. All men and women do not follow the Christian religion, but all are subject to natural law. The modern equation of religion with natural law is therefore false.

That conclusion would also have been heard and accepted by all students of the *ius commune* during the Middle Ages and through the age of the Enlightenment. It was placed at the outset of the Roman law's Institutes, as it also was in the Digest. Most famously, the Roman jurist Ulpian (d. 228) held that natural law was something that 'nature itself has taught to all animals' (Digest, 1.1.3), and what he wrote was stated and repeated in lectures at the very outset of every lawyer's education. Not a Christian, Ulpian mentioned no source of this teaching apart from nature itself, and he asserted that by some form of instinct even brute animals shared a measure of the knowledge of natural law. No religion there.

What Ulpian taught was echoed in the common learning of later centuries. For example, the famous thirteenth-century jurist Azo (c. 1150–1230) taught the identical lesson to his readers and students, although he also added 'God' to 'Nature' as the ultimate source of the knowledge of animals.[6] In fact he equated the two. Was this to

[5] See *Summa theologiae*, I.II.91.2.

[6] Azo, *Summa Institutionum* (n.p. 1533), Bk. I, tit. De iure naturali gentium et civili, no. 1: 'ius naturale est quod natura id est ipse Deus docuit omnia animalia.'

change the common understanding of natural law's character or of its source? No, as modern scholarship has shown. It made no difference.[7] In whatever ways natural law had first come into existence, it governed a significant part of the behaviour of all creatures, human beings and animals alike. That was the *communis opinio* among the jurists. It made no reference to Christianity.

This disjunction between natural law and the Christian religion was also the subject of an oft-quoted assertion by Hugo Grotius (d. 1645), the great natural lawyer. In the introduction to *De iure belli ac pacis* (1625), he wrote that 'a degree of validity' would exist in his conclusions 'even if we should concede that which cannot be conceded without the utmost wickedness, that there is no God, or that the affairs of men are of no concern to Him'.[8] Grotius surely meant this to stand as a strong statement of natural law's necessary place in all life, not as an invitation to atheism. Nevertheless, his words have sometimes been taken as a significant step in separating the realms of religion and law. A representative commentator has used it to assert that '[o]ne of [Grotius'] great achievements was to secularise natural law by detaching it from Christianity'.[9] This claims too much. An identical conclusion had been accepted among the so-called Second Scholastics in Spain, writers like Francisco de Vitoria (d. 1546) and Francisco Suárez (d. 1617), whose ties to religion were close. In fact, Grotius' statement merely restated in dramatic language something that had always been inherent in natural law thought. Jurists writing within the traditions of natural law in past centuries had never supposed that there was a perfect match between the teachings of the Christian religion and the tenets of natural law.

CHRISTIANITY IN NATURAL LAW JURISPRUDENCE

If the historical match between religion and natural law was not perfect, there was nevertheless a decided factual link between them. The link is readily apparent once one leaves the world of theory and enters into concrete legal questions. There, the two were not kept apart. They shared many features, and in practice they were usually identical in their consequences. This made sense. Both had their source in God's will. It is true that natural law was thought to extend beyond the bounds set by the Christian religion. It reached even animals, not just human beings. It also governed all men and women, not just Christians. However, it did not on this account exclude Christians. Quite the contrary. It embraced them. It gave them a head start. It had a direct impact on the law by which they were governed, so that in practice if not in theory the Christian religion long played a significant role in the working out of what natural law required. Making a connection between the two was

7 Brian Tierney, '*Natura id est Deus*: A Case of Juristic Pantheism?', *Journal of the History of Ideas* 24 (1963): 307–322.

8 *De iure belli ac pacis*, Proleg. no. 11.

9 Randall Lesaffer, *European Legal History: A Cultural and Political Perspective*, Jan Arriens, trans. (Cambridge: Cambridge University Press, 2009), 448.

easy; to all appearances it was all but inevitable in the historical conditions that existed in earlier centuries.

Statements and examples making the connection can be found in one treatise after another. Consider, for example, the following statement about the connection between law and religion. It was made by Thomas Rutherforth (d. 1771). He served as Regius Professor of Divinity in Cambridge University and was the author of a work drawn from his lectures which he called *Institutes of Natural Law* (1754–1756):

> The existence of a God is written throughout every part of nature in such legible characters; and the duty of honouring him is so plain to every capacity; that they who disbelieve his existence, or deny him that honour which is due to him, cannot but be understood to offend against the clearest precepts of the law of nature: they must be willfully blind if they do not see their duty, and perversely criminal if they do not practice it.[10]

Rutherforth would perhaps have admitted the existence of a theoretical divide between natural law and the Christian religion. They were not identical. In fact, however, he found it an easy divide to cross. There were many bridges. Only the 'willfully blind' would not make the journey. For purposes of convenience and analysis, I have divided the places where natural law and religion commonly intersected in the law into three categories. They are as follows: (1) Natural Law and the Bible, (2) Natural Law and the Canon Law and (3) Natural Law and Legal Problems.

Before coming to these subjects, however, one obvious but relevant factual point about the subject should be stated. It is that many of the most influential natural lawyers were in fact theologians, clerics or apologists for the Christian religion. Not all, of course. Some were mere lawyers. But many more writers on natural law were connected professionally with the promotion of religion. Of those mentioned so far, Thomas Aquinas was a Dominican friar, Hugo Grotius was author of a book entitled *On the Truth of the Christian Religion*, Francisco de Vitoria was a Dominican friar, Francisco Suárez was a Jesuit and Thomas Rutherforth was archdeacon of Essex. That these writers on natural law should have been interested in the Christian religion, finding it relevant to their own understanding of law and jurisprudence, is hardly surprising. They were servants of the author of natural law. It was fitting therefore, perhaps even inevitable, that these men should have made explicit connections between natural law and its author.

Natural Law and the Bible

The normal starting point for making these connections was the Christian Bible. That fact is of particular importance today because of the ecumenical perspective taken in this volume. One of the reasons that acceptance of natural law's place in

10 *Institutes*, Second American Edition Revised (Baltimore, 1832), Bk. I, c. 18 no. 9.

human life was shared by Christians of many stripes was that the Scriptures endorsed it. Whatever may be the case today and whatever may have been the disagreements then, historically its importance was not one of the issues that divided Protestants from Catholics. Biblical passages appear in most academic tracts on natural law, no matter the writer's religious affiliation. This common recognition was not without scriptural justification. The Old Testament affirms that God had said, 'I will put my law in their inward parts and write it in their hearts' (Jeremiah 31.33). The Psalmist proclaimed that he would 'delight to do thy will, O my God: Yea, thy law is within my heart' (Psalm 40.8). The Book of Isaiah recorded that God had promised salvation to those who kept his law (Isaiah 56.1). The New Testament also affirms the truth of the assertion that among God's creations the law of nature occupied a vital place. Speaking of his chosen people, God had declared, 'I will put my laws into their hearts, and in their minds will I write them, and their sins and iniquities will I remember no more' (Hebrews 10.16–17). What could these passages refer to but to a law meant to guide human conduct? That described the natural law's own purpose.

The contents of the Ten Commandments were an oft-cited illustration of natural law's close connection with Christianity. Moses had written the Commandments down as they had been revealed to him by God (Exodus 34.28). The jurists understood them as stating some of the principles of natural law. 'Thou shalt not kill' was one obvious example. 'Honour thy father and mother' was another. These were commands of God, stated in the Scriptures. In that sense they were parts of the divine law, particularly applicable to Jews and to Christians. They were also among the principles that God had inscribed in the hearts of all peoples, no matter their religion. But that they appeared in the Christian Scriptures gave further and particular reason for their observance and their close tie to the Christian religion.

The Ten Commandments were stated in general terms, of course, and they were subject to reasonable exceptions under the positive law, as were most of the principles of natural law. But as statements of principle, they did not change from one age to another or from one place to another, and they were not without force in the law applied in practice. An example was the Ten Commandments' prohibition against bearing false witness. It expressed one of natural law's principles. The proper task of the positive or municipal law was to put it into concrete form: making perjury a crime, ruling out the testimony of witnesses who had lied and perhaps even preventing enforcement of contracts tainted by one party's deceit. These instances were regarded as expressions of the commandment's larger intent. It was also found repeatedly in the Scriptures (e.g. Proverbs 16.19; Matthew 26.60). The intent was to provide guidance, ensuring that human law worked to secure fidelity to the aims of justice and the common good. Positive law might do this in various ways – that is one reason that different systems of positive law existed in the world – but the permissible ways were always controlled in scope by this part of natural law, one which God himself had given to men in the ninth of the Ten Commandments.

Such explicit uses of the Scriptures as statements of the natural law do not exhaust the subject. The jurists found natural law principles in many apparently unpromising parts of the Bible. Their use of the story of the expulsion of Adam and Eve from the Garden of Eden was long the textbook example. In it the canonists saw a basic pattern established for human law, one grounded in natural law. To modern readers, what they drew from the biblical account of mankind's earliest days may seem fanciful, if not absurd. But the story was used so often by jurists writing about natural law that we will be substituting our own prejudices for theirs if we dismiss out of hand what they found in the story of the Garden of Eden.

The starting point was God's command to Adam: '[O]f the tree of the knowledge of good and evil, thou shalt not eat' (Genesis 2.17). This statement contained one of the basic principles of what would become an accepted part of natural law: No one should be punished for an action that had not been prohibited and sufficiently defined by the law. God's express prohibition against eating from the tree of knowledge, issued in so many words to the first man, thus served as a model for all human law. It should conform to the principle illustrated by the story. Of course, Adam did eat the fruit of the tree. He disobeyed the command. As a consequence, we read: 'And the Lord God called unto Adam, and said unto him, Where art thou?' (Genesis 3.9). Here Adam was being called to answer for his violation of the very law God had given him. This passage too was read as establishing one of the basic elements of criminal procedure, the necessity of a sufficient citation. Did God not know where Adam was? That could not have been. Then why did God call out to Adam, seemingly pretending that he did not know? The reason was to demonstrate that every defendant must be summoned before he can be lawfully punished. It was a tenet of natural law that no person should be punished or deprived of his basic rights unless he had been summoned and given an adequate opportunity to speak on his own behalf. Under the impact of analytical jurisprudence, making use of this biblical example as its immediate source of reference, natural lawyers established this principle of due process. They treated it as required by the natural law.

It should be added that the Bible did not serve primarily as a handbook of civil rights, as might be said of the example of the need for proper citation prefigured in the Garden of Eden. Sometimes it worked the other way. The Bible contained some harsher lessons connected with, and seemingly even compelled by, both divine and natural law. An illustration is the biblical justification given in support of the medieval church's penal law. Sentences of excommunication – the principal sanction at the disposal of the courts of the church – separated the person sentenced from the sacraments of the church. In its strongest form, excommunication cut that person off from the company of other Christians. In theory, it could have devastating consequences. At least in the minds of the medieval canonists, this strong sanction was no mere human invention. They were necessary parts of the law. Excommunication's existence was based on teachings found in the New Testament. In Matthew 18.17, Jesus himself had directed that a sinning brother who refused to heed the church's voice should be treated as 'a heathen and a publican'. In the first letter of St Paul to the Corinthians, the Apostle had directed his readers to 'deliver to Satan' a man found guilty of serious moral transgressions; believers were 'not to keep company' with such transgressors (1 Corinthians 5.5). Indifference to wrongful conduct was not a lesson taught by natural law. Sometimes punishment was a necessary part of that law.[11] The fate of Adam and Eve also drove home that point. They were not let off with a warning.

Natural Law and the Canon Law

The canon law was the law of the medieval church, and it too was the site of connections between natural law and the Christian religion. Jurists who specialised in its study worked within the traditions of natural law no less than did contemporary theologians or medieval civilians who began with the Roman law. All of them accepted and cited natural law. They held that the canon law sometimes went beyond natural law not simply because the church had a freedom to enact rules of purely positive law. It also did so in the sense that God had added specific commands to which obedience was owed by Christians but not by all peoples. Those specific commands to Christians made up the *ius divinum*, properly speaking. An example was the prohibition against divorce (Matthew 19.9) – part of God's plan for Christians but not part of the natural law. There were always points of intersection, places where the two were identical. However, the overlap between these two fundamental sources of law was never complete. It was for this reason it was necessary to carve out a separate category for divine law, as we see elsewhere in this volume, keeping it separate from natural law.

The classical canon law, properly speaking, was the product of the scholastic revival of the twelfth and thirteenth centuries, although it built upon older traditions. Its formulation followed after the recovery of the texts and the start of the study of the Roman law at Bologna by a century or so. Many good introductions to how these events occurred now exist,[12] and a chapter on the history of the natural law is no place for attempting to improve on them. Let it be enough to say that the canon law consisted of several basic parts. The first was the *Concordia discordantium canonum*, called the *Decretum*, which was compiled by Gratian near to the year 1140. It was a schoolbook that brought together conciliar decrees and other authorities from the first millennium of the church's existence, seeking to state the church's law by reconciling contradictions within it. The second half included the papal decretals

[11] Richard Fraher, 'Preventing Crime in the High Middle Ages: The Medieval Lawyers' Search for Deterrence', in Stanley Chodorow and James Sweeney, eds., *Popes, Teachers and the Canon Law in the Middle Ages: Festschrift for Brian Tierney* (Ithaca, NY: Cornell University Press, 1989), 212–233.

[12] E.g. Wilfried Hartmann and Kenneth Pennington, eds., *The History of Medieval Canon Law in the Classical Period, 1140–1234* (Washington, DC: Catholic University of America Press, 2008); O.F. Robinson, T.D. Fergus and W.M. Gordon, *European Legal History*, 3rd edn (Oxford: Oxford University Press, 2000), 72–90; James A. Brundage, *Medieval Canon Law* (Harlow: Longman, 1995).

assembled by Raymond of Peñaforte for Pope Gregory IX and placed in a separate book called the *Liber extra* (1234), the *Liber sextus* (1298), then a further book of decretals compiled at the behest of Pope Boniface VIII, adding recent conciliar enactments and bringing the church's law up to date. It was completed by several minor collections added to this corpus in the later Middle Ages. Together these collections were called the *Corpus iuris canonici*, just as the Roman law was customarily referred to as the *Corpus iuris civilis*. The collections, together with the glosses that inevitably accompanied the texts themselves and later conciliar and papal decrees, remained the basic law of the Catholic church until the twentieth century.

After the Reformation, the texts of the *Corpus iuris canonici* were used by Protestant lawyers, in spite of the popish origins of its texts – origins that might seem to have rendered them obsolete or suspect. There were Protestants who wished to see them discarded root and branch, but the arguments for their continued use proved stronger. Prohibitions against simony – for example, the buying and selling of spiritual offices – were not held in monopoly by any one branch of the Christian church. Papal decretals could be used to demonstrate the incompatibility of simony with Christian values. They were. Many, perhaps most, of the papal decretals were similarly treated as statements of basic religious values in the centuries following the Reformation even within Protestant circles. English civilians like Thomas Ridley (d. 1629) held that many papal decretals possessed 'the authority of a law in themselves'.[13] Hugo Grotius was not out of line with other Protestant lawyers when he invoked the authority of a decretal of Pope Alexander III (d. 1181) to deal with the question, important in natural law, of the legal force of an oath taken under the constraint of fear.[14] Even Johann Oldendorp (d. 1567), much less given to citation to the law of the church than Grotius, resorted to the Gregorian decretals in dealing with the law of marriage and divorce.[15] To most Protestant lawyers in the late sixteenth and the seventeenth centuries, the origins of statements of rules of law seem often to have mattered less than their contents.

It may be that among the reasons Protestant lawyers accepted the authority of many canonical texts is that all the books of the *Corpus iuris canonici* incorporated references both to the Bible and to natural law. Gratian's *Decretum* begins with a description of natural law taken from Isidore of Seville's *Etymologies*: 'The law of nature is common to all nations, for it exists everywhere as proceeding from an instinct of nature' (D. 1 c. 7). The text goes on to give examples of its contents – the coming together of man and woman, the bringing up of children and the common possession of property are three of them. The *glossa ordinaria* added to the list and also sought to clarify their meaning. So, for instance, although common ownership of all property was part of the law of nature, its reach had everywhere been restricted

[13] *View of the Civile and Ecclesiasticall Law* (Oxford, 1662), Bk. I, c. 5 § 1.

[14] *De iure belli ac pacis*, Bk. II, c. 20, no. 3.

[15] *De sponsalibus*, no. 1, in Oldendorp, *Opera*, Vol. 2 (Basel, 1559, repr. 1966), 757.

by the *ius gentium*. It still existed only in a few areas of the law – the air in the sky and the waters in oceans and rivers. They were *res nullius*. However, common ownership had proved inconvenient for many aspects of human life. Men will not work to produce goods or crops if what they grow can be appropriated at will by strangers. Private ownership of land and chattels must therefore be accepted. It must be protected by human law. In times of scarcity, the original rule did come back into play; rights in private property were subject to a stronger obligation to share when lives were at stake. Then, a law of sociability which preserved human life and allowed it to flourish prevailed. This was common learning of the times. It was a view shared across denominational boundaries. It is only an example, but it may help to explain why it was that Protestant lawyers sometimes turned to the texts of the canon law for authority. Those texts stated and worked out some of the consequences of accepting the authority of natural law.

Any student of the church's law would have met the natural law almost from the first moment of his study. For the canonist, study began with the *Decretum*, which defined the kinds of law that existed, including natural law. Not only would any beginning student find that recognition clearly stated, he would soon have encountered a prominent example of one of natural law's limitations. As just noted, common possession of property remained among the tenets of natural law even though that regime's impact on human life had been restricted in fact. How had this happened? A student might well have asked that obvious question. A common answer then given was that at an early date all men had met together 'in a large plain' in order to effect an organizational change and decided to adopt a move towards property – a possibility that William Blackstone (1723–1780), the great English lawyer, described as 'too wild to be seriously admitted', though he went on to suppose that same result had been reached by an only slightly different route. Acceptance of this institution, he concluded, had been the gradual product of human experience and maturity.[16] An actual meeting may not have occurred, but the same decision had been reached in an equivalent way.

The subsequent books of the *Corpus iuris canonici*, principally the Gregorian decretals and the Sext, would have brought students of the canon law into repeated contact with natural law, although more by its application to specific parts of the church's existing laws than by treatments of the subject speculating on its origins. For the most part, these books contained decisions on specific points of law and procedure made in response to questions brought before the papal court for guidance. Some decisions by great councils of the church were included in the decretals and later books, and most of their content was not jurisprudential in nature. They were examples of its application. The decretals were applied law, most of it being taken from the decisions of actual cases, then brought together and edited to serve as a guide to the church's law. With reason, the contents of the

16 *Commentaries on the Laws of England*, Vol. 1 (1765–1769) 47.

decretals have sometimes been compared with leading cases in the English common law. They came to be more than records of past cases, because they had been taken into the general law of the church promulgated with the authority of the papacy, but they were still examples of how the law, including the natural law, had been applied in specific situations.

Most of what one finds in the decretals relevant to the historical study of natural law thus comes from situations where it had an impact on a specific area of religious law. A significant example of its impact arose within the question of the place of custom within the canon law. This treatment arose out of a query about two customary rules for the division and control of marital property that had been brought before Pope Honorius III (d. 1227). These established customs had the effect of enlarging the husband's ownership rights over property the wife had brought to the marriage, and Honorius took the occasion to declare them invalid as 'abusive' of the legitimate rights of wives (X 1.4.10). Application of the customs might leave the wife penniless. That was contrary to reason and good sense. The custom was therefore invalid. The following decretal, taken from Pope Gregory IX (d. 1241), enlarged on the prior text by stating clearly that all equivalent customs, being contrary to principles of natural law, were not to be followed. Prefigured in Gratian's *Decretum* (D. 1.8.3–5), this principle was one of the general contributions of natural law to the canon law. It provided a measuring stick to determine whether a long-established practice should persist. There were many that did not. As the *glossa ordinaria* to Gregory's decretal put it, 'No custom against the law of nature should prevail, even if all the men of the world were to act on it.'[17] Of course, this was a position the medieval church never succeeded in implementing fully. Not everyone, even among the clergy, agreed entirely on exactly what natural law required. Some 'odious' customs persisted. However, the rule did have some success as a religious principle put into practice. In the law of tithes, which were regarded as reserved for the clergy by God's command, it became the accepted law, one applied in practice, that the obligation to pay some form of tithes could not be abolished even by an immemorial custom of non-payment.

The contents of the decretals were not limited to subjects like the sacraments or the payment of tithes – matters we think of as closely related to religion. The canon law's jurisdiction ranged quite widely over many parts of human life, although normally with a limitation excluding purely temporal matters of the laity. Even with that limitation, a good deal of room was left for coverage of temporal matters, particularly those involving the clergy, and some of the canons invited attention to natural law. A good example is the law of homicide, to which a title of twenty-five separate decretals was placed in the fifth book of the *Liber extra* (X 5.12.1–25). The principal connections between this subject and the law of the church were two: clerics guilty of murder were to be defrocked and laymen guilty of the crime

17 *Gl. ord.* ad X 1.4.11, v. *Naturali iuri*: 'nulla consuetudo praevalet contra ius naturale, etiam si omnes homines de mundo contra facerent.'

were to be disciplined in the penitential forum. It was therefore necessary, or at least appropriate, for the canon law to take up the subject.

The greater part of the twenty-five decretals on the subject of homicide raised no issues related to natural law, but some of them did. Any student of the canon law would have seen the connection. For instance, the decretals made the obvious distinction between intentional and involuntary homicide. This invited attention to the sixth commandment: 'Thou shalt not kill.' It was taken to be a statement of natural law. Were it lawful to disobey this command, society would dissolve in turmoil. In the hands of commentators like Henricus de Segusio (Hostiensis) (d. 1271), the connection to principles of natural law was an evident one to make, and his commentary discussed it briefly but clearly. He also gave the standard exceptions to the commandment, exceptions recognised in natural law; they included the judge acting according to law, the person acting in self-defence and the soldier in a just war.[18] King David did justice in reigning over Israel and was blessed by the Lord even though he may not have observed the Commandments perfectly (1 Chronicles 18.14). Even biblical authority showed that the law of the church should make room for the legitimacy of such defences to the commandment's prohibition against murder. In the common view of the canonists, here the positive canon law tracked natural law principles.

Natural Law and Legal Problems

Treatments like that given to the sixth commandment recurred throughout the literature on the *ius commune*, in particular in the many commentaries on the law that came into existence from the thirteenth century onwards. In them, many practical problems involving both the Christian religion and natural law attracted the attention of generations of lawyers. Perhaps the most obvious examples are the now controversial prohibitions against sodomy and incest. Far from being matters of personal choice or even civil rights, they were condemned as violations of both the Christian religion and natural law. According to the Scriptures, for a man to lie with another man as he lies with a woman was an abomination (Leviticus 18.22), just as were sexual relations with close relatives (Leviticus 18.6). They were also regarded as contrary to natural law, as the common name given to buggery in English law – the 'crime against nature' – long attested. The fate of Sodom and Gemorrah awaited those who committed these crimes (Jude 7). It was the duty of the positive law to punish them, and this happened in fact.

These two offences are also good examples of the relationship between Christianity and natural law. God was the source of both. For him to have included express prohibitions of both in the natural law meant that these prohibitions applied more widely than in Christian lands. They applied everywhere. However, the commands of Scripture brought them home to Christians in a particularly

[18] *Summa aurea* (Venice, 1574) Lib. V, tit. *De homicidio voluntario*, no. 2.

compelling way. Both those commands and natural law required specific enactment in the positive law of Christian lands. And that is what they received. Statutes punishing sodomy are reminders that the tenets of natural law were never identical with evolving notions of human rights. They are also reminders of the effect that natural law principles might have in defining the positive law's contents.

Of such continuing links between Christianity and natural law, the example of usury also provides an illuminating (and more difficult) example. The subject's treatment in the writing of early medieval Christian thinkers had condemned the practice, and it remained the starting place in natural law discussion. Defined in the simplest case as taking back more than had been lent, usury stood condemned in the Old and New Testaments (Deuteronomy 23.10–20, Luke 6.34–35). It was also censured in the clearest of terms within the canonical half of the *ius commune* (X 5.19.4). Regarded as destructive of the sinews of a just society, usury was understood to be contrary to the law of nature. One reason commonly given for this conclusion was that in nature, money, unlike humans and animals, could not generate more money.[19] Coins are sterile. Aristotle himself had so stated, and many medieval jurists applied his analogy to contemporary commercial practice. Roman law had been more flexible on the subject, leaving some room for it (Digest, 22.1.17), but most of the medieval canonists rejected this laxist attitude towards a practice condemned by both religion and natural law. On this question, the connection between Christianity and natural law seems to have been tight.

Strains between the strength of the old prohibition and the needs of a more commercial society emerged from the twelfth century onwards, however, and scholarly efforts were made to reach an accommodation between them. Many sophisticated modern studies of those efforts have been made.[20] Most of the accommodation took the form of refinements in what was meant by the term 'usury'. Shared risk in a contract, for example, might take it out of the category of a usurious transaction. It may be said with some measure of truth that the subject did lead many of the late medieval Schoolmen into 'a quagmire of contradictions'.[21] The reply to this charge has been that usury was not an easy subject. The Schoolmen were working towards a sensible goal within the restraints of two traditions they had neither the wish nor the ability to discard.

19 Panormitanus (d. 1445/1453), *Commentaria super decretalium libros* (Venice, 1615) ad X 5.19.rubr. 'contra naturam rerum quoniam pecunia germinat pecuniam quae tamen naturaliter non est apta germinare.' The question was controversial, however, see José Barrientos García, *Un Siglo de moral económica en Salamanca, 1526–1629: Francisco de Vitoria y Domingo de Soto* (Salamanca: Ediciones Universidad Salamanca, 1985), 75–77.

20 See, e.g., John T. Noonan, Jr., *The Scholastic Analysis of Usury* (Cambridge, MA: Harvard University Press, 1957); Reiner Franke, *Die Entwicklung des (Darlehens-)Zinses in Frankreich* (Berlin: Duncker and Humblot, 1996), 17–90; Diego Alonso-Lasheras, *Luis de Molina's 'De Iustitia et Iure': Justice as Virtue in an Economic Context* (Leiden and Boston, MA: Brill, 2011), 125–183; James Davis, *Medieval Market Morality* (Cambridge: Cambridge University Press, 2012), 65–68.

21 Raymond de Roover, 'Scholastic Economics: Survival and Lasting Influence from the Sixteenth Century to Adam Smith', *Quarterly Journal of Economics* 69 (1955): 161–190, at 173.

A survey of evidence from the law courts has shown that the assertion that usury was contrary to both the Christian religion and natural law continued to be made. Traditional assumptions about its illegality did not disappear.[22] However, a tide of scholarly opinion was running in the opposite direction. It ran towards admitting the reasonability of less than total prohibitions of the practice of putting money out at interest. Most late medieval statutes that allowed a moderate rate were upheld even when they were challenged as contrary to both the natural law and the dictates of the Christian religion. A German constitution setting only a moderate penalty for usury – loss of a quarter of the profits – survived a challenge that it was contrary to natural law's prohibition of usury. So did an Italian statute allowing the taking of moderate interest on a loan, when challenged as contrary to natural law's strictures against usury. Both were defended successfully as both moderate in extent and useful in commerce.[23] On this score, it can be said that natural law remained intact, but it was also capable of adjustment to meet changed circumstances or more sophisticated analysis.

Allowing what once had been considered usury was also capable of being reconciled with the Christian religion. The true purpose of the church's prohibition, it was said, had always been to prevent men from taking advantage of the poor and the needy. From the start, this had been the immoral purpose being condemned by usury's prohibition in the law of the church. Experience and reason had shown, however, that allowing a moderate rate of interest (but no more) achieved that goal and also fit the needs of the community better than a widely evaded absolute prohibition against taking any rate of interest no matter how small. Such an approach could better serve the true purposes of Christian law than a total prohibition. There was thus room for development in the understanding of what was useful and what violated the laws of nature and religion. Both were supple enough to admit the validity of statutes that seemed to bring it into line with society's needs.

A further illustrative example of the practical connections between natural law and the Christian religion, one that had a definite impact on human life, comes from the law of last wills and testaments. At first sight, it appears to be an unpromising subject for investigation in this brief history. Although the Bible spoke to the subject of inheritance, stating, for instance, that 'A good man leaveth an inheritance to his children's children' (e.g. Proverbs 13.22), it had little to say about the mechanics of making a will that would accomplish that goal. Similarly, freedom of testation fits awkwardly with the natural law's recognition of the duty to provide for a testator's spouse and children. At best it could be no more than a bounded

[22] E.g. Julius Clarus, *Practica criminalis* (Venice, 1595) v. *usura*, no. 3: '[U]surae sunt omni iure prohibitae, et in primis quidem de iure naturali. Et est communis opinio.'

[23] These examples (along with some others) are taken from my *Natural Law in Court* (Cambridge, MA: Harvard University Press, 2015), 64–66. See also John F. McGovern, 'The Rise of New Economic Attitudes – Economic Humanism, Economic Nationalism – During the Later Middle Ages and the Renaissance', *Traditio* 26 (1970): 217–253.

permissive right, one open to substantial variants in practice. The Roman civil law, by contrast, had quite elaborate, detailed rules about the making of wills. They filled several titles in the Digest (e.g. Digest, 28–29), and they had a strong hold on law and life in Rome. Testation thus appears to be a subject that was left to the positive law, excluding influence from Christian jurisprudence.

This appearance turns out to be mistaken, however, and its history demonstrates one way in which the teachings of Christianity interacted with those from within the law of nature. This is shown in the requirement of formalities in the execution of last wills and testaments. Roman law required the presence of and subscription by seven legitimate witnesses to a testator's act of making a will (Institutes, 2.10.2; Digest, 28.1. 21–2). Without their presence, a last will and testament was invalid. There were always exceptions to this requirement, notably the wills of soldiers and sailors on active service. Civil lawyers recognised that military life's circumstances often could not accommodate ceremony, or even deliberation. Therefore, military wills were treated as valid even if they were out of compliance with the law's formal requirements. However, in most circumstances the requirement of seven witnesses remained the rule. It was a defensible requirement too. Formality plays a useful role in will making. It alerts testators to the seriousness of what they are doing. It often gives time for deliberation. It solves some difficult problems of proof. Requirements similar to those found in Roman law exist today, and they do not lack for modern proponents.

In the hands of early jurists steeped in natural law, however, the question arose: What was the true purpose of the requirement of seven witnesses? The answer they gave was that it was meant to secure that the last wishes of the dying person had been correctly ascertained. It did not exist for its own sake, but rather to secure the result desired by the testator. As stated in a decision of the *Rota Romana* in 1656, for example, the 'substance of the solemnities consists of making known the true wishes of the testator'.[24] The seven witnesses had been required 'only to make proof' of what those wishes were, and if those wishes could be reliably established some other way, the will would stand. Legal requirements should not stand as a barrier to the truth. It was safe to assume that the drafters of the requirement had not meant for this to happen.

Christian law also came into play. The Bible declared: 'In the mouth of two or three witnesses shall every word be established' (2 Corinthians 13.1). The decretals echoed the point. They held that the testimony of two or three reliable witnesses was sufficient to prove the truth of an assertion (X 2.20.23), and it was the truth that mattered to the canonists. Of course, there had to be at least two witnesses, at least under ordinary circumstances. The biblical story of Susannah and the Elders (Vulg. Daniel 13.51–59) illustrated the dangers of relying on fewer than two, and the jurists cited it repeatedly to make that point about last wills and testaments. The example

24 Joannes Zuffus, *Tractatus criminalis processus libri tres* (Rome: Ex Typographia Reveredae Camerae Apostolicae, 1665), Dec. 27, nos. 2–4: 'tota solemnitas et substantia huius testamenti consistat in nuda voluntate testatoris patefacta.'

was also taken *a contrario sensu* to show that with two witnesses in agreement, the truth would emerge. Other scriptural texts taught that same lesson (e.g. Matthew 18.16; John 8.17). In other words, the jurists saw this problem as one where the law of nature and the Christian Scriptures taught the same lesson. Purely formal rules should give way to the truth.

This line of reasoning led some jurists to a wider argument, one that now may seem directly contrary to the rules stated in civil law's texts. If what mattered under natural law was establishing the truth, as these lawyers assumed, it might be that fewer than two witnesses to a will could suffice to establish its validity, at least if there were other means of making sure of the truth. That is, if one took the seven-witness requirement to be merely a means by which the testator's true last wishes were to be ascertained, the way was opened up for a more elastic rule of proof. The existence of military wills obviously helped. It showed that Roman law itself was not dogmatic about the number seven, or even the number two. There were other reliable ways of establishing the truth.

The main 'work' of expansion in the law of proof was done by looking to the 'mind' behind the Roman law's provisions.[25] That was what might matter to a judge, not the particular words used in any particular legal texts. It was fair to assume that this 'mind' conformed to the tenets of the natural law, and that assumption opened legal development to the enforcement of wills that would not have passed muster under the positive law's rules stated in the Digest. This approach opened the way to the nuncupative will, the holographic will, and the will that failed to appoint an heir. The civil law's texts were not 'overruled' in the process. They were simply understood in a way that permitted this expansion of testamentary law to occur. Both the law of nature and the law of the church were understood as contributing to a result thought to be consistent with doing justice in individual cases.

CONCLUSION

The history of natural law's place in Christian thought surely supports its retention, or at least its recognition, in modern religious life. The natural law has played such an important role in shaping the ways in which Christians long thought about the goals and the details of the law that its exclusion today appears to be a radical change in the character of the law that governs the life of the church. Its history also shows that natural law, always assumed to be immutable, did in fact admit limitations and even changes of mind about what was permissible and what was forbidden in legal practice. It was a more protean source of law than is often supposed, but its goals, its achievements and its ways of thinking about law's inner character are not things Christians of today should carelessly discard. The chapters that follow respond positively to the contemporary challenge.

25 See Code, 1.14.5; this imperial decree declared: 'To follow the words of the law and not its mind is to offend against the law.'

2

Natural Law in the Roman Catholic Tradition

Helen Costigane

In the closing months of the Second World War, when it was clear that the Allies would defeat Nazi Germany, steps were taken to hide the evidence of the systematic extermination of Jews and others in the now-infamous concentration camps. Bodies buried were exhumed and burned in huge funeral pyres, camps were dismantled and crematoria were blown up. Such efforts to conceal mass murder in the name of the state demonstrated that, despite the rhetoric of leaders and the unquestioned obedience of those who followed them, there remained in the psyche, individual and collective, a recognition (even at a residual level) that some actions contradict our very understanding of what it means to be human. For the prosecutors at Nuremberg in 1948 putting on trial those involved in the extermination of Jews and others in the Holocaust, there was also the understanding that wrong was done, despite appeals to 'loyalty' and 'obedience'.[1] Responses to the Holocaust and other mass murders last century (such as those perpetrated by Ottoman Turkey, Cambodia, Stalinist Russia, North Korea and Rwanda) seem to suggest that there is an objective human morality which can, in principle, be known by any reasonable human being. In consequence, there are ways of acting required or prohibited by our very humanity that are not relative to history, culture, religion or geography. As Stephen Pope puts it: 'The horrors of the [twentieth] century – from the Holocaust to Rwanda – point to a level of moral perversity that is unimaginable. There is widespread recognition by all but the most indifferent and cynical that these evils amount to something more than a violation of mere social customs, aesthetic taste or sentiment.'[2]

Moral condemnation of murder, genocide, slavery, sex trafficking, torture, rape and child abuse presupposes that there is an objective human morality. The natural law tradition tries to provide a basis for such a universal morality which is not conditioned by, or can appeal to, human law, societal convention, authority or subjective preference. Used in a number of different ethical fields (social, medical

[1] For the first part of this chapter, I am indebted to Dr Nicholas Austin SJ (Heythrop College, University of London) whose insights and teaching notes on 'natural law' have been of enormous assistance to me.

[2] Stephen J. Pope, 'Natural and Christian Ethics', in R. Gill, ed., *The Cambridge Companion to Christian Ethics* (Cambridge: Cambridge University Press, 2006), 77–95, at 92.

and sexual ethics; human rights; just war theory; and international law), natural law theory claims that moral obligations can be derived from reflection upon human nature. Natural law, therefore, is a form of ethical naturalism, the theory that morality is grounded in human nature. This chapter considers the idea of natural law in the Roman Catholic tradition, beginning with one of the foremost exponents of natural law, Saint Thomas Aquinas, the Dominican Friar (1225–1274), as his thought forms the basis of much of the understanding of the concept today. From there we consider authoritative and alternative views of natural law, how the concept is understood by the International Theological Commission and the use of the concept in the canon law of the Latin Church.

AQUINAS: FORERUNNER OF CATHOLIC NATURAL LAW THEORY

Before looking in more detail at Aquinas' understanding of natural law, it is helpful to consider some presuppositions of his theory, because this is reflected to a degree in the church's canon law. First, the human person is made in the image of God and has the power of genuine agency; in other words, the individual has free will and power over his actions, and morality consists in fulfilling and perfecting that agency. Ethics, therefore, is essentially about the imitation of God – yet the starting point of Aquinas' ethics is not one of 'dependency' (where a person is merely a creature depending on God for directing his life), but one of a child who is growing up, with power over his own actions.[3] Secondly, for Aquinas, moral actions and human actions are the same thing, in the sense that 'human actions' proceed from intention and will rather than an involuntary action such as blinking. As such, those actions arising from a deliberative will can be either morally good or morally bad. A *human* act, derived from reason, is good with the goodness proper to human acts (moral goodness) insofar as it is truly rational. Reason or rationality, therefore, is constitutive of moral goodness. The function of reason is to know the truth and to direct actions to an end. Thirdly, Aquinas claims that human actions derive their morality from conformity to a standard, the first rule of morality being the eternal law itself, the directive wisdom of God:

> A law is nothing other than a certain dictate of practical reason in the leader who governs some complete community. It is clear, however, given that the world is ruled by divine providence ... that the whole community of the universe is governed by divine reason. Therefore the very concept of the governance of things in God, as existing in the leader of the universe, has the nature of a law (*Summa theologiae*, I.II.91.1c).

This eternal law, then, is the governance by which God directs each thing to its ultimate end, but this is a moral direction that preserves free will. Having looked at

3 See Ignatius Theodore Eschmann, *Ethics of St Thomas Aquinas*, Edward A. Synan, ed. (Toronto: Pontifical Institute of Medieval Studies, 1997), 163–164.

these underpinnings of Aquinas' treatment of natural law, we move to a consideration of his understanding of it.

Aquinas defines law as 'nothing else than an ordinance of reason for the common good, made by him who has care of the community, and promulgated' (I.II.90.4c). First, law is rational and induces someone to act in accord with it, not through brute force, but because it is intelligible. He says:

> [L]aw is a certain rule and measure of acts, whereby man is induced to act or is restrained from acting: for *lex* (law) is derived from *ligare* (to bind), because it binds one to act. Now the rule and measure of human acts is the reason, which is the first principle of human acts ... since it belongs to reason to direct to the end, which is the first principle in all matters of action ... Consequently it follows that law is something pertaining to reason (I.II.90.1c).

Therefore, if a law has no rational basis, then it cannot bind and so is not truly a law. Additionally, a law must be for the sake of the common good and as such binds *only* because it is directed towards this end. Next, if the purpose of the law is the good of the community, then it must be promulgated either by the whole community or by someone whose role is to act for the good of that community. While this would mean that law made by a tyrant for his own advancement would not be valid, it would suggest that an intelligible law made by a benevolent despot for the common good would be valid. Finally, a law has to be promulgated as those who are to be subject to it without finding out what it prescribes would be unable to obey it.

He then suggests four kinds of law – eternal, divine, natural and human positive law. The eternal law is the divine wisdom which guides all creatures to their respective ends: as the whole universe is governed by divine reason, which has the nature of a law, and as 'the Divine Reason's conception of things is not subject to time but is eternal ... therefore it is that this kind of law must be called eternal' (I.II.91.1c). The divine law is the positive, revealed law. This consists in what Aquinas terms the 'Old Law' of the Israelites, which includes the Ten Commandments, and the 'New Law' of the gospel. These are not seen as separate laws, but the latter is a progression of the former, with the Old Law being concerned with an earthly good and more focussed on obedience through fear of punishment, and the New Law focussing on a heavenly good and appealing more to 'the love poured into our hearts by the grace of Christ' (I.II.91.4c).

In turn, Aquinas defines natural law as the rational creature's participation in the eternal law. Non-rational creatures have a natural logic inscribed within them directing them to their end. (Today we might call this natural inclination 'instinct'.) On the other hand, human beings, being rational, grasp the nature of the good and so can exercise free will in determining how to attain this end. In this way, humans participate in God's wisdom through their own rationality. The fourth category, human law, is a more particular determination of the natural law. For Aquinas: '[I]t is from the precepts of the natural law, as from general and demonstrable principles, that the human reason needs to proceed to the more particular determination of certain matters. These particular determinations, devised by human reason are called human laws' (I.II.91.3c). While human law may be to an extent culturally relative, it cannot escape the imperative to conform to the natural law.

In terms of the interaction of the four categories of law (and it is important to understand that 'law' is an analogical concept), each kind of law is a 'law' by relation to its proper context. Rather than being only a list of precepts (for example, like the Ten Commandments of the positive, revealed 'divine' law or human law), natural law is a 'law' in the sense of an underlying order of nature oriented towards a particular end. What is this order and what is its particular end? What follows explores this in connection with the precepts of natural law.

Aquinas states that the foundational precept of the natural law is that 'good is to be done and pursued and evil is to be avoided' (I.II.94.2), all other precepts of the natural law being based upon this. This is very abstract, but we can reach more specific precepts, first, by understanding the concept of 'good' by means of the natural inclinations of survival (possessed by all created beings) and procreating and rearing offspring (possessed by animals), and possessing rational inclinations such as knowing God and living in society. These natural tendencies incline a human being towards his natural good and therefore form the foundation for the natural law. These precepts are universal and naturally knowable by all human beings. Moreover, there are more derived precepts and the grounds of these. The inclination of self-preservation grounds the prohibition of suicide. The proclivity for reproduction forms the basis for the right exercise of sexuality and marriage. The predisposition towards knowing God is the obligation to offer God due worship. And the inclination to living in society harmoniously grounds the basic precepts expressed in the Decalogue, prohibiting stealing, murder, adultery, covetousness and bearing false witness.

Is natural law in Aquinas' mind, then, a system of moral precepts? The answer is yes and no. He distinguishes between negative and positive precepts. The negative precepts, which include prohibitions against theft, adultery, murder and rape, are universally true without exception. However, the positive precepts require prudential reason in order to be applied at the right time and in the right way. This is addressed in the thought of Thomist moral theologians such as Jean Porter, who says that rather than a system of moral precepts, natural law is identified by Aquinas as the capacity for moral discernment. However, this capacity is developed through certain moral precepts. In a key passage, Porter states:

> [N]atural law is fundamentally a capacity or power to distinguish between good and evil; it is intrinsic to the character of the human soul as made in the image of God, and therefore it cannot be altogether obliterated; and it is expressed or developed through moral precepts which are confirmed as well as being completed and transcended, through the operation of grace. Even though the natural law

> understood in its primary sense does not consist of specific moral rules, it does find immediate expression in the fundamental precepts of the Golden Rule or the two great commandments of love of God and neighbour; these in turn yield the more specific norms of the Decalogue, which can be further specified as warranted by the circumstances of human life. Hence, the natural law more broadly understood does include specific moral norms as well as a fundamental capacity for moral judgment, although there is considerable room for both legitimate variation and sinful distortion at the level of particular norms.[4]

On Porter's view, therefore, Aquinas' concept of the natural law is much less rationalist than modern versions. In fact, Aquinas is clear that ethics cannot hope to be an immediate guide to action. As Aquinas states in his *Commentary on the Ethics*:

> And since the conversation concerning morals even in general matters is uncertain and variable, even more uncertainty is found when we descend to the solution of singular cases specifically. For this does not fall under art or tradition, because, the cases of individual actions vary in infinite ways. Hence the judgment concerning singulars is left to the prudence of each, and so [Aristotle] adds that it is necessary that each agent attends by his prudence to the consideration of what is to be done according to the present time, with all the particular circumstances having been considered. A doctor bringing about a cure and a captain steering a ship must act in the same way. However, although this conversation is of this kind, that is uncertain in general aspects and incapable of precision in particular matters, nevertheless we ought to attend to it in order that we may confer upon men some help, through which they may be directed in their actions (*Commentary on the Nicomachean Ethics*, Bk II, L.2).

Therefore, for Aquinas, ethics can never completely guide action in the particular case. As Armand Maurer puts it:

> Moral science or ethics is a practical science because its purpose is to direct human action; but it guides man only in a remote way, because as a science it deals with human actions in general and not directly with the particular action to be done here and now. The moral virtue of prudence is the immediate guide to action in the moral order.[5]

Ethics should not attempt to usurp the role of on-the-spot prudential judgment, since it cannot consider the concrete singularity of any given action. Similarly, the

[4] Jean Porter, *Nature as Reason: A Thomistic Theory of the Natural Law* (Grand Rapids, MI: William B. Eerdmans, 2005), 14.

[5] Thomas Aquinas, *The Division and Methods of the Sciences*, Armand Augustine Maurer, trans. (Toronto: Pontifical Institute of Mediaeval Studies, 1986), 19, n. 36. The term 'moral science' is used by Roman Catholic moral theologians such as Charles E. Curran, *The Catholic Moral Tradition Today: A Synthesis* (Washington, DC: Georgetown University Press, 1999), 176. It is worth noting, however, that others such as James F. Keenan suggest that there has been a move from 'defining moral theology as the fixed science of human action to becoming a guide for the personal and communal development of the conscientious disciples of Christ': see *A History of Catholic Moral Theology in the Twentieth Century* (London: Continuum, 2010), 7.

Thomist philosopher Yves Simon claims that even the articulation of moral laws does not do away with the need for individual, prudential judgment:

> Between law and action there always is a space to be filled by decisions which cannot be written into law. And the number of steps needed to connect the last word of the legislative reason and the ultimate form of action is itself determined by contingent particularities: [the space] may be large.[6]

Simon admits there is a tension here: on the one hand, the law aims for necessity and universality; on the other hand, prudence and practical wisdom attempt to take into account the particularity of times, persons and circumstances. This idea of prudential judgment underpins the idea of *epikeia*, where the letter of the law may be set aside for the sake of justice and the common good.

A FRAMEWORK FOR REFLECTION

As we see later in Chapter 6 in connection with the 'Wesleyan Quadrilateral', many Christian moral theologians appeal to four entities – Scripture, tradition, reason and experience – as a framework for moral reflection,[7] and it is especially in its use of the first two that Christian ethics is distinguished from philosophical ethics. While there are many issues about how Scripture is to be interpreted, most (if not all) Christians would acknowledge the importance of divine revelation for the way that life ought to be lived. For the Latin Church, tradition refers to the writings of the early church fathers, the doctors of the church, key figures such as Aquinas and Alphonsus Liguori (1696–1787) and the magisterium, that is, the official teaching office of the Roman Catholic Church. Some would widen the idea of tradition to include the *sensus fidelium*, the 'wisdom of the Christian community' or the 'ongoing, living faith of the communion of saints whose members include both the living and dead'.[8] Reasons can include reflection on the natural law as well as engagement with the human sciences such as sociology, psychology and anthropology, which give us much information about human life and can enrich moral reflection. Finally, experience (personal or general) is an important source for Christian ethics; as Bretzke notes: '[A]ny reflection on moral theology that ignores or pays insufficient attention to experience will build its system in an unreal world, constructing an abstraction with no correlation to actual human reality.'[9] Each source has its own strengths and weaknesses,[10] and some

6 Yves R. Simon, *The Tradition of Natural Law*, Vukan Kuic, ed. (New York: Fordham University Press, 1965), 83.

7 Don Thorsen, *The Wesleyan Quadrilateral* (Lexington, KY: Emeth Publishers, 2005); W. Stephen Gunter, *Wesley and the Quadrilateral: Renewing the Conversation* (Nashville, TN: Abingdon, 1997).

8 James Bretzke, *A Morally Complex World: Engaging Contemporary Moral Theology* (Collegeville, MN: Liturgical Press, 2004), 23.

9 Ibid., 25.

10 An unduly simplistic or fundamentalist interpretation of scriptural texts must be avoided. Tradition has been slow to accept insights of human thought (one notable example is that of Galileo).

Roman Catholic moral theologians would give equal weight to all, while others suggest that some are more important than others.[11] It is with this in mind that we explore different approaches to natural law and the balance given to these four entities. To do so, it is helpful to consider a particular contemporary issue, that of same-sex relationships, to illustrate the ways in which natural law thinking is employed today in relation to a topic at the heart of so many fierce theological, cultural and other battles.

The Natural Law Approach of the Magisterium

Teaching on natural law is expounded by the magisterium, the teaching authority of the Catholic Church.[12] Recent documents show a more or less consistent approach to natural law. *The Catechism of the Catholic Church* notes that, written and engraved in the soul of every person, natural law 'expresses the original moral sense which enables man to discern by reason the good and the evil, the truth and the lie' (paragraph 1954). This law

> shows man the way to follow so as to practice the good and attain his end. The natural law states the first and essential precepts which govern the moral life. It hinges upon the desire for God and submission to him, who is the source and judge of all that is good, as well as upon the sense that the other is one's equal. Its principal precepts are expressed in the Decalogue (paragraph 1955).

Universal in its precepts and its authority extending to all, the natural law 'expresses the dignity of the person and determines the basis for his fundamental rights and duties' (paragraph 1956) and is immutable and permanent throughout the variations of history (paragraph 1958), and yet its application can vary greatly and require reflection that takes account of various conditions of life (paragraph 1957). On this view, ethics is grounded in normative (rather than 'descriptive') human nature. Corresponding to the modern scientific concept of nature, the 'descriptive' human notes the behaviours that humans engage in with some statistical regularity, but it makes no moral evaluation. The normative view corresponds to a teleological concept of human nature and determines the behaviours which humans may or should engage in.

The operation of reason can be distorted by ignorance or emotion. And experience on its own can lead to a very subjective morality.

11 For example, Germain Grisez would put authoritative teaching and Scripture foremost before (and often against) experience: see 'Revelation versus Dissent', in John Wilkins, ed., *Understanding Veritatis Splendor* (London: SPCK, 1994), 1–8. Feminist theologians such as Susan F. Parsons argue that the experiences and reasoning of women can shed new light on ethical analysis: see 'Feminist Ethics', in Bernard Hoose, ed., *Christian Ethics: An Introduction* (London: Cassell, 1998), 135–148. Much discussion of the Roman Catholic understanding as to the four aspects of moral reflection focusses on the idea of 'conscience' and the tensions often arising between official church teaching and the individual's personal judgment: see Linda Hogan, *Confronting the Truth: Conscience in the Catholic Tradition* (New York: Paulist Press, 2000), 28–33.

12 The magisterium comprises the pope and the bishops of the church (see Code of Canon Law, canons 749ff).

This normative human nature is disclosed in revelation and interpreted by the magisterium. In terms of same-sex relationships, the teaching authority, in the *Catechism*, moves from an understanding of the human person and the place of sexuality to virtue and then sin and bases its teaching on homosexuality within its discussion of the sixth commandment and the prohibition against adultery (paragraphs 2331–2400). This approach, then, puts a strong emphasis on the complementarity of the sexes, that they are equal but different, and that it is in relation to each other that these differences reach their fulfilment in the goods of marriage[13] and the flourishing of family life (paragraph 2333). Thus, sexuality 'becomes personal and truly human when it is integrated into the relationship of one person to another, in the complete and lifelong mutual gift of a man and a woman' (paragraph 2337).

In turn, the magisterium places an emphasis upon the immutability of certain aspects of the natural law. *Persona Humana* (1975), a declaration of the Sacred Congregation of the Doctrine of the Faith, states:

> Of course, in the history of civilization many of the concrete conditions and needs of human life have changed and will continue to change. But all evolution of morals and every type of life must be kept within the limits imposed by the immutable principles based upon every human person's constitutive elements and essential relations – elements and relations which transcend historical contingency . . . Hence, those many people are in error who today assert that one can find neither in human nature nor in the revealed law any absolute and immutable norm to serve for particular actions . . . *Now in fact the Church through her history has always considered a certain number of precepts of the natural law as having an absolute and immutable value* (III–IV).

The argument from natural law against homosexual acts is based upon 'the finality of the specific function of sexuality'. *Persona Humana* prays in aid various magisterial documents (including those of the Second Vatican Council) and biblical texts, and declares: 'It is respect for its finality that ensures the moral goodness of this act.' Consequently, 'the use of the sexual function has its true meaning and moral rectitude only in true marriage' (V). The position of the magisterium might be summed up in Stephen Pope's observation that what is 'natural', normatively speaking, is not what we are given, but what we are called to become:

> The central moral issue, then, is not genetic or statistical naturalness, but rather whether homosexuals can respond (at least, that is, as well as heterosexuals) to the universal challenge to train and habituate their sexual passions – naturally oriented to various goods but existentially disordered by concupiscence – in a way that contributes to their flourishing.[14]

[13] 'The goods of marriage' refer to the ends or blessings that come from marriage. Augustine listed them as the *bonum prolis*, the good of offspring who are to be loved and educated, the *bonum fidei*, the good of fidelity between husband and wife and the *bonum sacramenti*, which is a bond of indissolubility and a sign of Christ's union with his spouse, the church.

[14] Quoted in James Keenan, op cit., 141.

So, we can see that natural law is invoked here by the magisterium, which elucidates and interprets its precepts, doing so alongside both other magisterial documents and biblical texts. Natural law thinking is thus part and parcel of magisterial practice and reasoning.

Responses Critical of the Magisterial Approach

However, to illustrate the vitality of natural law thinking, some moral theologians, often grouped under the description of 'revisionists',[15] have criticised the magisterium's understanding of natural law as being too rigid and inflexible and, in the sexual sphere, one which ignores 'the broad spectrum of sexuality, the many types of friendship, and the experiences of women'.[16] A 'revisionist' approach to natural law has a number of characteristics, including an emphasis on experience and contemporary science (including the social sciences) as important sources of moral knowledge, an openness to change and development in moral teaching, the autonomy of individual conscience and the importance of prudential judgment in the particular situation. There is also recognition of the need to take into account social and historical circumstances, as well as the need to evaluate critically magisterial teaching. Therefore, in terms of the question of same-sex relationships and natural law, revisionist moral theologians would question the way in which the four entities outlined earlier – namely, Scripture, tradition, reason and experience – are used, and also the priority that is given to each of them. Critically, revisionists would give greater weight to moral sources of knowledge other than current magisterial teaching.[17]

Having looked at the way in which biblical texts are used to prohibit homosexual acts,[18] Salzman and Lawler turn their attention to the natural law arguments, claiming first that 'nature' is not directly experienced but rather socially interpreted and constructed. Therefore, what is claimed to be the reality of 'nature' is always subject to scrutiny, even if that interpretation has emanated from the magisterium. Rejecting the argument from sexual complementarity, Salzman and Lawler conclude: 'Homosexual sexual acts are "natural" for people with a homosexual orientation, just as heterosexual sexual acts are "natural" for people with a heterosexual orientation.'[19] Drawing upon human experience which affirms that homosexual couples do experience affective complementarity, they argue that the view 'that

15 Such moral theologians form a loosely connected movement, rather than what might be styled a school of moral theology; they are concerned with the revision of certain elements, as well as the overall method, of moral theology. These include Peter Knauer, Joseph Fuchs, Bruno Schuller, Louis Janssens and Richard McCormick.

16 James F. Keenan, 'The Open Debate: Moral Theology and the Lives of Gay and Lesbian Persons', *Theological Studies* 64 (2003): 127–151, at 130.

17 For example, see Todd A. Salzman and Michael G. Lawler, *The Sexual Person: Toward a Renewed Catholic Anthropology* (Washington, DC: Georgetown University Press, 2008), 214.

18 Ibid., 216–217. 19 Ibid., 227.

homosexual acts, by definition, cannot contribute to the good of the human person seems to contradict the relational experiences of committed, monogamous, homosexual couples'.[20] With this approach, they exhibit the central characteristics of the revisionist approach to natural law: an emphasis upon human experience and the natural sciences, a willingness to question magisterial teaching and the recognition of historicity and context.[21]

NATURAL LAW AND THE INTERNATIONAL THEOLOGICAL COMMISSION

Having identified how natural law is understood, its relationship to other 'laws', who may expound it and some of the criticisms made against its use, we move to a brief discussion of the document *In Search of a Universal Ethic: A New Look at Natural Law*, issued by the International Theological Commission of the Roman Catholic Church in 2009.[22]

The commission maintains that there are objective moral values 'which can unite human beings and bring them peace and happiness' (paragraph 1). The search for a common ethical language concerns all, and Christianity has no monopoly on this; moreover: 'the natural law is the basis of collaboration among all persons of good will, whatever their religious convictions' (paragraph 9).[23] While it is clear that there are many misunderstandings about the term itself, there are 'convergences' in the great religious and wisdom traditions that 'bear witness to a largely common moral patrimony that forms the basis of all dialogue on moral questions' (paragraph 11).[24] It is therefore possible to speak of the perception of common moral values, beginning with their insertion into a network of human relationships from birth, which

[20] Ibid., 229.

[21] There are many other writers on the subject of natural law, such as Russell Hittinger, who lament the collapse of natural law in modern Catholic moral theology and explore what he claims is a failure to teach what natural law is in terms of three foci: namely, the human mind, nature and the mind of God. As to using natural law as a framework for moral reflection, he reminds us of the delicate balance between reason and faith in Aquinas' view of human knowledge; see his *The First Grace: Rediscovering the Natural Law in a Post-Christian World* (Wilmington, DE: ISI Books, 2003), and *A Critique of the New Natural Law Theory* (Notre Dame, IN: University of Notre Dame Press, 1987). Stephen Brock's interpretation of Aquinas explores inconsistencies in natural law theories which place an exclusive emphasis on the morality of subjective intention; see *Action and Conduct: Thomas Aquinas and the Theory of Action* (Edinburgh: T & T Clark, 1998). A third notable scholar, Alasdair MacIntyre, looks at whether a persuasive case can be made for a foundational morality if God does not exist, thus putting moral reflection into another and different framework; see *Intractable Disputes about the Natural Law*, Lawrence S. Cunningham, ed. (Notre Dame, IN: University of Notre Dame Press, 2009).

[22] For responses to the document, see John Berkman and William C. Mattison III, eds., *Searching for a Universal Ethic: Multidisciplinary, Ecumenical, and Interfaith Responses to the Catholic Natural Law Tradition* (Grand Rapids, MI: William B. Eerdmans, 2014).

[23] *In Search of a Universal Ethic: A New Look at Natural Law* (Vatican: International Theological Commission of the Catholic Church, 2009), Introduction.

[24] Chapter 1, Convergences: the wisdom traditions and religions; Greco-Roman thought; Scripture and natural law; the development of the Christian natural law tradition; and natural law and the magisterium of the church.

allow individuals to become aware of themselves, of others, and of the context within which they live (paragraph 38). Attaining self-awareness and responsibility, a person is capable of perceiving the call to do good and avoid evil, and by searching for the moral good, a person 'contributes to the realization of his nature, beyond impulses of instinct or the search for a particular pleasure' (paragraphs 39–40). In searching for this good, a person will consider the fundamental inclinations of his nature (which are not the 'simple blind impulses of desire') and formulate 'under the form of practical commands, the moral duty of actualizing them in his own life'. These are expressed in the form of general precepts shared with all other human beings, 'the content of that which we call natural law' (paragraph 45).

These fundamental inclinations include the preservation and development of one's own existence (including the need for food, clothing, housing and work); the survival of the species realised through procreation, which implies the permanence of the union of a man and a woman; the inclination to care for and educate children; a consideration for that which may threaten life, such as global warming; and the inclination to live in society, to form relationships, to overcome individual limitations and to cooperate in the search for truth. Additionally, there is a need to form societies built on natural justice, respect for humanity and the recognition of equal dignity for everyone. From this emerges the 'Golden Rule' – 'do not do to another that which you would not want done to you' – which is the 'very principle of a morality of reciprocity' (paragraphs 48–51). However, morality is not just about producing norms for action, and natural law is not 'an already established set of rules that impose themselves a priori on the moral subject'; individual formation and the acquisition of moral virtues such as prudence are essential. Thus, natural law becomes 'a source of objective inspiration for the deeply personal process of making a decision' (paragraph 59).[25]

While having recourse to the wisdom of experience, 'an experience that integrates the contributions of the other sciences and is nourished by contact with men and women' (paragraph 54), the moralist also must look to theology, philosophy and other branches of knowledge (human, economic and biological) 'in order to discern clearly the given facts of the situation and to identify correctly the concrete requirements of human dignity'. However, he must always at the same time 'be particularly attentive to safeguard the fundamental givens expressed by the precepts of the natural law that remain valid despite cultural variations' (paragraph 54). Natural law involves moral experience; it is discoverable and universal; it consists of precepts; and these precepts are capable of application through the moral dispositions of persons and their use of practical reason applied to concrete actions.[26]

[25] Chapter 2, The Perception of Common Moral Values.

[26] Chapter 3, The Theoretical Foundations of Natural Law: the role of society; moral experience (one must do good); the discovery and universality of natural law; the precepts of natural law; the application of these precepts (and the historicity of natural law); and the moral dispositions of persons and concrete action.

The commission also advocates deepening understandings of the philosophical, metaphysical and religious dimensions of natural law, and the use of natural law precepts in the regulation of political life. The commission maintains that the person 'is at the centre of the political and social order because he is an end and not a means' (paragraph 84). This being the case, the end of society is 'to promote, consolidate and develop its common good' (paragraph 85). This common good allows a person to be a more human person, its external aspects among other things being security, social justice, education, access to employment and spiritual searching. In short, following from the natural inclinations of the human being, society must pursue the values of freedom, truth, justice and solidarity (paragraph 87).[27]

Above all, natural law acquires its full meaning in the history of salvation, and the 'new law of the Gospel includes, assumes and fulfils the requirements of the natural law'. In turn, 'the orientations of the natural law are not therefore external normative demands with respect to the new law. Rather, they are a constitutive part of it, even if they are secondary and completely ordered to the principal element, which is the grace of Christ' (paragraph 112).[28]

In summary, the commission maintains that there is a need for humanity to seek common rules for living together in justice and peace, that natural law is the foundation of a universal ethic and yardstick against which to measure the political order and that it is discoverable from observing and reflecting on a common human nature. Inscribed on the human heart, the natural law is dynamic rather than static and, instead of being a list of definitive and immutable precepts, 'it is a spring of inspiration always flowing forth for the search for an objective foundation for a universal ethic' (paragraph 113). In all this, the commission draws upon the theological inheritance and teaching of the church, including Aquinas.[29]

NATURAL LAW AND CANON LAW

Bearing in mind Aquinas' view of law, which is (i) an ordinance of reason, (ii) for the common good, (iii) made by the one who has care of the community and (iv) promulgated, we turn now to a consideration of how natural law ideas are used in canon law. At the time of the promulgation of the *Pio-Benedictine Code* of 1917, the question of church-state relations was dominated by the model of the 'perfect society',[30]

[27] Chapter 4, Natural Law and the City: the person and the common good; natural law as the measure of the political order; the norm of natural justice and positive law; the political order is a temporal and rational order.

[28] Chapter 5, Jesus Christ: the fulfilment of the natural law.

[29] As well as its extensive use of conciliar material and recent papal teaching, interestingly, the document also contains many citations to Aquinas, e.g. in footnotes 33, 45, 48, 50, 56–58, 62–63, 76, 82, 84, 94, 102 and 104.

[30] The model of the church as a perfect society was a paradigm that was popular in Catholic ecclesiology from the early 1600s to the 1950s. See Avery Dulles, *Models of the Church* (Dublin: Gill and MacMillan, 1988).

and canons 100 §1 and 1495 §1 of that Code are expressions of this juridical theory.[31] A reading of these canons demonstrates an understanding of natural law in terms of the right of the church to exist independently of any will on the part of the state and that it must be allowed to do so. The Second Vatican Council (1962–1965) led to a new self-awareness of the church in terms of a renewed ecclesiology of *communio*, which was reflected in the revised Code of Canon Law of 1983. This new Code for the Latin Church, governing internal ecclesial life in relation to areas such as the administration of sacraments, temporal goods and ministry,[32] was designed to provide the conditions for human flourishing in terms of the anthropology, ecclesiology and Christology articulated in the council's documents. It was promulgated by Pope John Paul II, the supreme legislator,[33] on 25 January 1983, for whom the Code was not to replace faith, grace, charisms or charity but 'looks towards the achievement of order in the ecclesial society ... such that it facilitates at the same time an orderly development in the life both of the ecclesial society and of the individual persons who belong to it'.[34] The idea, derived from natural law, that society exists to serve individual human flourishing and the common good at the same time has been a constant theme in Papal Allocutions.[35] Often mentioned within these are themes relating to natural law principles of freedom, justice, truth and solidarity.[36]

31 Canon 100 §1: 'The Catholic Church and the Apostolic See have moral personality by reason of divine ordinance; other inferior moral persons in the church arise in her either by prescription of the law itself or by special concession of the competent ecclesiastical Superior granted by formal decree for a religious or charitable purpose'; canon 1495 §1: 'The Catholic Church and the Apostolic See have the native right freely and independently from any civil power of acquiring, retaining, and administering temporal goods for the pursuit of their own ends.' Translation from E.N. Peters, *The Pio-Benedictine Code of Canon Law* (San Francisco, CA: Ignatius Press, 2001), 57, 500 – hereafter Peters 2001.

32 The Code comprises 1752 canons, divided into seven books: General Norms, The People of God, The Teaching Office of the Church, The Sanctifying Office of the Church, Temporal Goods, Sanctions and Processes. The Code governs the Latin Church only; the Eastern Catholic Churches are governed by a separate Code promulgated in 1990.

33 Canon 331 asserts that the pope is the pastor of the universal church who 'has supreme, full, immediate, and universal ordinary power' which he can always exercise freely.

34 The official language of the Code is Latin; this translation is from the *Code of Canon Law Annotated*, E. Caparros, M. Theriault, J. Thorn and H. Aube, eds. (Montreal: Wilson & Lafleur, 2nd edn, 2004), 7 – hereafter CCLA.

35 Successive pontiffs have given allocutions to the Roman Rota (the supreme marriage tribunal) on an annual basis. These are published in volumes edited by William Woestman, from the Faculty of Canon Law, St Paul University, Ottawa, on a periodic basis. They can also be found on the Vatican website (www.vatican.va).

36 Some examples: Pius XII noted that Rotal judgments 'do not discriminate between the humble and the mighty in proclaiming truth and justice' (2 October 1939); John XXIII: 'The thing that distinguishes your work is the devotion to the cause of justice ... It is your great merit to work for the triumph of a virtue, which supposes all the others, and completes them for the common good' (19 October 1959); on the work of the Roman Rota, Paul VI said: 'It exemplifies the justice that the Church conceives, professes and defends; that is, the justice founded on moral principles coming from the objective moral order of law – divine, natural and positive – not less than from the subjective conscience, which confers upon the juridic order, besides the force of law, its stability and social dimension' (23 January 1967).

Three areas illustrate general and particular applications of natural law theory in the Code itself. First, there is an implementation of the precepts of natural law, focussing on specific issues. Secondly, it is used in the relationship between church and state, not least when there is a clash of civil law with canonical legislation derived from natural law. Thirdly, there is Aquinas' idea of 'intention and will', specifically in relation to canonical sanctions.

Precepts of Natural Law in the Code

Canonists often connect natural law and divine law; typically, natural law, 'the root and rule of canon law', is 'a source of law in those cases where its precepts are common to all mankind', having 'God as its author', so 'in its own way [it] is a kind of divine law', namely that law which is 'established by God and made known to us by revelation'.[37] The Code commonly presents norms in its canons as being derived from divine law or as being of divine institution; for example, the right of the church to govern itself is one of divine institution (canons 129 and 331); all Christ's faithful are obliged by divine law – *ex lege divina tenentur* – to do penance (canon 1249); and 'No custom which is contrary to divine law can obtain the force of law' (canon 24). In addition, we find in the Code many norms which are re-presentations of, or else implement, the negative precepts of natural law.

Discussed earlier was Aquinas' identification of negative precepts of natural law which included adultery, rape, murder and theft. While these are clearly prohibited in the moral law – as expressed within the *Catechism of the Catholic Church* – there is also either implicit or explicit reference to them in canon law. For example, in the canons relating to marriage, a partnership for the whole of life (canon 1055) gives an expectation of permanence and exclusivity (canon 1134) to one person, and this also rules out polygamy (canon 1148). While there is no explicit reference to rape, the requirement that the consummation of a marriage be *in humano modo* (in a human manner) rules out conjugal acts committed with violence.[38] As to murder (defined as the illegal killing of innocent life), the canons are much more specific. Procuring or enabling an abortion carries with it the penalty of automatic excommunication (canons 1329 and 1398) and excludes the perpetrators from the reception of orders (canon 1041). This exclusion also applies to one who has committed wilful homicide, and for such an act a range of penalties are available (canons 695, 1397 and 1401).

With regard to theft, canon law concerns itself with the temporal goods of the church and asserts an 'innate right' to acquire, retain, administer and alienate property (canon 1254); again, 'The Church can acquire temporal goods by every

37 Robert Ombres, 'Faith, Doctrine and Roman Catholic Canon Law', *Ecclesiastical Law Journal* 1 (1989): 33–41, at 38.

38 As the CCLA reflects, this innovation in the revised Code of 1983 makes it clear that *humano modo* is equivalent to a human act; in Aquinas' terms, this makes it a moral action which proceeds from intention and will: CCLA, 810.

just means of natural and positive law' (canon 1259). The claim is rooted in centuries of conflicts between the Catholic Church and civil governments over the church's material possessions. However, the right to acquire property and funds is exercisable provided that (as the Second Vatican Council put it) 'the just requirements of public order are preserved'.[39] This appears to reflect natural law values of justice, peace and concern for the overall common good. Moreover, while the church's capacity to acquire temporal goods is asserted, as is its independence from the state, ecclesiastical stewards are exhorted to protect property by civilly valid means. However, given that history relates many attempts to appropriate unlawfully the church's goods, acquired for specific purposes,[40] from those persons who belong to the ecclesial community, there are a number of checks and balances set up within the canons in Book V of the Code, and while 'theft' is not explicitly mentioned, it is clear that any abuse of ecclesiastical office which causes loss to the church is potentially punishable by deprivation of office.[41]

Canon Law and Civil Law

What happens, when our human positive law goes against what we understand as moral requirements derived from natural law, and what is the canonical response? Historically, there has been a long interaction between canon law and the law of the state. For example, until recent years, there has been a common understanding of marriage as a union between a man and a woman (canon 1055) and that children adopted in accordance with the civil law are also considered such in canon law (canon 110).[42] Where the civil law specifies an age for marriage which is higher than that in canon law, then the latter should yield to the former.[43] Catholic schools, too, have generally had a level of autonomy, recognising that parents have the right and obligation to educate their children and to provide for their faith formation (either inside or outside of school).[44] The canons on the church's temporal goods are a most obvious connection between the two systems of law; for example, in the British Isles, church organisations (dioceses, religious congregations, and other voluntary entities) are registered as charities in the civil sphere and urged to be so by canon law.[45] Again, there has to be compliance with civil legislation, such as on employment

39 *Dignitatis Humanae*, 4. See also J.P. Beal, J.A. Coriden and T.J. Green, eds., *New Commentary on the Code of Canon Law* (New York: Paulist Press, 2000), 1454 – hereafter 2000 *New Commentary*.

40 Canon 1252 §2: 'principally the regulation of divine worship, the provision of fitting support for the clergy and other ministers, and the carrying out of works of the sacred apostolate and of charity, especially for the needy'.

41 For a canonist's analysis of natural law, see Javier Hervada, *Critical Introduction to Natural Law*, Mindy Emmons, trans. (Montreal: Wilson & Lafleur, 2006).

42 The main canonical effect of adoption is that it gives rise to a marriage impediment (canon 1094).

43 Canon 1083 specifies that a man must have completed his 16th year of age, and a woman her 14th year.

44 See canons 796–800.

45 Canon 1284 §2 specifies that administrators are to ensure that the ownership of ecclesiastical goods is safeguarded in ways which are valid in civil law and urges observance of any civil law requirements.

(canon 1286), maintaining financial records and producing accounts at the end of the fiscal year (canon 1284). In short, there has been a reasonable coherence between the 1983 Code and state law as to understandings of marriage, family life, education, employment, charitable work and financial accountability.

What is known as 'public ecclesiastical law' derives from the recognition of this interaction and common understanding, and it seeks to avoid conflict between the two legal systems. An important canon in this respect is canon 22:

> When the law of the Church remits some issue to the civil law, the latter is to be observed with the same effects in canon law, *in so far as it is not contrary to divine law*, and provided it is not otherwise stipulated in canon law (emphasis added).

This is the so-called canonization of secular law,[46] and it refers to cases where deference to civil law is given so that it might be applied within canon law.[47] In other words, wherever canon law yields to civil law, the civil law must be observed and its effects are the same in canon law. In respect to most legal matters regulated by civil law, canon law says nothing.

However, though the church teaches that, morally, citizens are bound to observe legitimate civil laws, the faithful are obliged to disobey any laws or directives contrary to the demands of the moral order, to the fundamental rights of persons or to the teachings of the Gospel.[48] For example, the church understands abortion to be an abominable wrong, a violation of the right to life, and as something which is forbidden by the faith, by church teaching, by canon law and by divine and natural law. According to a declaration on procured abortions, issued by the Sacred Congregation for the Doctrine of the Faith in 1974, where

> civil law cannot expect to cover the whole field of morality or to punish all faults . . . it cannot act contrary to a law which is deeper and more majestic than any human law; the natural law engraved in men's hearts by the creator as a norm which reason clarifies and strives to formulate properly . . . which it is always wrong to contradict

Thus, 'human law can abstain from punishment, but it cannot declare to be right what would be opposed to the natural law, for this opposition suffices to give the assurance that [such] a law *is not a law at all*' (emphasis added). For the Congregation, therefore, 'it must in any way be clearly understood that a Christian can never conform to a law which is in itself immoral, and such is the case of a law which would admit in principle the liceity of abortion'. Christians should not 'campaign in favour of such a law, or vote for it', and they 'may not collaborate in its application'.[49]

46 CCLA, 47.

47 It is interesting to note that there are differences in translation, with some translating the Latin as 'remit', while others use 'yield'.

48 See *Catechism of the Catholic Church*, promulgated by Pope John Paul II by the apostolic constitution *Fidei Depositum* (London: Geoffrey Chapman, 1994), paragraphs 2238–2242.

49 *Quaestio de abortu*, Congregation for the Doctrine of the Faith, Declaration on Procured Abortion (18 November 1974).

Ordinarily, then, the two systems of law oblige simultaneously, but the view that canon law always prevails whenever it conflicts with civil law[50] does not always hold, as a distinction needs to be made as to whether civil law is contrary to divine law, or to natural law, or not. If there is no breach of divine law, or natural law, the civil law applies. For example, under canon law a parish has the status of a public juridical entity, enjoying rights and obligations, and in charge of its own finances.[51] However, in Britain, for the purposes of the civil law, all dioceses are incorporated as charities and, whenever there is a dispute over property or finance, the civil law applies and the diocesan charity has rights over parish finances.

Nevertheless, problems continue to arise in cases where civil legislation may be understood to challenge the natural law ideas underpinning canon law. Britain, again, is a case in point. For instance, canonically, marriage is a union between a man and a woman, for the procreation and education of children. However, under civil legislation same-sex couples may now contract a civil marriage, as well as adopt and raise children. While this has not affected the conduct of marriages under canon law,[52] it has had significant repercussions for Catholic adoption agencies.[53] Civil law promoting equality has also challenged admission policies of Catholic schools, and what is taught in the religious education curriculum, thus undermining the role of parents and bishops in Catholic education.[54] Similarly, the right to freedom of religion and conscience has been challenged by midwives being required to participate in the scheduling of abortions.[55] And, in what is seen by many as a step too far, there have been proposals for legislation in Ireland and Australia to require priests to delate paedophile-penitents to the police, so violating the sacramental seal of the confessional.[56]

50 2000 *New Commentary*, 85. 51 See canons 515, 532, 1255 and 1284.

52 'Every person enjoys the natural right to marry' (2000 *Commentary*, 1254). However, while the 1983 Code recognises that there is a right to marry derived from natural law, it may (only) be restricted for serious and just reasons, i.e. prohibition by law (canon 1058). The 1995 *Commentary* describes this as 'one of the most basic of human rights' (575). Another commentary giving a more detailed discussion of this right draws a distinction between the right to marry (which is inherent, is permanent and cannot be waived) and the right to exercise the right, which may be subject to regulation. See A. Marzoa, J. Miras, R. Rodriguez-Ocana and I.M. de Azpilcueta, eds., *Exegetical Commentary on the Code of Canon Law*, Vol. III/2 (Montreal: Wilson & Lafleur, 2004), 1076 – hereafter *Exegetical Commentary*. As the marriage of Catholics (even if only one party is Catholic) is governed by divine law and canon law, prohibitions would arise if the couple were of the same sex. A demand for a sacramental marriage in this case would also suggest that there was a lack of the 'proper disposition' required under canon 843.

53 For a discussion on this see Helen Costigane, 'Catholic Adoption Agencies and "Gay adopters"', *Law & Justice: The Christian Law Review* 161 (2008): 98–110.

54 See canons 803 etc. See Helen Costigane, 'Catholic Education in England – What Is to Be Taught?', *Law & Justice: The Christian Law Review* 163 (2009): 103–109.

55 Canon 1329 §2.

56 Canon 983 says that the sacramental seal is inviolable and that it is 'absolutely wrong' for a confessor to break it. This English translation of *nefas est* does not convey the strength of the Latin, which suggests that breaking the seal is contrary to divine law. The penalty stated in canon 1388 is automatic excommunication reserved to the Apostolic See (which means that recourse has to be made to the Apostolic Penitentiary in Rome). That there are only five such crimes/sins carrying this penalty gives

In sum, as Benedict XVI said to the Bundestag in Berlin (22 September 2011):

> Unlike other great religions, Christianity has never proposed a revealed law to the State and to society, that is to say a juridical order derived from revelation. Instead, it has pointed to nature and reason as the true sources of law – and to the harmony of objective and subjective reason, which naturally presupposes that both spheres are rooted in the creative reason of God.[57]

Intention and Will

Earlier we noted Aquinas' view that proper human actions proceed from intention and will as compared with an involuntary event such as blinking. The individual must have free will and power over their actions. This is expressed in various parts of the Code in positive terms. For example, individuals must have the right intention and the requisite freedom to embrace a state of life, such as orders, marriage or membership of an institute of consecrated life.[58] The Code, reflecting many of the insights of the Second Vatican Council, and particularly its emphasis on human dignity and rights, also demonstrates this in its provisions on sanctions: the faithful are not liable in church penal law if their prohibited acts are not freely willed.

The Code states: 'The Church has its own inherent right to constrain with penal sanctions Christ's faithful who commit offences' (canon 1311). The focus of the *ius puniendi* is certain sins that are also exterior actions. These are designated crimes to which sanctions are attached to 'redress the disorder caused by the offence',[59] and to protect 'sanctity and unity, governance and liberty, the sacraments, special obligations, human life and liberty'.[60] However, canon 1321 states: 'No one can be punished for the commission of an *external violation* of a law or precept unless it is *gravely imputable* by reason of *malice* or of *culpability*' (emphasis added).[61] Moreover, canon 1322 states: '[T]hose who habitually lack the use of reason (*qui habitualiter rationis usu carent*) are considered to be incapable (*incapaces*) of a delict, even if they violated a law or precept while seemingly sane.' It is understood that the force of *incapax* means that a 'person habitually deprived of the use of reason is viewed as incapable of a delict despite appearing normal when breaking the law';

an indication of its seriousness. For a discussion on this see Helen Costigane, 'A Protected Rite?' *America*, 30 July 2013.

57 Martin Rhonheimer, 'The Secular State, Democracy, and Natural Law', in Marta Cartabia and Andrea Simoncini, eds., *Pope Benedict XVI's Legal Thought: A Dialogue on the Foundation of Law* (New York: Cambridge University Press, 2015), 79, at 80.

58 For example, see canons 597, 865, 1029, 1057, 1089, 1095, 1098, 1101 and 1103.

59 *Catechism of the Catholic Church*, paragraph 2266.

60 *Exegetical Commentary*, 211.

61 This is a juridical and not simply a moral imputability: '[T]hat which is damaged by the violation of the law or precept is not specifically the moral order, the order of sin, but rather the public or social order … This juridical imputability must be rooted in either malice or culpability': *The Canon Law: Letter and Spirit*, The Canon Law Society of Great Britain and Ireland (London: Geoffrey Chapman, 1994), 754.

such a person is not in possession of his faculties and therefore does not function 'freely and deliberately'.[62] The following canon (1323) deals with those who violate a law and are normally in possession of their faculties, but who are not subject to penalty when there are certain factors that significantly diminish their knowledge or freedom, such as age (not yet having completed the sixteenth year), grave fear or physical force. However, this defence cannot be made if reason is lacking 'because of culpable drunkenness or other mental disturbance of a similar kind' (canon 1324 §1, 2) or where one has sought to excuse the offence by deliberately seeking 'drunkenness or other mental disturbances' (canon 1325). These provisions too may be understood to reflect not only the teaching of the church on the proper nature of human action and moral responsibility but also the precepts of natural law.

CONCLUSION

The concept of natural law has an important place in the teaching of the Roman Catholic Church. Not only did Aquinas provide a systematic account of natural law for the medieval church. His position on natural law continues to shape modern Roman Catholic thought. Natural law provides a universal ethic for the whole of humanity. The discovery of its precepts involves the observation of and reflection on common human nature and moral experience. It may also function as a yardstick against which to measure the legitimacy of the political order and its positive law which, if contrary to natural law, fails to obtain the status of law properly so called and as a result may lose its capacity for obedience by the faithful. The concept of natural law is deployed today by the magisterium on a range of complex and contested contemporary issues, though such deployment is not free from debate and criticism. Natural law thinking also plays a part in the legal life of the Latin Church. The Code of Canon Law explicitly presents many of its canons as of divine institution or as required by divine law. However, whilst it contains no systematic or discrete treatment of natural law as such, it does contain norms which mirror precepts of natural law as the teaching of the church understands to have been inscribed by God on the human heart. This is the case in such fields as church penal law, marriage law and church-state relations law, in all of which 'the supreme law of the Church is the salvation of souls' (Code, canon 1752).

62 2000 *New Commentary*, 1541–1542.

3

Natural Law in the Orthodox Tradition

Paul Babie

A recent visit to the tiny island of Iona off the coast of western Scotland brought with it the opportunity not only to spend some time immersed in the spiritual tradition of St Columba, whose shrine is found in the church there, but also to reflect upon the early Christian Church.[1] My visit stimulated an interest in the *Life of St Columba*,[2] written in 597 by St Adomnán, one of Columba's successors as abbot of Iona. As I explored the work of Adomnán, I discovered that he had also written a somewhat less well-known 'law' in the seventh century, entitled the *Law of the Innocents* or, in Gaelic, *Cáin Adomnáin*,[3] an early law for the protection of non-combatants in war enforced by many kings, bishops and abbots in Ireland, Gaelic Scotland and Pictland.

What struck me most as I read Adomnán's *Law* was the diversity of the early Christian world. Celtic Christianity, active also in Wales, and today remembered only for its rich spiritual tradition,[4] was, in the first millennium, a rival to Roman Christianity, only succumbing to it at the Synod of Whitby, 664, following its advance through the south of England from Canterbury. St Adomnán's *Law*, an early form of natural law thought in the Western Christian world, demonstrates how differently the early Christians treated war and non-combatants. The Celtic position took a relatively more (although not entirely) pacifist approach, while the Roman world developed the theory of *jus in bello*, or just war.[5]

One finds a similar diversity of Christian approaches to natural law, not amongst those churches which became part of the Western, Roman world, but between the two traditions that grew from the Great Schism of 1054, the principal division which

[1] Sincere thanks to Jerome Squires (LLB, 2014), who provided outstanding research assistance and comments in the preparation of this chapter. Any errors and omissions, of course, are entirely my own responsibility.

[2] St Adomnán of Iona, *Life of St. Columba*, Richard Sharpe, trans. (London: Penguin, 1995).

[3] St Adomnán, *Law of the Innocents (Cáin Adomnáin): A Seventh Century Law for the Protection of Non-Combatants*, Gilbert Markus, trans. (Kilmartin: Kilmartin House Trust, 2008).

[4] See Oliver Davies and Thomas O'Loughlin, eds., *Celtic Spirituality* (Mahwah: Paulist Press, 2000).

[5] See Michael Walzer, *Just and Unjust Wars: A Moral Argument with Historical Illustrations* (New York: Basic Books, 4th edn, 1977).

has scarred the second millennium of Christianity – the rift that has developed between East and West, Orthodox and Catholic (and the numerous splits that have occurred since in the Western Catholic tradition, leading to a proliferation of Protestant confessions). Norman Doe in Chapter 10 of this volume notes that 'natural law has played an important part historically in Christian theology, ethics, and jurisprudence. By way of contrast, traditionally, it has played only a small part in Judaism and Islam'.[6] Yet the same variation in treatment identified by Doe as amongst the monotheistic traditions might also be said to exist between the Eastern (Orthodox) and Western (Roman and its many variants) Christian traditions, for natural law in the Orthodox world has played nothing like the dominant role it has in the Christian West, and this was true from the very earliest emergence of Christianity. The treatment of natural law in the Orthodox tradition – or, more to the point, the lack of it – will seem as alien to Western Christians today as was Celtic Christianity to Roman Christians over 1000 years ago.

But in addition to the diversity of approaches to natural law within the Christian world, it is worth remembering that there is a similar diversity of churches within the Orthodox world itself. What, then, do I mean by the 'Orthodox tradition'? A number of Christian churches claim to be Orthodox, of which there are two main divisions, the Eastern Orthodox and the Oriental Orthodox churches, each containing a number of further divisions into particular churches, largely orientated around national lines, such as the Russian and Greek Orthodox churches within Eastern Orthodoxy and the Syriac, Coptic and Ethiopian churches of Oriental Orthodoxy.[7] Within each of these groupings, the concept of communion among churches serves, in some cases loosely, in others more rigidly, to bind them together into the relevant grouping. And, compounding this diversity for present purposes is the lack in the Christian East of a Western Christian systematisation of theology. Every Orthodox church can take its own approach to theological questions that might otherwise be dealt with in a common way in the West. Natural law is no exception to this rule of the Christian East. Thus, in the interests of space, this chapter considers the place of natural law largely as it is found within the Eastern Orthodox group or communion of churches. But even here, as we will see, there is still a diversity of opinion as to the status and role of natural law.

This chapter, then, to the extent that it is possible to do so, provides a brief overview of the key features of natural law in the teaching, tradition and canon law of the Orthodox tradition. There is little doubt that the way in which natural law is used in the Christian East differs from its treatment in the Christian West. One of the fundamental differences, for example, is found in the way in which canon law, or ecclesiastical law, operates in Eastern and Western Christianity; in the case of the latter, systematisation and codification dominates, while in the former, 'unlike the

[6] See below, Chapter 10.

[7] See Elizabeth A. Livingstone, ed., *The Concise Oxford Dictionary of the Christian Church* (New York: Oxford University Press, 2nd rev. edn, 2006), 'Orthodoxy'.

canon law of the Roman Catholic Church ... [Orthodox canon law] has not been codified. Neither is it prescriptive in character, anticipating a situation before it actually takes place; instead, it is corrective in nature, responding to a situation once it has occurred';[8] the canon law of the Christian East is therefore contained in collections, the most widely used today being the *Pedalion* (or *Rudder*), which is discussed later in this chapter. What ultimately emerges, then, from the analysis presented here is a picture of four unresolved disputes concerning the natural law in the Christian East. And, because there is no Western-style systematisation in the Christian East, these disputes will remain unresolved.

The first of these disputes is simply this: can it even be said that the Orthodox tradition recognises natural law, or, conversely, does any conception of natural law even have a place within the Orthodox tradition? While asking such a question may seem odd to Western ears, there is real disagreement about the existence of natural law in the Christian East. Concluding, though, as this chapter does, that natural law has a place in the Orthodox tradition only leads to a second unresolved dispute: how can one define natural law in the Orthodox tradition? The third dispute concerns the structure – origin, sources and content – of natural law in the Orthodox tradition. The final dispute is how, if at all, can natural law which already rests on so many contingent conclusions – the prior disputes concerning existence, definition and structure – be applied in the modern world? The conclusion of this chapter offers some reflections on future directions for research in this field, specifically, in order further to outline the place and role of natural law in the modern Orthodox tradition.

THE FIRST DISPUTE: EXISTENCE

The first dispute concerns the existence of natural law within the Orthodox tradition. Put another way, can it even be said that there *is* natural law in the Orthodox tradition? Some of the most influential and accessible modern Orthodox theology (in English) is that emerging from the early to mid-twentieth-century Neo-Patristic synthesis[9] of the Parisian School led by George Florovsky and Vladimir Lossky.[10] Yet

8 Lewis J. Patsavos, *Spiritual Dimensions of the Holy Canons* (Brookline: Holy Cross Orthodox Press, 2003), 6.

9 Father Georges Florovsky and Vladimir Lossky were the founders of Neo-Patristic thought. 'Florovsky and Lossky sharply rejected the religious-philosophical approach to theology practiced by Soloviev and those whom he inspired ... as Florovsky and Lossky saw it, Soloviev and his heirs were bad expositors of the mind of Orthodoxy because of the heavy dose of nineteenth-century German idealism and other modern tendencies in their thought. The antidote was to return to the church fathers, hence the name neopatristic': Paul Valliere, 'Introduction to Modern Orthodoxy', in John Witte Jr. and Frank S. Alexander, eds., *The Teachings of Modern Christianity: On Law, Politics, and Human Nature*, Vol. 1 (New York: Columbia University Press, 2006), 505.

10 This phrase seems to originate with Butler, by which it is likely that in using 'Parisian School', he meant the 'Neo-Patristic synthesis', which refers to theologians such as Vladimir Lossky, the émigré

its pre-eminent position notwithstanding, one searches in vain for anything like a systematic approach to natural law in the work of these scholars.[11] This failure to deal systematically with natural law seems to have promoted a common view among many Orthodox clergy denying the existence of natural law, concluding that it does not form part of the Orthodox tradition.[12] Yet, it may be that the only evidence for this stance is the very paucity itself of writing on natural law in the Orthodox tradition,[13] unlike the situation that pertains in the Catholic Church and other Western Christian traditions.[14]

This failure directly to mention natural law cannot be taken, though, for evidence that it does not exist. Indeed, there is scant Patristic or modern theological authority for reaching either conclusion: that natural law either does or does not exist as part of the Orthodox tradition. As such, we must exercise caution in accepting the absence of a systematic approach as evidence for the non-existence of natural law in the Orthodox tradition. As Michael Butler states:

> [P]eople who do not read contemporary Orthodox authors carefully, may come away with the idea that the Orthodox Church does not have a theory of natural law. Father John Romanides is sometimes cited in this regard, but what Romanides says, in fact, is this: 'Within Greek patristic thought, there is no room for theories concerning natural law, in terms of physical, social and moral laws being copies of eternal and immutable forms in the mind of God.' So we see Romanides is not objecting to the notion of natural law *per se*, he's objecting to Augustine's theories of the *rationes eternae*, of pre-existing ideas in the mind of God.[15]

Nonetheless, notwithstanding the lack of authority on the point, and the failure to take care in interpreting that authority which does exist, one of the leading Orthodox theologians of the late twentieth century, Stanley Harakas, concludes that 'the

theologian who settled in Paris, and Vladimir Lossky. Nikolay Lossky writes: 'Father Georges Florovsky termed Lossky's *Mystical Theology of the Eastern Church* a "neopatristic synthesis",' which provides support for the view that the phrase is synonymous with the Neo-Patristic synthesis: see N.O. Lossky, *History of Russian Philosophy* (New York: International Universities Press, 1951).

11 Michael Butler, 'Orthodoxy and Natural Law' (Lecture delivered at Acton University, 21 June 2013): www.ancientfaith.com/specials/episode/orthodoxy_and_natural_law.

12 See, e.g., George Morelli, *Pastoral Considerations on Current Problems: Sex, Natural Law and Orthodoxy* (Orthodox Research Institute, April 1976): www.orthodoxresearchinstitute.org/articles/ethics/morelli_sex_natural_law.htm; Gregory Jensen, *Orthodox Criticism of Natural Law* (23 February 2009): http://palamas.info/orthodox-criticism-of-natural-law/; Gregory Jensen, *Criticizing the Critics* (29 February 2009): http://palamas.info/criticizing-the-critics/.

13 Stanley S. Harakas, 'The Natural Law Teaching of the Eastern Orthodox Church', *Greek Orthodox Theological Review* IX (1964): 215–224, at 215 – hereafter Harakas 1964.

14 On the major traditions and their size, see F.L. Cross and E.A. Livingstone, eds., *Oxford Dictionary of the Christian Church* (Oxford: Oxford University Press, 3rd rev. edn, 2005); Pew Research Center, *Global Christianity – A Report on the Size and Distribution of the World's Christian Population* (The Pew Forum, 19 December 2011): www.pewforum.org/2011/12/19/global-christianity-traditions/-protestant.

15 Butler, op cit. (no citation to Romanides is provided in the original).

natural moral law . . . in Eastern Orthodox Christian Ethics is *generally accepted*' (emphasis added).[16]

This chapter, then, rejects the absence of sustained scholarship as evidence for the non-existence of a conception of natural law in Orthodox theology. Instead, it assumes that it is generally accepted to form part of the Orthodox tradition. And it argues that through an excavation of Patristic sources, along with a careful reading of modern scholarship, we can construct a tentative outline of natural law in the Orthodox tradition. Still, in doing so, one ought to consider that any such attempt not only suffers from the paucity of sources but also opens itself to outright hostility in some quarters.[17] And so, while we can turn to the matter of definition, we must remember that this first dispute remains unresolved.

THE SECOND DISPUTE: DEFINITION

The second dispute concerns the definition of natural law itself. In the Western tradition, natural law is often associated with 'moral standards which, on a long-dominant but now disfavoured account of morality, political philosophy, and law, can justify and guide political authority, make legal rules rationally binding, and shape concept-formation in even descriptive social theory'.[18] John Finnis, perhaps the foremost natural law scholar of the last fifty years,[19] has modified this monolithic, objective approach to natural law so as to apply to 'theories of ethics, theories of politics, theories of civil law, and theories of religious morality'.[20] In other words, natural law today tends to avoid taking a dogmatic stance, opting instead for an inclusive approach, both encompassing a range of different theories and taking account of the role played by ethical, legal, moral, political, etc., standards. Thus, modern Western approaches to natural law tend to draw upon a diversity of sources, taking a multidisciplinary stance.

How, though, given the paucity of the sources, can we even begin to build a definition of natural law in the Orthodox tradition, even allowing that we might

16 Stanley S. Harakas, 'Eastern Orthodox Perspectives on Natural Law', *American Journal of Jurisprudence* 24 (1979): 86–113 – hereafter Harakas 1979.

17 See Dylan Pahman, 'Orthodoxy and Natural Law: A Reappraisal' (7 March 2013): http://blog.acton.org/archives/51078-orthodoxy-and-natural-law-a-reappraisal.html; Dylan Pahman, 'Fr. Michael Butler: Orthodoxy and Natural Law' (21 June 2013): http://blog.acton.org/archives/56420-fr-michael-butler-orthodoxy-and-natural-law.html.

18 Ted Honderich, ed., *The Oxford Companion to Philosophy* (Oxford: Oxford University Press, 2nd edn, 2005), 642.

19 Although an alternative claim to that title may be made by Germain Grisez; see 'The First Principle of Practical Reason: A Commentary on the Summa Theologiae, 1–2, Question 94, Article 2', *Natural Law Forum* 10 (1965): 168–201.

20 John Finnis, 'Natural Law Theories', in Edward N. Zalta, ed., *The Stanford Encyclopaedia of Philosophy* (Fall 2014 edn): http://plato.stanford.edu/archives/fall2014/entries/natural-law-theories/. See also John Finnis, *Natural Law and Natural Rights* (Oxford: Oxford University Press, 2nd edn, 2011).

draw what we can from the existing material? The Orthodox approach to theology, and so to natural law, is complicated, at least in the modern context, by the need to begin, as with all Orthodox theology, with the Patristic Fathers. With the awakening of modern Orthodox theology in the twentieth century came also a heuristic for 'doing theology', which can be summarised as the 'return to the Fathers'.[21] This emerged during the

> First Orthodox Theological Conference, which was held in Athens in 1936, [where George] ... Florovsky, perhaps the greatest Orthodox theologian of the 20th century ... proclaimed Orthodox theology's need to 'return to the Fathers' and to be released from its 'Babylonian captivity' to Western theology in terms of its language, its presuppositions, and its thinking.[22]

And it led to the 'return to the Fathers' heuristic becoming

> the hallmark of and the dominant 'paradigm' for Orthodox theology for the better part of the 20th century, and for many its primary task, to such a degree that this celebrated 'return to the Fathers' and the efforts to 'de-westernize' Orthodox theology overshadowed all other theological questions.[23]

Though doubtless an extreme position, recent scholarship questions the ongoing viability of the Neo-Patristic synthesis in contemporary theology,[24] with some calling for

> a new way for modern Orthodox theology, which combines fidelity to tradition with renewal and innovation, boasting in the Lord about the positive things that Orthodox theology has offered up to this time, but also including an element of self-criticism and openness to the future. Primarily, however, [this] ... advocates [for] a free space for open-minded dialogue, where all views can be expressed and considered, with respect for the diversity of 'the other', who is an icon of the Other par excellence, God.[25]

Nonetheless, such calls for modification of the 'return to the Fathers' heuristic does not diminish the extent to which contemporary Orthodox theology must eschew a mechanistic acceptance of Western theology and begin with the Fathers, advert regularly to the Fathers and bring any conclusions back to the Fathers. And herein lies the dispute: do we return to the Fathers, or move towards the West? Or, we might take a middle path: whatever natural law is, it must be authentically Orthodox, in the sense that it originates with and returns to the Patristic Fathers,

21 See Pantelis Kalaitzidis, 'From the "Return of the Fathers" to the Need for a Modern Orthodox Theology', *St Vladimir's Theological Quarterly* 54(1) (2010): 5–36.

22 Ibid. 23 Ibid.

24 Metropolitan Kallistos Ware, 'The "Neo-Patristic Synthesis"' (Lecture delivered at the Cambridge Orthodox Forum Lectures, Cambridge, 1 May 2012): www.ancientfaith.com/podcasts/cambridge/the_neo_patristic_synthesis.

25 Kalaitzidis, op cit., at 36.

while allowing for innovation to meet modern conditions. Whichever route one chooses, though, there will be nothing like uniformity of opinion.

So, we might begin, first, by 'returning to the Fathers'. Amongst the Patristic Fathers, the most authoritative are the Three Great Hierarchs or Ecumenical Teachers – St Basil the Great (d. 379), St Gregory the Theologian or Nazianzus (d. 390) and St John Chrysostom (d. 407). The latter wrote:

> [I]n creating man at the beginning, God placed within him a natural law. *And what is this natural law?* He structured our conscience and made it so that our knowledge of good acts and those which are not so, was self-learned (*autodidakton*).[26]

And we might then look to modern Orthodox theologians. They seem to have added little. Michael Butler, for instance, drawing upon the Western approach – placing the term in its religious milieu and moral application, provides a tentative definition of natural law that goes little further than Chrysostom: 'the rule of conduct which is prescribed to us by God and by our constitution as rational creatures'.[27] Stanley Harakas expands upon this, writing:

> [T]he Eastern Orthodox Church accepts and teaches the reality of natural law found in the rational nature of man through which man may know the fundamental laws and rules of human moral and social life.[28]

Butler therefore concludes that 'natural law understanding is basically the same in the Orthodox Church as it is in the West'.[29] This seems to bring us full circle, rejecting Western theology to 'return to the Fathers', only to find ourselves back at our Western starting point. Yet, this fails to address the fact that there is little evidence, Patristic or modern, for a comprehensive approach to natural law. As such, we need to take Chrysostom and Butler as providing the best definition that we have, albeit sparse. And with that, we can turn to a consideration of the existing sources, both Patristic and modern, to begin constructing a rudimentary structure of natural law in the Orthodox tradition. But here we find another dispute: to which sources do we give priority, Patristic or modern?

THE THIRD DISPUTE: STRUCTURE

Is the structure of natural law to be developed using solely Patristic sources, or is it possible that such development may begin with those sources and be adapted to meet modern concerns? Whatever the answer to that question, there is one point of agreement: the origin of natural law is in the will of God. As such, we now turn, first, to the divine origin and, second, the sources, Patristic and modern, of Orthodox natural law. From that analysis, we will find that the two sources, engaged

[26] St John Chrysostom, *Homilies on the Statues*, 12.3 (emphasis added). [27] Butler, op cit.
[28] Harakas 1964, 215–216. [29] Butler, op cit.

in dispute, nonetheless come to a largely consistent conclusion concerning the structure of natural law in the Orthodox tradition.

Origin

In the Orthodox tradition, the sources of the natural law are to be found in 'the writings of Saint Paul and in the writings of the Fathers of the Church of the first five centuries of the Christian era'.[30] The divine revelation of natural law, though, originates in Holy Scripture, which 'indicated to patristic writers the existence of natural law precepts'.[31] The prescriptions of natural law therefore originate in the Old and New Testaments.

In the Old Testament, the Decalogue affirms that 'the essential right to life is protected by "You shall do no murder" ... property is protected by "You shall not steal" and "you shall not covet" and so forth'.[32] The principal New Testament sources are Romans 2.12–15 and 13.1, Peter 2.13, John 19.11, Acts 5.20 and 29 and Luke 12.15 and 57.

While each of the New Testament sources contains important scriptural authority forming the basis of the Patristic exposition of natural law,[33] the main New Testament source is Romans 2.12–15:

> [A]ll who have sinned without the law will also perish without the law, and all who have sinned under the law will be judged by the law ... When the Gentiles who have not the law, do by nature what the law requires, they are a law to themselves, even though they do not have the law. They show that what the law requires is written on their hearts, while their conscience also bears witness.[34]

And while both the Christian West and East take this as a primary source of natural law, the two traditions treat it differently. Thus:

> [T]he Roman Catholic understanding of natural law turns on a rationalistic interpretation of elements of the original Christian teaching. St Paul speaks of the Gentiles having 'the requirements of the law ... written on their hearts' (Romans 2:15). The Orthodox interpretation is that Paul was in fact talking about the human heart, a facility of the soul able, with proper disposition, to appreciate the guidance of God. The Roman Catholics, in contrast, came to hold that reason, not the heart, could discern the law of God.[35]

30 Harakas 1964, 216. 31 Ibid., 217. 32 Harakas 1979, 106.

33 Harakas 1964, 217 and 1979, 94. While Harakas' 1979 article contains a section on 'Natural Law and the New Testament', in which he considers the biblical basis for natural law teachings, a subsequent section entitled 'Natural Moral Law and the Fathers' does not examine the heuristic employed by the Fathers in using those sources.

34 Romans 2:12, 14–15 as quoted in Harakas 1964, 216.

35 H. Tristram Engelhardt, Jr., *The Foundations of Christian Bioethics* (Oxford: Oxford University Press, 2nd edn, 1996), 93, citing John S. Romanides, *Franks, Romans, Feudalism, and Doctrine* (Brookline, MA: Holy Cross Orthodox Press, 1981), 45ff.

The origin of the natural law therefore lies in 'the will and intelligence of God ... [and] the Orthodox Church teaches that all of creation is an act of the intelligence and will of God alone. This refers to all of creation and not alone to the natural and moral law'.[36]

As we might expect, though, while the origin is clear, the human ability to discern and understand the law is itself a matter of dispute. Romanides sees it as a matter of the heart, while Harakas, without rejecting that position, adds that it 'may be discerned through experience and reason'.[37] That dispute notwithstanding, with the origin of natural law clear, it is possible to consider its content.

Content

Drawing upon its divine origin in the will and intelligence of God, the Patristic tradition discerned a rudimentary content of the natural law. The Neo-Patristic synthesis provides a minimal supplement to that content. This section examines each source.

Patristic: From its divine origin, Patristic theology relied upon Holy Scripture and reason in order to expound the content of natural law. Harakas explains that

> the effort of unaided reason is seen by the Fathers of the first five centuries as the main and central means by which man discerns the content of natural law. Man's rational nature is effective for this purpose because he shares in the rational nature or Logos of God ... Thus, the basic elements of natural law ought to be clear and evident to all men, though such understanding is subject to development.[38]

Perhaps the most significant Patristic statement is that of St John Chrysostom:

> We use not only Scripture but also reason in arguing against the pagans. What is their argument? They say they have no law of conscience, and that there is no law implanted by God in nature. My answer is to question them about their laws concerning marriage, homicide, wills, [and] injuries to others, enacted by their legislators. Perhaps the living have learned from their fathers, and their fathers from their fathers and so on. But go back to the first legislator! From whom did he learn? Was it not by his own conscience and conviction? Nor can it be said that they heard Moses and the prophets, for Gentiles could not hear them. *It is evident that they derived their laws from the law which God ingrafted in man from the beginning.*[39]

Using this approach, the Patristic Fathers mention 'natural law' or the 'law of nature'; they also often speak of that which is 'according to nature' or 'contrary to nature'.[40] In relation to the former, we find representative examples in Origen (d. 254):

> As there are, then, generally two laws presented to us, the one being the law of nature, of which God would be the legislator, and the other being the written law of

36 Harakas 1964, 220. 37 Ibid., 215–216. 38 Ibid., 222.
39 Ad pop. Ant., XII, 4 (emphasis added). 40 Butler, op cit.

> cities, it is a proper thing, when the written law is not opposed to that of God, for the citizens not to abandon it under pretext of foreign customs; but when the law of nature, that is, the law of God, commands what is opposed to the written law, observe whether reason will not tell us to bid a long farewell to the written code, and to the desire of its legislators, and to give ourselves up to the legislator God, and to choose a life agreeable to His word, although in doing so it may be necessary to encounter dangers, and countless labours, and even death and dishonour.[41]

And likewise in St John Chrysostom:

> [W]hen God formed man, he implanted within him from the beginning a natural law . . . And what then was this natural law? He gave utterance to conscience within us; and made the knowledge of good things, and of those which are the contrary, to be self-taught.[42]

He elaborates:

> Now we have a natural law implanted in us, by which we distinguish between what is virtue, and what is vice. Hence it follows, And as ye would that men should do unto you, do ye also to them. He does not say, Whatever ye would not that men should do unto you, do not ye. For since there are two ways which lead to virtue, namely, abstaining from evil, and doing good, he names one, signifying by it the other also. And if indeed He had said, That ye may be men, love the beasts, the command would be a difficult one. But if they are commanded to love men, which is a natural admonition, wherein lies the difficulty, since even the wolves and lions observe it, whom a natural relation compels to love one another. It is manifest then that Christ has ordained nothing surpassing our nature, but what He had long before implanted in our conscience, so that thy own will is the law to thee. And if thou wilt have good done unto thee, thou must do good to others; if thou wilt that another should show mercy to thee, thou must show mercy to thy neighbor.[43]

In relation to what is according to nature or contrary to nature, four of the Fathers provide examples. Origen writes:

> But we maintain, at the same time, that God cannot do what is disgraceful, since then He would be capable of ceasing to be God; for if He do anything that is disgraceful, He is not God. Since, however, he lays it down as a principle, that 'God does not desire what is contrary to nature', we have to make a distinction, and say that if any one asserts that wickedness is contrary to nature, while we maintain that 'God does not desire what is contrary to nature', – either what springs from wickedness or from an irrational principle – yet, if such things happen according to the word and will of God, we must at once necessarily hold that they are not contrary to nature. Therefore things which are done by God, although they may be, or may appear to some to be incredible, are not contrary to nature. And if we must press the force of words, we would say that, in comparison with what is generally

41 Origen, *Against Celsus*, 5.37.

42 St John Chrysostom, *Homilies Concerning the Statues*, 12.9.

43 Ibid., 13.

> understood as 'nature', there are certain things which are beyond its power, which God could at any time do; as, e.g., in raising man above the level of human nature, and causing him to pass into a better and more divine condition, and preserving him in the same, so long as he who is the object of His care shows by his actions that he desires (the continuance of His help).[44]

St John Chrysostom says this:

> This much only do I enjoin: (I say) not fast, but abstain from luxury. Let us seek meats to nourish, not things to ruin us; seek meats for food, not occasions of diseases, of diseases both of soul and body: seek food which hath comfort, not luxury which is full of discomfort: the one is luxury, the other mischief; the one is pleasure, the other pain; the one is agreeable to nature, the other contrary to nature. For say, if one should give thee hemlock juice to drink, would it not be against nature? If one should give thee logs and stones, wouldest thou not reject them? Of course, for they are against nature. Well, and so is luxury. For just as in a city, under an invasion of enemies when there has been siege and tumult, great is the uproar, so is it in the soul, under invasion of wine and luxury.[45]

St Dionysius the Areopagite (d. early sixth century) says this:

> Everything that is according to nature comes into being from a defined cause. And if the Evil is without cause, and undefined, it is not according to nature. For there is not in nature [that which] is contrary to nature ... It remains then that the Evil is a weakness and a falling short of the Good.[46]

And, finally, Oecumenius of Trikka (d. late tenth century) tells us:

> Everything against nature is false. Virtue is according to nature, since from the beginning the Creator has implanted in our makeup the seed of virtue, and so vice is against nature. For just as health is natural to our bodies and sickness is unnatural, and just as seeing and hearing are natural while blindness and deafness are unnatural, so also virtue in our souls is natural and evil is unnatural. Health is, then, analogous to virtue, and vice analogous to sickness. In a corresponding way, falsehood is evil, for it often falsely presents itself as virtue. Temerity masquerades as courage, dishonourable conduct as prudence, sloth as wisdom, and false modesty as righteousness. All of these things are evils, cloaking themselves with a mask of virtue, to those who fall in with them, and therefore he casts outside the divine walls those who pursue such lying deceit.[47]

The most significant Fathers who wrote on natural law in the first five centuries of Christianity, though, are Justin Martyr (d. c. 165), Irenaeos (d. 202), Clement of Alexandria (d. 215), Origen (d. 254), Tertullian (d. 225), St Athanasius (d. 373),

44 Origen, *Against Celsus*, 5.23.

45 St John Chrysostom, *Homilies on the Acts of the Apostles*, 27 (on Acts 12.18–19).

46 St Dionysius the Areopagite, *On the Divine Names*, 4.30.

47 Oecumenius of Trikka, *Commentary on the Apocalypse*, 22.15–19.

St Basil (d. 379), Gregory of Nazianzus (d. 390), Gregory of Nyssa (d. 395), St John Chrysostom (d. 407), Cyril of Alexandria (d. 444) and St Maximus the Confessor (d. 662).[48] This last Father stands out from all the others as providing the fullest account of natural law and may be seen as an Orthodox equivalent to Aquinas or Luther. Yet here again disagreement exists as to which of these Fathers enjoys the greatest prominence in relation to the Orthodox position on natural law. Harakas identifies Justin Martyr as father of Patristic natural law thinking,[49] while Butler attributes this place to St Maximus the Confessor because he provides the only systematic teaching on natural law among all of the Greek Patristic Fathers.[50]

While avoiding the dispute over the pre-eminence of either Justin or Maximus, we can nonetheless provide a summary of the major points found in each of the Fathers' work which touches on natural law. Justin Martyr, Harakas writes, expounds

> the conviction that men are rational ... With this emphasis on a common human God-given rationality, he emphasizes that 'in all persons, there appear to be seeds of truth'. The existence of these 'seeds' is explained by the doctrine of Christ as the pre-existent 'Logos' (word, reason, rationality). The 'logos' is reason. Christ is the 'logos'. Man's reason is Christ in man ... This view naturally leads to the natural law position.[51]

Irenaeos battled

> Gnostic heretics who used platonic and neo-platonic concepts to blur the distinction between the Creator and the creation ... For Irenaeos, God created the world freely by His own will and design ... One of the things which the Creator has done is to implant in human beings a perception of the moral law. In creating humanity, God naturally gave to all the knowledge of good and evil.[52]

According to Clement of Alexandria, 'God gave the "rule of right" to humanity alone in the world. "Whether, then he speaks of the law given at birth, or of that given afterwards, whatever the case, it is from God; the law of nature and the law which is learned, are one" (*Stromata*, 2, xxix).'[53]

Origen provides a significant contribution to natural law

> 'by differentiating the natural law from conscience by noting that the first is a rational power of the soul for discovery of the content of the law while the second is a spiritual power which serves as a guide to the moral life, praising the good and condemning evil'. In criticizing those who called positive enacted law 'the king of all', Origen counters, saying 'we Christians, who have come to the law by which nature is the "king of all", which is the very same as the law of God, attempt to live according to it, having bid a long farewell to laws which are not laws.'[54]

48 Harakas 1979, 98. For a full list of the writings of the Patristic Fathers on natural law and human nature, see Butler, op cit.

49 Harakas 1979, 98–99.

50 Butler, op cit.

51 Harakas 1979, 98–99.

52 Ibid., 99–100.

53 Ibid., 100.

54 Ibid., 100–101.

Tertullian 'makes a special effort at diagnosing the content of natural law, and without ignoring the older tradition of the rational nature of natural moral law, he does add the observation that all of nature is included within the structure of natural law and that nature itself is law and requires obedience'.[55]

St Athanasius 'emphasized the natural law idea in connection with the creation of man in the image and after the likeness of God',[56] while St Basil '[i]n his *Hexaemeron* … argues that the general order and harmony existing in creation is a prototype for the ordering of human life. He holds that the social order of human society is an expression of the natural moral law (29, 193)'. He 'teaches that "within us there are virtues by nature to which the soul conforms itself, not through the teaching of man, but out of nature itself, in which it exists" (*Hexaemeron* 29, 196)'.[57]

While at one end of a spectrum, Gregory of Nazianzus and Gregory of Nyssa 'both touch upon but do not elaborate in detail natural law concepts';[58] at the other, it is perhaps St John Chrysostom 'of all the Eastern Christian Fathers, who elaborated most on the natural law'. Moreover:

> Though he did not contribute new understandings, he did express more clearly than any other Eastern Father the teaching of the Church on the question of natural law, the '*nomos physeos*' or law of nature, as he preferred to call it. The law of nature, for Chrysostom, is a true law and any positive law opposed to it is not worthy of obedience as false. The law of nature is general, eternal, and immortal. Special revelation is not needed to understand its precepts; it is known naturally.[59]

And Cyril of Alexandria 'follows the teachings of Chrysostom generally but he also makes mention of the eternal law in God which will play an important role in later thought, especially in Augustine'.[60]

The great contribution of St Maximus the Confessor was to outline a hierarchy within the moral or divine law, which is knowable by all people, the Jew through the Mosaic law or Decalogue and the Gentile through the natural law.[61] Other Fathers made clear this understanding of the place of natural law:

> Cyril of Alexandria refers to 'three laws, the natural, and the Mosaic, and the evangelical'. And Theodoretos, in his commentary on Psalm 18:1 writes: 'There are three kinds of divine law … the first is without letters, given to human beings through creation and nature … the other … through Moses in writing … and the third … the law of grace.'[62]

St Maximus the Confessor wrote, in relation to the law of grace, that natural law and the written law are equally valuable in coming to the law of grace,[63] the three categories corresponding to a progressive revelation to humanity of the Word of God.[64] In the Orthodox tradition, in other words, 'the natural moral law, the Old

55 Harakas 1964, 218. 56 Ibid., 218. 57 Harakas 1979, 102. 58 Harakas 1964, 219.
59 Harakas 1979, 102. 60 Harakas 1964, 219. 61 Ibid., 218; Harakas 1979, 93. 62 Ibid., 88.
63 Butler, op cit. 64 Ibid.

Testament moral law, and the ethical teaching of the New Testament are not sharply divided, but rather, point to different dimensions of the same reality'.[65]

Based upon Maximus' teaching, revelation proceeds (i) from natural law, which leads to the recognition of the Golden Rule, to (ii) the written law, which leads to love of neighbour, and finally to (iii) the law of grace/Christ, which leads to loving our neighbour more than ourselves.[66] Mikhail Kulakov summarises Maximus this way:

> In his *Five Centuries of Various Texts*, Maximus drew a clear distinction between 'natural law', 'written Law' (meaning Mosaic law), and the 'law of grace'. He emphasized the social function of the natural law and saw its task in bringing 'into harmony all men's voluntary relationships with one another' and in granting 'equal rights to all men in accordance with natural justice'. He described the function of the 'written law' as that of 'preventing wrongdoing through fear' and as making one accustomed to doing what is right. He regarded the law of grace as superior to the other two laws because it directly teaches the attainment of 'similitude to God, in so far as it is possible for man'. Thus the law of grace, by contrast, describes not a rational ascent to an intellectual principle, but a transformation of human nature through deification without 'altering its fundamental character'. It is a revelation of the archetype of human nature and union with Him.[67]

It is in large part due to Maximus the Confessor's magisterial position in Patristic theology that later Orthodox tradition has added little in the subsequent centuries, content to leave the understanding of natural and written laws and the law of grace, their relationship to one another and their role in divine revelation to the potent Maximian distinctions.[68]

Neo-Patristic Synthesis: The development of Orthodox theology, in every area, including natural law, languished in the second millennium of Christianity, having missed all of the major developments of philosophy and theology that have so influenced the West and Western Christianity in the last 1000 years. Indeed, the natural law itself, as part of this larger neglect, re-emerges as worthy of attention only within the last 100 years. Kulakov observes:

> [T]he notion of natural law is present in the Eastern patristic tradition, yet it has not been developed in the East into a comprehensive theory comparable to the natural law theory in Catholic theology ... Today, natural law teaching does not have the

65 Harakas 1979, 88.

66 Butler, op cit. This appears very similar to natural law in the Catholic tradition. See Brian Tierney, 'Natural Law and Natural Rights', in John Witte Jr. and Frank S. Alexander, eds., *Christianity and Law: An Introduction* (Cambridge: Cambridge University Press, 2008), 89, at 92: 'The very first words of Gratian's work gave a definition of natural law as the Golden Rule of Scripture.'

67 Mikhail Kulakov, 'Vladimir Nikolaievich Lossky', in John Witte Jr. and Frank S. Alexander, eds., *The Teachings of Modern Christianity: On Law, Politics, and Human Nature*, Vol. 1 (New York: Columbia University Press, 2006), 612, 636–637.

68 Ibid.

> same status in the Eastern Orthodox theology as it does in the Western Thomistic system, where it forms the basis for the development of positive law.[69]

As such, our account of the sources of Orthodox natural law jumps from the first millennium of Christianity, with the Patristic Fathers, to the last 100 years, with the Neo-Patristic synthesis. For this reason, it is here that the Orthodox position on natural law becomes difficult. What one finds in the Neo-Patristic synthesis is sketchy, providing little guidance on how to make the Fathers relevant to the modern world and to allow anything like engagement with the much more fully developed understanding of natural law in the Christian West.

Thus, for example, we might ask: why does one find so little reference to the ancient Greek philosophers, particularly Plato and Aristotle, in the modern Orthodox writing on natural law? Indeed, while the early Patristic Fathers were engaged with the philosophy of their time,[70] the Neo-Patristic Synthesis and the 'return to the Fathers' heuristic has rejected anything that may seem to lead towards Western philosophy; and while the Greek philosophers were not, of course, writing in the Christian tradition, their association with Western Christian theology today has rendered the use of those sources, at least as the state of contemporary Orthodox theology currently stands, out of bounds. And that has been aided by the fact that the Patristic Fathers made little direct reference to the ancient Greeks. For that reason, modern Orthodox theology returns to the Fathers, and not to the Greeks.

That said, what can the Neo-Patristic synthesis provide in terms of a modern understanding of the natural law? The pre-eminent modern theologian to attempt an elucidation of the Orthodox position on natural law is Stanley Harakas. Harakas identifies '[K.B.] Kyriazis, [Vasileios] Ioannides, [John] Romanides, [Vladimir] Lossky and [Sergius] Bulgakov [as having] made substantial contributions in natural law studies', but, he writes, 'as yet a full and complete and authoritative study of a definitive character has failed to appear'.[71] Moreover, Harakas himself fails always to cite these scholars as providing an understanding of Orthodox natural law. Thus, no mention, or footnote to the works, of Ioannides, Lossky and Bulgakov appears in Harakas' 1964 article; rather, only Kyriazis and Romanides are cited. Still, Harakas' conclusion about these Neo-Patristic scholars suggests that their work may be a fruitful area for further research, which Michael Butler summarises as: (1) St Maximus the Confessor; (2) Greek scholars/theologians of

69 Ibid.

70 See, e.g., Jaroslav Pelikan, *What Has Athens to Do with Jerusalem? Timaeus and Genesis in Counterpoint* (Ann Arbor, MI: University of Michigan Press, 1998).

71 Harakas 1964, 215. Father John Romanides (1927–2001) was a prominent twentieth-century Orthodox priest, Sergii Bulgakov (1871–1944) was a significant Russian Orthodox theologian and Vladimir Lossky (1903–1958) has been described as the 'best exponent' of the 'Neopatristic synthesis': see Andrew Louth, 'The Greek Tradition', in Augustine Cassiday, ed., *The Orthodox Christian World* (Abingdon: Routledge, 2012), Chapter 1.

the late thirteenth and early fourteenth centuries (Aquinas' *Summa Theologiae* was translated into Greek at this time); (3) scholars/theologians of late Imperial Russia (pre-revolutionary): Nicholas Alexeyev and Vladimir Soloviev (author of *The Justification of the Good*); and (4) the Russian Orthodox Church today: Patriarch Kirill of Moscow and 'Bases of the Social Concept of the Russian Orthodox Church'. To this list might be added a more detailed assessment of natural law in the Orthodox canonical tradition[72] as found in the *Pedalion* or *Rudder*.[73]

Still, notwithstanding the daunting task facing Orthodoxy if it cares to develop its own natural law position, some scholars do provide elucidation of the approach taken by the modern Orthodox Neo-Patristic synthesis to defining natural law. Mikhail Kulakov, for instance, provides this summary of Vladimir Lossky's work, which is worth citing in full for its clear statement of the differences between the Orthodox and Western Christian positions on the development of natural law, its purpose and the role of the Fathers today:

> In order to assess better the major objections of the Eastern Orthodox to the Western natural law theory, it would be helpful to recall that in the Roman Catholic system the human attribute of reason or intelligence plays an essential role. Angela Carmella rightly points out: 'The conviction that we can know natural law is based upon the premises that the person is intelligent, that nature is intelligible, and that nature's intelligibilities are laws for the mind that grasps them'. Thus, in the Roman Catholic philosophy of law, the natural law or the intelligible moral order becomes the criteria of the ethical content of the positive law of society. 'An intelligible moral order,' continues Carmella, 'means that the positive law of a society can be measured against those moral principles'.

However:

> The Greek Fathers operated on a different understanding of the nature of human reason. They distinguished between spiritual intellect and discursive reason. Discursive reason is incapable of direct apprehension of spiritual reality. Spiritual reality is of a principally different nature from the phenomena perceived by the senses. Moreover, the Eastern Orthodox and particularly Lossky's understanding of divine order in the universe is expressly personalist, apophatic, and experiential in contrast to the Catholic rational notion of natural law. Discursive reason is incapable of direct apprehension of dynamic divine economy. Truth is also understood experientially, rather than rationally. Following Khomyakov, Lossky insists on two specific attributes of the truth. First, the 'Truth can have no external criteria'. It stands on the basis of its own internal evidence. Second, 'gnosis [authentic knowledge] is inseparable from love'. Thus, by connecting gnosis with love

72 Butler, op cit.

73 *The Rudder* (or *Pedalion*) (see more fully below) was originally compiled by Agapius a Hieromonk and Nicodemus a Monk in 1800 and is now available in translation by D. Cummings, based upon the 5th edition published by John Nicolaides (Kesisoglou the Caesarian) in Athens, Greece, in 1908 (The Orthodox Christian Educational Society, repr. 1957; Luna Printing Co., 1983).

> Lossky highlights the ethical and communitarian dimensions of the Eastern Orthodox epistemology. He follows Khomyakov, who insisted that the 'Truth can only be apprehended in brotherly love'. At the foundation of Catholic legal consciousness and ethics lie the rational notion of natural law and the key role of human reason in the apprehension of this natural law. Lossky's ethics, by contrast, could be described as the internalized and experiential ethics of transfiguration through participation in the divine nature. *Theosis*, or deification, is at the heart of Lossky's ethics.[74]

And Paul Valliere provides an equally important summary of Vladimir Soloviev's account of natural law:[75]

> [Soloviev] sought a middle way between utopianism and Romantic conservatism in a formula acknowledging both the free-personal and the social aspects of law: '*Law is freedom conditioned by equality*', or '*the synthesis of freedom and equality.*'

Moreover:

> The crafting of a definition of law provided Soloviev with an occasion to clarify his concept of natural law. Soloviev rejected the concept in the sense of an actual ordering of life preceding the rise of political associations in a supposed state of nature. To think of natural law in this way is 'to take an intellectual abstraction for reality'. But the concept is useful as an expression of the necessary formal properties which positive law must reflect, 'to the extent that it is really law and not something else'.

Thus:

> The concepts of personhood, freedom, and equality constitute the essence of so-called natural law. The rational essence of law is distinguished from its historical manifestation, namely positive law. In this sense, natural law is that general algebraic formula into which history inserts the various real quantities of positive law; it exists in reality only as the general form of all positive legal relations, in them and through them.

A key theme emerging, then, from the Neo-Patristic synthesis is that of theosis – that whatever the natural law is, it involves the process of theosis. For Orthodox theology generally, theosis represents a central concept, the belief that one may be transfigured through participation in the divine nature. And this participation is made possible as part of the divine oikonomia/economy through living the Christian life. Part of this life of theosis and the demands it makes of the Christian is Orthodox canon law found in the *Pedalion* and other collections of canon law.[76]

74 Mikhail Kulakov, op cit., 638–639.

75 Paul Valliere, 'Vladimir Soloviev', in John Witte Jr. and Frank S. Alexander, eds., *The Teachings of Modern Christianity: On Law, Politics, and Human Nature*, Vol. 1 (New York: Columbia University Press, 2006), 533, 545.

76 See, e.g., Panteleimon Rodopoulos, *An Overview of Orthodox Canon Law*, W.J. Lillie, trans. (Rollinsford, NH: Orthodox Research Institute, 2007), 10.

Drawing on the metaphorical ship of the Orthodox Church, the *Rudder* contains all of the sacred and divine canons of the Apostles; the Holy Councils, ecumenical as well as regional; and of individual Fathers of the Church. And it is here that the Orthodox Christian finds the keys to the nature of theosis. In other words, by following the strictures of the *Rudder*, principally the sacraments of the church, one can follow the path of theosis.[77] Thus, the *Rudder* mediates the divine law to humans, rather than the natural law, as part of the relationship of oikonomia/economy in the context of theosis. Or, put another way: '[T]he Orthodox sense of natural law draws more on transformative noetic experience related to theosis, than a more static sense of natural laws in our fallen world.'[78]

In sum, then, we may make two claims drawing upon both Patristic and Neo-Patristic scholarship. First, the natural law is *not* synonymous with the divine law/law of God/moral law.[79] Rather, it forms a *part* of the latter form of law, without being a complete statement of it. Still, 'the core of the Mosaic Law, the Decalogue [the Divine moral law], and the core of natural law written in the hearts of all men coincide, the contents being essentially the same'.[80] The relationship between the divine/moral law and natural may be captured thus:

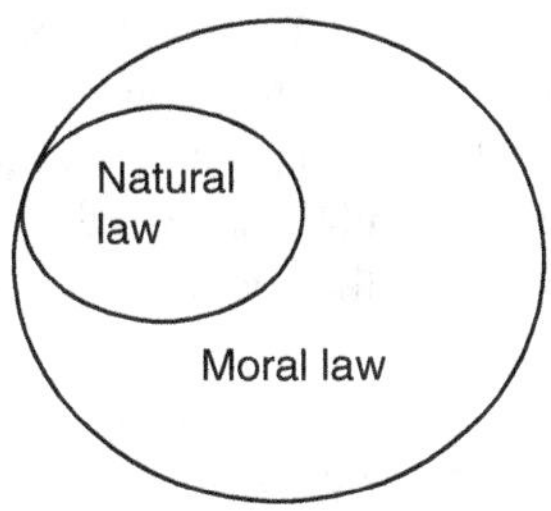

Figure 1

Secondly, based upon Patristic thought we know that natural law *per se* is sufficient to order human relationships; it, together with the Decalogue, makes it possible for all people to know the divine moral law, the law of grace/Christ. Modern scholarship affirms this view and adds that natural law may either guide the development of positive law or, more importantly, reflect its essence, through ordering human relationships as a matter of theosis.

77 On the operation and interpretation of, and for some of the canons on the sacraments found in, the *Rudder*, and for the modern regulatory instruments of Orthodox churches, see Norman Doe, *Christian Law: Contemporary Principles* (Cambridge: Cambridge University Press, 2013), 23–24, 33, 233–273.

78 Alfred Kentigern Siewers, *Secular Privilege and Natural Law* (Orthodox Christian Network: The Sounding, 7 July 2014): http://myocn.net/secular-privilege-and-natural-law/.

79 See Harakas 1979.

80 See Harakas 1964, 215–216.

THE FOURTH DISPUTE: RELEVANCE

The final dispute concerns the relevance of natural law: its purpose and its application.

Purpose

What, then, can we say about the purpose of natural law in modern Orthodox thought? Here again, we run up against a dispute over the contemporary relevance of natural law for the Orthodox Church. On a narrow view, natural law may not have a purpose *per se*, but, rather, it may be a consequence of (or incidental to) creation, making it possible for humanity to participate in the divine nature through the transfiguration of theosis.

Taking a broader approach, however, it is also possible to attribute a two-fold purpose to natural law. First, the natural law may ensure that humankind has knowledge of what is right and wrong (at least to a limited extent) and therefore possesses the capacity to make moral choices and to avoid sin. And this applies to all people, as Romans 2.12 makes clear and Patristic authority confirms; as Harakas puts it:

> The general patristic interpretation is, in the words of Kyriazis, 'that the place which the Mosaic Law has for the Jews, that is the knowledge of the law and therefore of good and evil, is the very same taken amongst the gentiles by their naturally given capacity for the knowledge of God and the knowledge of the main requirements of ethics which they are able to find in the law written in their hearts.'[81]
>
> The fact that the recipient of this ethical endowment is subject to judgment and condemnation on the same level as the recipient of the Mosaic Law, is reason enough to identify the ethical endowment as *a legally binding requirement of life for those who are without the written law* (emphasis added).[82]

So, natural law not only applies to all people but is also prescriptive in its own right, its basic content deriving from the Mosaic Law, and arising from prescriptions found within people's hearts. In short, natural law creates a sense of obligation and conscience in humankind.

Second, and perhaps more importantly, the natural law operates within basic social relationships so as to make possible social life and the maintenance of human community.[83] It is 'an expression of the basic conditions permitting and protecting the existence of human society'[84] and 'articulates the absolutely necessary modes of

[81] Ibid., 216. [82] Ibid., 217.

[83] On community in the Orthodox tradition see John Zizioulas, *Being as Communion: Studies in Personhood and the Church* (New York: St Vladimir's Seminary Press, 1997) and Paul Babie, 'Looking East to the Concept of Property: A Review Essay of Witte and Alexander, *Christianity and Law: An Introduction*', *Adelaide Law Review* 30 (2009): 175–184.

[84] Harakas 1979, 104.

behaviour for the maintenance of the human community.'[85] K.B. Kyriazis summarises this purpose thus:

> The task of the natural law is to establish surely the foundational rules which make up the necessary basis of social life. Because of this it is characterized as a necessity for life and consequently it is said by some Fathers that without it the world would have long ago been destroyed.[86]

How, then, is this law applied in the modern context?

Application

While Orthodox tradition tends to hold that natural law does not lead directly to positive law, as may be the case in Western thinking, there are some who take another position. For instance, the canonist Panteleimon Rodopoulos argues:

> Naturally, in any specific society, human authority must also have independent powers. In the exercise of its authority, however, and in the adoption of its laws, it must conform totally to the natural law implanted by God in people's conscience and of which St Paul speaks in his Epistle to the Romans (2:14–15) . . . Therefore, every law and every human judicial institution must be formulated in accordance with divine justice (*jus divinum*), that is with unwritten divine justice or natural justice (*jus naturale*) or the natural law (*lex naturalis*) and with the written divine law.[87]

Still, there is little contemporary evidence that points to a usage, either in the church itself or more broadly by legislators and policy makers in the design of positive law that would suggest that the Orthodox stance on natural law plays a large part in ordering social relations, notwithstanding that this seems to represent one of its principal functions.

Three tentative examples of the contemporary application do exist, though, which may demonstrate a possible influence of natural law on (i) the internal discipline of the church, (ii) the ordering of church-state relations and (iii) positive law-making.

In relation to church discipline, it may be that the natural law, such as it is in the Orthodox tradition, forms the basis of bioethics.[88] In this context, Harakas writes that, on the one hand, natural law 'refers primarily to the elementary relationships that are necessary for the constitution and maintenance of human society', the foundation of which, as we have seen, is the Decalogue. On the other hand, however, and balancing natural law, it is important to remember that 'there are

85 Ibid., 107.

86 K.B. Kyriazis, *To Physikon kei to Kanonikon Dikeion ex Epooseos Orthodoxou*, Vol. 1 (Athens: Apostolike Diakonia Press, 1957), 69, quoted in Harakas 1979, 104.

87 Rodopoulos, *An Overview of Orthodox Canon Law*, op cit., 10.

88 Stanley S. Harakas, *For the Health of Body and Soul: An Eastern Orthodox Introduction to Bioethics* (Greek Orthodox Archdiocese of America): www.goarch.org/ourfaith/ourfaith8076.

modes of behavior that are either prescribed or proscribed for the lives of Christians growing in the image and likeness of God toward theosis or full humanity. These positive and negative injunctions are found in the Holy Scriptures, in the writings of the Fathers and in [the *Rudder*]'. In turn:

> For the Orthodox these statements are normative in the sense that they embody the mind of the Church and reflect standards of behavior that are appropriate and fitting for the members of the Church and, potentially, for all human beings growing in the image and likeness of God – for the full realization of personhood. This . . . level of ethical direction is saved from legalism and rigid prescriptivism by the fundamental emphasis on love as a motive of action.

Thus, for Harakas, 'both order [the more objective natural law] and compassion [the more flexible nature of theosis with its emphasis on love] are harmonized in an approach to Christian ethics that seeks to avoid the extremes of legalism and relativism.'[89] And it is in this duality of order/objectivity and compassion/flexibility/love that, as part of the divine oikonomia/economy, and mediated through the *Rudder*, there exists a balance of natural law as against the divine law, leading the way perhaps to an emergent bioethics.

Similarly, in 2000 the Russian Orthodox Church released 'Bases of the Social Concept of the Russian Orthodox Church', outlining social doctrine on a wide variety of issues including church-state relations, private property, crime and punishment, war and peace, family life, bioethics, environmental issues, globalisation and secularisation.[90] This outline may contain a natural law foundation for discussions of marriage, contraception and abortion, biomedical and scientific advances, death and dying and homosexuality, and 'several considerations that assume natural law arguments even though natural law is never explicitly cited'.[91]

As to relations between church and state, early twentieth-century Russian lawyer and political scientist Nicholas Alexeyev 'supporte[d] . . . natural law rather than any form of constitutionalism'; he maintained that 'free consent should be the basis of relations between those who are governed and those who govern. This consent is attained through a common concept of virtue, rather than contract or any formal law or guarantee of rights'.[92] Like the Bases document, this too may constitute an example of natural law ideas being used to suggest not only how the faithful, but also the church itself, should relate to the state.

Finally, two scriptural passages suggest that the natural law has authority over humanly created juridical norms, or positive law: the Apostolic dictum that 'it is better to obey God than to obey man' (Acts 5.29), and Jesus' teaching in the form of the negative question 'and why do you not judge for yourselves what is right' (Luke 12.15). Stanley Harakas nonetheless suggests, though, that even if one ought to obey the positive law of the state, the natural law retains 'a binding and legal character to

[89] Ibid. [90] Cassiday, ed., *The Orthodox Christian World* (op.cit.), 32. [91] Butler, op cit.
[92] Ibid.

which all positive laws, secular and ecclesiastical, are subject and from which they obtain their authority',[93] following Chrysostom who believed 'the law of nature . . . is a true law and any positive law opposed to it is not worthy of obedience as false'.[94] Still, there is little evidence that the natural law as mediated through these two texts has any operation in relation to the positive law of any particular state where the Orthodox Church exists.

CONCLUSION

An exploration of the Orthodox position on natural law, rather than allowing any definitive statements, produces a number of unresolved disputes surrounding its existence, definition, structure and contemporary relevance. Having examined these disputes, it remains only to offer two concluding reflections on directions which future research in this field might take. These two reflections 'book-end', if you will, the development of the Orthodox treatment of natural law, such as it is, in the Patristic and Neo-Patristic eras.

As one book-end, we might explore the pre-Patristic period. The absence of scholarship on the relationship between Classical Greek philosophy and the Patristic tradition, while eschewed in the Neo-Patristic synthesis, seems necessary in order to engage with what happened in the Christian West in the second millennium of Christianity. Exploring these connections in the early Patristic engagement of Greek philosophy may prove a rich source of possible connections to the development of natural law in the West and so of extending the Patristic tradition to modern global challenges.

The other back-end lies at the other end of the chronological spectrum; in order for the Orthodox tradition to engage with the rich Western Christian tradition, it will be necessary to understand modern liberalism and its approach to human rights. Much modern scholarship centres on the relationship between natural rights and the liberal category of 'human rights'. There is an obvious relationship between the two in the Christian West, but it is as yet unexplored in the Orthodox tradition. Of course, this requires asking Orthodox theology to 'catch up' with the developments of the second millennium of Christianity, which itself spawned the liberalism that has given rise to the human rights movement. It will be no easy task to develop in short order in the Christian East what it took the West 1000 years to achieve.

93 Harakas 1964, 215–216. 94 Ibid., 219.

4

Natural Law in the Anglican Tradition

Will Adam

Anglicanism is, at the same time, of ancient origin, a creature of the sixteenth century, and a more modern phenomenon. The well-documented break with Rome in the first half of the sixteenth century produced a church separate from the Roman Catholic Church and named the Church of England. This church developed in England through further political and religious upheavals in the sixteenth and seventeenth centuries and then began to expand out of the boundaries of the British Isles,[1] as British trade, imperial and missionary activity spread around the globe. The churches that were founded in this expansion, beginning with early imperial and trade expansion into the Americas and India, have become known as the Anglican Communion. What follows traces the legal dimension of institutional Anglicanism, particularly in England but also globally, and the extent to which natural law has a place within it.

THE LEGAL FOUNDATIONS OF ANGLICANISM

The essential structures of the Church of England in the sixteenth century were those of the medieval Western church, reformed. The reform of church law was piecemeal. The key tool of legal reform was parliamentary statute, enacted to regulate various areas of church life and to alter or repeal the existing (Roman) canon law as it applied in England. However, statute law was not comprehensive and, in order for the church to function properly, officials had to rely on the law that they inherited. Indeed, statutory provision was made for the continuance of such laws as they were not contrary or repugnant to the laws, statutes and customs of this realm, nor to the damage or hurt of the king's prerogative royal.[2] One consequence of this was that legal thought and practice continued to develop out of pre-reformation legal traditions.

[1] The Church of England remains the established church in England; the Church in Wales is disestablished (1920) as is the Church of Ireland (1870); and the Scottish Episcopal Church has never been established.

[2] Act for the Submission of the Clergy 1533. See also Canon Law Act 1543, which explicitly permitted the continuance of such canons etc. that were not contrary to English law.

Natural Law, Common Law and Legal Positivism

Natural law was an important theme in the legal thinking of the time. Richard Helmholz traces a long list of English common lawyers who asserted that natural law formed part of, or was a source for, the common law of England. This list starts with 'Bracton' (in the thirteenth century), can be seen to extend at least to Blackstone (in the eighteenth century) and is certainly not dominated in later years by students and practitioners of the civil law, who might be thought to have had more exposure to the natural law outlook than students and practitioners of the common law.[3]

However, developments in legal thought, particularly under the influence of the nineteenth-century philosopher John Austin, led to an increasing dominance in English law of legal positivism: the separation of law and morals. Despite the existence of a branch of the English legal profession, Doctors' Commons, whose members were schooled primarily in the civil law and who practised in the ecclesiastical courts, the influence of common law and legal positivism took hold in English law. The waning of the influence of Doctors' Commons meant that, during the years of the nineteenth century, more and more ecclesiastical suits were being argued and adjudicated by advocates and judges whose practice was in the king's courts. For instance, the long-running disputes over the reintroduction of Catholic ritual practice into the Church of England during the second half of the nineteenth century were heard in a variety of forums: diocesan consistory courts and the appellate ecclesiastical Court of Arches, but also the Queen's Bench, Privy Council and House of Lords. As early as 1809 the Dean of the Arches (president of the appeal court of the Province of Canterbury, the Court of Arches) judicially stated that the task of the court was to administer law, not theology. The practice of the civilians of Doctors' Commons, whilst it included ecclesiastical suits, was dominated by probate, admiralty and family law matters.

Following the demise of Doctors' Commons, those barristers who argued and those judges who adjudicated in ecclesiastical suits, therefore, were individuals who were not trained in civil law, let alone in canon law (the teaching of which was abolished at the time of the Reformation) but in the Inns of Court, the 'universities' of common law. In his recent book, *Natural Law in Court*, Helmholz develops his survey of the influence of natural law in the field of legal education. Whilst he finds some references to the law of nature as a source for the law of England, they are not common. Some lawyers may have, in a previous classical education, come across some of the principles common to natural law and classical philosophy. Others may have come across them through reading legal writers and commentators who wrote on the law of nature or who at least acknowledged its place in the legal tradition.[4]

3 Richard H. Helmholz, 'Natural Law and Human Rights in English Law: from Bracton to Blackstone', *Ave Maria Law Review* 3 (2005): 1–22.

4 Richard H. Helmholz, *Natural Law in Court: A History of Legal Theory in Practice* (Cambridge, MA: Harvard University Press, 2015), 82–93.

However, as time passed so the growth of positivist thinking began to take hold. Legal positivism generally rejects the principles on which natural law is based. David Hume (d. 1776) was of the opinion that natural law could never be objectively or empirically determined, and thus it relied wholly on the subjective viewpoints of the observer of nature. Jeremy Bentham (d. 1832) famously described Blackstone's concept of natural law as a source of English law as 'nonsense upon stilts' and natural law itself as 'a hodgepodge of confusion and absurdity'. In common with other proponents of legal positivism, for Bentham law could only become law when enacted by a sovereign authority. It is pointless, in this school of thought, to think what the law *ought* to be rather than simply looking to what the law *is*. For John Austin (d. 1859), the sovereign was supreme, and law (commands issuing from the will of the sovereign) was enforceable by means of sanctions available in the event of its breach. The introduction of the authority of God into this world view has the effect of reducing the sovereign to the level of viceroy. A viceroy could not truly be sovereign, neither could any authority that acknowledged external limits on sovereign power. In 1891, Henry Sidgwick, in looking back, was confident enough to state that the fundamental concepts of government and law 'held by the majority of instructed persons in England at the present day ... is derived in the main from Austin'.[5]

Church law, however, by definition has to acknowledge and accept the existence of God and divine sovereignty revealed to humankind. The Tudor view of church and state saw the combination of godly prince, faithful parliament and compliant clergy as the divinely instituted way of things. However, it did not take long for cracks to appear and for people of faith to distrust Parliament as the true or best interpreter of the divine will. In successive generations Roman Catholics, Puritans, Independents, Baptists, Quakers, etc., dissented from this point of view – to them the revealed divine law led them in a different direction. Nevertheless, the official view of Anglicanism remained that, whilst, in the words of the Thirty-nine Articles of Religion, it is not 'lawful for the Church to ordain any thing that is contrary to God's Word written', yet that which is enacted by the Church of England *is* 'agreeable to God's Word'.

As we have seen in earlier chapters, for Aquinas, 'the validity of law depends upon its justice,' and 'if a human law is at variance in any particular with the natural law, it is no longer law, but rather a corruption of law'.[6] Whilst some who found themselves outside the tent of the English expression of church-state relations would have sided explicitly with Aquinas, others would not. For the puritan or evangelical the result might be the same (i.e. belief that the law enacted by Parliament did not reflect revealed divine law), but the source of authority might be different. It is generally understood that for the puritan or evangelical, the source of divine law was not nature or natural law but the divine law as revealed in Scripture. This is explored in more detail below.

5 Henry Sidgwick, *The Elements of Politics* (London: Macmillan, 1891), 15.

6 *Summa theologiae*, I.II.95. 2.

The Obligation to Obey the Law

Those who consider themselves justified, or even compelled, by faith not to obey what they consider an unjust law frequently find themselves face to face with the coercive force of the law. Bentham was characteristically robust in his view that a legal obligation to do a certain thing 'is said to attach upon a man . . . when in the event of his performing the act at the time and place in question he will not suffer any pain, but in the event of his not performing it he will suffer a certain pain'.[7] The modern commentator Trevor Allan suggests that an individual is able to choose whether or not to conform to obligations which are laid down by the law, adding that such obligation is the 'product of a personal moral judgment that obedience is justified'. Allan references the work of John Finnis, suggesting that legal authority is necessary in society and, thus, people seldom fail to observe the law, but, at the same time, a good citizen has no moral duty to comply with a bad law even if that law is treated as valid by the courts, one function of which is to enforce law.[8] H.L.A. Hart points to a more communal view that individuals take – that of being 'under obligation': this is a sense of duty in the individual to obey the law, arising from a critical reflective attitude to the law and an appreciation of its value; Hart also writes of the need for law to have a minimal moral content.[9] Lon Fuller considers this obligation to be a moral duty.[10] Austin, on the other hand, concentrated more even than Bentham on the force of coercive sanction to enforce obedience to the law.

That there is a general duty of obedience is familiar to the Christian legal tradition. The Mosaic Law features large in the Old Testament, and obedience to the law is both coercive and incentive-based. On the one hand: 'And if in spite of this you will not obey me, I will continue to punish you sevenfold for your sins. I will break your proud glory, and I will make your sky like iron and your earth like copper' (Leviticus 26.18–19). On the other hand: 'Now therefore, if you obey my voice and keep my covenant, you shall be my treasured possession out of all the peoples' (Exodus 19.5); Jesus said 'If you love me, you will keep my commandments' (John 14.15) and that 'All authority in heaven and earth has been given to me' (Matthew 28.18); and St Paul states that 'obeying the commandments of God is everything' (1 Corinthians 7.19). The New Testament also enjoins obedience to non-Christian state authority. St Peter states 'Honour everyone. Love the family of believers. Fear God. Honour the emperor' (1 Peter 2.17), having already stated:

> For the Lord's sake accept the authority of every human institution, whether of the emperor as supreme, or of governors, as sent by him to punish those who do wrong

7 Amanda Perreau-Saussine, 'Bentham and the Boot-Strappers of Jurisprudence: The Moral Commitments of a Rationalist Legal Positivist', *Cambridge Law Journal* 63(2) (2004): 346–383, at 360.

8 T.R.S. Allan, *Constitutional Justice* (Oxford: Oxford University Press, 2001), 67–68.

9 See Hilaire McCoubrey, *The Obligation to Obey in Legal Theory* (Aldershot: Ashgate, 1997), 5.

10 Lon L. Fuller, 'Positivism and Fidelity to Law', *Harvard Law Review* 71(4) (1958): 630–672.

and to praise those who do right. For it is God's will that by doing right you should silence the ignorance of the foolish (1 Peter 2.13–15).

St Paul likewise states:

Let every person be subject to the governing authorities; for there is no authority except from God, and those authorities that exist have been instituted by God. Therefore whoever resists authority resists what God has appointed, and those who resist will incur judgment. For rulers are not a terror to good conduct, but to bad. Do you wish to have no fear of the authority? Then do what is good, and you will receive its approval; for it is God's servant for your good. But if you do what is wrong, you should be afraid, for the authority does not bear the sword in vain! It is the servant of God to execute wrath on the wrongdoer. Therefore one must be subject, not only because of wrath but also because of conscience (Romans 13.1–5).

As we saw in Chapter 1, issues such as these were the object of deep debate amongst medieval jurists and theologians, and Aquinas himself holds that 'man has a natural aptitude for virtue' and 'men who are well disposed are led willingly to virtue by being admonished better than by coercion: but men who are evilly disposed are not led to virtue unless they are compelled'.[11] And, as we have seen in Chapter 2, modern Roman Catholic sources are clear that obedience to civil authority is the norm, but the church's teaching contained in the *Catechism* recognises that conscience (noted above in Romans 13 as leading to obedience to the law) might, at times, oblige a citizen not to obey civil authority if that authority's command contradicts the law of God.[12]

In the Church of England obedience to lawful authority is normative. Under its canon law, individuals are obliged to take various oaths (such as at ordination and when clergy take up offices) of allegiance to the sovereign and canonical obedience to the bishop (namely, to obey the lawful and honest directions of the diocesan bishop). However, there have been numerous examples of clerics failing to live up to the promises made, especially where, like others over the centuries, their interpretation of divine law, however revealed, clashes with the enacted will of otherwise lawful authority.[13]

In short, the relatively recent dominant legal culture applicable to the Church of England seems to have been that of the philosophical posture of positivism: the separation of law and morals in terms of issues of the validity of law, its enforcement in court and obedience to it. It is submitted that this marginalisation, so to speak, of natural law thinking would seem to be due to the supremacy of the common law tradition, with its practical rather than theoretical focus, in which certainly from the nineteenth century the natural law outlook has played so very little a part.

[11] *Summa theologiae*, I.II.95.1.1.

[12] *Catechism of the Catholic Church*, paragraph 144; Code of Canon Law (1983) canon 22.

[13] See, e.g., Norman Doe, *The Legal Framework of the Church of* England (Oxford: Clarendon Press, 1996), 209–217, on obedience and sanctions.

NATURAL LAW IN ANGLICAN THOUGHT

Seeking out explicit natural law influences in the practice of English ecclesiastical law, then, is difficult. However, natural law is not entirely absent from Anglican theological or social thought, historical or contemporary. Perhaps the most influential Anglican thinker to make explicit use of natural law is the Elizabethan divine, Richard Hooker (1554–1600). Hooker was Master of the Temple (the church of two Inns of Court, Inner Temple and Middle Temple) and, whilst in that post, became embroiled in a long-running dispute with the Reader of the Temple Church who was a puritan who leaned towards Calvin and Geneva. The Reader, Walter Travers, occupied the pulpit at Sunday afternoon services and used this opportunity to preach sermons critical of that which Hooker had preached in the morning. Travers was a leading figure in the puritan movement of the day, representative of a more extreme strand of that movement. He was a keen exponent of a Presbyterian form of church government (he had refused ordination in the Church of England) and a close ally of the acknowledged leader of the Presbyterian party, Thomas Cartwright. Cartwright had lived through the turbulent years of the Reformation and, like Travers, had spent time in Geneva. Hooker's masterwork, *Of the Lawes of Ecclesiastical Politie*, was published in eight books (three posthumously) and can be credited as the principal source of the Anglican *via media* between the catholic and the puritan.

Richard Hooker and Natural Law

Hooker knew and engaged with the classical natural law thinking of Thomas Aquinas which itself depends ultimately on Aristotle. Joan Lockwood O'Donovan concludes that Hooker's outlook was decidedly 'Thomistic-Aristotelian', as opposed to the earlier 'Franciscan-Augustinian' approach of John Wyclif (d. 1384). It was Hooker's approach to the nature of the church in general, and the character of the English church in particular, which, ultimately, took hold and underpinned subsequent Anglican thought: 'amply endowed with the spirit of probity, moderation, and charitable compromise'.[14] Aquinas' view of the acts and ends of creatures as a reflection of the eternal law of God is picked up by Hooker although he often uses the term 'law of reason' as synonymous with 'natural law'. Thus, Aquinas describes natural law as 'the sharing in the Eternal Law by intelligent creatures',[15] and Hooker talks of 'creatures reasonable in this world'.[16] Hooker was convinced that the law of reason pointed reasonable people to the truths of Christianity:

> Men do both, as the Apostle teacheth, yea, those men which have no written law of God to show what is good or evil, carry written in their hearts the universal law of

[14] Joan Lockwood O'Donovan, *Theology of Law and Authority in the English Reformation* (Grand Rapids, MI: William B. Eerdmans, 1991), 129.

[15] *Summa theologiae*, I.II.91.2. [16] Richard Hooker, *Of the Lawes of Ecclesiastical Politie*, I.3.1.

> mankind, the law of reason, whereby they judge as by a rule which God hath given unto all men for that purpose.[17]

Rowan Williams, writing during his time as Archbishop of Canterbury, states:

> Hooker takes it for granted that recognition of God's existence is part of what is 'natural' to human being in this way; and so is the sense of moral responsibility, the connection between actions and rewards and punishments. This basic grasp of what we are in relation to creator and creation would dictate human behaviour even if human beings didn't live together. But as a matter of fact we are also by nature sociable; our good can never be fully realised by any one of us living alone. So we next have to discern how common life is to be regulated so as to allow us to do to each other the good we are capable of doing and to restrain the damage we are equally capable of doing.[18]

Thus, by nature, human beings are societal. Law is necessary; it consists of 'rules of action', and it exists to serve an end. Hooker sees law, at its root, as coming from God. He terms God's own law, to which all creation is inevitably subject, 'first eternal law'. Then, however, there is the 'second eternal law' which is itself divided into a number of classes of law: 'Nature's law', which is the law all creation obeys without having to choose; the 'law celestial', which is the law observed by heavenly beings; the 'law of reason', which is the natural law by which reasonable people believe themselves bound; the 'divine law', which is likewise binding but revealed by God's specific revelation and found in Scripture; and 'human law', which is made by human beings for human beings and arises from the consent of the community to which it applies (as, he argues, was the case with English ecclesiastical law). These categories of law are distinct but connected, not least in the connection between the law of nature and the law of reason and, then, between the law of reason and human law.

Hooker is also clear that 'the authority of the Bible is unique and unparalleled within the Christian life',[19] but his views on the interpretation of Scripture and its relationship with reason and natural law are complex. His *Lawes* argues against more extreme puritan understandings of Scripture, the church and the relationship between church and state and probably represents a synthesis and refining of his views as they were affected by the long-running disputes with the puritan Travers in their years as Master and Reader of the Temple. In Book II of *Lawes* Hooker argues systematically against an understanding that Scripture is the *only* source of authority for the Christian and for godly society. Such arguments had been put forward forcibly by Cartwright, who, in his published debate with Archbishop Whitgift, had claimed that anything done other than in accord with God's revealed word is

17 Ibid., I.16.5.

18 Rowan Williams, 'Richard Hooker: The Laws of Ecclesiastical Polity Revisited', *Ecclesiastical Law Journal* 8 (2006): 382–391, at 384–385.

19 Alison J. Joyce, *Richard Hooker and Anglican Moral Theology* (Oxford: Oxford University Press, 2015), 106.

sinful. However, Cartwright and Travers stand at one end of the spectrum of puritan thought. The Westminster Confession, dating from the mid-seventeenth century, is more nuanced. The opening words of the first chapter refer to 'the light of nature and the works of creation and providence' as manifestations, albeit insufficient, of the 'goodness, wisdom and power of God'. Later in the first chapter there is an acknowledgement that there is a place in the ordering of Christian worship, church government and human society 'by the light of nature and Christian prudence' and in the nineteenth chapter mention is made of 'general equity' contained in the judicial laws of the Old Testament.[20] For Hooker, reason and human law which conforms to reason are necessary and not necessarily contrary to the will of God. Joan Lockwood O'Donovan puts the relationship thus:

> Albeit God's revealed Word supplies the churches with manifold directives in matters of government, discipline and ceremonies, both general principles to follow and particular models to emulate, laws of nature and divine imperatives; still, man's natural reason is permitted a broad latitude in the interpretation, application, and combination of divinely revealed laws and examples. Moreover, in its liturgical, disciplinary, and administrative judgments, a church is most often led by the natural principles of reason, which may or may not be explicitly contained in the Scriptures.[21]

And, to return to Williams:

> The 'sufficiency' or perfection of Scripture, argues Hooker, is a matter of its perfect capacity to do what it is meant to do. If we try to make it do more than it is meant to, we destroy its credibility; if we suggest, for example, that nothing except what is commended in the Bible can be other than sinful, we paralyse a great deal of ordinary human life.[22]

In the words of Hooker himself:

> [M]en being enabled to know truth from falsehood, and good from evil, do thereby learn in many things what the will of God is; which will himself not revealing by any extraordinary means unto them, but they by natural discourse attaining the knowledge thereof.[23]

Thus, without belittling the importance of Scripture, there is something God-given about the divinely created natural world and order. Natural law gives the means to demonstrate and fathom the will of the creator. God is, for Hooker, active in the world. Scripture, the witness of the natural world, and the application of human reason all combine to reveal this divine action. That this may be described as 'law' is because there is regularity in God's will and action; it is not capricious or arbitrary.

20 *The Westminster Confession of Faith*, I. vi and XIX. iv.
21 Joan Lockwood O'Donovan, op cit., 147.
22 Rowan Williams, op cit., 386.
23 Richard Hooker, *Lawes*, I. 8. 3.

Scripture, Reason and Tradition

Hooker is given credit for the Anglican approach to decision-making, resting on Scripture, reason and tradition. The seventeenth-century divine Daniel Whitby (1638–1726), who was sympathetic to nonconformists, puts it thus: 'Reason in judging of the sense of Scripture is regulated partly by principles of Faith, partly by Tradition, partly by Catholic maxims,'[24] and the seventeenth-century Cambridge Platonist Benjamin Whichcote (1609–1683) acknowledges and commends the use of reason:

> [I]ndeed this is a very profitable work to call upon men, to answer the principles of their creation, to fulfil natural light, to answer natural conscience, to be throughout rational in what they do; for these things have a Divine foundation.[25]

In the eighteenth century Hooker's treatment of natural law was also developed by Joseph Butler (1692–1752), Bishop of Bristol (1738–1750) and an exponent of natural theology whose chief work was his *Analogy of Religion* (1736). For Butler true morality consists in living in accordance with one's nature, and the fundamental principles in human nature are self-love, benevolence (love of neighbour) and conscience – and in a series of sermons (he was preacher at the Rolls Chapel 1718–1726), by means of scriptural exegesis, he argued for the primacy of conscience in moral thinking and for a cosmology and ethic based on the love of God.[26]

The relationship of Scripture, as revealed by divine law, to natural law and conscience has, however, periodically raised its head in Anglican debates, particularly in moral decision-making and ethics. Some classical Anglican scholars have argued that there is no distinction between divine and natural laws. This is explicitly seen in the work of the English cleric, Christian apologist and natural theologian William Paley (1743–1805), who criticised philosophers for their propensity to

> divide too much of the law of nature from the precepts of revelation; some authors industriously declining the mention of scripture authorities, as belonging to a different province; and others reserving them for a separate volume: which appears to me much the same defect, as if a commentator on the laws of England should content himself with stating upon each head the common law of the land, without taking any notice of acts of parliament; or should choose to give his readers the common law in one book, and the statute law in another.[27]

[24] Daniel Whitby, 'An answer to Sure Footing' (1666), reproduced in Gillian R. Evans and J. Robert Wright, eds., *The Anglican Tradition: A Handbook of Sources* (London: SPCK, 1991), 263.

[25] Benjamin Whichcote, 'Several Discourses', reproduced in Evans and Wright, ibid., 284.

[26] See generally Christopher Cunliffe, ed., *Joseph Butler's Moral and Religious Thought: Tercentenary Essays* (Oxford: Oxford University Press, 1992).

[27] William Paley, *Principles of Moral and Political Philosophy* (1785), 8th American edn (Boston: West and Richardson, 1815), Preface, viii. See also Thomas Rutherforth (1712–1771), especially his *Institutes of Natural Law* (1754), cited in Chapter 1 above.

However, there has been constant, it seems, debate within the Church of England, and then the wider Anglican Communion, about the balance in authority between the threads of Scripture, tradition and reason. The contemporary Anglican theologian Nigel Biggar explores natural law extensively in his book *Behaving in Public*. Biggar argues that Christians share with those outside of the church certain common understandings of right ethical behaviour – something that can be explained by natural law whereby even sinful human beings are able to discern basic moral goods in society. He acknowledges, however, that this sits uncomfortably with a Christian world view which claims a divine source for that which is explained as 'natural' by the non-believer.[28] That said, he is wary of treading a path that sets up too great a distinction between an exclusively Christian moral view and that of the wider world.

Some of Biggar's predecessors in the Regius Chair of Moral and Pastoral Theology at the University of Oxford contributed to the quiet debate on natural law over the course of the last century. Kenneth Kirk (later Bishop of Oxford) was critical of Thomist thought to the extent that he (Kirk) mistrusted immutable truths and saw all law and moral principle as defined by and subject to developing community consensus. Oliver O'Donovan deals comprehensively with natural law in setting a framework for moral decision-making in his book *Resurrection and Moral Order*.[29] In an earlier work he coined the phrase 'natural ethic' and softens the stark distinction in some Protestant thought between the 'natural' and the 'revealed'.[30]

This introductory survey has shown a general trajectory of Anglican thought away from the extremes of over-reliance on either revealed divine law or communitarian natural law. The careful *via media* approach that has its foundation largely in the work of Richard Hooker has continued in the work of Anglican theologians in more recent years. However, a question remains as to the extent to which this understanding of natural law is made manifest in the practices of Anglicans. The next section explores briefly some examples of how the age-old tension between divine and natural laws has been worked out in relation to well-known concrete, practical issues.

DIVINE LAW, NATURAL LAW AND CONCRETE ISSUES

One of the principal recurring questions in natural law is to what extent that which can be observed represents that which is perfect or even good – namely, the relationship between what 'is' and what 'ought to be'. In the nineteenth century the Church of

[28] Nigel Biggar, *Behaving in Public: How to do Christian Ethics* (Grand Rapids, MI: William B. Eerdmans Publishing, 2011), especially chapter 2.

[29] Oliver O'Donovan, *Resurrection and Moral Order: An Outline for Evangelical Ethics*, 2nd edn (Leicester: Apollos, 1994).

[30] Oliver O'Donovan, 'The Natural Ethic', in David F. Wright, ed., *Essays in Evangelical Social Ethics* (Exeter: Paternoster Press, 1979), Chapter 1.

England and the burgeoning presence of what would become Anglicanism overseas faced the same moral and theological pressure points as others in church and society. Natural law arguments have been advanced in relation to the following.

The Social Order

Historically, in the Church of England, there are many popular examples of writing which suggested that the inherited social order was ordained by God. In the seventeenth century, George Herbert penned a verse now sung as a hymn: 'A servant with this clause makes drudgery divine. Who sweeps a room, as for thy laws, makes that and the action fine.'[31] The hymn-writer Cecil Frances Alexander portrayed a similar outlook in the still popular hymn 'All things bright and beautiful', written as part of a series of hymns for children explaining clauses of the Creed: 'The rich man in his castle, the poor man at his gate. God made them high and lowly and ordered their estate.'[32] The 'is' of the social order becomes, in this, the 'ought'. That which is observed as the status quo is given the status of divine writ. The biblical image of the rich man and the poor man at the gate is drawn from the parable of the rich man and Lazarus in Luke 16.19–31. Unfortunately for the rich man in the parable, he is taken to eternal torment, having already received his reward on earth whereas the poor man, Lazarus, is carried by angels to Abraham's bosom. Jesus' harsh parable does not, on a plain reading, advocate the status of the rich man and Lazarus as divinely ordered. Placed within St Luke's general thrust of argument about the social order the link becomes weaker still – the divine will is more plainly seen in the words of Mary in Luke 1.52–53: 'He has brought down the powerful from their thrones, and lifted up the lowly; he has filled the hungry with good things, and sent the rich away empty.'

Slavery

The example that is often cited in sources is that of slavery, the state of servitude by which one person is treated as the property of another. The New Testament can be read as recognising the reality of slavery, and Paul exhorts slaves to 'obey your earthly masters in everything': not challenging the status quo,[33] whilst claiming that there was an essential unity in Christ – 'all are one in Christ Jesus', whether Jew or Greek, slave or free, male or female.[34] Thus, there is a sense in which the 'is' of the status quo does not reflect the 'ought' of the divine order, that the provisional status of the

[31] George Herbert, *The Elixir*, 1633. The popular hymn goes under the title of its first line 'Teach me, my God and King in all things thee to see', which is, itself, a statement of natural law and the evidence of the work of the creator in creation.

[32] 'All things bright and beautiful', first published in *Hymns for Little Children*, 1848.

[33] Colossians 3.22. There are similar examples in the deutero-Pauline Ephesians 6.5 and in the first letter of Peter: 1 Peter 2.18.

[34] Galatians 3: 28.

slave in fallen creation is not ultimately God's will. As a result, slavery has been much discussed by theologians, their position moving ultimately to the idea that slavery is opposed to human dignity which does not allow a person to be treated as a chattel; that it violates innate rights to liberty of conscience, the integrity of the soul and body and the stability of family life; and that it fosters vice and cruelty.[35] In the common law world the issue of slavery was most closely argued in the United States. Helmholz outlines the use of natural law arguments in the developing law on slavery in eighteenth- and nineteenth-century America.[36] The leading case at the beginning of this story was *Somerset's Case* (1771), in which Lord Mansfield gave judgment to the effect that slavery could be permitted by positive law, but it was, in effect, not lawful in the absence of positive law (albeit holding at the same time that the contract for the purchase of a slave was good in English law): 'The state of slavery is of such a nature, that it is incapable of being introduced on any reasons, moral or political; but only [by] positive law.'[37] In turn, natural law thinking was employed by the abolitionists, including the Clapham Sect, the Evangelical Anglican group which included as a member William Wilberforce, who in his *Appeal to the Religion, Justice and Humanity of the Inhabitants of the British Empire in Behalf of the Negro Slaves in the West Indies* (1823) claimed that the total and unqualified emancipation of slaves was a moral and ethical 'duty before God'. Wilberforce died in 1833 just as Parliament abolished slavery in the British Empire.

Contraception

The advent of artificial birth control stimulated debate across the worldwide Anglican Communion in the early part of last century, not least at the Lambeth Conference, the assembly of Anglican bishops which meets every ten years or so. The issue of contraception appeared on the agenda of the Lambeth Conference more than once. Its resolutions evolve from a restrictive approach to a more liberal approach, and natural law thinking is used to justify both. In 1908, Conference Resolution 41 stated:

> [T]he Conference records with alarm the growing practice of the artificial restriction of the family and earnestly calls upon all Christian people to discountenance the use of all artificial means of restriction as demoralizing to character and hostile to national welfare.

Moreover, in 1920, Resolution 68 was emphatic that

> [the] primary purpose for which marriage exists [is] the continuation of the race through the gift and heritage of children and we utter an emphatic warning against the use of unnatural means for the avoidance of conception, together with the grave

35 F.L. Cross and E.A. Livingstone, eds., *The Oxford Dictionary of the Christian* Church, 3rd edn rev. (Oxford: Oxford University Press, 2005), 1519.

36 Richard Helmholz, *Natural Law in Court*, op cit., 161–165.

37 (1771) 98 English Reports 499.

> dangers – physical, moral and religious – thereby incurred, and against the evils with which the extension of such use threatens the race.

However, in the ten years that followed the bishops changed their minds. Resolution 13 of the Lambeth Conference 1930 stated:

> The Conference emphasises the truth that sexual instinct is a holy thing implanted by God in human nature. It acknowledges that intercourse between husband and wife as the consummation of marriage has a value of its own within that sacrament, and that thereby married love is enhanced and its character strengthened. Further, seeing that the primary purpose for which marriage exists is the procreation of children, it believes that this purpose as well as the paramount importance in married life of deliberate and thoughtful self-control should be the governing considerations in that intercourse.

However, Resolution 15 acknowledges:

> [W]here there is clearly felt moral obligation to limit or avoid parenthood, the method must be decided on Christian principles. The primary and obvious method is complete abstinence from intercourse (as far as may be necessary) in a life of discipline and self-control lived in the power of the Holy Spirit. Nevertheless in those cases where there is such a clearly felt moral obligation to limit or avoid parenthood, and where there is a morally sound reason for avoiding complete abstinence, the Conference agrees that other methods may be used, provided that this is done in the light of the same Christian principles. The Conference records its strong condemnation of the use of any methods of conception control from motives of selfishness, luxury, or mere convenience.

Whilst there is no explicit appeal to natural law as a source or authority for either position taken in the preceding resolutions of the Lambeth Conference, Bishop Charles Gore responded to the *volte face* in 1930 using terms derived from the vocabulary of natural law,[38] and Pope Pius XI issued an encyclical *Casti connubii* (1930) which, *inter alia*, responded to the Lambeth resolution and restated Catholic opposition to contraception. The tit-for-tat dialogue continued in that Resolution 22 of the Lambeth Conference 1968 stated that the bishops assembled did not agree with Pope Paul VI's encyclical *Humanae vitae*; it was a matter of conscience:

> The Conference believes that the responsibility for deciding upon the number and frequency of children has been laid by God upon the consciences of parents everywhere; that this planning, in such ways as are mutually acceptable to husband and wife in Christian conscience, is a right and important factor in Christian family life and should be the result of positive choice before God.

The story is expanded in *Life in Christ*, the Second Anglican-Roman Catholic International Commission's statement on 'Morals, Communion and the Church'.[39]

38 Charles Gore, *Lambeth on Contraceptives* (London: Mowbray, 1930), §3.
39 ARCIC II, *Life in Christ* (1994), paragraphs 78–82.

However, natural law does not feature at all in this document as an argument one way or the other. Indeed, the evolution of the authoritative but not binding Resolutions of the Lambeth Conference on the subject shows a diminution of explicit natural law arguments: in 1920, contraception is classified as 'unnatural' and, today, a matter of 'conscience'.

Human Sexuality

The subject of human sexuality or, more accurately, the attitude of the church towards homosexuality, has been a major topic in the life of the Anglican Communion in recent decades. The debate is far from settled. However, there is less reliance on natural law on either side of the debate than there is on revealed law in the form of Scripture or argument about the interpretation of Scripture. The Church of England, in its study document *Some Issues in Human Sexuality*,[40] does not reference natural law save (in an ecumenical spirit) for a quotation from the *Catechism of the Catholic Church*. However, there is considerable treatment of biblical texts.

The more recent Church of England contribution to the human sexuality debate, *Report of the House of Bishops' Working Group on Human Sexuality*, The Pilling Report,[41] considers the use of reason in the debate; it draws on Hooker, stating: '[T]he exercise of rational thought is required in order to understand and apply the teaching of the Scriptures.' It also draws on Alasdair MacIntyre, for whom 'tradition constituted' suggests that reason is informed by 'the traditions and narratives through which ... communities make sense of the world around them'. Conscience also finds its way into the thinking of the working group, in particular in the acknowledgement that people may have 'in good conscience' entered into same-sex relationships.

It is difficult to find specific examples of the pleading of natural law as an argument in this debate. *Life in Christ* states that both Anglicans and Catholics 'appeal to Scripture and the natural order as the sources of their teaching on the issue' and, leading on from this, that both 'reject ... the claim ... that homosexual relationships are morally equivalent'.[42] In 2003, the then Bishop of Carlisle, Graham Dow, stated on the BBC's *Newsnight* programme: '[O]bviously the penis belongs in [or in some accounts "to" or "with"] the vagina; that this is something fundamental to the way God has made us.'[43] From a different perspective the contemporary Anglican ethicist Sean Doherty states in relation to his own experience: 'As a gay man, my sexual desires nonetheless certainly still expressed something good and

[40] *Some Issues in Human Sexuality: A Guide to the Debate*, General Synod 1519 (London: Church House Publishing, 2003).

[41] *Report of the House of Bishops' Working Group on Human Sexuality*, General Synod 1929 (London: Church House Publishing, 2013).

[42] *Life in Christ*, para. 87.

[43] *Newsnight*, 16 June 2003. Quote taken from Lois S. Bibbings, 'The Heterostate: Hegemonic Heterosexuality and State Power', in Roy Coleman, Joe Sim, Steve Tombs and David Whyte, eds., *State, Power, Crime* (London: Sage, 2009), 35–48, at 37.

beautiful about the way God had made me – both in terms of desire for a sexually intimate relationship and in terms of desire for non-sexual intimacy with other men.' However, Doherty then goes on to point out that '[t]he problem, as I saw it and still do, was the fallen conflation of these two originally separate but good and godly desires.'[44] So here we have an implicit appeal to natural law (sexual preference is part of the way God makes the human being) counteracted by a greater prohibition – in this case the belief that 'sex is a good gift given by a good God to humanity for marriage, and that marriage is the union between a woman and a man'. Indeed, the concept of 'reason' also played an important part in debates surrounding the proposal for churches of the Anglican Communion to adopt a covenant to regulate their relations of ecclesial communion, the exercise of autonomy by each church and the resolution of conflict – the proposal itself grew in part from disputes about human sexuality.[45]

Human Rights

The issue of human rights has featured frequently on the agenda of Lambeth Conferences and, as a topic, is too broad for more than cursory treatment here. The concept of human rights is embodied in various resolutions of the conference, some of which invoke ideas broadly associated with divine law and natural law thinking. The conference recognises the existence of human rights and regards them as of 'capital and fundamental importance' for human dignity.[46] Moreover, it calls upon 'all the Churches to press upon governments and communities their duty to promote fundamental human rights and freedoms among all their peoples'.[47] Human rights involve freedom to enable humankind to develop its relationship with God, to ensure that 'the divine dignity of every human being is respected and . . . justice is pursued'.[48] The conference commonly attacks breaches of human rights on the basis that such breaches are contrary to 'the teaching of Christ'.[49] It classifies human rights in terms of political rights, which include 'a fair and just share' for people in government, and economic rights, in so far as 'human rights must include economic fairness and equity, and enable local economies to gain greater control over their own affairs'.[50] Fundamental is the idea that all humans are created in the image of God.[51] Consequently, '[t]he Christian must . . . judge every social system by its effect on human personality'.[52] Therefore, Anglican churches are

44 Sean Doherty, '"Love Does Not Delight in Evil, but Rejoices with the Truth": A Theological and Pastoral Reflection on My Journey Away from A Homosexual Identity', *Anvil* 30(1) (2014): 14.

45 Norman Doe, *An Anglican Covenant: Theological and Legal Considerations for a Global Debate* (Norwich: Canterbury Press, 2008), 8, 94, 114, 158.

46 See, e.g., Lambeth Conference (hereafter LC) 1998, Res. 1.1.

47 LC 1968, Res. 16.

48 *The Official Report of the Lambeth Conference* 1998 (Harrisburg, PA: Morehouse Publishing, 1999), 77.

49 LC 1978, Res. 3.

50 LC 1920, Res. 75; LC 1920, Res. 78; LC 1958, Res. 110; *Called to Full Humanity*, LC 1998, *Official Report*, op cit., 79.

51 LC 1958, Res. 110; and LC 1968, Res. 16.

52 LC 1948, Res. 5.

'to speak out' against breaches of human rights, 'support all who are working for [the] implementation of human rights instruments'[53] and 'urge compliance with the United Nations Declaration of Human Rights by the nations in which our various member Churches are located, and [by] all others over whom we may exercise any influence'.[54] Individual Anglicans also have a responsibility to promote and protect human rights.[55] Indeed, on the fiftieth anniversary of its proclamation of the Lambeth Conference of 1998 they formally affirmed and adopted the Universal Declaration of Human Rights.[56]

NATURAL LAW AND ANGLICAN CANON LAW TODAY

As Hooker can be understood to have taken the explicit doctrine of natural law of the Thomist tradition and repackaged it as the law of reason, so echoes of natural law may be identified in the law governing Anglican churches, but often under other guises. Certain principles, such as 'natural justice', continue to form an established part of Anglican legal thinking, but explicit use of 'natural law' is less conspicuous.

In the laws of Anglican churches, both the complex law of the Church of England (and, to a lesser extent, the disestablished Church in Wales, the law applicable to which contains some vestiges of the former establishment of the Church of England in Wales), bound up as it is with the law of England, and the constitutions, canons and other regulatory instruments of Anglican churches worldwide, there is little if any specific reference to natural law.[57] Rather, Scripture is understood as the dominant normative source; for example, as to doctrine, Canon A5 of the Church of England states:

> The doctrine of the Church of England is grounded in the Holy Scriptures, and in such teachings of the ancient Fathers and Councils of the Church as are agreeable to the said Scriptures. In particular such doctrine is to be found in the Thirty-nine Articles of Religion, *The Book of Common Prayer*, and the Ordinal.[58]

Nevertheless, the regulatory instruments of Anglican churches do sometimes employ a number of categories historically associated with the natural law tradition. One such category is that of conscience: individual and collective.[59] For example,

53 LC 1988, Res. 33. 54 LC 1998, Res. 1.1(a).

55 LC 1920, Res. 77; however, 'the Church is not to be identified with any particular political or social system': LC 1958, Res. 104.

56 LC 1998, Res. 1.1. For more on the Lambeth Conference's treatment of the matter, see Norman Doe, 'Canonical Approaches to Human Rights', in Mark Hill, ed., *Religious Liberty and Human Rights* (Cardiff: University of Wales Press, 2002), 185–206.

57 Norman Doe, *Canon Law in the Anglican Communion* (Oxford: Clarendon Press, 1998).

58 See also similar provisions in, *inter alia*, Constitution of the Anglican Church in Aotearoa, New Zealand and Polynesia, Further Provisions, B. 1; Constitution and Canons of the Anglican Church of Canada, Declaration of Principles 1; Constitution of the Anglican Church of Australia, part 1.1.

59 Norman Doe, *Canon Law in the Anglican Communion*, op cit., 34, 96, 144, 167, 175, 235, 237, 252, 253, 258, 275, 288, 335 and 358.

according to the law applicable to the Church of England, an individual minister retains a conscientious right not to solemnise a marriage where one party is divorced with a former spouse still living or, in the case of an incumbent, the right to not make their church available for the solemnisation of such a marriage.[60] The concept of collective conscience is used in the constitution of the United Church of North India: 'No form of worship or ritual to which they conscientiously object shall be imposed on any congregation.'[61] Like the category 'reason', conscience has also been invoked in the global debate about the adoption of an Anglican Communion Covenant.[62]

The Principles of Canon Law Common to the Churches of the Anglican Communion also employs categories associated with the natural law tradition, but nowhere in the document is there express reference to natural law *per se*. The document, which was launched at the Lambeth Conference 2008, is a statement of principles of law induced from the profound similarities between the laws and other regulatory instruments of Anglican churches worldwide. First, 'All persons are equal in dignity before God'; as such, 'All persons have inherent rights and duties inseparable from their dignity as human beings created in the image and likeness of God and called to salvation through Jesus Christ'.[63] Secondly, 'human law [is] distinct from the will or law of God'; above all, 'Law should reflect the revealed will of God';[64] and the laws of churches present Holy Scripture as the ultimate standard and rule in matters of faith.[65]

Thirdly, the exercise of ecclesiastical governance is to be characterised by Christian virtues, transparency and the rule of law, which is to be applied with 'natural justice'.[66] Fourthly, the document appeals to 'conscience'; for example, '[l]ay persons who do not hold ecclesiastical office are free, subject to their own consciences, to perform any act not prohibited by law',[67] and provision may be made available for alternative episcopal oversight for those 'parishes which in all conscience cannot accept the ministry of their own bishop',[68] typically for those who in conscience cannot accept the ordination of women as bishops and priests. Fifthly, many of the principles may be understood to echo or equate with the precepts of natural law and reason as historically understood; for example, '[l]aws cannot oblige a person to do the impossible';[69] '[p]ersons cannot give what they do not have';[70]

60 Matrimonial Causes Act 1965, s. 8(2). This also covers clergy and churches of the Church in Wales. See also Constitution and Canons of the Anglican Church of Canada, Canon XXI. IV. 29. D.
61 Constitution, I.I.IV.
62 Norman Doe, *An Anglican Covenant*, op cit., 55, 66, 67, 68, 97, 102, 114, 160, 188.
63 *Principles of Canon Law Common to the Churches of the Anglican Communion* (London: Anglican Consultative Council, 2008), Principles 26.1 and 2.
64 Ibid., 95, Definitions, 'Law', and Principle 2.
65 Norman Doe, *Canon Law in the Anglican Communion*, op cit., 198ff.
66 *Principles*, 29. The constitution of the Anglican Church of North America, which is not part of the Anglican Communion, refers specifically to 'natural justice' in its canons: Constitution and Canons of the Anglican Church of North America (2012), Canon IV.5.7.
67 Principle 6.3. 68 Principle 38.5. 69 Principle 7.3. 70 Principle 7.4.

a declaration to comply with ecclesiastical jurisdiction binds the person who makes that declaration;[71] 'bodies or persons who exercise ecclesiastical functions may delegate to others only such functions as they are not required to perform themselves';[72] the judges of church courts are 'to exercise their office impartially, without fear or favour';[73] and church trustees are not liable for any financial loss resulting from an investment 'unless such loss is due to their own wilful default or culpable negligence'.[74] However, there is no obvious evidence in the principles themselves, or in the regulatory instruments of Anglican churches from which they are drawn, indicating a general practice that natural law (or divine law) binds directly in a juridical sense, nor that natural law (or divine law) vitiates contrary canon law.[75]

Finally, incidences of familiar natural law principles under other guises may also be discerned in secular law in the present day. Denise Myerson, for instance, considers that so-called common law principles have been used in English courts as a 'proxy' for natural law.[76] Cameron Stewart points out that the 'rule of law' has often been used to show that even parliamentary sovereignty is subject to a higher authority.[77] In the United Kingdom, 'public interest' has acquired a similarly high status where, for instance, it has been called on to justify a decision by the director of public prosecutions not to prosecute in the circumstances of a particular case.[78] Defamation law requires that a statement, to be classified as defamatory, seeks to 'lower the plaintiff in the estimation of right-thinking members of society generally'.[79] Rafael Domingo considers 'God' to have acquired the status of a 'meta-legal' concept. He points out, *inter alia*, that morality is recognised by courts and that God and religion, though intertwined, are ontologically separate. It is possible for a court to be neutral in terms of recognition of religion whilst accepting the concept of God. Such thinking is redolent of natural law.[80] Judicial review enables the court to exercise jurisdiction over public officials or organisations (but not, in the UK, the content of parliamentary statutes). Among the grounds for the judicial review are that an action violates natural justice,[81] proportionality, legitimate expectation and reasonableness or rationality. The standard in the latter is drawn from the

71 Principle 5.6.

72 Principle 17.4; VI.68: 'Whatever someone can do by himself, he can do it by another (unless the power to act cannot be delegated).'

73 Principle 24.7; VI.12: 'Justice should be rendered without respect to persons.'

74 Principle 89.4; VI.62: 'No liability arises from advice given provided it was not fraudulent.'

75 Mark Hill, 'Gospel and order', *Ecclesiastical Law Journal* 4 (1996): 659–663.

76 Denise Meyerson, *Understanding Jurisprudence* (London: Routledge Cavendish, 2007), 36–38.

77 Cameron Stewart, 'The Rule of Law and the Tinkerbell Effect: Theoretical Considerations, Criticisms and Justifications for the Rule of Law', *Maquarie Law Journal* 4 (2004): 135–164.

78 *Decision On Prosecution – The Death by Suicide of Daniel James*, 9 December 2008, para 1: www.cps.gov.uk/news/articles/death_by_suicide_of_daniel_james/.

79 *Sim v Stretch* [1936] 2 All ER 1237, (1936) 52 TLR 669, *per* Lord Atkin.

80 Rafael Domingo, 'The Metalegal God', *Ecclesiastical Law Journal* 16 (2014): 147–167.

81 *Lloyd v McMahon* [1987] AC 625.

Wednesbury case,[82] and the *dictum* of Lord Diplock in the case of *Council of Civil Service Unions v Minister for the Civil Service*, that an unreasonable decision is one which is 'so outrageous in its defiance of logic or of accepted moral standards that no sensible person who had applied his mind to the question to be decided could have arrived at it'.[83] In other words, the language of logic, morality and common sense echoes the language of natural law in these arrangements though without any specific pleading of natural law.

CONCLUSION

The concept of natural law, and its derivative – the law of reason, played a central role in the thought of Richard Hooker at the close of the sixteenth century in his exposition of the ecclesiastical law of the established Church of England. However, despite the profound influence of Hooker on the thinking and methodology of what was to become global Anglicanism, and the examples of Anglican moral theologians engaging with the natural law tradition, natural law does not feature prominently in modern Anglican decision-making, at least at the global level of the Lambeth Conference. Rather, Anglican jurisprudence today is largely characterised by legal positivism – by legislation that is the product of parliamentary-style drafting and, at least in the Church of England, by legal precedent laid down in the decisions of judges whose day-to-day work, style and legal language is that of the common law. Moreover, in recent years, the weight in Anglican thought generally has shifted in the balance between Scripture and natural law. Nevertheless, 'reason' is still acknowledged as necessary in the interpretation of Scripture, but Scripture may be seen to have gained for itself a status further along the road towards the puritan understanding that Hooker sought to nuance. This is most clearly seen in the current debate on human sexuality where certain key biblical texts become touchstones. That said, it is not possible to conclude that natural law thinking has been banished irretrievably from the laws of the Church of England or the other churches of the Anglican Communion. It may be, however, that it is just more difficult to find.

82 *Associated Provincial Picture Houses Ltd v Wednesbury Corporation* [1948] 1 KB 223.
83 [1984] UKHL 9, [1985] AC 374.

5

Natural Law in the Lutheran Tradition

Antti Raunio

In Western thought, historically, natural law is an idea which seeks to combine morality and law. In the 'natural law tradition', the concept of natural law has been used to refer to certain moral principles recognisable to all. These very same principles form also the foundation of just laws for communal life. Because natural law is seen as a common and objective foundation, all human law should be based upon it, even though concrete laws may differ between different peoples. However, this traditional approach which brings together morality and law no longer enjoys the dominant position it once held. Nevertheless, today, the Western understanding of the relationship between morality and law is still influenced in part by particular aspects of the natural law tradition; these include the idea that people have a natural consciousness of what is right and just. This chapter examines these approaches as they have developed in Lutheranism, from the time of the Reformation in the sixteenth century, until today, in Lutheran theology and juridical thought.

NATURAL LAW AND THE LUTHERAN REFORMATION

In general terms, the Lutheran Reformation did not depart from traditional ideas on the relationship between natural law, humanly created law and morality.[1] However, understandings of this relationship were applied to Reformation views on the relation between God, the human being and other creatures. In this sense, the Reformation understanding of natural law diverges somewhat from, for example,

[1] For Lutheran legal thought, see John Witte Jr., *Law and Protestantism: The Legal Teachings of the Lutheran Reformation* (Cambridge: Cambridge University Press, 2002) – hereafter Witte 2002; Harold J. Berman, *Law and Revolution II: The Impact of the Protestant Reformations on the Western Legal Tradition* (Cambridge, MA: Belknap University of Harvard Press, 2003). For connections between Patristic, medieval and Reformation views of natural law, see Antti Raunio, *Summe des christlichen Lebens: 'Die Goldene Regel' als Gesetz der Liebe in der Theologie Martin Luthers 1510–1527*, Veröffentlichungen des Instituts für europäische Geschichte (Mainz: Zabern Verlag: Wiesbaden, 2001) – hereafter Raunio 2001; and Antti Raunio, 'Divine and Natural Law in Luther and Melanchthon', in Virpi Mäkinen, ed., *The Lutheran Reformation and the Law* (Leiden, Boston: Brill, 2006), 21–61 – hereafter Raunio 2006.

Thomas Aquinas' conception of natural law. Yet, both Luther and Melanchthon propose that natural law is discoverable by human reason and that it forms the basis for moral life and just laws. On the other hand, as we shall see, their conceptions of the content of natural law are not identical but differ significantly. Therefore, the Lutheran version of the natural law tradition at the time of the Reformation contains some inherent tensions and vagueness. This conceptual imprecision can be explained, at least in part, by the fact that, following on from theological agreement in the Lutheran Confessions, little attention was paid to the differences between Luther and Melanchthon. But these differences exist, and they have influenced Lutheran theology since. Scientific research on Reformation thought has brought these differences back into debate.

It is commonly understood that Lutheranism has a 'worldly' view of society and a distinct 'spiritual' outlook, both grounded in the Bible, and therefore it has no place for the concept of natural law. Indeed, since the nineteenth century, many Lutheran thinkers have been very critical of natural law ideas.[2] This understanding, however, gives a misleading view of the main strands of Lutheran thought. The idea that morality and law should be based on natural law *is* to be found in Lutheranism. However, there has been ambiguity as to what 'natural law' exactly means. This ambiguity follows from the different approaches of Luther and Melanchthon. To understand their different views, it is necessary to take a short look at the medieval and Renaissance antecedents.

The Medieval and Renaissance Antecedents

In medieval theology, natural law thinking was based in the main on a combination of Augustinian and Aristotelian frameworks. From Augustine, medieval theology adopted the *ordo caritatis*,[3] a conception of the correct structure of the created world and the place of human beings in it. The understanding of natural law was closely connected with this structure.[4] Its starting point is that God is the Supreme Being and the highest good. As such, God is the aim and end of all creatures. In other words, the created world is oriented towards the highest good. For human beings, this orientation is both a movement that takes place within them as created beings and a moral law which commands them to love God above all else. In this sense,

[2] See, for example, Jacob Corzine, 'Friedrich Julius Stahl: A Lutheran's Rejection of Natural Law', in R.C. Baker and R.C. Ehlke, eds., *Natural Law. A Lutheran Reappraisal* (St Louis, MO: Concordia Publishing House, 2011), 99–115.

[3] Augustine expresses the idea of *ordo caritatis*, for example, in De doct. Christ. I, XXIII, 22, I XXVI, 27.

[4] See, for example, Klaus M.S.C. Demmer, 'Ius caritatis: Zur christologischen Grundlegung der augustinischen Naturrechtslehre', *Analecta Gregoriana,* Vol. 118, Series Facultatis Theologicae: Section B, n. 40 (Liberia Editrice dell'Università Gregoriana: Roma, 1961), 141–143; Demmer especially examines the connection between natural law, the created natural order and love in Augustine's thought.

natural law is at the same time something that is happening in nature and a moral commandment that should be followed.

God is also the first and highest object of love, and human beings should love God wholeheartedly, that is, through their understanding and affection. Even though our created being is oriented towards the highest end, each human being should join in this orientation consciously and willingly. Natural law demands this. And so natural law concerns not only outward deeds but also the inner orientation of a human being. At the same time, natural law commands us to love the objects of love in the right order, depending on the nearness of that object to God. After God, the highest good, the second object of love is one's own soul and the souls of our neighbours, then our own body and that of our neighbour and, thereafter, those of other creatures. Natural law commands love in this order. In the Aristotelian-Thomistic tradition, natural law was understood as a participation of the eternal divine law. Therefore, natural law connects all creatures with the divine will but demands rational creatures to live according to God's commandment of love.[5]

In the late Middle Ages, the Franciscans understood this order in a new way. They gradually abandoned the idea of the created and, in a sense, necessary orientation towards the highest end and, rather, saw creation as a contingent order that could also be other than it is. This led to the idea that the natural moral law did not reflect the order of creation but, rather, that it consisted of rational commandments based on right reason. For example, William of Ockham (d. 1347) maintained that one should live morally either by following God's commandments or the dictates of right reason.[6] These two possibilities are parallel and compatible, but their existence is one consequence of the fact that a human being, endowed with reason and will, is not by any necessity connected with the final end. This change influenced the Western world view deeply, as well as the foundations of legal and ethical thought. Since the late Middle Ages there have been (at least) two different approaches to natural law: the 'classical' teleological conception of natural law and ethics, and the 'modern' deontic model. Indeed, the Augustinian order of love may be combined with both.

Many scholars see Luther as a representative of the deontic, or 'Divine Command', model – this is a view, though, which is subject to qualification. However, Melanchthon (who scarcely adheres to nominalist thinking in this respect) seems to follow more the classical model. What makes both the classification and the evaluation of the Lutheran tradition even more complicated is that Luther, in spite of his Augustinian background, explicitly rejects the order of love, whereas Melanchthon seems to maintain it. So, Luther may have some nominalist assumptions at least in philosophical questions but he cannot be characterised as a straightforward follower of nominalist natural law thinking. Melanchthon – as has

[5] For an overview of Aquinas, see Raunio 2006, 32–33.

[6] See Raunio 2001, 100–105; and Lucas Freppert, *The Basis of Morality According to William Ockham* (Chicago, IL: Franciscan Herald Press, 1988), 44–45, 77–78, 82, 92.

often been stated – is more a Lutheran Renaissance humanist, who follows the Aristotelian way of thinking not only in philosophy but also in theology. At the same time, Melanchthon accepts the views of Luther in most questions of Christian doctrine.

Luther and Natural Law

Martin Luther (1483–1546), in his basic concept of natural law, is traditional.[7] For him, natural law is expressed in the 'Rule of Love' (often styled the 'Golden Rule'), in the Double Commandment of Love (of God and of neighbour) and in the Ten Commandments. That the Rule of Love and the Ten Commandments are expressions of natural law is clearly part of the Augustinian inheritance.[8] There may thus be different formulations of natural law – but they say the same thing, and they are 'written in the human heart', so that everybody is able to recognise natural law in their own minds. Yet, this does not mean that everyone is able to understand its demands correctly.[9]

However, Luther's interpretation of the content of natural law differs from the traditional views based on the *ordo caritatis*. He says that if the Golden Rule and the Commandment of Love are formulations of natural law, they express the 'law of pure and uncorrupted love'.[10] In other words, natural law is not based on human nature but on the nature of divine love. For Luther, divine love is a continuous giving (by God) that does not attend objects for their goodness (which deserve to be loved) but gives its objects what they lack: '[T]o be God is not to receive but to give [good things].'[11] God gives himself continuously as Father, Son and Holy Spirit as well as all He has. In short, for Luther, natural law is the commandment to follow the self-giving divine love. This makes its radical demands impossible to fulfil on the basis of human capacity alone.

Luther reads the commandments 'to do to others as we wish others to do to us' and 'to love our neighbour as our self' in the following way. Everyone knows how to love one's self, and everyone wishes others to do them good. This provides an example as to how to love our neighbour and to seek good for our neighbour. The precepts do not command but rather presuppose self-love. In proper neighbour-love, the focus of love is turned from oneself to our neighbour. Luther also proposes how to speak

7 See Antti Raunio, 'Natural Law and Christian Love in Luther's Theology', in Kees van Kooten Niekerk and Ulrik Nissen, eds., *Lidenskab & Stringens: Festskrift til Svend Andersen* (København: Forlaget Anis, 2008), 249–261 – hereafter Raunio 2008; Raunio 2001 and 2006.

8 De vera rel. XLVI, 87; De doct. Christ. III, XIV, 22; En. in Ps. LVII, 1; En. in Ps. LVII, 2; En. in Ps. CXVIII, sermo XXV, 4.

9 For the view that Luther did not neglect natural law, see Knud Haakonssen, *Natural Law and Moral Philosophy: From Grotius to the Scottish Enlightenment* (Cambridge: Cambridge University Press, 1996), 37.

10 *Weimarer Ausgabe* (Weimar Edition of Luther's Works) 1, 502, 16–26 – hereafter WA.

11 'Hoc est esse deum: non accipere bona sed dare', WA 4, 269, 25–26.

about love of self. We may love ourselves correctly, if we love ourselves 'in God'; that is, if we want for ourselves exactly the same as that which God wills for us. This kind of willing and loving cannot start from human nature. And love of God does not mean seeking after the highest good in order to attain it, but the love of God's will, and uniting with it, prepares us for everything that God wills. This also means loving God incarnated in all who need our help, support and care. Christ is present in them receiving all our works performed for them. So, the demands of natural law concern both inward orientation and outward action, in so far as natural law requires the practice of divine love in order for its precepts to be fulfilled. Natural law concerns the whole person, and good deeds should be performed out of the divine self-giving love.

Alongside his strong theological interpretation of natural law, Luther also sees natural law as concerned with moral reasoning. He considers that human reason is capable of practical reasoning which may be used in working out the implications of the Golden Rule. A human person may perform morally good deeds even without fulfilling the proper (theological) demands of natural law. In other words, one may follow natural law in outward action, without the inward activity of divine love; humans have different capacities to apply natural law in their diverse circumstances.

A decisive factor in applying the Golden Rule is the human capacity and willingness to put oneself in the position of the other, our neighbour. For Luther, the Golden Rule does not presuppose that we should transfer our own wishes and preferences directly to our neighbour. We should first put ourselves in the shoes of the other and then determine what we would wish if we were in a similar situation to that of our neighbour. This is designed to understand what is best for our neighbour. One cannot know what is good for our neighbour beforehand solely on the basis of one's own preferences and intentions. Nevertheless, there are some very basic wishes and preferences, which all people share, which are implicit in the Ten Commandments. Luther often interprets these with the aid of the Golden Rule which enables us to see what we should do if we were in the position of God and our neighbour. So, the Commandments verbalise and concretise the content of natural law.

Luther also adheres to the traditional view that civil laws have to be based on natural law. When treating questions of law and right, he refers both to the Commandment of Love and to the Ten Commandments. In concrete decisions, he stresses the equity or moderation of the strict law. His conception of equity (επιεικεια) has several aspects. First, he sometimes combines equity and natural law so that they are actually one and the same thing.[12] In his tract *On the Worldly Authority*, Luther considers that the strict application of human law may sometimes be contrary to the will of God, natural law and love. People may not demand a more

[12] WA 51, 344, 13–14: 'Darumb, ists billich auch der vernunfft vnd naturlichem recht nach'. This equation of natural law and equity is also to be found in Calvin: see Chapter 7.

severe decision than they are ready to accept if they find themselves in a similar situation.[13] Here Luther clearly presents the Golden Rule as a principle which requires the equitable application of the law. He also relates equity to the principle of love: in applying the law one has to take into account the differences between and particular circumstances of individuals. The strict positive law cannot do this.[14] Because all positive civil laws have to be based on the natural law of love, it follows that they should also be equitable. And so natural law provides the criterion against which to measure the legitimacy of all legal prescriptions.[15] Rules which are against love are not valid and others should be applied so that the consequences do not violate the rule of love.[16] Such reasonable deliberation is needed at all times. Luther calls such deliberations on the part of princes and judges the 'living law'.[17]

Melanchthon and Natural Law

Philip Melanchthon (1497–1560) developed what has been called a theory of natural law. In his later works he integrates his ideas about natural law into his whole scheme of theology.[18] He distinguishes divine law and natural law – in contrast to Luther – and this distinction became very influential in the later Lutheran tradition. For Melanchthon, divine law concerns both the inward disposition and outward action; natural law consists of those aspects of divine law which may be discovered and understood through the use of human reason. In other words, for Melanchthon, unlike for Luther, natural law consists only of rationally comprehensible outward acts. He considers that the inward element of love is not commanded by natural law but only by divine law. Therefore, natural law forms the basis for moral life and social legislation, but it does not have a direct relation with spiritual life. With Melanchthon, then, the spiritual and social aspects of human life are (at least conceptually) more remote from each other than with Luther.[19] In this sense, Melanchthon has probably given impulses to the 'modern' view of the relation between religious life and civil society based on human reason, even though his focus was the visible Christian order.

For Melanchthon, natural law consists of ten principles which closely resemble the Ten Commandments. God has written these principles in the human heart and the Decalogue confirms and elucidates their content.[20] As John Witte suggests (at least implicitly), Melanchthon's view of the uses of natural law is somewhat

13 WA 11, 279, 16–25.

14 WA 20, 147, 36–148, 13. For Luther's view of equity, see Ulrich Duchrow, *Christenheit und Weltverantwortung: Traditionsgeschichte und systematische Struktur der Zweireichelehre* (Stuttgart: Klett-Cotta, 1980), 498–499.

15 WA 37, 134, 3–4.

16 WA 8, 664, 22–39.

17 WA 11, 272, 13–24; WA 14, 554, 32–555, 19; WA 44, 704, 30–39.

18 Clemens Bauer, 'Melanchthon's Naturrechtslehre', *Archiv für Reformationsgeschichte* 42 (1951): 64–100.

19 For a detailed analysis, see Raunio 2006.

20 Ibid., 49–50.

ambiguous. On the one hand, natural law is useful for the earthly kingdom and civil life. On the other hand, it serves theological and pedagogical uses: it makes people conscious of their inability to fulfil the divine law, and it teaches morality.[21] The civil utility of natural law may be understood by the use of reason; the second function may not.

According to Melanchthon, law consists of commandments which seek to effect moral discipline in terms of external conduct. These commandments bind and generate obedience. Indeed, God wills that all human beings live under an external discipline, and He punishes external vice, typically through the sword of worldly authorities.[22] In turn, Christian magistrates promulgate 'rational positive laws for the government of the earthly kingdom', positive laws, that is, which must be based on the principles of natural law, practical considerations of social utility and the common good. The magistrate is the 'custodian of both tables of the Ten Commandments', as Melanchthon puts it. The commandments of natural law have to be protected, maintained and elaborated. So positive laws based on the First Table govern spiritual morality and relations between persons and God. The Second Table is the foundation for laws which govern civil morality, the social relationships between persons. Thus, civil authorities must support with law the teaching of right doctrine and prohibit violations of the three first commandments of the Decalogue.[23] Here, again, Melanchthon differs from Luther, for whom religion and faith cannot be coerced by worldly laws; for Melanchthon, governments may not be able to rule the inner life of people, but in the world of external action, all should obey the laws, even in religious matters. This view dominated the Lutheran countries of northern Europe for centuries: all citizens were obliged to participate in church life, through attendance at church, receiving Holy Communion and learning the Catechism.

The concept of natural law is also relevant to the development of church law and the absorption of norms applicable to the church into the civil laws of these countries. Whilst Luther was critical of the idea of church law, he gradually accepted that church life too has to be regulated. In due course, Lutheran and Evangelical church ordinances were formulated. Whilst Johannes Bugenhagen (1485–1558) was the main architect of these in northern Germany and Denmark, Luther himself was involved in the preparation of the first reformatory church ordinance of the town of Leisnig, and he wrote its preamble. The ordinance places a strong emphasis on Christian love as the basis of common life, and similar ordinances mention natural law in their norms, for example on marriage. Alongside the church ordinances, the doctrinal instruments known as the Lutheran Confessions were also normative and they too invoked natural law thinking. For instance, the Large Catechism (1529) presents the Ten Commandments as

[21] Witte 2002, 127–128. [22] Corpus Reformatorum 22, 250: quoted in Witte 2002, 127–128.
[23] Ibid., 129–131.

natural law; the Apology of the Augsburg Confession (1530) provides that natural law contains both tables of the Decalogue which govern relations with God and our neighbours[24] and that human reason understands this law 'in some way' (*aliquo modo*);[25] and the Book of Concord (1580) presupposes the existence of natural law, and the view that the divine law is 'written in the human heart'.[26] Moreover, the content of the First Table concerning love to God goes far above the rational capacity of humans, because reason is able only to concern itself with outward deeds.[27] Without the Holy Spirit, one cannot love God above all.[28]

Natural Law in German Lutheranism

John Witte describes two early schools of Lutheran jurisprudence. The first was formed in the University of Wittenberg, centred on Melanchthon, and the second a little later in the University of Marburg, whose leading scholars included Johannes Eisermann and Johann Oldendorp. These scholars were also involved in church and political life, and they developed laws for both areas.

The main work of Eisermann (1486–1558), published in 1533, is *Von dem gemeinen Nutze*, 'On the Common Good'; it was later expanded and republished in 1556 as *De republica bene instituendo parenesis*, 'On the Good Ordering of a Commonwealth'. Eisermann combines natural law with Lutheran teaching, especially with that on the three estates: *ecclesia, oeconomia* and *politia* – these have complementary roles in teaching and enforcing the norms of natural law, especially the Golden Rule and Ten Commandments.[29] A question for Eisermann is: how might fallen mankind form a good society? His answer is based on the idea that, even though human beings as a result of the Fall are prone to sin, traces remain of the (original) human being as created by God. As such, humans still have the capacity to recognise natural law and the precepts to love God, neighbour and self. They also possess a natural sense of equity, by which these laws should be applied. However, natural law needs to be studied, taught and enforced continuously – because people easily ignore and forget it – as an important foundation of communal life, morality and law.[30]

According to Eisermann, there have always been 'wise men', who have carefully studied the sparks of natural law. Such people have from the beginning had the capacity to form 'covenants of human society' following laws based on the reasonable natural law. These covenants differed according to 'nature, custom, and reason', and their common foundation in natural law was applied to local

[24] Bekenntnisschriften der Evangelisch-Lutherischen Kirche (Göttingen: Vandenhoek and Ruprecht, 1983), 160, 7–8 – hereafter BSELK.

[25] BSELK 160, 7.

[26] BSELK 661, 67; 793–794, 2; 963–964, 5. See also Ronald Ziegler, 'Natural Law in the Lutheran Confessions', in R.C. Baker and R.C. Ehlke, eds., *Natural Law: A Lutheran Reappraisal*, op cit., 65–78.

[27] BSELK 163, 18. [28] BSELK 160, 9. [29] Witte 2002, 142–143. [30] Ibid., 143–144.

circumstances and laws formed for these differing conditions.[31] For John Witte, *On the Common Good* represents the first detailed social contract theory in evangelical Germany. Although its influence on subsequent social contract theories developed in Protestantism has not been carefully studied, there are traces of similar ideas in, for example, the work of Martin Bucer (1491–1551).[32]

For Eisermann, even though the classical commonwealths were often good societies, in relative terms, they lacked something that only a Christian commonwealth could have. Such commonwealths may have attained only a 'civil goodness', and an 'outward conformity' to natural law, but not a 'spiritual goodness', and an inward renewal of their citizens – they provide only the goods of the mind and body, not the goods of the soul and heart. Therefore, echoing Luther, for Eisermann the model for the earthly commonwealth should be the heavenly kingdom, and this is possible only on the basis of biblical teaching. He used the metaphor of the Body of Christ to describe the form and function of a Christian *politia*, which is instructed by nature but especially by the Bible, and in which charity is a duty, teaching hospitality even to its enemies. Again resonating Luther, Eisermann writes that in the practice of charity, 'man is a veritable god to his fellow man.'[33]

Johann Oldendorp (1486–1567) was at the beginning of his career a representative of legal humanism, but during the 1530s he became a supporter of the Reformation. In 1516 he was appointed professor at the University of Greifswald, but from 1543 to his death, he worked as a professor of law at the University of Marburg; he had come into personal contact with Melanchthon, whom he greatly admired.[34] Oldendorp established an Evangelical legal and civil order in the Protestant German states in which, for him, the common good was the highest ideal.[35] Like his Lutheran contemporaries, Oldendorp adhered to the view that there is a natural moral law inscribed in the human heart, which he also styled the 'instruction of conscience'. Natural law is actually divine law in the human reason. It contains general moral principles: the love of God and neighbour, the Golden Rule and the Ten Commandments. According to Witte, Oldendorp taught that all individuals are inclined towards these moral principles, which the Bible also teaches.[36] This may suggest that, for Oldendorp, natural law does not consist solely of moral precepts but also of an inclination to follow them. Such a trait could well have been influenced by his humanist education.

The conscience, which instructs natural moral principles, is a form of practical reason. It is implanted by God and is therefore unchangeable and independent of an individual's personal powers. If our conscience is studied and followed diligently it will be an infallible guide. However, fallen human beings are not able to engage in an unbiased consultation of their own consciences. For a better understanding of God's law, they need the Bible and guidance of the Holy Spirit. Moreover, all civil

[31] Ibid., 146. [32] Ibid., 153. [33] Ibid., 147, 149. [34] Ibid., 155–156. [35] Raunio 2006.
[36] Witte 2002, 160.

laws must conform with natural law and through it with divine law. Oldendorp gives a list of laws which in his view were illegitimate because they contradicted natural law, such as laws which permit divorce and remarriage. He also discussed laws which conform to natural law, such as laws which require owners to use their private property for social purposes and those which do not exclude others from use of it when such use does the owner no harm.[37]

Oldendorp's special contribution to Lutheran jurisprudence was his theory of equity, namely, equity should pervade the substance or content of all law; equity is not merely a principle to be applied in such cases where strict law leads to immoderate conclusions. Here, Oldendorp seems to be close to Luther, for whom, as we have seen: (1) *epieikeia* also involves the implementation in law of the Golden Rule and the Commandment of Love, which presupposes that the legislator must take into account the particular positions of those who are affected by the law;[38] (2) the Golden Rule is included in all the precepts of the Decalogue;[39] and (3) divine and natural laws, identical in content, are the most equitable.[40] Equity is thus already present in natural law and all positive laws should be evaluated by it; as positive laws cannot take all possible situations into account, so the 'living law' is needed, that is, the equitable judgment of all who apply the laws in practice.

Perhaps Melanchthon held the same view. Whilst some of his texts seem to restrict the use of equity to special cases which necessitate the relaxation of strict law, the principle 'what is not right and equitable, cannot be law' implies that equity should pervade all laws in terms of their content. Certainly, Melanchthon's Swedish students, such as Olaus and Laurentius Petri, learnt this when studying at Wittenberg. They too used the idea when they formulated laws and church ordinances for the emerging Lutheran kingdom of Sweden. Though Oldendorp on the relation between law and equity may not be as novel as Witte suggests, this does not diminish his achievement in proposing a theory of equity which neither Luther nor Melanchthon fully developed.

Natural Law in Swedish Lutheranism

Melanchthon had been the principal teacher of those Swedish theologians who became influential in the development of legislation for the emergent Swedish kingdom. Olaus Petri (Olof Persson, 1493–1552) was the most important in this respect. He absorbed reforming ideas as he studied at Wittenberg (1516–1518). His influence grew in the kingdom of Gustav Vasa where he was the king's chancellor from 1531 to 1533 and then as pastor of the Great Church (Storkyrkan) in central Stockholm. Influenced by Melanchthon, Luther and even Thomas Aquinas, for Olaus Petri all the positive laws should be based on natural law, which was summarised in the Golden Rule.

[37] Ibid., 160–163. [38] WA 8, 664, 22–39. [39] See Raunio 2001, 259–293.
[40] WA 15, 321, 25–27.

Here, Petri seems to follow Luther rather than Melanchthon: natural law is reasonable and common for all, whereas the Decalogue is the product of divine revelation and sharpens natural law.[41] This, in turn, resembles Melanchthon's view that the Decalogue is a refinement of natural law. Central to the thought of Olaus Petri was the idea that 'the advantage of the common people is the best law'; as with Luther and Melanchthon, this required reciprocal service between authorities and subjects.[42] Olaus Petri's younger brother Laurentius (Lars Persson 1499–1573), the first Lutheran archbishop of Sweden in 1531, also uses the concept of natural law in his theological and juristic thought.[43]

In the practical sphere of sixteenth-century Swedish civil law, the concept of 'God's law' is sometimes understood and used as the source and ground of positive law. Sometimes 'God's law' is synonymous with natural law; sometimes they are distinguished; sometimes it signifies the Decalogue, sometimes the whole Mosaic Law.[44] Indeed, the expression 'God's and Sweden's law' (Guds och Sveriges lag) was commonplace in the seventeenth century and is used, for example, by Laurentius Paulinus Gothus (1565–1646), bishop (1608) and archbishop (1637), in his *Ethica Christiana* (1615–1630), which also discusses divine, natural and positive laws, and equity.[45] In 1687 Sweden adopted its own Church Law, which remained in force until 2000 (and its equivalent in Finland lasted until 1867). This invokes divine law only indirectly when it apprehends the Bible and the Lutheran Confessions as sources of correct doctrine.[46] Indeed, later, the preamble of the book of Swedish Law of 1735 combines divine law and natural law, on the basis of the idea that the natural knowledge of the will of God is written deeply in the hearts of all men.[47] It is to natural law theory in the thinkers of the seventeenth and eighteenth centuries that we now turn.

NATURAL LAW IN PUFENDORF AND LEIBNIZ

After the Reformation, Lutheran teaching on natural law followed broadly the lines set out by Melanchthon and the Lutheran Confessions. The seventeenth century saw the formation of the modern natural law theory by leading Protestant thinkers such as Hugo Grotius, Thomas Hobbes and Samuel Pufendorf and, later, by the jurist Christian Thomasius and the philosopher Gottfried Wilhelm Leibniz. Grotius

41 Martti Takala, *Lex Dei – Lex Politica Dei: teos ja Kaarle IX:n lainsäädäntö* (The *Lex Politica Dei* and King Karl IX's legislation) (Helsinki: SHS/SKHS, 1993), 34–35.

42 Ibid., 33. Takala sees here a difference to Luther, but at this point his view is clearly erroneous. Luther writes explicitly about the mutual serving between worldly authorities and the subjects.

43 Ibid., 38–42. 44 Ibid., 1993, 45–47.

45 Ruben Josefson, *Guds och Sveriges lag: Studier i den lutherska socialetikens historia* (Uppsala: A.-B. Lundequistiska bokhandeln; Leipzig: Otto Harrassowitz, 1950), 19–22.

46 Kyrkolag och ordning 1867, Cap. I, § I, § IV: Kyrkio-lag och Ordning/Kircko-Laki ja Ordningi 1687 (Church Law and Ordinance).

47 Hannu Juntunen, *Oikeuden idean teologiset perusteet* (The Theological Foundations of the Idea of Right) (Helsinki: Kauppakaari Lakimiesliiton Kustannus, 2000), 243.

and Hobbes had a more or less Reformed background, whereas Pufendorf, Thomasius and Leibniz were Lutherans – even though Leibniz was very critical of Pufendorf's legal thought, which Thomasius for his part defended. According to Kari Saastamoinen, the Lutheran heritage in Pufendorf's moral and legal thinking is stronger than has previously been thought.[48] However, Pufendorf was critical of Lutheran orthodoxy and developed his natural law theory mostly through engagement with other modernists like Grotius and Hobbes. They all have a common starting point: natural law exists and its focus is the basic need of human beings to survive through peaceful social life. They elaborate and justify this in different ways.[49]

Modern theory makes a clear distinction between philosophy and theology – and it presents natural law without prominent theological or at least biblical dimensions. Nevertheless, at this time, faith in God was common and considered natural, and atheism was rare and considered unnatural.[50] For example, Pufendorf (1632–1694) – like Grotius before him (1583–1645) – seeks to avoid biblical argumentation but nevertheless justifies the existence of natural law by reference to God. Pufendorf sees the world as consisting of two kinds of entities: physical and moral. A moral entity is a quality, or mode (*modus*), which has been settled in physical entities. God has not given moral laws as inborn ideas, but humans are able by their reason to determine natural law, the normative aspect, which God through the divine will has placed in the world. All morality is based on the duty to obey the precepts of natural law. By observing the circumstances of the real world and human nature, one may understand the precepts of natural law. The basic commandment of natural law is that everyone should promote peaceful sociality so far as is possible. Hence, everything that endorses sociality has to be understood as commanded by natural law.[51]

For Pufendorf, natural law is based on the human condition *after* the Fall, whereas prior Lutheran orthodoxy saw the basis for natural law in the original state *before* the Fall. Pufendorf agrees with Hobbes in part but denies Hobbes' view that the original state of humankind is that of strife and selfishness. Pufendorf considers that humans at one and the same time have the capacity for both wickedness and for acknowledging the obligations of natural moral law to promote sociality and not doing harm. The precepts of the natural law concern only the outward deeds of humans in a society. As seen above, this distinction between moral and theological concepts of law was present in Melanchthon's thought, and Pufendorf offers this distinction even more clearly.

[48] Kari Saastamoinen, 'Morality of the Fallen Man: Samuel Pufendorf on Natural Law', *Studia Historica* (1995): 52.

[49] Petter Korkman, 'Valtio ja sen lait modernissa luonnonoikeusperinteessä' (The State and Its Laws in the Modern Natural Rights Tradition), in Jarkko Tontti, Kaisa Mäkelä and Heta Gylling, eds., *Filosofien oikeus* (Helsinki: Suomalainen Lakimiesyhdistys, 2001), 96–97.

[50] Ibid., 97.

[51] Heikki Haara, 'Pufendorf, Samuel', *Logos-ensyklopedia* (2014): http://filosofia.fi/node/6580/.

Pufendorf also proposes a particular understanding of the Golden Rule on the basis of his ideas about the natural equality of all men. Whatever a person expects from others, others may demand exactly the same from that person: as all are equal, like should be treated alike – when a person decrees a judgment for another, that person is obliged to submit himself in like case.[52] This 'equality of right' belongs to natural law because humans, the most sociable of creatures, should grant the same rights to others as they desire for themselves. Pufendorf here resembles to some degree Luther on the Golden Rule, even though Pufendorf discusses it in the context of rights, and not in the context of the duty to love our neighbour. As everyone knows their own human nature, and therefore at least on a common level the natures of others, so each one of us, as a social being, should also know and acknowledge for others the same rights as we claim for ourselves.[53]

The influence of Pufendorf on morality, law, the state and the separation of church and state has been considerable. His major works were republished and translated into French, English and German. He was also well-known in Sweden and worked as professor in the University of Lund, where he published his main works on natural law. For a long time, study of his *De Officio* – a shorter version of his understanding of natural law – was required in the universities of northern Europe. It was reprinted on over seventy occasions. In Prussia, Christian Thomasius (1655–1728) promoted, defended and developed Pufendorf's legal thought, and in France his approach to the original state of humankind was refined by the Huguenot scholar Jean Barbeyrac (1677–1747).[54]

Another influential Lutheran natural law theorist in this period was Gottfried Wilhelm Leibniz (1646–1716). The distinctly Lutheran dimension of his approach, however, is less obvious. Nevertheless, there is at least one inherited feature: charity as the basis of natural law. Leibniz maintains that the highest principle of natural law is the 'charity of the wise man, that is, charity which follows the dictates of wisdom', and this charity or universal benevolence is both the source and limit of law. And Leibniz associates charity with justice: justice is charity or love, the source of which is the wisdom and will of God.[55] The main difference between Pufendorf and Leibniz concerns the foundation of morality. While Pufendorf roots morality in God's free will, Leibniz bases it on God's rational nature, not on the divine will. Leibniz also criticises the view that external actions and internal affects or movements of the soul are separate from each other.[56]

52 Samuel von Pufendorf, *The Whole Duty of Man According to the Law of Nature* [1673], trans. Andrew Tooke 1691, and by Basil Kennett (London, 1729), 226.

53 Ibid. 227. 54 Petter Korkman, op cit., 101.

55 Roger Berkowitz, *The Gift of Science: Leibniz and the Modern Legal Tradition* (Cambridge, MA: Harvard University Press, 2005), 64–65.

56 Knud Haakonssen, op cit., 48.

Leibniz proposes a teleological understanding of the human being.[57] All humans seek happiness, and science aims at the attainment of happiness. The divine wisdom, which is the rational source of justice, may be comprehended through the science of happiness. This science, exercised by the wise, reveals natural law with its three degrees or levels, each governed by its own rule. The lowest degree of natural law is the strict law (*ius strictum*), or commutative justice. Strict justice regulates relations among persons according to the rule: harm no one (*neminem laedere*). On this lowest level of justice legal persons encounter each other formally as equal bearers of rights. The second degree of natural law is equity (*aequitas*), or distributive justice, and it directs political relations among citizens in their external actions, according to the rule: 'give to each his own' (*suum cuique tribuere*); the rule 'what you do not want to have done to yourself, do not to others' (*quod tibi nolis, alteri non faciendum*) belongs to equity. Indeed, *ius strictum* arises from the 'principle of the conservation of peace', seeks not the attainment of virtue but the avoidance of harm and is required by equity, 'except when an important consideration of a greater good makes us depart from it'.[58] The highest degree of natural law is *pietas*, or universal justice, which governs the internal forum in the rule: 'live virtuously' (*honeste vivere*). This level of natural law perfects the other levels and it makes them effective – and so God ensures and actualises charity through his wisdom and will.[59]

Not unlike Luther, Leibniz also proposes that consideration of 'the position of the other' is the right approach in politics and morality. Leibniz also applies the Golden Rule to the juridical sphere. Although he prefers the negative formulation of the rule, *quod tibi non vis fieri*, he argues that this not only prohibits harm to the other but also requires or commands, as well as doing, good to the other. The prohibition of harm is a requirement of the *ius strictum*, and the precept to do good, is required by equity. Leibniz applies this principle, for example, to criminal law and punishment, in which a judge must take into consideration the positions of all those involved in the case.[60]

The Lutheran rationalist philosopher, Christian Wolff (1679–1754), influenced in part by Leibniz, also connects natural law with the duty to strive to perfection: all are obliged by the law of nature to instantiate perfection in their lives; actions tending towards perfection produce pleasure and those towards imperfection displeasure.[61] In short, natural law thinking among the leading Lutheran scholars in the seventeenth and eighteenth centuries reflects Melanchthon rather than Luther.

57 Markku Roinila, 'Leibnizin oikeusfilosofia' (Leibniz's Philosophy of Right), in Jarkko Tontti, Kaisa Mäkelä and Heta Gylling, eds., *Filosofien oikeus* (Helsinki: Suomalainen Lakimiesyhdistys, 2001), 133–152, at 137, based on Leibniz's *Theodicée* § 278.

58 Roger Berkowitz, op cit., 65.

59 G.W. Leibniz, *Frühe Jugendschriften zum Naturrecht*, trans. into German, H. von Hubertus Busche (Hamburg: Felix Meiner Verlag, 2003), 75–83, 203.

60 G.W. Leibniz, *Filosofisia tutkielmia* (Philosophical Studies), trans. into Finnish by Tuomo Aho, Kimmo Jylhämö, Sari Kivistö, Petter Korkman, Mika Oksanen, Arto Repo, Markku Roinila, Jyrki Siukonen, Hannu Sivenius and Risto Vilkko (Helsinki: Gaudeamus Helsinki University Press, 2011), 62–63, 270–272.

61 Matt Hettche, 'Christian Wolff', *Stanford Encyclopedia of Philosophy* (2014): 103–132.

THE CRISIS FOR NATURAL LAW IN THE ENLIGHTENMENT

The so-called crisis of natural law thinking began with the French Enlightenment. The result was that its role in debate about the foundations of morality and law diminished but did not disappear. Immanuel Kant (1728–1804) was indebted to the voluntarist natural law tradition – which sought to separate nature and values – but he did not address natural law fully, preferring to use instead the categories of practical reason and human freedom to set their own ends. From the theological point of view, Kant was a Protestant but not a Lutheran. However, he was to influence Lutheranism greatly in the form of the work of G.W.F. Hegel (1770–1831). Hegel was a Lutheran, but was critical of orthodox Lutheran theology, which he studied at Tübingen. He considered it unable to answer the questions which the Enlightenment posed and, like many other Protestant theologians, turned to Kant. Nevertheless, he did appreciate and use the Lutheran heritage in his work.[62]

In *The Philosophy of Right and Law, or Natural Law and Political Science Outlined* (1821), Hegel develops, *inter alia*, the concept of 'natural rights';[63] the 'original state' was one in which (like Pufendorf) egoism and sociability exist simultaneously but also in which humans had a basic need to be acknowledged as spiritual persons.[64] For Hegel, therefore, '[t]he basis of law and right is altogether the spiritual, its starting point the will which is free. Freedom constitutes its substance and its end, and the legal system is the realm of actualized freedom, the world of the spirit created by the spirit as its second nature' (§ 4); moreover, '[r]ight and law, then, result from the fact that any human existence is an existence of free willing beings. Right and law are altogether freedom as an idea' (§ 29); and:

> To consider something rational does not mean to apply reason to such a matter from the outside and thus to work upon it [*bearbeiten*], but to recognize that the object is by itself rational; here it is the spirit in its freedom, the highest summit of self-conscious reason, which gives itself reality and creates itself as the existing world; science has only the task of making conscious this labour of reason (§ 31).[65]

In all this, there are three versions, so to speak, of 'right'; each version is larger than the preceding ones and encompasses them: abstract *right* (*Recht*), in which Hegel sees 'non-interference' as necessary but insufficient in order to respect others; *morality* (*Moralität*), under which humans reflect their own subjectivity of others in order to respect them; and *ethical life* (*Sittlichkeit*), the integration of individual

62 Gary Badcock, 'Hegel, Lutheranism and Contemporary Theology', *Animus* 5 (2000): 144–158.

63 Shlomo Avineri, *Hegel's Theory of the Modern State* (Cambridge: Cambridge University Press, 1972), 82–83.

64 Juha Manninen and Markus Wahlberg, 'G.W.F. Hegelin oikeusfilosofian synty ja asema' (The Formation and Status of Hegel's Philosophy of Right), in G.W.F. *Hegel, Oikeusfilosofian pääpiirteet eli luonnonoikeuden ja valtiotieteen perusteet*, Suomentanut ja selityksin varustanut Markus Wahlberg (Oulu: Kustannus Pohjoinen, 1994), 12–13.

65 See Carl Joachim Friedrich, *The Philosophy of Law in Historical Perspective*, 2nd edn, 5th impression (Chicago: University of Chicago Press, 1963), 136–138.

subjective feelings and universal notions of right. In turn, the free will can only be realised fully in the social context of property rights and relations, contracts, moral commitments, family life, the economy and the law. A person is not truly free unless that person is a participant in all of these different aspects of the life of the state. Hegel also argues that the state itself is subsumed under the higher totality of world history, in which individual states arise, conflict with each other and eventually fall. The course of history appears as moving to an ever-increasing actualisation of freedom; each successive historical epoch corrects certain failures of the earlier ones. Today, some argue that Hegel is hostile to natural law, that he is a legal positivist, others that he is a natural law theorist in the conventional sense and Tony Burns argues that both interpretations are incorrect – rather, Hegel is a natural law theorist, but not in the conventional sense; like several medieval thinkers, he subscribes to what is by current standards an unconventional natural law theory, which derives ultimately from Aristotle.[66]

Both Kantian and Hegelian influences penetrated academic Lutheran theology so as to distance itself from earlier conventional natural law thinking. It became more and more common to make a clear distinction between the different realms of nature and the person or spirit. This distinction was understood as identical with that between necessity and freedom. As a result, 'natural law' came to be comprehended in its scientific sense as the (physical) laws of nature, and these do not belong to the spiritual or personal realm.[67] Another possibility was to connect with 'natural rights' theory, and 'human rights', which are considered to belong to every human. Both the Hegelian and the Neo-Kantian world view see the aim of a human being as rising from the level of nature to real personhood, where freedom reigns. For Hegel the created world divides into the realms of nature and finite spirit or humanity. God works in both realms, but a free and conscious relationship to God is possible only in the latter. Hegel sees the achievement of the realm of spirit as a stage in the self-development of the absolute spirit whereas Neo-Kantianism emphasises the personal freedom and the ability of individuals to determine their own values. A crucial question for both schools is: how might a human became a truly religious and Christian person? This takes place in the personal encounter between God and the human soul, an encounter in which natural law plays no part.[68]

THE GRADUAL RETURN OF NATURAL LAW THEORY TO LUTHERANISM

Given these earlier developments, it is not surprising that in the twentieth century Lutheran theology had difficulty with the concept of natural law. However, the end of the nineteenth century saw publication of the new scientific edition of Luther's

66 Tony Burns, 'Hegel and Natural Law Theory', *Politics* 15 (1995): 27–32.

67 E.g. the well-known Lutheran theologian Wilhelm Herrmann represents this kind of view: see Raunio 2001, 16–17.

68 Raunio 2001, 14–15.

works, the *Weimarer Ausgabe* (WA). With this new edition, Lutherans soon came to observe the incidence of natural law thinking in Luther himself. Three particular explanations were given. One – quite common – was that the concept of natural law was a vestige of Roman Catholic thought, which did not belong to genuine Reformation theology. A second was that Luther used the traditional concept but meant something different. Thirdly, it was also possible to think that actually it was to be expected that there was continuity between the medieval understanding of natural law and Luther. As a result, the role of natural law in Lutheran ethics and social ethics has been the focus of much discussion during the last century.

Modern discussion about the role of the natural law in Lutheran theology and ethics begins with Ernst Troeltsch (1865–1923),[69] and his book *The Social Teachings of the Christian Churches and Groups*, published in Germany, 1912. Troeltsch has dominated images of Lutheranism for a long time. However, he did not use sources from the time of the Reformation but rather based his views on observations about nineteenth-century German Lutheranism. Thus Troeltsch considers that Luther presupposes a distinction between absolute and relative natural laws. Absolute natural law operates in the original state and Christ renews it. It functions as a religious animation and as the nature-penetrating spiritualisation of all natural circumstances. The religious animation of nature, that is, the love of God and neighbour, is all that natural law demands. Relative natural law stands in philosophical ethics, jurisprudence and the natural conscience. For Troeltsch, the problem of Luther's ethics is that the two forms of natural law are in conflict. From this it follows that, for Christians, inward personal morality and outward morality are in conflict.[70]

At the beginning of the twentieth century, this sort of distinction meant that the realm of personal freedom left little room for the inner religious life. What happened in society and politics was understood as the world of natural necessities. Many Lutheran academics at the time shared this view. Therefore, for example, war was seen as an inevitable occurrence in the process of history. This understanding of the 'natural' and 'personal' spheres actually provides the background to the conception that the Lutheran position is to submit humbly to worldly authorities. All criticism of the temporal order is misplaced and against the will of God, which realises itself inevitably in the natural sphere. Many Lutherans represented these sorts of views in the first decades of the twentieth century. This may be seen as the second crisis of the Lutheran understanding of natural law, at least in central Europe. Thus, after the Second World War, German Lutheranism was very careful in its approach to natural law. For example, Gerhard Ebeling (1912–2001) proposed an existential interpretation of Luther's theology, and this hardly mentions natural law. Many

69 He had a keen interest in the history of natural law; see, e.g., Ernst Troeltsch, 'Christian natural law', in his *Religion in History*, James Luther Adams and Walter F. Bense, trans. (Minneapolis, MN: Fortress Press, 1991), 159–167.

70 Raunio 2001, 17–18.

have seen Karl Barth's theology and Christian ethics, which copes without the concept of natural law, as a better alternative. And so some Lutheran theologians, like Ernst Wolf, sought to combine Luther on natural law with Barth who is hostile to natural law theory.[71] Johannes Heckel analyses Luther's concept of natural law from a juridical point of view. He distinguishes 'secular natural law' and 'Christian natural law', the latter merely a Christian version of the former. The two forms of natural law are not identical in content. Neither the Golden Rule nor the Decalogue is as such a spiritual law but they belong to secular natural law and address the state of corrupted nature. They are the foundations of the secular laws but have nothing to do with the kingdom of Christ.[72] Heckel tries to argue carefully for his view – but nevertheless it jars against Luther's accentuation of the unity of law and also against his statement that the worldly kingdom is the image and shadow of the kingdom of Christ. The historical Lutheran sources know no such distinction between these two kinds of natural law, but they clearly presuppose an analogy of being between the two kingdoms.

Nordic Lutheranism sees natural law as the foundation of ethics more than does central European Lutheranism. Perhaps the best-known representatives of a Nordic point of view are the Danish philosopher K.E. Løgstrup and the Swedish theologian Gustaf Wingren. Both see a confluence between natural law and the Christian message, though Wingren's understanding of natural law appears to be somewhat unclear.[73] The Swedish Luther scholar Herbert Olsson and his Finnish pupil Lauri Haikola also deserve to be mentioned as modern scholars of Luther's concept of natural law. Both have done thorough work with the sources but nevertheless they – like many others – have difficulties with Luther's accentuation of the unity of law, a principle not always in focus in their thinking. This means that natural law as a rule of morality and law does not presuppose love in the Christian sense. The difference is not only that the first demands outward action whereas the latter extends to the inward disposition of love and therefore these laws allow different motivations. What is problematic is that these observations are often combined with the view that secular natural law and the Christian natural law are different in content. Natural law is, then, a principle of reciprocity, which accepts at least a moderate egoism but the Christian natural law demands more, namely unselfish love. As has been shown, this is a common Lutheran interpretation, which divides the worldly kingdom and the kingdom of Christ. This view still obscures foundations for the view that the worldly sphere with its morals and laws is quite different in comparison to the Christian spiritual sphere, and therefore there cannot be any direct Christian

[71] See Chapters 7 and 10.

[72] Johannes Heckel, *Lex Caritatis: Eine juristische Untersuchung über das Recht in der Theologie Martin Luthers* (München: Abhandlungen der bayerischen Akademie der Wissenschaften, 1953), 67, 75–76; Raunio 2001, 28–28.

[73] For Wingren, see John T. Pless, 'After Barth: Three Lutheran Appraisals of Natural Law', in R.C. Baker and R.C. Ehlke, eds., *Natural Law: A Lutheran Reappraisal*, op cit., 117–134, at 126–134.

contribution to the worldly issues. On the other hand, this conclusion is not inevitable. For example, the Finnish Evangelical-Lutheran Church has assumed that because natural law, that is the Golden Rule, is common and recognisable to all people, so the church may and should elaborate its content in the contemporary world – and say something about what seeing things from another's point of view could mean today, especially for disadvantaged, suffering and oppressed people, but not only them.[74]

Despite these theological discussions about natural law, the modern laws and other regulatory instruments of Lutheran churches do not refer directly to natural law. German Lutheranism grounds church law on the distinction between the two regiments, according to which the law belongs to the world. The church is understood on the one hand as a spiritual community and on the other hand as an organisation. So a Lutheran Church has both spiritual and temporal aspects and belongs to both regiments.[75] For example, the Basic Regulations (*Grundbestimmungen*) of the United Evangelical-Lutheran Church of Germany (VELKD) provide that the foundation of the church is the Gospel of Christ as witnessed in the Holy Scripture of the Old and New Testaments and the Confessions of the Evangelical-Lutheran Church, especially the Augsburg Confession and Luther's Small Catechism; the Confessions do not mention natural law in any detail, as we have seen.

Much the same pertains in the Swedish Church Order which also opens with a reference to the Bible, Ecumenical Confessions and Lutheran Confessions (as did the Church Law of 1687). In Finland too, this is the position: the Church Law regulates relations between church and state, and the Church Council decides on matters of Church Order: the object of the Evangelical-Lutheran Church is to preach the Gospel, administer the sacraments and engage in the practice of the love of neighbour. Natural law makes no appearance, but the concept of divine law does – all church doctrine must be evaluated by reference to the Word of God.[76] Outside Europe, the regulatory instruments of Lutheran churches also make occasional reference to concepts associated with the historical Lutheran concept of natural law, such as 'equity', 'conscience' and 'natural justice'.[77]

CONCLUSION

Today in Lutheranism, the concept of natural law appears only in the theoretical discussions of scholars, not in the concrete laws of Lutheran churches, though the

74 See *Towards the Common Good*, Statement on the Future of the Welfare Society by the Bishops of the Evangelical Lutheran Church of Finland, March 1999.

75 See Kirche und Recht, Friedrich Hauschild and Udo Hahn, *Kirche und Recht – theologische und juristische Annäherungen* (Hannover: Amt der VELKD, 2008).

76 Kirkkolainsäädäntö (Church Legislation): Kirkkolaki, § 1, § 2. Kirkkojärjestys, § 1; Kirkon vaalijärjestys; Kirkon säädöskokoelma (Helsinki: Kirkkohallitus, 2013).

77 Norman Doe, *Christian Law: Contemporary Principles* (Cambridge: Cambridge University Press, 2013), 34.

Word of God is a category which appears in these juridical instruments. The absence of natural law in these documents is not surprising: natural law was meant to be the foundation of civil law, not internal church law. But natural law thinking is invoked sometimes by church leaders when they address contemporary ethical issues. In the Lutheran tradition, at the time of the Reformation and beyond, natural law was commonly invoked by the leading thinkers, and much of its content is traceable back to the medieval inheritance. Lutheranism abandoned much of its historical understanding of natural law at the time of the Enlightenment. However, there is evidence that scholars today are taking greater interest in the concept of natural law, particularly as they deal with contemporary ethical issues. One trait of Lutheran natural law thinking has remained in Nordic Lutheranism, even though civil law is no longer justified by its connection with natural law. This trait is the reference to equity in the sense that the equity should be – at least in principle – contained in the law itself.

There is an ambiguity in Lutheran natural law thinking from the time of the Reformation. For Luther, the commandment of love, the Golden Rule and the Decalogue all say the same thing concerning love of (and faith in) God and love of neighbour. Furthermore, as expressions of natural law they concern *both* inner orientation and external action, and they demand selfless, divine love. However, for Melanchthon, natural law consists of precepts, which resemble the Ten Commandments, and they demand *only* external action, not inner orientation. As such, for Melanchthon, natural law is not a law of love as it is for Luther. This difference has led to a certain lack of clarity on the role of natural law in social ethics. For Luther a theological natural law can form the basis of social and political life; Melanchthon would deny this. These two lines lead to somewhat different views as to whether the church and Lutherans possess any means to criticise worldly authorities. In both cases, the content of natural law may offer some grounds to criticise civil authorities which violate its precepts. But, according to the approach of Melanchthon, such criticism may be rationally argued on principles of natural law. Following Luther, one needs to put oneself in the shoes of our neighbour; so, both reason and love are needed to formulate criticism.

Lutheran natural law theorists in the seventeenth and eighteenth centuries seldom refer to Luther, Melanchthon or the early Lutheran jurists. Nevertheless, traces of both views can be found in their writings. On the one hand, for example, Leibniz combines natural law with the idea of divine love, and, on the other hand, Pufendorf's approach resembles more that of Melanchthon.

An understanding of the content of natural law depends on conceptions of the so-called natural or original state of human beings. Views changed remarkably. For the Reformers, the human being in the original state was pure, sinless and loving. But natural law theorists understood the human being in the natural state as selfish and striving to survive. However, the most prominent Lutheran natural law theorists thought that a human being was not only selfish but also capable of taking others into account. So, natural egoism and self-preservation were not the only basis for natural moral law. The basic idea among the Lutherans was, despite their differences, that natural law is based both on the natural selfishness of humans and their natural inclination towards others. As far as natural law functions as a basis for social ethics, this seems to be the case even today. One version of this approach is the – as such problematic – differentiation between the secular natural law and the Christian natural law. The secular natural law allows a certain amount of selfishness if the advantage to our neighbour is also taken into account. The Christian natural law demands even more concentration on altruistic or selfless deeds. This interpretation raises the question: should a Christian follow different morals in the worldly and spiritual contexts? If Lutherans deny the idea of double ethics, they have two possible solutions. Either, to follow the Christian natural law and let the world follow its own standards or else to consider that in the end the law is one and the same for all. It is easy to see that these solutions lead also to different attitudes towards the 'world'.

6

Natural Law in the Methodist Tradition

John A. Harrod

'Slavery is contrary to the laws of God, man and nature, and hurtful to society; [and] contrary to the dictates of conscience.'[1] So the early American Methodist Church's conference declared in 1780. This is echoed by the words of Wesley himself, appealing to the principle *Lex injusta non est lex*: 'Can law, human law, change the nature of things? ... Notwithstanding ten thousand human laws, right is right and wrong is wrong still.'[2] These quotations evidence the use of the concept 'natural law' in Methodist tradition. That said 'natural law' is an elusive concept, employed in different senses and sometimes employed only vaguely. For this reason I begin by trying to clarify, and to defend, a particular approach to and understanding of natural law theory. With that understanding in mind, I then attempt to ask to what extent this approach receives expression in the Methodist tradition, also arguing that even if not given explicit expression, this approach to natural law still resonates with many themes characteristic of Methodist theology. It follows that this chapter will not simply offer cameos in the history of ideas. It seeks also to engage critically and creatively with natural law ideas themselves, all be it with an eye to the Methodist tradition.

Natural law theory maintains that the fundamental values we hold aspire to have in some sense 'objective validity'. They are attested by reason, recognised rather than invented, and they make a 'claim' upon us – in all this we struggle to find the right language. Thus, judgments of value are not 'simply expressions of emotion which can be neither true nor false'.[3] It follows, therefore, that the positive law of a particular jurisdiction is subject to critique by 'natural law'. But how can this be so? For Ayer, just quoted, and a near contemporary J.L. Mackie, the opponents of choice are so-called intuitionists. In the full-leaded version we simply 'know' or 'see' that it is morally wrong, say, to torture or to rape. The apprehension is immediate and compelling. There might even be the claim that 'moral values' inhabit some

[1] Quoted by J. Philip Wogaman, *Christian Ethics: An Historical Introduction* (London: SPCK, 1994), 181.

[2] John Wesley, *Thoughts on Slavery* (1787).

[3] Alfred Jules Ayer, *Language Truth and Logic*, 2nd edn (London: Gollancz, 1946), 103.

transcendent sphere, apprehended by some 'moral sense' or 'intuition'. Intuitionism is rather like an atheistic version of a 'divine command' approach. Instead of moral values and obligations being grounded in the command of God, they are grounded in our *sui generis* intuitions.

It is not clear how much of this description an intuitionist would own and how much is a caricature. That said, discussions of difficulties constitute well-trodden ground in moral philosophy. Critics insist the theory is unintelligible. Mackie maintains we cannot make sense of such a 'queer' notion as a universe populated by transcendent values alongside empirical reality.[4] Moreover, there is no way of checking our intuitions or of resolving disagreement. Again, why should I accept the demands of this strange realm of transcendent values? As Hume objected, how is it that 'the calm and indolent judgments of the understanding' may 'excite the passions'?[5]

Natural law does not ground moral values in 'intuitions' but rather in the way things are and, in particular, fundamental truths of the human condition. After the puzzles of appeals to inscrutable intuition, this has an immediate appeal – but then a cluster of problems quickly presents itself.

First, can we give a credible account of what is in fact 'natural'? This is a question which is especially urgent if we use the provocative concept 'human nature'. Contrary to essentialist conceptions, it is urged, human nature is not a given but is radically malleable. It is largely a cultural construct moderated by our choices. 'Existence precedes essence,' as the existentialist sound bite has it. There is also a dimension of protest. Why should I be constrained by what is supposed to express my 'nature'? I demand freedom to decide what I wish to be!

And the protest goes deeper. Not only is the 'natural' merely conventional. The conventional is largely a construct to validate and secure those in power. Is it not natural for women to be subordinate to men? But as John Stuart Mill remarked, this surely derives 'from the worse rather than the better parts of human nature'.[6] Not perhaps conventional, but certainly serving those with power and wealth is an 'evolutionary ethic' which takes what is deemed to be natural in the biological sphere as a guide to ethics. Thus, laissez-faire capitalism is justified because the fittest survive. Eugenics may likewise be justified. Evolution is about bleaching out those who are neither swift nor strong. Eugenics simply hurries along the process. It appears that the concept of human nature, after all, is a large holdall containing the good, the bad and the indifferent. Any equivalence between what is deemed natural and what is judged to be right/good is contingent, not necessary.

No credible natural law philosophy can ignore these familiar challenges or fail to offer a nuanced approach that takes them into account. Natural law theories have

[4] John L. Mackie, *Ethics: Inventing Right and Wrong* (Harmondsworth: Penguin, 1977), 38.

[5] David Hume, *Treatise of Human Nature*, III.I.I, L.A. Selby-Bigge, ed. (Oxford: Clarendon Press, 1888), 457.

[6] John Stuart Mill, *On the Subjection of Women* (1869) (Oxford: Oxford World's Classic, 1912), 430.

invariably recognised this, speaking only of our 'true' nature, or some such phrase. In this chapter, I focus upon a style of natural law thinking that seeks to find a way through. This is guided by two fundamental principles.

First, ethics is about discovering that which serves our mutual well-being. The morally 'good' is what nourishes. The bad is what damages. Given that we are social animals, ethics is about pursuing what is wholesome in our relationships with one another – thus, the criterion is our mutual and corporate well-being. It might be objected this involves an elicit jump from 'fact' to 'value'. For some, the famous protest of Hume is holy writ.[7] But is the charge a real offence? We may grant that the languages of factual description and of moral evaluation are different and that there is no logically tight movement from the one to the other. However, that does not mean that there is no legitimate movement at all. It is not clear that it makes any sense to deny the goodness of our mutual flourishing or that it is our obligation to pursue any course that does not have a rationale in terms of our common good. As for G.E. Moore's 'open question' – maybe the question, 'But is our common flourishing *really* good?' makes grammatical sense but it is not clear how such a question could have any sense beyond that.[8] Differences between descriptive and prescriptive language need not entail the dogma that our values neither need nor receive a foothold in the way things are. Moreover, we are not here making a *deduction* from fact to value. The claim is rather that our common well-being is self-evidently good and should be pursued. The failure to grasp this led to the sterility of much Anglo-Saxon moral philosophy in the middle of the last century and led to the legitimate protest of writers such as Philippa Foot and Martha Nussbaum.[9]

Secondly, however, we cannot say that *anything* may serve our mutual flourishing since our ethical values must relate to the human condition, to the kind of creatures we are. It is morally wrong to rape, steal and pillage not because of some inscrutable fiat deriving from some transcendent realm of values but because such actions damage people and cause hurt and distress. One could even call the bluff of the uncomplicated intuitionist by asking if they would indeed feel under an obligation to rape, steal and pillage if their intuitions so demanded. They are likely to reply that such an intuition would be inconceivable. But why is it inconceivable if our intuitions are inscrutable, unattached to any empirical foothold? It is inconceivable rather because of 'natural law'. Our moral commitments are rooted in our commitment to our mutual wholeness and decent and just relationships which express this, and all this guided by the kind of creatures human beings are – their needs and what serves their well-being. The voluntarist philosophy of William of Ockham appears to have entailed believing that if God were to command adultery then adultery would

7 David Hume, op cit., 469 in Selby-Bigge edn (see above n. 5).

8 George Edward Moore, *Principia Ethica* (Cambridge: Cambridge University Press, 1903), 15.

9 Philippa Foot, *Virtues and Vices* (Oxford: Blackwell, 1978): 'Goodness and choice' and 'Moral Beliefs'; and *Natural Goodness* (Oxford: Clarendon Press, 2001); Martha Nussbaum, *Love's Knowledge* (Oxford: Oxford University Press, 1990), 95–96, 389–390.

become obligatory – to which natural law theorists might reply that God would not command adultery *without changing our human nature*; in other words, without changing us into the kind of creatures for whom relationships of mutual commitment make no contribution to our well-being or creatures who have no concept of disloyalty or betrayal.[10] As Philippa Foot remarked, what is good for a human being is not the same as what is good for honey bees. In other words, the focus is not on some vague human 'nature' but, rather, on *human good*.[11]

But what are these constants? We are haunted by the way in which human freedom has been restrained and the weak and vulnerable oppressed by the powerful, on the basis of the excuse that 'nature' demands it be so. Indeed, part of our 'nature' is that we are free, that our futures are to a degree open. This, natural law must take into account. We cannot produce a blueprint for what constitutes our flourishing – and that is a mercy. Bentham's hedonism is erroneous in offering a shallow and impoverished – and even a menacingly controlling – definition. And yet there are limits beyond which we cease to be living with the 'grain of our nature'. It seems difficult to deny that strong candidates include the following: the acquisition of knowledge, bodily and mental health, an appropriate measure of self-determination, aesthetic enjoyment, relationships of love, loyalty, cooperation and justice and the opportunity for creativity and play. Such an approach to natural law leaves yet to be made specific moral judgments and is very different from the approach that too confidently draws moral conclusions from certain biological specifics, such as the inseparability in nature of the procreative and personal dimensions of a sexual relationship. In that sense natural law has 'no history'.[12] By contrast, ethics has, as it struggles with the ambiguities of the specific. Nonetheless, natural law gives ethics a sufficient mooring – but the anchor chain remains long.[13]

In summary, for natural law theory the object of morality is our mutual well-being – or where that might seem too ambitious it is about avoiding harm and the 'amelioration of the human condition'.[14] The imperatives are compelling, indeed overriding, because nothing is more important to us. That is why they 'excite the passions', in Hume's phrase. And yet the 'human' is not infinitely malleable. There are human needs and constraints imposed by the kind of creatures we are that set a limit to our ethical thinking whilst also offering resource. These provide the

[10] Daniel John O'Connor, *Aquinas and Natural Law* (London: Macmillan, 1967), 18ff.

[11] Space does not permit a discussion of whether or not environmental ethics can be adequately addressed simply in consequentialist terms focussed on human good – as Kant claimed in *Lectures on Ethics*, Louis Enfield, ed. (London: Methuen, 1930), 241. Nor does space permit discussion of our responsibility towards animals.

[12] The phrase is that of John Finnis in *Natural Law and Natural Rights*, 2nd edn (Oxford: Clarendon Press, 2011), 24.

[13] On this note the argument of Finnis, ibid., and Jean Porter, *Natural and Divine Law* (Grand Rapids, MI: William B. Eerdmans, 1999), 306–307, 309.

[14] The phrase is Geoffrey Warnock's in *The Object of Morality* (London: Methuen, 1971), 16.

'evaluative substratum of all moral judgement'.[15] Herein we find both the rationality of our ethical thinking and its universal appeal. For the purposes of this chapter we need to draw out two central features. First, on this understanding natural law thinking gives ethics an appropriate autonomy and locates it firmly in the public realm. Rooted in a commonality in the human condition, its insights may be available and compelling to all on the basis of reason. Such a universal ethic can go some way towards adjudicating parochial and individual differences. Crucially, the insights are independent of any theological foundation. However, secondly, whilst all this remains true, natural law thinking can readily be incorporated into a theological ethic, receiving what Maclagan spoke of as 'lateral enrichment',[16] although the 'enrichment' will invariably include a constructive critique.

THE EARLY METHODIST TRADITION: WESLEY

The Methodist tradition illustrates various ways in which these claims have been accepted, presupposed, contested, ignored or developed. To explore this, I glance at a number of indicative Methodist writers and cameos of Methodist tradition, asking how natural law is addressed. What follows is not a balanced or comprehensive history of thought – merely a number of representative portraits. The focus is on Britain and the United States – a restriction imposed by lack of both space and my competence. But it needs to be remembered that Methodism is now a network of churches worldwide – although in countries such as South India and Australia part of united churches. In the light of these brief portraits, I will offer some reflections on how those in the Methodist tradition might, consistently with their tradition, value and develop insight derived from natural law thinking.

Inevitably, we begin with John Wesley (1703–1791), since Methodism is distinctive in British Christianity in being founded by one person who towers over all others. A typical eighteenth-century polymath, Wesley read, wrote and corresponded widely, had broad sympathies and interests, and commented on what he read with untroubled self-confidence. Far from being a rebel who founded an opposing movement, he remained to his death a loyal Anglican and his calibre betokens the vitality of the Anglicanism in which he was nurtured. Recent scholarship has exploded the myths about Wesley, saving him from hagiography and sentimentalism, and establishing him as a significant theologian and man of affairs.

At first sight there appears little connection between Wesley and natural law thinking. Typical of his age he had no evolutionary perspective. The world was created in a state of perfection, but all went wrong with the 'fall'. As with Augustine, the fall of humanity incurred also the fall of the physical creation. Before the fall the lion did indeed lie with the lamb, and he quaintly speculates that worms were then

15 Finnis, op cit., 59. 16 W.G. Maclagan, *The Theological Frontier of Ethics* (London: GAU, 1961).

as intelligent as elephants.[17] Wesley does not mince his words when he spoke of the resulting 'total depravity'. Not much hope, it appears, for a credible natural law philosophy.

However, the picture is more complicated. A closer look reveals much in Wesley's theology which is open to natural law approaches. In this we may keep in mind three related loci. There is first the conviction that there are basic moral values, 'objectively valid' and potentially universally recognised. Second, these values are rooted in our nature as humans. Thirdly, 'natural law' serves our mutual well-being since this well-being is, in Warnock's phrase, the 'object of morality'.[18]

In Wesley's thought, despite the 'fall', God has not abandoned us. 'His mercy is over all his works.'[19] Wesley had a strong theology of 'prevenient grace'. The grace of God is not given only to a few or becomes operative only at the offer of the Christian gospel. Rather, the mercy and goodness of God are woven into the fabric of the human condition, nurturing genuine goodness whether or not people recognise its source. The widespread manifestation of conscience and an awareness of the difference between good and evil are examples of the work of prevenient grace.[20] His view of the 'state of nature' is thus not as pessimistic as is that of Hobbes.

Wesley believed that we enjoy a measure of freedom – a further manifestation of prevenient grace mitigating the 'total depravity' following the fall. Such a freedom is required by an Arminianism which, whilst insisting the grace of God is offered to all, recognises that all do not respond. Our response or refusal depends – in part – upon how we exercise our freedom. Our nature is not so utterly corrupt that there is nothing to which the love of God can appeal. Wesley resisted such a grim portrait of the human condition. We are able to respond to 'justifying grace', only because it can appeal to something in our nature and condition which is owed to 'prevenient grace'.

Thus, Wesley refuses to see the human person as nothing more than a musical instrument upon which an omnipotent God through irresistible grace plays a tune. God's offer of grace is compelling and attractive – but we may still resist. It follows that, for Wesley, grace is 'responsible'.[21] Inspired and empowered but not controlled by the divine love, we accept the discipline of an attention to the manner of our living. He therefore opposed the 'quietism' associated with his Moravian contemporaries. God awaits our continuing and ever deepening and maturing response. God's grace is not only a grace showing pardon – as in some strands of Protestantism. It is also a grace which gives power to heal our fallen nature by our participation in God.[22]

Famously, controversially and even notoriously, he speaks not only of a growth in holiness but also of the possibility of sanctification or perfection. But this is only the logical implication of his belief that God's grace is renewing and not simply

[17] Sermon 60, 'On General Deliverance', paragraph III.3. [18] Geoffrey Warnock, op cit.

[19] Sermon 60, 'On General Deliverance', paragraph I.

[20] E.g. Sermon 105, 'On Conscience'; see also Sermon 12, 'The Witness of Our Own Spirit', paragraph 3.

[21] Randy Maddox, *Responsible Grace* (Nashville, TN: Abingdon Press, 1994).

[22] Sermon 12, 'The Witness of our own Spirit', paragraph 15.

justifying. He was extremely reluctant to identify perfection and he never claimed it for himself. And in any case it was emphatically a perfection only *in love*, consistent with imperfection in moral insight, intellectual judgment, etc. His preferred term was in fact 'perfect love'. Wesley put great emphasis on his belief that God is love. God's love inspires our own and so love is central to human relationships. Presumably by 'love' Wesley understood a rich complex of commitment and sentiment. There is both a warm delighting in the person loved, but also a staunch commitment, involving sacrificial giving, to the well-being of the other. And his emphasis on 'grace' means that love, rather than 'sovereignty', is at the heart of his understanding of God.

In none of this is Wesley developing a philosophy of natural law. He is rather working within a traditional Protestant scheme of salvation. Yet this characteristic Wesleyan theology contains many strands that resonate with natural law thinking or at least offer an opening for natural law thinking as characterised earlier in this chapter. The divine image in humanity has not been completely obliterated. God's prevenient grace is at work within fallen creation. This is evident in the ubiquity of conscience. And Wesley's Arminianism – deeply rooted in his Anglican heritage, as represented for instance in the Caroline divines – offers a universal embrace which also resonates with natural law thinking.

Stepping back a little from the 'scheme of salvation', there are three other areas where Wesley offers an opening to a natural law perspective. First, rooted in his Anglicanism, Wesley spoke of two books: the 'book of God's works' and the Scriptures, the 'book of God's words'. His interest in the natural world is seen in his *Compendium of Natural Philosophy* (1776ff.), a guide to current understanding for Methodists – Wesley had a firm commitment to furthering education and learning amongst his followers. Indeed, the *Arminian Magazine* carried regular reports on the proceedings of the *Royal Society*. Although critical of an evidential preoccupation, such as that represented by John Ray, he nonetheless said in the preface to the *Compendium* that our study of nature does not merely satisfy 'idle barren curiosity' but gives insight into 'the invisible things of God, his power wisdom and goodness'. Despite the priority he professed to give to Scripture, it appears he does not allow Protestant zeal for revelation in Scripture to eclipse entirely the 'book of nature'.[23]

All of this connects with Wesley's deep awareness of our physicality. Whilst rejecting ostentatious and excessive consumption because it robs the poor, he insisted it is our Christian duty to care for our bodies. He set up charities for poor relief and was keenly committed to developments in medicine.[24] Christian care is for

[23] Thus Randy Maddox, 'Wesley's Engagement with the Natural Sciences', in Randy Maddox and Jason Vickers, eds., *Cambridge Companion to John Wesley* (Cambridge: Cambridge University Press, 2010), 160ff.

[24] Despite John H. Plumb's rather dismissive remark, Wesley's *Primitive Physick* was in tune with the medical understanding of the day: John H. Plumb, *England in the Eighteenth Century* (Harmondsworth: Pelican, 1950), 95–96.

the whole person, not just their 'souls'. All this is consistent with his dissatisfaction with the idea that once we enjoy a 'spiritual' heaven, the physical creation is discarded. In a later sermon he speculates about God's redemption for the whole cosmos, in which indeed animals will continue to have their place.[25]

Secondly, Wesley claimed to be a man of reason. It is true that he routinely insisted that theology is not based on reason or experience. He was a *homo unius libri*, deriving all entirely from Scripture. Reason and experience have a subordinate role only in 'confirming' Scripture.[26] It is not clear whether his practice was consistent with this claim; indeed, it is difficult to see how it could be, given that it is we as readers who select from, interpret and appropriate Scripture. Moreover, Scripture itself explores the resources of reason and invites readers to exercise their own reasoning powers. To say the least, Wesley's insistence that our consciences are a gift of the prevenient grace of God, together with his emphasis on reason, provide an opening for natural law thinking. Theology cannot be based wholly upon a gratuitous fideism. In addition, Wesley's rejection of a doctrine of predestination is not based simply on marshalling biblical texts. It is based also on his reasoning that such a doctrine is unworthy of God.

Later Methodist tradition has sometimes embraced an 'Epworth Quadrilateral' which identifies 'scripture, tradition, reason and experience' as four sources of theological understanding. This conception is flawed insofar as it appears to separate four things which are inextricably related. But it has the strength of containing an implicit critique of a straightforward *sola scriptura* approach. A natural law ethic will not appeal to authoritative texts or some specific religious 'revelation' but will appeal to 'reason and experience' – be it with the Kantian proviso that the two cannot really be separated. Such an approach will find a place in a strong strand of Methodist tradition.[27]

Finally, I have argued that for natural law thinking the 'good' and the 'right' correspond with the 'well'. The good life is not about submitting ourselves to life-diminishing prohibitions. It is about living in accord with our nature and thereby finding wholeness – or at least what wholeness is available. For Wesley, God's will is not received as an alien fiat. God is love and God's love inspires our own since we are made for love, and that nourishes our well-being. We are following the grain of our nature, being like 'trees planted beside still waters'.[28] There is the invitation to discover our 'true' nature as made for love and to find in love our salvation: 'He made you; and he made you to be happy in him ... gratitude to our creator and supreme benefactor, and benevolence to our fellow creatures.'[29]

[25] Sermon 60, 'On General Deliverance', paragraph III.3.

[26] E.g. Sermon 107, 'On God's Vineyard', paragraph IV.1.

[27] E.g. the British Methodist Conference report on *Human Sexuality* (1980) appeals to the 'Epworth Quadrilateral'.

[28] Psalm 1.3; Jeremiah 17.8. [29] Sermon 114, 'The Unity of the Divine Being', paragraphs 9 and 16.

All that said, we look in vain for any explicit discussion of 'natural law' or use of the concept. His 'Christian Library', whilst drawing from many strands of Christian tradition, overlooks Aquinas and even Hooker, although his definition of conscience at one point is strikingly similar to Joseph Butler's in his sermons in the Rolls Chapel.[30] Probably one reason for this neglect is that Wesley is uncomfortable with a stark contrast between the realms of 'nature' and of 'grace'. For Wesley, all is of grace. So, paradoxically, perhaps his doctrine of prevenient grace whilst, on the one hand being open to the insights of natural law, also tends to prevent him from using the concept. Nevertheless, his strong objection to John Hutchinson (1674–1737), and his 'moral sense' philosophy,[31] might be taken as implying a sympathy for natural law thinking on account of it better integrating with a theological perspective. Furthermore, Wesley's critique of J.J. Burlamaqui's *Principes du Droit Naturel* (1748) is probably less of the idea of natural law itself as of the work's failure to give it a theological interpretation.[32] And Wesley did speak of a 'natural' right to liberty, all be it a right that is a gift from God.[33]

Moreover, we do not find Wesley explicitly drawing upon the resources of natural law when actually making moral judgments. Indeed, we do not find him agonising much over moral dilemmas at all, and maybe it is anachronistic to expect that of him. His approach to ethical issues and life style is that of fairly conventional eighteenth-century cleric. Accepting an essentially Malthusian perspective, he tended to think in terms of perpetual scarcity; consequently it is a Christian duty to live frugally so that any surplus may be given to the poor; and he certainly practised what he preached. In his early years he focussed on individual charity as a solution for the world's ills. Even his vehement opposition to slavery initially confined itself to exhorting individual slave owners to free their slaves. But later he did come to think in terms of statutory abolition and his tract *Thoughts on Slavery* (1787) shows an impressive grasp of the socio-economic dimensions involved – betraying in his thinking a growing awareness that 'sin' has an institutional and not simply an individual manifestation. Similarly, his *Thoughts on the Present Scarcity in Provisions* (1773), shows an awareness of economic matters alongside individual action.

At the same time there are implicit in Wesley resources for offering constructively critical perspectives on natural law philosophy. First, given that the physical creation, after the fall, is no longer in a state of perfection, a natural law approach cannot point to a straightforward correspondence between facts about nature and the right and the good. If nature is to inform our ethical thinking our approach must be critical and nuanced. There is much about the empirical reality of 'human nature' which we must resist. This insight abides even though it is no longer plausible to

30 Sermon 12, 'The Witness of our own Spirit', paragraph 3. For Hooker and Butler, see above Chapter 4.
31 E.g. Sermon 90, 'An Israelite Indeed'; and Sermon 105, 'On Conscience'.
32 Sermon 114, 'The Unity of the Divine Being', paragraph 18.
33 John Wesley, *Thoughts upon Liberty* (1772).

posit a prelapsarian perfection. Furthermore, his realism about sin keeps us alive to the possible abuse of natural law – in particular encouraging what today we might call a 'hermeneutic of suspicion'. Natural law can easily be employed by those in power to validate their power and its use. But as always in Wesley 'realism about sin' is combined with 'optimism about grace'.

Indeed, his emphasis on freedom and growth in grace might connect with those who protest against (or develop?) natural law theory, by insisting that we are not constrained by limitations imposed by over-tight definitions of what the 'human condition' might entail. Wesley's emphasis on freedom and growth sees the human condition as enjoying a wide open future, offering a whole range of possibilities, which for him, on account of God's grace and gift, are wonderfully compelling.[34]

Secondly, natural law may help us discern what is right and good. But where is the motivation to pursue it? How do we cope with the weakness of our wills? And how do we justify and find motivation for a magnanimity and commitment to fairness beyond our immediate circle? For this Wesley would appeal to his understanding of grace – especially a vision of the love of God, which embraces all, inspiring and enabling our own. 1 John 4.19 is an often-quoted text.

In sum, we find in Wesley little that is explicit concerning natural law. Nevertheless, it needs to be remembered that he produced no systematic treatise – our source for Wesley's theology is found largely in his sermons, inevitably addressed to specific situations. Moreover, it is not clear that he had a single mature position, that his thinking contained no ambivalence or that he addressed our questions. It is not surprising, therefore, that different scholars offer different perspectives. Some, such as Theodore Runyon, point to Wesley's emphasis on experience as indicative of openness to Lockean empiricism.[35] This might suggest on his part openness to what was later to be dubbed the 'autonomy of ethics' and therefore to the development of an ethic based on reason and aspiring to have universal appeal. By way of contrast, Stephen Long locates Wesley more within 'the mediaeval and Anglican sacramental world' of a moral theology where things are based firmly in God, Scripture, creed, sacrament, Christ and church.[36] But, even if this is so, there remain – as I have argued – themes in Wesley wide open to natural law thinking.

LATER METHODISM AND NATURAL LAW THINKING

Despite the range of his interests and sympathies, Wesley remains focussed upon a Protestant 'scheme of salvation', and this continues in Methodism after his death. We obtain a feel for the character of early Methodism from the hymns. This source is

34 See Angela Shier-Jones, *A Work in Progress: Methodists Doing Theology* (Peterborough: Epworth, 2005), 164ff.

35 Thomas Runyon, *The New Creation: John Wesley's Theology Today* (Nashville, TN: Abingdon Press, 1958), 150ff.

36 D. Stephen Long, *John Wesley's Moral Theology* (Nashville, TN: Abingdon Press, 2005), 10.

far more significant than what Methodist thinkers might occasionally write. Just as Anglicans might be 'formed by how they pray',[37] so Methodists were formed by what they sang. It is striking how Wesley's collection of hymns focussed upon this scheme. The opening section is about 'Exhorting sinners to return to God'. There follows a section on 'Praying for repentance' and then, rather quaintly, 'For persons convinced of backsliding' and next, another 'For backsliders recovered'. For Arminians, the fear of backsliding is real. Calvinism offered the assurance of the eternal preservation of the saints. But the Arminian knows that on account of 'backsliding' they may cease to be in a state of grace.

The collection nonetheless includes some hymns, by Isaac Watts (1674–1748), focussed on creation. And a hymn by John's brother Charles Wesley (1707–1788) on a less familiar theme might keep company with a natural law perspective:

Far off we need not rove
To find the God of love;
In his providential care
Ever intimately near,
All his various works declare
God, the bounteous God is here!

We live, and move, and are,
Through his preserving care;
He doth still in life maintain
Every soul that moves and lives;
Gives us back our breath again,
Being every moment gives.[38]

In the remainder of this chapter I look at a number of indicative writers – and some official Methodist documents – which might be supportive of, critical of, or complementary to, natural law thinking. Brief cameos are grouped together to illustrate four distinct stances or styles.

Stance One: The Continuing Wesleyan Tradition

Our first example is William Burt Pope (1822–1903), tutor at the Wesleyan Didsbury College in Manchester, and probably the most significant British Methodist theologian of the nineteenth century. Like Wesley, he does not focus on natural law, but we find similar resonances and similar openings. He claimed to write Christian Theology, not a sectarian Methodist theology, since the theology of Methodists is 'scriptural, catholic and orthodox'. His work displays thoroughness and wide learning, engaging with others often with generous sympathy and openness, if at other times somewhat peremptorily. That said, he works mostly within a received

[37] Preface to *Alternative Service Book* (1980), 10.
[38] There is also Charles Wesley's hymn on conscience: 'I want a principle within.'

tradition, lacked somewhat sympathy with developing biblical scholarship and, in contrast with his contemporaries William Arthur and William Dallinger,[39] engaging little with contemporary thought.

Pope emphasises the anthropological character of theology: 'Theology is concerned with the things of God as they relate to man [*sic*] ... God has come down in the likeness of men, and speaks to them in their own language.' He continues: 'With what profound human interest does this invest the whole! Our life, our hope, our destiny, our all, is bound up with it.' Echoes of natural law thinking are found in his affirmation concerning 'the law written on the heart, or reason, of universal man'. Like Wesley, he speaks of a 'preliminary grace' which 'explains the secret desire of man to be restored; and thus lights up the whole sphere of universal ethics'.[40]

Human beings are essentially creatures of this material world – and that defines certain parameters. In particular, Pope emphasises dependence, limitation and vulnerability. But in addition to being 'from the earth his nature is that he is a living soul'. Humanity is made in the image of God. The 'natural image' is found in our freedom, but 'a few particulars are not enough ... It includes the whole sum of man's prerogative as a creature, and it brings all that belongs to God into some relation with man.' It follows, Pope insists, that a Christian anthropology must affirm 'the unity of the race, or human species'.[41]

There is much here that connects implicitly with the three loci of natural law thinking identified earlier. However, Pope – insofar as he has a natural law philosophy in mind – takes his argument further. How, we might ask, are we to envisage the 'human nature' to which natural law might appeal? Implicitly Pope denies a 'given' human nature, easily identified, and certainly not necessarily wholesome. He introduces a Christological focus. Christ is the true Adam, the one in whom the image of God in humanity is restored: 'He has confirmed and supplemented natural theology ... He has consummated the preliminary disclosures of his own earlier dispensation.' Implicitly, there is the warning that a natural law philosophy might encourage complacency about a natural *status quo*, deriving from a nature corrupted by sin. Grace opens opportunities of ever greater richness. We should never allow 'the Fall to be forgotten, amidst the triumphs of grace'.[42] All this is consonant with a Wesleyan 'realism about sin' combined with 'optimism about grace'.

Furthermore, Pope offers a theology of grace that takes us beyond a natural law, in particular adding motivation where the will is weak or where sympathies are lacking. He speaks of the liberation of forgiveness: 'Vain is all the teaching of morality without preliminary forgiveness ... The sense of pardon gives birth to a new order

39 William Arthur, *Religion without God* and *God without Religion* (London, 1885–1888); William Dallinger offers an early theological appropriation of Darwin's theory of natural selection in *The Creator and What We May Know of the Methods of Creation* (London, 1887).

40 William Burt Pope, *Compendium of Christian Theology* (London: Wesleyan Conference Office, 1875), 4–5, 7, 186.

41 Ibid., 173, 177, 181. 42 Ibid., 6, 576.

of ethics, emotions and obligations and duties.' He also speaks of the 'future life, with its powers and terrors and hopes . . . as the ground of ethics'. Strikingly and perhaps influenced by F.D. Maurice, he does not threaten the punishment of hell understood as retributive torment. Rather, 'the only sanction of law is the displeasure of God . . . the penalty of separation from God is the great Christian ethical argument'. Thus, 'what natural theology is to . . . supernatural revelation, moral philosophy is to Christian ethics. They agree on the fundamentals . . . but the Christian system of morals supplies what is essentially lacking'.[43]

Few read Pope today. But the chords he strikes, writing very much in the Wesleyan tradition, are heard repeatedly in later Methodist thought, all be it transposed into different cultural and intellectual keys. An Arminianism combined with a strong belief in prevenient grace resonates with many themes in natural law thinking, even if rarely made explicit. At the same time, 'realism about sin' and the Christological focus caution against too easy a correspondence between the 'natural' and the right and the good. We find this also in John Scott Lidgett, who had been a pupil of Pope.[44]

In a similar vein, early North American writers such as Nathan Bangs (1778–1862) focus upon prevenient grace. This mitigates the disaster of the 'fall' allowing a continuing affirmation of the essential goodness and coherence of creation and our place within it. Along with giving an awareness of right and wrong, this grace gives an ability to know, and freedom to respond to, God.[45] In all this reason has a proper place. Later Methodist theologians in the USA, such as John Miley, spoke of 'ethical Arminianism', a theme continued by Randy Maddox in his *Responsible Grace*.[46] Typically Methodist, a theology of God's free grace and human free will allows a gracious God to evoke our willing and thankful response. This is offered in explicit contrast to a Calvinism which allegedly spoke of God controlling by irresistible power. Charles Wesley had penned the line, 'By thy pardoning love compelled.' But it was the compulsion *of love*. Miley was part of the early development of 'Boston Personalism' exemplified also in Borden Parker Bowne, Edgar Sheffield Brightman and Albert Knudson. This philosophy easily resonated with a Methodist emphasis on grace. The God 'in whom we live and move and have our being' is the supreme personhood. The 'personal', therefore, becomes a fundamental category for Christian understanding. There is a complementary focus on divine immanence and a Christology which emphasises Jesus as the true Adam, the model of true humanity. All this allowed a sense of the connectedness and coherence of reality within which natural law can easily find a place. Such a philosophy encourages confidence in a certain correspondence between the 'natural' and the 'good', all be it a correspondence carefully defined and nuanced. The feel of this perspective is very

43 Ibid., 576, 579.
44 John Scott Lidgett, *The Christian Religion* (London: Robert Cully, 1907), 370, 437ff., 483.
45 Nathan Bangs, *Predestination Examined* (New York: J.C. Totten, 1817).
46 Randy Maddox, op cit.

different from the radical discontinuities found – for instance – in the later thought of Barth and Niebuhr.

It is not surprising that the later 'process philosophy' was attractive to Methodist thinkers such as Schubert Ogden, John Cobb and David Pailin. Indeed, Brightman had been a mentor of Charles Hartshorne. God is related to the 'processes of reality', in Pailin's phrase, by way of persuasion and cooperation rather than overruling control. God relates to us through the 'lure of love' and Christology is understood in such anthropological terms.[47] That said, although consistent with a natural law philosophy, generally these writers tend not to focus on ethics.[48]

Stance Two: An Autonomous Ethic

Some Christian thinkers maintain a complete separation between ethics and theology. An example is the British philosopher – not a Methodist – H.D. Lewis. Although a theist, he defended the full autonomy of ethics: our values derive from intuition alone and require no rationale or wider context from theology or any other area of thought. There is no such thing as 'Christian Ethics' any more than 'Christian Mathematics'. This was in part a reaction against the perceived theological imperialism of Brunner and Barth.[49]

Writing earlier, American Methodist Borden Parker Bowne (1847–1910) is an example – though more qualified – of this style of thinking, despite being a key figure in Boston Personalism. In contrast to the later Lewis, and his ethical intuitionism, Bowne is more in the natural law tradition. Ethics is about applying universally valid ethical principles to the ambiguities of real life situations, recognising that this can often be done only imperfectly. Yet, our freedom allows us to do the best we can. Crucial for Bowne, however, is that the universally valid ethical principles are such because they are not based on any 'subjective' choice or perspective. They have objective grounding because they express what is good for human beings. Morality is thus rooted in 'the nature of things' – by which he means the nature of the human condition and what constitutes our good.[50] Ethics, being universal, is prior to theology. There are echoes here of a Wesleyan emphasis upon human freedom, allowing us to act in the world, and in a confidence that progress is possible. But any sustained analysis of a possible integration with a theological perspective is lacking.[51] For this, the North American Methodist tradition has to wait for writers such as Paul Ramsey and Philip Wogaman.

47 For example, David A. Pailin, *God and the Processes of Reality* (London: Routledge, 1989), 193.

48 An example of an exception is Methodist John B. Cobb who considers issues in moral theology in *A Christian Natural Theology* (London: Lutterworth, 1965), 108ff.

49 For example, H.D. Lewis, *Our Experience of God* (London: GAU, 1959), 265ff. See also his earlier *Morals and the New Theology* (London: Gollancz, 1947). For Brunner and Barth, see Chapter 7.

50 Borden P. Bowne, *The Principles of Ethics* (New York: Harper, 1892), 143.

51 Edgar Sheffield Brightman, *The Moral Laws* (New York: Abingdon, 1943), 265–266.

Stance Three: 'Natural Law' or 'Divine Command'

We move now to a starkly contrasting approach to Christian ethics which bypasses natural law and in its unqualified form rejects it. Our moral judgments are based on scriptural injunctions, the 'plain sense' meaning of specific texts which are, being the inspired word of God and therefore the final authority, binding upon us today. This approach might presuppose a grim estimate of our human capacity, without the aid of divine revelation, to discern the right and the good.

That such approach may be in direct opposition to any natural law thinking is clear from two examples, although neither is Methodist. The first example is John Hopkins, Episcopalian bishop of Vermont, who in 1861 declared that were he to be guided by 'personal sympathies, tastes or feelings', he would support the abolition of slavery: his 'education, habit and social position stand entirely opposed to it'. But he continues: 'As a Christian I am compelled to submit my weak and erring intellect to the authority of the almighty.' Scripture never challenges the institution of slavery and so neither might he.[52] The second example is Anglican. The 1966 Church of England report *Putting Asunder* proposed a change in English civil law, later accepted by parliament, making irretrievable breakdown of marriage the principal ground for divorce and the civil dissolution of a marriage. Consistent with an Anglican tradition rooted in Hooker, the report appeals to natural law, reason and a commitment to the common good. Some, however, were uncomfortable. Whilst not seeking to impose a specifically Christian position on the rest of society, for Christians divorce is permitted only on the grounds of the 'Matthean exception' and the 'Pauline privilege'. These are the two grounds sanctioned in the New Testament and irretrievable breakdown is not one of them.[53] Both examples reflect a voluntaristic ethic based purely upon the divine will.

The British Methodist Conference supported the recommendations of *Putting Asunder*.[54] Any opposition on scriptural grounds is rarely heard if ever. That said, in British Methodism there have always been those who will appeal to scriptural injunctions as a basis for ethics, so circumventing and overruling an approach based on reason and natural law. In modern British Methodism, it is rare to hear opposition, based on the household texts of the New Testament epistles, to the mutual partnership and equal social power of women and men. Homosexuality, however, is a different matter. Those who are gay are mandated to lifelong celibacy, and this view will be held on the basis of the 'plain sense' of specific texts. It is rare for a Methodist to appeal to a natural law argument that the procreative and unitary dimensions of sexuality are rooted in nature, such that what nature has joined we may not put asunder. Such a position also rules out the use of contraception.

52 John Hopkins, *A Scriptural, Ecclesiastical and Historical View of Slavery* (New York: Pooley and Co., 1861), 2.

53 Thus, John Stott, *New Issues Facing Christians Today* (London: Marshall Pickering, 1990), 50ff., 305.

54 British Methodist Conference, 1967.

Critics of this approach will question a reliance upon the 'plain sense' of a text, urging that it ignores the historical and cultural context and that it begs massive questions concerning how Scripture can inform our moral judgments, why some texts are highlighted but not others and generally how we understand the 'authority' of Scripture. These questions, however, will be heard as loudly within Methodism as outside. This *sola scriptura* approach is no more common in the broad church of British Methodism than in the broad church of, say, the Church of England.

At first sight a 'divine command' ethic might appear to be in direct conflict with natural law thinking. And this is indeed the case with an unqualified version of the former. But if we start smoothing away the sharp edges we can easily find resources for reconciliation. For a start, there is nothing incoherent in claiming that what is grasped by our reason to be right and good may also be judged to express the divine will and thereby indeed receiving greater urgency and stronger motivation. The fact that a Christian speaks of the divine will need not entail that this will fails to commend itself to us as right and fitting. Indeed, might not God reveal the divine will *through* our reason and experience and through what is manifest in the human condition as part of the divine creation? Much of Scripture appears to follow this approach. Moreover, few Christians would resist the claim that God's will is for our good, and that is close cousin to the claim that it is for our good because it is in accordance with the grain of our nature. Methodist writer Esther Reed speaks of the authority of God as being 'dialogic' and 'relational'.[55] Again, there is no reason why a natural law approach should deny – indeed it may embrace – a theological understanding which may clarify and inform and indeed demand a radical rethinking of our perception of what is right and fitting. This is not so much a teleological *suspension* of ethics, as a clarification and deepening. Scripture might expose how our high sounding moral posturing might simply cloak our self-seeking ideologies. For all these reasons, language about the divine will or divine command in no way necessarily implies 'blind obedience'. We may still 'taste and see that the Lord is good' and so 'love what is commanded and desire what is promised'.

Critics of what they claim is 'Christian ethics', such as Anthony C. Grayling, need not therefore have the last word. Grayling accuses 'people of the book' of basing ethics on the inscrutable commands of the deity. These require the response of unthinking and servile obedience. Even worse we obey because we fear punishment. We do not understand *why* something is good or required of us. We simply listen and obey. The attitude of Abraham is typical of the ethics of 'people of the book'.[56] The command of God might violate even our most compelling of obligations, the obligation of a father to care for his son.[57] To be fair to Grayling, there is a sufficiency of Christian intent on firing proof texts like missiles to warrant his criticism.

55 Esther D. Reed, *The Genesis of Ethics* (London: Darton, Longman and Todd, 2000), 58ff.

56 Genesis 22.1–14.

57 Anthony C. Grayling, *What Is Good?* (London: Weidenfeld and Nicolson, 2003), 56ff.

Grayling regards Plato's *Euthyphro* dilemma (whether the pious is loved by the gods because it is pious or whether it is pious because it is loved by the gods) as a killer – as does Simon Blackburn.[58] But this dilemma is misconceived. It makes sense only if we toy with two abstract concepts. On the one hand is the command of an all-powerful deity and on the other hand is the right and the good. But Christians are rarely satisfied with thinking of God simply as omnipotent will. As Richard Price has observed: 'What can be more preposterous than to make the Deity nothing but will . . . on the ruin of all other attributes?'[59] A natural law approach will speak of the purposes of God as being for our good and woven into the fabric of the human condition, ultimately dependent upon God as creator. This radically reconfigures the matter so that the Euthyphro dilemma loses pertinence. The dilemma is real for a simplistic voluntaristic ethic, but misses the point for natural law.

The thinking of Stanley Hauerwas represents a distinctive version of a 'divine command' approach. Although now an Episcopalian, he is a cradle Methodist and ordained in the American United Methodist Church, whilst acknowledging many ecumenical debts, especially to Mennonite John Yoder. Hauerwas challenges as a liberal myth the idea of the autonomous individual. By the same token, he is suspicious of natural law thinking which cherishes the hope of finding a universally persuasive ethic based on reason and our experience of being human. Following MacIntyre, a one-time colleague, he sees our moralities as embedded within the various traditions and communities in which we are formed. A Christian ethic will not seek to connect with a universally applicable ethic: 'The first task of the church is to be the church.' And the church is a community of moral formation in which Christians are nurtured in characteristically Christian virtues.

Pivotal to this – although not only this – is the charge to live peaceably. Few Christians would resist this as a *prima facie* obligation. Hauerwas goes further. The charge to live peaceably is absolute in all circumstances. This is not based on a sentimental belief that our peaceable witness will melt every heart. He recognises that the vulnerable may become unprotected and tyranny remain unchecked – at least in the short and medium term. We can but trust that in the long term God will surprise us with the powerful effect of the church's prophetic countercultural stance. All this is in tension with a natural law ethic which invariably takes seriously the nature of the human condition as requiring structures to hold evil in check – hence the tradition of the just war found in Augustine and Aquinas. For Hauerwas it is not the church's role to make common course with others of 'good will'. Its ethic is based ultimately upon obedience to the ethic of peace discerned in Christ.

He certainly believes in the church's countercultural witness to the wider society, although it is not clear what society is supposed to do with it. Neither is it clear how

58 Anthony C. Grayling, *The God Argument* (London: Bloomsbury, 2013), 105, 157–158; Simon Blackburn, *Being Good: An Introduction to Ethics* (Oxford: Oxford University Press, 2001), 15–16.

59 Richard Price, 'A Review of the Principal Questions in Morals', in L.A. Selby-Bigge, ed., *British Moralists*, Vol. II (Oxford: Clarendon Press, 1897), 151.

Christians are to conduct themselves when in the wider community and not within the church's fellowship. This muting of a natural law tradition is perhaps why Hauerwas gives little attention to the need for the church to expose itself to the scrutiny of, and to be chastened by, the prophetic witness of 'the world'. And perhaps we see in his optimistic vision of the church as a 'community of character' an overemphasis upon Wesleyan perfectionism and an underemphasis upon Wesley's realism about sin.[60]

We thus illustrate a style of Christian ethics which emphasises what is distinctive about a Christian approach, in contrast to a natural law ethic which aspires to that which may be apprehended by all human beings. We have followed other writers who offer Christian insights which might enrich and develop a natural law approach. But sometimes the tension becomes so great that the connection snaps. Wesley believed that reason and experience will confirm what we read in Scripture. But suppose it does not? Suppose there is a genuine teleological suspicion of ethics? Gay partnerships that are loving, faithful and equal are a case in point. Do we accept the testimony and experience (both concepts deeply rooted in Methodist tradition) of those who are gay that their partnerships are a blessing from God and a means of grace? Or do we accept the 'plain sense' meaning of highlighted scriptural texts? Which trumps the other? Some contemporary British Methodists would say the former and some the latter. Neither stance has official endorsement from the Conference. And probably neither is significantly more represented in Methodism than in the Church of England.

On a wider front, the default position of post-war British Methodism sides more with Niebuhr than with Hauerwas, and in this it manifests its Anglican roots. In other words, it seeks to make common cause with wider society with a view to furthering the common good, recognising the ideal is rarely achievable, and that invites grounding in some style of natural law ethics. This has been true of contributions made, from time to time, by the Methodist Conference on social issues, as it has been the case with its significant charitable sector. Kenneth Greet and Lord Soper of Kingsway were distinguished pacifists, but pacifism has always been a minority stance. Representative of this perspective is a Methodist report on *The Ethics of Wealth Creation*.[61] It accepted that a free enterprise market economy is the most efficient way we know for creating wealth. The discipline of the market, the price mechanism and the profit motive, provide incentives and encourage innovation. The market honours the freedom of both entrepreneur and consumer. There are of course significant downsides. The market is bad at distributive justice, can be harsh on the environment and can manipulate demand in an inappropriate way. The human cost of 'creative destruction' is considerable. But we may enjoy the

60 Of the voluminous writings of Stanley Hauerwas, I have selected *A Community of Character* (Notre Dame, IN: University of Notre Dame Press, 1981); *A Peaceable Kingdom* (Notre Dame Press, 1983) and, with William Williman, *Resident Aliens* (Nashville, TN: Abingdon Press, 1993).

61 British Methodist Conference, *The Ethics of Wealth Creation* (1990).

market's amazing blessings whilst seeking to moderate the downside through state partnership and regulation and the culture of civil society. There was some opposition – presumably seeking a radical shift to some kind of command economy or guild socialism – but from a minority, and the Conference adopted the report.

Stance Four: Human Nature or the Nature of God?

Natural law theories focus on the nature of the human condition. However, a strong strand of Methodist thinking puts the focus on our understanding of the nature of God. A good example is the American Methodist Philip Wogaman. Certain convictions about the nature of God establish certain moral presumptions; they predispose the mind to embrace, as a fitting response to our belief in God, certain value commitments. One such presumption is the goodness of created existence, encouraging positive attitudes towards our physicality, creativity, sexuality and environmental responsibility. A second is the dignity of each individual life. Such a conviction is not self-validating: 'It is because we have our being from God and sustained by God.'[62] Connected with this is 'the unity of the Human Family in God ... To be truly human is to be a "fellowman" [*sic*], not a rugged selfish individualist'.[63] This excludes any kind of racism 'and other kinds of social barriers' and so requires of Christians a commitment to a fundamental equality.[64] He speaks also of a 'negative presumption' in the recognition of human finitude and sinfulness. This should warn us against an unrealistic perfectionism and the absolution of any particular. We are guarded against both naivety and self-righteousness – for instance 'the absolutized goodness of the revolutionary class, the evil of the exploiting classes, and the goodness of a planned for future'.[65] In all this, he acknowledges his indebtedness to both Reinhold and Richard Niebuhr.

Wogaman says little about natural law, and the references in Methodist Richard Jones are generally critical rather than constructive.[66] By way of contrast, writing decades later against a very different intellectual milieu, the present author appeals to both our understanding of God and also a natural law ethic: 'Ethics is about discovering our mutual well-being, and discovering appropriate relationships, given the kind of creatures human beings are.'[67] He insists that ethics is fundamentally a common human concern and that any 'Christian' ethic must incorporate this recognition. It is because ethics is a human concern that ethics belongs to the public realm and can be the subject of intelligible debate across ideological differences. It can be such a human concern because ethics is about our corporate well-being. Given a basic commonality of human needs and aspirations there can be a public

[62] J. Philip Wogaman, *A Christian Method of Moral Judgment* (London: SCM, 1976), 80.
[63] Ibid., 87. [64] Ibid., 93. [65] Ibid., 9, 111–112.
[66] Richard G. Jones, *Groundwork of Christian Ethics* (London: Epworth, 1984), 173–174.
[67] John A. Harrod, *Weaving the Tapestry of Moral Judgement: Christian Ethics in a Plural World* (London: Epworth, 2007), 4.

7

Natural Law in the Reformed Tradition

Mary Anne Plaatjies van Huffel

More than 80 million Christians in 108 countries around the world belong to churches of the Reformed tradition. The World Communion of Reformed Churches (WCRC) consists of some 230 Reformed, Presbyterian, Congregational and United churches. However, these do not have a single understanding of natural law or of its implications for church polity. As such, one should be cautious in speaking of a Reformed tradition on a contentious issue like natural law. Therefore, this chapter examines those positions which embrace natural law wholeheartedly as well as those which do not. Indeed, when I told my colleagues about my involvement in a project about the Reformed understanding of natural law, and its place in church polity, this was met with a considerable degree of scepticism. This chapter provides an overview of the key historical and contemporary features of the natural law outlook as it appears in Reformed teaching, tradition and church order (and in church order scholarship).[1]

JOHN CALVIN AND NATURAL LAW

The ambiguity of the Reformed approach to natural law is encapsulated in diverse modern interpretations of John Calvin himself (1509–1564), a humanist-influenced lawyer by training,[2] whose theological position has been so influential in the development of the Reformed tradition. There are scholars today who consider that the approach of Calvin to natural law has proved to be one of the major battlegrounds of twentieth-century Reformed scholarship (see below): for some, natural law plays no part in Calvin's teaching, and these scholars, who propose the sufficiency of divine revelation, deny that Calvin considered it was possible to have a natural knowledge of what is right and wrong outside this, and, for others, Calvin built the edifice of his social, ethical and political ideas on the foundation of natural law.[3]

[1] I am grateful to Norman Doe for his assistance in making substantial changes to this chapter possible in the circumstances of the tight schedule set for the timely production of this book.

[2] Calvin was a student of law at Orléans in 1528–1529.

[3] William Klempa, 'John Calvin on Natural Law', in George Timothy, ed., *John Calvin and the Church: A Prism of Reform* (Westminster: John Knox, 1990), 72–76.

Calvin wrote a great deal about natural law and his concept of it may be treated as an aspect of his account of the natural knowledge of God possessed by humans. Moreover, the concept of equity plays a pivotal role in his understanding of natural law. On the one hand, some read Calvin as proposing that obedience to the divine commands revealed in the Word of God is a sufficient basis for the human judgment of what is right and wrong; Calvin himself states:

> The Lord, in giving the rule of perfect righteousness, has referred all its parts to his will, thereby showing that nothing is more acceptable to him than obedience. The more inclined the playfulness of the human mind is to dream up various rites with which to deserve well of him, the more diligently ought we to mark this fact.[4]

On the other hand, Calvin maintains:

> It is a fact that the law of God which we call the moral law is nothing else than a testimony of natural law and of that conscience which God has engraved upon the minds of men. Consequently, the entire scheme of this equity of which we are now speaking has been prescribed in it. Hence, this equity alone must be the goal and rule and limit of all [positive] laws (*Institutes*, 4.20.16).

In this critical passage he invokes a multiplicity of related abstract juridical concepts: natural law, the law of God, the moral law, conscience, equity and positive laws of humans.

For Calvin, natural law is normative (it sets out values and standards), accessible to humans in general (its norms recognisable without recourse to special divine revelation) and universal (its norms apply to all regardless of particular circumstances like time and place). The goodness of natural law is grounded in the character of God and in human nature and it allows humans to have knowledge of good and bad, so promoting their flourishing – in short, for Calvin, God endowed humankind with a knowledge of natural law at creation – this is one expression of the grace of God and His gift of a moral sense to humankind.[5] And so these ideas also impact on conscience, equity and positive law. The degree to which Calvin adopts or departs from the medieval inheritance in this regard has been keenly debated by scholars.[6]

First, natural law is normative – a central aspect of it is the Golden Rule; Calvin writes:

> Furthermore, seeing that we should not operate in such a way by either finesse or subtlety, it is crucial for us to return to that natural law which is, that we ought to do

[4] John Calvin, *Institutes of the Christian Religion*, John T. McNeill, ed., Ford Lewis Battles, trans. (Philadelphia, PA: Westminster Press, 1960), 2.8.5 – hereafter, *Institutes*. For interpretations of this passage see Paul Helm, *John Calvin's Ideas* (Oxford: Oxford University Press, 2004), 347–354.

[5] The relationship between natural law and common grace is much debated: see Paul Helm, op cit., 382–388.

[6] Thomas F. Torrance, *Calvin's Doctrine of Man* (London: Lutterworth Press, 1949), 29, cited in Paul Helm, op cit., 367.

> unto others as we want them to do unto us. When we follow that rule, it is unnecessary to have thick tomes in order to learn not to steal, for, in brief, everyone knows how he ought to walk with his fellowman, that is, that he should not harbour malice, or attempt to enrich himself at his neighbour's expense, or gain for himself substance which is not his own (*Institutes*, 4.20.16).

Natural law also forbids doing to others that which we would not want them to do to us.[7] The worship of God, as well as love of neighbour, is also an essential of the 'moral law':

> The moral law [which is] contained under two heads, the one of which simply enjoins us to worship God with pure faith and piety, the other to embrace men with sincere affection, is the true and eternal rule of righteousness prescribed to the men of all nations and of all times, who would frame their life agreeably to the will of God. For His eternal and immutable will is that we are all to worship Him, and mutually love one another (*Institutes*, 4.20.16).

Obedience to the moral law is a matter of both freedom and obligation (*Institutes*, 3.19.3, 7).

Secondly, natural law is accessible to all: it is not verbally revealed by God, but it is, rather, implanted by God in the human nature. For Calvin, 'to begin with, God's image was visible in the light of the mind, in the uprightness of the heart, and in the soundness of all the parts' (*Institutes*, 1.15.4; see also 2.8.1). The human reason plays a key role here: 'Man in his first condition excelled in these pre-eminent endowments, so that his reason, understanding, prudence, and judgment not only sufficed for the direction of his earthly life, but by them men mounted up to God and eternal bliss' (*Institutes*, 1.15.8). However, in their sinful state, humans are unable of their own powers alone to know fully the natural law of God in its entirety. Nevertheless, humans may be assisted by God to ascertain the precepts of this divine natural law, not only by means of reason: through the exercise of conscience each person knows enough of this natural law so as to be rendered inexcusable before God for their sin; that is, one end of natural law 'is to render man inexcusable before the judgment of conscience distinguishing sufficiently between just and unjust, and by convicting men on their own testimony depriving them of all pretext for ignorance' (*Institutes*, 2.2.22).

In his *Commentary on the Epistle [of Paul] to the Romans*, Calvin bases his view of the accessibility of natural law on Romans 2.14–15 and, once again, assigns a special place to the human conscience in its apprehension: 'When the Gentiles, which have not the law, *do by nature* the things contained in the law, these, having not the law, are a law unto themselves: which show the work of the law written in their hearts, their conscience also bearing witness, and their thoughts the meantime accusing or else excusing one another.' Yet, humans may not always be disposed to comply with natural law: only some seeds of what is right and just are implanted in the human

7 John Calvin's *Sermons on the Ten Commandments*, 247; See Paul Helm, op cit., 371.

nature. Therefore, all people 'of themselves and without a monitor, are disposed to make laws for themselves', 'laws to punish adultery, and theft, and murder, they commended good faith in bargains and contracts' which mirror the Decalogue.[8]

However, natural law alone cannot lead a person to God:

> For the natural man refuses to be led to recognize the diseases of his lusts. The light of nature is extinguished before he even enters upon this abyss. While the philosophers label the immoderate incitements of the mind as 'vices', they have reference to those which are outward and manifest by grosser signs. They take no account of the evil desires that gently tickle the mind (*Institutes*, 2.2.24).

Yet, '[t]here is nothing more common than for a man to be sufficiently instructed in a right standard of conduct by natural law' (*Institutes*, 2.2.22). Here he addresses other legal forms.

Of particular relevance are his ideas about the 'judicial law' (i.e. positive law), which in turn is connected to his idea of the two kingdoms, the 'spiritual and inward Kingdom of Christ, and civil government', itself instituted and ruled by God (*Institutes*, 4.20.2), an idea still used in the Reformed tradition (as we shall see below). The spiritual kingdom concerns the soul – its inner and eternal life (enjoyed by the grace of Christ) – and civil government concerns the temporal, mortal life and outer conduct (*Institutes*, 3.19.15; see also 4.20.1). Positive law exists *inter alia* to combat sin, to provide the basis for peaceful life and to enforce natural law – and it is obeyed by people because of the threat of sanction under which they live:

> But they are restrained, not because their inner mind is stirred or affected, but because, being bridled, so to speak, they keep their hands from outward activity and hold inside the depravity that otherwise they would wantonly have indulged. Consequently, they are neither better nor more righteous before God. Hindered by fright or shame, they dare neither execute what they have conceived in their minds, nor openly breathe forth the rage of their lust. Still, they do not have hearts disposed to fear and obedience toward God (*Institutes*, 3.7.10).

However, religion too is a proper object of positive law: '[A]ll have confessed that no government can be happily established unless piety is the first concern; and that those laws are preposterous which neglect God's right and provide only for men.' Therefore, since 'among all philosophers religion takes first place, and since this fact has always been observed by universal consent of all nations, let Christian princes and magistrates be ashamed of their negligence if they do not apply themselves to this concern' (*Institutes*, 4.20.9).[9]

Thirdly, natural law is universal. Calvin develops this theme in his treatment of equity: the moral sense possessed by all human beings. Equity is also an idea associated with natural law in the work of Calvin. The law of God is equitable: 'The ordinance of God . . . has its own equity – unknown, indeed, to us but very sure'

[8] *Commentary*, V.15, 96, 98. [9] For different types of government, see *Institutes*, 4.20.8.

(*Institutes*, 3.23.9). Equity is synonymous with and prescribed by natural law and so accessible by the use of reason and conscience (*Institutes*, 4.20.16). Equity is 'the goal and rule and limit of all [positive] laws' (*Institutes*, 4.20.16). Thus, equity is sufficient as a yardstick against which to measure positive law, and if positive laws are not inconsistent with the dictates of equity, those laws are valid:

> Whatever laws shall be framed to that rule, directed to that goal, bound by that limit, there is no reason why we should disapprove of them, however they may differ from the Jewish law, or among themselves (*Institutes*, 4.20.16).

Calvin develops this last idea – namely, that different systems of law may reflect equity in different ways – in relation to his division of the Mosaic laws, in a manner reminiscent of Aquinas, into moral, ceremonial and judicial laws.[10] When he proposes that the ceremonial and judicial laws of Israel were appropriate to it, Calvin states:

> But if this is true, surely every nation is left free to make such laws as it foresees to be profitable for itself. Yet these must be in conformity to that perpetual rule of love, so that they indeed vary in form but have the same purpose (*Institutes*, 4.20.15).

This also is of course reminiscent of Aquinas in his treatment of natural law: 'Owing to the great variety of human affairs the common principles of natural law do not apply stiffly in every case. One outcome is the diversity of positive laws among different peoples.'[11]

However, for Calvin, if a positive law fails to accord to justice, it loses its quality as law:

> For I do not think that those barbarous and savage laws such as give honour to thieves, permit promiscuous intercourse, and others both more filthy and more absurd, are to be regarded as laws. For, they are abhorrent not only to all justice, but also to all humanity and gentleness (*Institutes*, 4.20.15).

Nevertheless, Calvin is cautious about overthrowing unjust government: '[W]e must . . . be very careful not to despise or violate that authority of magistrates, full of venerable majesty, which God has established by the weightiest decrees, even though it may reside with the most unworthy men, who defile it as much as they can with their own wickedness.' Indeed, if 'the correction of unbridled despotism is the Lord's to avenge, let us not at once think that is it entrusted to us, to whom no command has been given except to obey and suffer' (*Institutes*, 4.20.31).

In any event, for Calvin, then, equity is a moral sense that all humans possess, and as such equity is itself a principle of natural law; this may represent further evidence of Calvin's recognition of natural law.[12] Calvin also uses equity as a corrective medium to justify the relaxation of positive law when its application produces unjust consequences – that is, to intensify or enlarge the scope of positive law when this may

[10] William Klempa, op cit., 77. [11] *Summa theologiae*, I.II.95.2. [12] Paul Helm, op cit., 363.

be inferred. He uses this idea in his discussion of the Decalogue as it applies to particular cases:

> We must, I say, inquire how far interpretation ought to overstep the limits of the words themselves so that it may be seen to be, not an appendix added to the divine law from men's glosses, but the Lawgiver's pure and authentic meaning faithfully rendered.

As such:

> Obviously, in almost all the commandments there are such manifest synecdoches that he who would confine his understanding of the law within the narrowness of the words deserves to be laughed at. Therefore, plainly a sober interpretation of the law goes beyond the words; but just how far remains obscure unless some measure be set (*Institutes*, 2.8.8).[13]

Again:

> Equity, because it is natural, cannot but be the same for all, and therefore, this same purpose ought to apply to all laws, whatever their object. Constitutions have certain circumstances upon which they in part depend. It therefore does not matter that they are different, provided all equally press toward the same goal of equity (*Institutes*, 4.20.16).

Thus, some scholars consider that for Calvin the 'basic ethical principle … is equity'.[14] In turn, as John Helm observes: 'In his treatment of some Old Testament legislation Calvin does use equity as a corrector of such legislation not (as with Aristotle) merely on account of its generality but because as it stands it is an inadequate measure of the true meaning of the law of God as revealed in the Decalogue and supremely in Christ.'[15]

Elements of natural law thinking present in Calvin also surface in the historical confessions of the Reformed tradition. These confessions are statements of the Christian faith which reflect understandings of the faith at particular times and places. As such, they contain 'subordinate standards' (subordinate that is to the Bible), and fifty or so were written in the first 150 years of the Reformed tradition.[16] For example, the Belgic Confession (1561) indicates two sources for human knowledge of God, namely the general revelation and the special revelation. Article 2 of the Belgic Confession presents the distinction thus:

[13] A synecdoche is a figure of speech in which a term for a part of something refers to the whole of that thing, and *vice versa*.

[14] Allen Verhey, 'Natural Law in Aquinas and Calvin', in Clifton J. Orlebeke and Lewis B. Smedes, eds., *God and the Good* (Grand Rapids, MI: William B. Eerdmans, 1975), 86, cited in Paul Helm, op cit., 365.

[15] Paul Helm, op cit., 366.

[16] John H. Leith, *Introduction to the Reformed Tradition: A Way of Being the Christian Community* (London: Westminster John Knox Press, rev. ed. 1981), 133–136.

> First, through the creation, preservation, and government of the universe, since that universe is before our eyes like a beautiful book in which all creatures, great and small, are as letters to make us ponder the invisible things of God: God's eternal power and divinity, as the apostle, Saint Paul, says in Romans 1:20. All these things are enough to convict humans and to leave them without excuse. Second, God communicates to us more clearly through the holy and divine Word, as much as we need in this life, for God's glory and for our salvation.

The latter, the special revelation, is elaborated in Article 3 of the Belgic Confession:

> We confess that this Word of God was not sent nor delivered 'by human will', but that 'men and women moved by the Holy Spirit, spoke from God', as Saint Peter says. Afterward our God because of a special care for us and our salvation commanded the prophets and apostles, God's servants, to commit this revealed Word to writing. The two tables of the law were written with God's own finger. Therefore we call such writings holy and divine Scriptures.[17]

Moreover, Reformed thinkers continued to associate natural law with other abstract normative entities after Calvin. For example, the great German jurist and Calvinist political philosopher Johannes Althusius (1563–1638) recognised the existence of a (cosmic) legal order consisting of a multiplicity of related entities: divine law, moral law, natural law, natural justice, natural equity, the law of conscience, the law of the mind and the law of reason or right reason; this legal order also embraced: the law within people, the immutable law, the supreme law, the general law, the common law and other categories.[18] Moreover, natural theology has to do with what can be known or rationally believed about the existence and nature of God on the basis of human reason; it consists of moral standards embedded in human nature by God and is therefore part of God's divine wisdom and his eternal law.[19]

Biblical law was another important category for Althusius: (1) the moral law, the enduring moral teachings of the Decalogue and the New Testament; (2) judicial law, the rules by which the ancient Israelites and apostolic Christians governed their religious and civil communities; and (3) ceremonial law, the Mosaic laws of personal diet, ritual sacrifice, priestly life, and the like, which again governed the religious life of the ancient Israelites. Althusius sees the Decalogue as the clearest and most comprehensive confirmation and codification of natural law, that is, of every person's inner and natural inclination to piety and justice, to faith and order, to love of God, and to love of neighbour.[20] Natural law juxtaposes the inability of human beings to do the good due to sin with the moral responsibility to obey God.

17 See Ernst M. Conradie, 'All Theology is Natural Theology: The Hermeneutic Necessity of Natural Law?', *Dutch Reformed Theological Journal* 52 (2011): 58–65, at 61.

18 John Witte, 'Natural Rights, Popular Sovereignty, and Covenant Politics: Johannes Althusius and the Dutch Revolt and Republic', *Mercy Law Review* 87 (2007): 565–627.

19 Johan Buitenbag, 'Die wêreld as gelykenis: 'n Trajek om die middelterm van die "teologie" te vind', *HTS Theological Studies* 59(4) (2003): 1063–1064.

20 John Witte, op cit., 565, 583.

Althusius regarded the moral laws of the Bible and the common laws of nations as two visible manifestations of the same invisible natural law hidden within each person's reason and conscience. He viewed the laws of ancient Israelites and of the institutional churches of his day as two types of positive law which stood alongside the positive laws of historical and contemporary civil communities. Every person, he maintained, by their very nature thus has knowledge (*notitia*) of and an inclination (*inclinatio*) to natural law born within them.[21]

The great Dutch jurist and theologian Hugo Grotius (1583–1645) also famously used natural law as the basis of his work on international law; his great work *De Jure Belli ac Pacis* severs law from theology but fixes the principle of justice in the Law of Nature which has as its principal source man as a social being – as such, natural law is derived from pure human reason, and it binds civil government only through the conscience of the sovereign; however, his place as a classical thinker within the Reformed tradition is the subject of some considerable debate.[22] According to Grotius natural law is a rational principle of morality and social justice which 'is so unalterable, that it cannot be changed even by God himself'; moreover, 'even if we were to say that there is no God', there would still be natural justice: 'Natural law is the dictate of the right reason indicating that an act, according as it conforms to or is in disagreement with nature, individual and social, is either morally wicked or morally necessary and in consequence such an act is commanded or forbidden by God, the author of nature.'[23] Grotius inferred five rules of natural law: do not take things that belong to others; restore to other people anything that we might have of theirs; fulfil promises; compensate for any loss that results through our own fault; and punish people as deserved. These are not only at the core of all morality, but form the essentials of social and political obligation – within countries and also between countries internationally.[24]

NATURAL LAW IN LATER REFORMED TRADITION

Natural law later became the focus of much debate in the Reformed tradition: some embraced it,[25] others did not.[26] A celebrated debate took place on the matter between

[21] Ibid., 579–580.

[22] See, e.g., Oliver O'Donovan and Joan Lockwood O'Donovan, eds., *From Irenaeus to Grotius: A Sourcebook in Christian Political Thought* (Grand Rapids, MI: William B. Eerdmans, 1999), 783–792.

[23] *De Jure Belli ac Pacis*, 1.1.

[24] See, e.g., Carl Joachim Friedrich, *The Philosophy of Law in Historical Perspective*, 2nd edn, 5th impression (Chicago and London: The University of Chicago Press, 1963), 65–66.

[25] See, e.g., Nelson D. Kloosterman, 'A Response to "The Kingdom of God is Twofold": Natural Law and the Two Kingdoms in the Thought of Herman Bavinck by David VanDrunen', *Calvin Theological Journal* 45 (2010): 165–177, at 166. See also John Bolt, 'Herman Bavinck on Natural Law and Two Kingdoms: Some Further Reflections', *The Bavinck Review* 4 (2013): 64–93.

[26] See, e.g., Cornelius Van Til, 'Common Grace', in Edward Heerema, ed., *Proceedings of the Calvinistic Philosophy Club* (1941), 61.

the Swiss theologians Karl Barth (1886–1968) and Emil Brunner (1889–1966) – a key issue in the debate concerns the attitude of Calvin to natural theology and the rational knowledge of God.[27]

For Brunner, '[T]he proclamation of the Church has not two sources and norms, such as, e.g. revelation *and* reason or the Word of God *and* history, and that ecclesiastical or Christian action has not two norms, such as e.g. commandments *and* "Ordinances."' However, in his treatment of the 'general revelation', on the one hand, Brunner argues that in reading the Bible humans cannot fail to recognise that God's world 'speaks' of His work: 'Wherever God does anything, he leaves the imprint of his nature upon what he does. Therefore the creation of the world is at the same time a revelation, a self-communication of God.'[28] Sin may indeed blind human beings, but the revelation of God in the natural world does not cease with sin; our image of God has not been fully obliterated by human sin. In point of fact, our conscience provides the consciousness of responsibility, of what we 'ought' to do, etc.; no matter how imperfectly we perceive it, or how much we rebel against it, this moral consciousness of God's law is present in sinful humanity. Thus, the key question is not whether there are two kinds or levels of revelation (from a single source, God), but how the two that do exist (in creation and in Christ) are related:

> [T]aking our stand upon the revelation in Jesus Christ, we shall not be able to avoid speaking of a double revelation: of one in creation which only he can recognise in all its magnitude, whose eyes have been opened by Christ; and of a second in Jesus Christ in whose bright light he can clearly perceive the former. This latter revelation far surpasses that which the former was able to show him.[29]

Karl Barth rejects this position:

> [K]nowledge of God occurs in the fulfilment of the revelation of His Word by the Holy Spirit, and therefore in the reality and with the necessity of faith and its obedience. Its content is the existence of Him whom we must fear above all things because we may love Him above all things; who remains a mystery to us because He Himself has made Himself so clear and certain to us.[30]

For Barth:

> By natural theology I mean every (positive and negative) *formulation of a system* which claims to be theological; that is, to interpret divine revelation whose *subject*, however, differs fundamentally from the revelation of Jesus Christ and whose method the revelation of God in nature can be known 'in all its magnitude' only by him 'whose eyes have been opened by Christ'. But it is 'somehow' recognisable –

[27] Karl Barth and Emil Brunner, *Natural Theology*, Peter Fraenkel, trans. (London: Geoffrey Bles, 1946). The debate started in 1934, at the time of the 'Barmen Declaration' 1934, which rejects the subordination of the church to the state and the subordination of the Word and Spirit to the Church.

[28] Barth and Brunner, *Natural Theology*, op cit., 18–25. [29] Ibid., 26–27.

[30] Karl Barth, *Church Dogmatics*, G.W. Bromiley and T.F. Torrance, eds. (Edinburgh: T. & T. Clark, 1956), II.I.3.

> though but distortedly and dimly – even by those of whom this cannot be said ... Hence real knowledge of God through creation does not take place without revelation though only 'somehow' and 'not in all its magnitude'. (emphasis added)[31]

Rather, God is known only by God:

> We do not know Him, then, in virtue of the views and concepts with which in faith we attempt to respond to His revelation. But we also do not know Him without making use of His permission and obeying His command to undertake this attempt. The success of this undertaking, and therefore the veracity of our human knowledge of God, consists in the fact that our viewing and conceiving is adopted and determined to participation in the truth of God by God Himself in grace.[32]

In other words, natural theology is itself a system which claims to be theological, to interpret divine revelation, whose subject, however, differs fundamentally from the revelation in Christ and whose *method* thus differs from the exposition of Scripture.

The debate between Barth and Brunner greatly influenced subsequent discourse about natural law in Reformed circles[33] and has led in part to revival of interest in the subject, particularly during the past decade.[34] Typical is the work of Stephen J. Grabill. According to Grabill, the Brunner-Barth debate had two significant consequences for Protestant systematic and historical theology on the subject of natural law. On the one hand, the debate brought into question the legitimate and circumscribed use of natural law in Reformed theological ethics by identifying it as an essentially Roman Catholic and neo-Protestant doctrine, and so Grabill explores the possibility that Barth 'displaced' natural law from the Reformed tradition. On the other hand, the debate meant that subsequent discussions of natural law failed to examine how Protestant orthodoxy had actually modified the medieval natural law tradition as received through the Reformers. There is clear evidence, for Grabill, that the Reformers, starting with John Calvin and his attitude to natural theology, and others, particularly Peter Martyr Vermigli (1499–1562), Johannes Althusius (1563–1638) and Francis Turretin (1623–1687), reiterated and developed the medieval doctrines concerning natural law. Grabill, therefore, seeks to rehabilitate natural law for Reformed theological ethics, and he calls on Christian ethicists, theologians and laypersons to take another look at this vital element in the intellectual history of Christian ethics. A rediscovery of natural law enables us to explore whether knowledge of right and wrong is written on the human heart, how people might know God from the world around them and the extent to which natural knowledge contributes

31 Karl Barth, 'No! An answer to Emil Brunner', in Barth and Brunner, *Natural Theology*, op cit., 80–81.

32 Karl Barth, *Church Dogmatics*, op cit., II.1.179.

33 The debate has generated an abundant literature: see, e.g., Trevor Hart, 'A Capacity for Ambiguity: The Barth-Brunner Debate Revisited', *Tyndale Bulletin* 44(2) (1993): 289–305.

34 See, e.g., J. Daryl Charles, *Retrieving the Natural Law: A Return to Moral First Things* (Grand Rapids, MI: William B. Eerdmans, 2008).

to Christian teaching. In short, natural theology and natural law represent a valuable part of historical Reformed theological reflection which has been eclipsed by the twentieth-century dominance of special revelation resulting from the Barth-Brunner debate.[35]

David VanDrunen is another scholar of the Reformed tradition who advocates natural law thinking for the development of Reformed social teaching.[36] He also sets out a biblical case for natural law.[37] First, there is a 'moral order inscribed in the world and especially in human nature'; it is 'an order that is known to all people through their natural faculties', in particular 'conscience' and 'reason', 'even apart from supernatural divine revelation that binds morally the whole human race'.[38] Secondly,

> human nature at the beginning was one of righteousness and holiness, of knowledge of God and himself, of a moral commission to rule over creation in a way imitating God's rule. This image of God carried along with it a natural law, a law inherent to human nature and directing human beings to fulfill their royal commission in righteousness and holiness.[39]

Thirdly, in a traditional interpretation of Romans 2.14–15, 'natural law continues to exist in the fallen world', and 'it continues to have positive usefulness today'.[40] Fourthly, natural law is the law of God for 'civil' matters, whereas supernatural revelation is His law for 'spiritual' matters: the civil kingdom 'pertains to temporal, earthly, provisional matters' (e.g. politics, law and cultural life), and the ends of the civil kingdom are 'not salvation and eternal life but a relatively just, peaceful and orderly existence in the present world in which Christians live as pilgrims away from their heavenly homeland'. However, the spiritual kingdom 'is also ruled by God, but he rules it not only as creator and sustainer, but also as redeemer in Christ. This kingdom pertains to things that are of ultimate and spiritual importance'; moreover, 'Insofar as this spiritual kingdom has earthly existence, Calvin believed it must be found in the church and not in the state or other temporal institutions.' These two kingdoms exist together and have 'some mutual interaction in this world', but each enjoys 'a measure of independence so that each can pursue the unique work entrusted to it'.[41] Fifthly, the civil kingdom receives its institutional foundation in God's covenant with Noah, a 'covenant of common grace', and 'God has established the civil kingdom in the sinful world, a common realm constituted of all people, whatever their religious commitment, in which temporal affairs of justice,

35 Stephen Grabill, *Rediscovering the Natural Law in Reformed Theological Ethics* (Atlanta, GA: Emory University Studies in Law and Religion, 2006).

36 David VanDrunen, *Natural Law and the Two Kingdoms: A Study in the Development of Reformed Social Thought* (Grand Rapids, MI: William B. Eerdmans, 2010).

37 David VanDrunen, *A Biblical Case for Natural Law*, Studies in Christian Social Ethics and Economics, No. 1 (Grand Rapids, MI: Acton Institute, 2006).

38 Ibid., 1. 39 Ibid., 14. 40 Ibid., 16. 41 Ibid., 24.

procreation, and cultural development are regulated. These affairs are a common enterprise.'[42]

For VanDrunen, 'in a certain sense, Scripture is not the appropriate moral standard for the civil kingdom'; rather:

> Biblical morality is characterized by an indicative-imperative structure. That is, all of its imperatives (moral commands) are proceeded [*sic*] by and grounded in indicatives (statements of fact), either explicitly or implicitly. The most important indicative that grounds the imperatives in Scripture is that the recipients of Scripture are the covenant people, that is, members of the community of the covenant of grace.

Thus, 'Since membership in the civil kingdom is not limited to believers, the imperatives of Scripture do not bind members of that kingdom. These imperatives are not directly applicable to non-Christians.'[43] Lastly, 'The present, earthly existence of the spiritual kingdom cannot be at odds with that good creation and its natural law; it far transcends them.'[44] VanDrunen's position on natural law is not without its critics.[45]

NATURAL LAW THINKING AND SYSTEMS OF CHURCH ORDER

In the context of the spiritual realm of the church, it is a fundamental of the Reformed tradition that the kingdom of God is not limited to the ministry of Word and Sacrament. Nor is it part of the Reformed tradition to view external church government as a matter for the kingdom of the world so coming under the control of the civil magistrate. Rather the tradition emphasises that Christ's kingship over his church includes its government and other visible organisational structures. Therefore, Reformed churches have their own regulatory systems of church order or polity designed on the basis of theological reflection on the nature of the church. Systems of church order are forms of applied ecclesiology. Moreover, from their earliest days Reformed churches have defended their right to exercise discipline and to administer their own affairs, again a position developed from the early Reformers' view of the political and ecclesiastical powers under the doctrine of the twofold kingship of Christ.[46]

Natural law thinking may be recognised in the early systems of church polity of the Reformed tradition. The Ecclesiastical Ordinances 1541, formulated by Calvin himself for the church community in Geneva (but with modifications insisted on by the civil government, indicated below in square brackets) make no explicit reference to natural law. However, they do invoke broad ideas of divine institution: '[T]here are four orders of offices instituted by our Saviour for the government of his Church: namely, the pastors, then the doctors, next the elders *[nominated and appointed by*

[42] Ibid., 28. [43] Ibid., 39–40. [44] Ibid., 57. [45] E.g. Nelson D. Kloosterman, op cit.

[46] Pieter Coertzen, *Church and Order: A Reformed Perspective* (Leuven: Peeters, 1998).

the government] and fourthly the deacons. If we wish to see the Church well-ordered and maintained we ought to observe this form of government'; 'Pastors are ... to proclaim the Word of God, to teach, admonish, exhort and reprove publicly and privately, to administer the sacraments and, with the elders or their deputies, to issue fraternal warnings.' Moreover:

> There must be some means available to discipline ministers ... to prevent scandalous living. In this way, respect for the ministry can be maintained and the Word of God not debased by any minister bringing it into scorn and derision. Those who deserve it must be corrected, but at the same time care must be taken to deal with gossip and malicious rumours which can bring harm to innocent parties.

The Golden Rule of natural law is implicit in the duty of deacons: one deacon is 'to receive, distribute and care for the goods of the poor (i.e. daily alms as well as possessions, rents and pensions); the other has to tend and look after the sick and administer the allowances to the poor as is customary'; there are also norms on hospital administration and 'Of the order which must be observed in obedience to those in authority, for the maintenance of supervision in the Church' in the form of a Consistory. Also:

> If anyone teaches things contrary to the received doctrine he shall be summoned to a conference. If he listens to reason, let him be sent back without any scandal or disgrace. If he is obstinate, he should be admonished several times until it is apparent that greater severity is needed: then he shall be forbidden to attend the communion of the Supper and shall be reported to the magistrates.[47]

The Synod of Emden (1571) approved adjustments to Calvin's Ecclesiastical Ordinances, and its church order was revised at the Synods of Dordrecht (1574 and 1578), Middelburg (1581) and The Hague (1586), before being adopted by the Synod of Dordrecht (1618–1619). Like the Ecclesiastical Ordinances of 1541, these instruments make no explicit use of natural law, but rather, in a functional fashion, regulate the life and conduct of members and officers, property, services and discipline of members and officers. However, there are elements of natural law thinking in these instruments. For example, the Canons of Dort (1619) imply elements of natural law thinking at two points. First, under the doctrine of general revelation, the light of nature provides humans with an image of God, good and evil, albeit distorted:

> There is, to be sure, a certain light of nature remaining in man after the fall, by virtue of which he retains some notions about God, natural things, and the difference between what is moral and immoral, and demonstrates a certain eagerness for virtue and for good outward behaviour. But this light of nature is far from

47 J.F. Bergier and R.M. Kingdon, *Registres de la Compagnie des pasteurs de Geneve au temps de Calvin*, 2 vols. (1962–1964), G.R. Potter and M. Greengrass, trans., *Jean Calvin* (London: Edward Arnold, 1983), 71–76.

> enabling man to come to a saving knowledge of God and conversion to him – so far, in fact, that man does not use it rightly even in matters of nature and society. Instead, in various ways he completely distorts this light, whatever its precise character, and suppresses it in unrighteousness. In doing so he renders himself without excuse before God.[48]

Secondly, therefore, the Canons recognise the human conscience in those who have not turned to God:

> Those who do not yet actively experience within themselves a living faith in Christ or an assured confidence of heart, peace of conscience, a zeal for childlike obedience, and a glorying in God through Christ, but who nevertheless use the means by which God has promised to work these things in us ... ought to continue diligently in the use of the means, to desire fervently a time of more abundant grace, and to wait for it in reverence and humility.[49]

The Canons also underline, however, that in the church, decisions are to be made in accordance with the law of God – natural law, again, is not mentioned: '[W]e must make judgments about God's will from his Word.'[50] Similarly, justice is rooted in God (not natural law): 'God is not only supremely merciful, but also supremely just. His justice requires (as he has revealed himself in the Word) that the sins we have committed against his infinite majesty be punished with both temporal and eternal punishments, of soul as well as body. We cannot escape these punishments unless satisfaction is given to God's justice.'[51]

Today, the principles of church polity of all Reformed churches include the principle of the autonomy of the church (its right of self-government under the sole headship of Christ), the equality of the faithful, the participation of the laity in church government and discipline – and the discipline of all church members is to be exercised by a court which consists of ministers of the gospel and the ruling elders; church government is a gift from God that must remain distinct from civil government.[52] In all this, 'the external juridical order of the church should be at the service of the proclamation of the Word'; consequently, 'the external order must be tested ever anew by the confession of faith, and on no level of legal church life can juridical questions be solved without relation to the church's confession'; church law is not a 'constitutive', but a 'consecutive' and 'regulative' element of the reality of a church.[53] On the basis of these fundamental principles, the systems of

48 Canons of Dort, The Third and Fourth Main Points of Doctrine: Human Corruption etc., Article 4.

49 Canons of Dort, The First Main Point of Doctrine: Divine Election and Reprobation, Article 16.

50 Canons of Dort, The First Main Point of Doctrine: Divine Election and Reprobation, Article 17.

51 Canons of Dort, The Second Main Point of Doctrine: Christ's Death and Human Redemption, Article 1.

52 Mary Anne Plaatjies van Huffel, *Principles of Reformed Church Polity* (Zurich: Lit Verlag, 2014), 42.

53 Statement made at the Barmen Synod 31 May 1934 on the German Evangelical Church: quoted by Marc Reuver, *Faith and Law: Juridical Perspectives for the Ecumenical Movement* (Geneva: World Council of Churches, 2000), 4.

church order and other regulatory instruments of the Reformed, Presbyterian, Congregational and United churches,[54] within the membership of the World Communion of Reformed Churches, use a range of ideas broadly associated with natural law,[55] the moral law and, more commonly, with the law of God.

First, systems of church order and polity invoke the idea of divine law, embodied in the Word of God as revealed in Scripture, as a yardstick for decision-making in the church. In Reformed churches, ordained ministry is conceived as instituted by Christ;[56] and in Presbyterianism, typically, '[o]ur blessed Saviour, for the edification of the visible Church ... has appointed officers not only to preach the Gospel and administer the Sacraments, but also to exercise discipline for the preservation both of truth and duty'; moreover, '[t]hough the character, qualifications and authority of church officers are laid down in the Holy Scriptures, as well as the proper method of office investiture, the power to elect persons to the exercise of authority in any particular society rests with that society'.[57] Thus, Presbyterian norms acknowledge that the church receives its authority from Christ,[58] that 'the Word of God' is the supreme 'rule of faith and life'[59] and that church courts and officers must 'uphold the laws of Scripture' or 'the rules contained in the Word of God' and have 'the right to require obedience to the laws of Christ' and hear cases involving 'violations of the divine law';[60] and it is 'the duty of everyone to accept and obey' the will of God as revealed in Scripture.[61] Also, scriptural texts are cited expressly in these legal instruments.[62]

Secondly, the norms of churches sometimes invoke the concept of moral law, justice, ethics and conscience. Typically, 'the moral law of God, summarized in the Ten Commandments, testified to by the prophets, and unfolded in the life and teachings of Jesus Christ, stands for ever in truth and equity', and God requires, for

54 See Norman Doe, *Christian Law: Contemporary Principles* (Cambridge: Cambridge University Press, 2013).

55 E.g. there is an express reference to natural law in James L. Weatherhead, ed., *The Constitution and Laws of the Church of Scotland* (Edinburgh: The Board of Practice and Procedure, 1997), 3.

56 Reformed Church in America: The Book of Church Order (2010), Preamble: 'their authority derives from Christ though they are elected by the people'; 'he distributes these functions among those whom he calls to serve'.

57 Presbyterian Church in America: The Book of Church Order (2005), Preface, II.6; 1.1, 7.1.

58 Presbyterian Church in Ireland: The Code: Book of the Constitution and Government (2010), I.I. IV.15: 'Christ is the sole King and Head of the Church'.

59 Presbyterian Church of Aotearoa New Zealand: The Book of Order (2011), 1.1(2): 'The supreme rule of faith and life and the supreme standard of the Church is the Word of God contained in the Scriptures of the Old and New Testaments.'

60 Presbyterian Church in America: The Book of Church Order (2005), Preface, II.3: also II.7: 'laws of Scripture'; 1.3: members profess Christ and 'promise submission to His laws'; 11.2: laws of Christ; 29.3: violations of divine law; 59.6: 'laws of God'.

61 Presbyterian Church in Ireland: The Code: Book of the Constitution and Government (2010), I.I. III.11.

62 United Congregational Church of Southern Africa: Constitution (2007), Procedure 15: Sacraments are 'remedies for sin (Romans 6.4 and Matthew 26.29)'.

instance, 'every man to do justly'.[63] Presbyterian laws sometimes invoke 'the principles of natural justice'[64] and contain 'ethical standards', 'standards of practice', 'values' and 'norms'.[65] Indeed, the Golden Rule is implicit in norms on the 'rights and privileges' of church membership; for instance, Christian service implies 'mutual and outgoing care and responsibility'.[66] Importantly:

> God alone is Lord of the conscience and has left it free from any doctrines or commandments of men (a) which are in any respect contrary to the Word of God, or (b) which, in regard to matters of faith and worship, are not governed by the Word of God. Therefore, the rights of private judgment in all matters that respect religion are universal and inalienable;

and, as a result, '[n]o church judicatory may make laws to bind the conscience'.[67]

Thirdly, the concept of equity occasionally surfaces in norms,[68] as does the idea of moderation in discipline, that church laws should be applied 'with pastoral prudence and Christian love' or 'the law of love'.[69] Indeed, in the United Free Church of Scotland, the General Assembly has a *nobile officium*: 'the power of the General Assembly, as Supreme Court to act in special circumstances beyond or even against its own rules or forms of procedures' as 'shall seem to the General Assembly right and needful for doing justice in the particular case'.[70]

Fourthly, moral standards (sometimes with explicit reference in the legal text to the idea of divine law) are prominent in relation to norms on church discipline, which itself is conceived as of divine institution: 'Discipline is the exercise of the authority which . . . Christ has given to the church to promote purity, to benefit the offender, and to vindicate [His] honour.'[71] Thus, '[s]ince ecclesiastical discipline must be purely moral or spiritual in its object, and not attended with any civil effects, it can derive no force whatever, but from its own justice, the approbation of an impartial public, and the countenance and blessing of the great Head of the Church'.[72] Consequently, discipline is to be administered with mercy and gentleness: it is to be exercised under 'the dispensation of mercy' and in faithfulness, meekness, love and tenderness for 'the condemnation of offences and the recovery

[63] United Church of Canada: Manual (2010), Basis of Union 2.14.

[64] Presbyterian Church of Aotearoa New Zealand: The Book of Order (2011), 15.1: disciplinary process.

[65] United Reformed Church (in Great Britain): Manual (2008), E: Guidance [on] Baptism and the Basis of Union; United Church of Canada: Ethical Standards and Standards of Practice for Ministry Personnel (2008): this is 'a common set of values' and 'a set of norms for the education and formation of ministry personnel' to 'enable [them] to be accountable to self, church, and community'.

[66] United Reformed Church (in Great Britain): Manual (2008), A.19.

[67] Presbyterian Church in America: The Book of Church Order (2005), Preface II.1; II.8.

[68] United Church of Christ in the Philippines: Constitution and Bylaws (2002), Article II.5: 'justice' is at the heart of its witness to the world; II.6: the church must ensure 'equitable representation' of its general membership in terms of, e.g., gender and age.

[69] Presbyterian Church in America: The Book of Church Order (2005), Preface, II; 8.3.

[70] Manual of Practice and Procedure (2011), Glossary of Latin Terms and V.II.8.

[71] Reformed Church in America: The Book of Church Order (2010), Chapter 2, Part I, Article 1.

[72] Presbyterian Church in America: The Book of Church Order (2005), Preface, II.8.

of offenders'.[73] In turn, conduct which may be the subject of disciplinary process includes, typically, in one United Congregational Church: anything in teaching or conduct of a person under church jurisdiction which has been declared censurable by the Word of God;[74] 'grave moral misconduct unworthy of a minister'; conviction of a minister in a secular court for 'any grave criminal charge'; and teaching contrary to Scripture and church doctrine.[75] Equally, in the Presbyterian Church in America, an elder must ensure that 'no corruption of doctrine or of morals' enters the life of the members, and the Presbytery must ensure that the elder has 'full freedom to maintain and teach the doctrine of our Church'.[76]

In short, the discipline of the church is seen as of a spiritual nature and as one of the keys of the kingdom of heaven;[77] for example:

> Christian discipline is exercised exclusively by spiritual means, which are: (1). Admonition: Tenderly and solemnly confronting the offender with his sin, warning him of his danger and exhorting him to repentance and to greater fidelity to the Lord Jesus Christ. (2). Rebuke: A form of censure more severe than admonition, which consists in setting forth the serious character of the offence, reproving the offender, and exhorting him to repentance and to more perfect fidelity to Christ.[78]

However, anyone who obstinately rejects the admonition by the consistory or who has committed a public sin can be suspended from the church.[79] When those who have been excommunicated repent and desire to be again received into the communion of the church, they may be reinstated. Ministers, elders or deacons who have committed a public or otherwise gross sin or refuse to heed the admonitions may be suspended or deposed.[80] The church orders make provision that the consistory should exercise discipline regarding sins of a public nature or those brought to its attention according to the rule of Matthew 18.15–17.[81] The concurrence of the presbytery is required.[82]

Finally, there are vestiges of natural law thinking in norms on church-state relations. But it is the concept of divine law, rather than natural law, which is the dominant idea here. Calvin's notion of freedom of conscience, the separation of church and state and religious tolerance are still influential.[83] For the Reformed

73 Presbyterian Church in Ireland: Code, paragraph 131; Presbyterian Church in America: The Book of Church Order (2005), 27: it is exercised under 'a dispensation of mercy and not of wrath'.

74 Presbyterian Church in Ireland: Code, paragraphs 131–132: (e.g. I Corinthians 5.9–11).

75 United Congregational Church of Southern Africa: Constitution (2007): Procedure 13 and 15.

76 Presbyterian Church in America: The Book of Church Order (2005), 8.3 and 8.7.

77 Canadian Reformed Churches: Church Order (2015), Articles 66–76.

78 Reformed Church in New Zealand: Church Order (2015), Articles 67–94.

79 Canadian Reformed Churches Church: Order (2015), Articles 66–76.

80 Christian Reformed Church in North America: Church Order (2015), Article 81.

81 Christian Reformed Church in North America: Church Order (2015), Article 80.

82 Reformed Church in New Zealand: Church Order (2015), Articles 67–94.

83 Gerard Mannion and Eddy Van der Borght, eds., *John Calvin's Ecclesiology: Ecumenical Perspectives* (London: Bloomsbury, 2011).

churches, 'Christ, the only ruler and head of the Church, has therein appointed a government distinct from civil government and in things spiritual not subordinate thereto, and that civil authorities, being always subject to the rule of God, ought to respect the rights of conscience and of religious belief and to serve God's will of justice and peace for all humankind.'[84] The church should therefore exercise no authority over the state nor does the state over the church.[85] Generally, churches must comply with state law.[86] United and Congregational churches also distinguish themselves from the state[87] but seek 'to uphold the just authority of the State'.[88] And the members of United churches should not approach the courts of the 'civil power' in order to resolve their disputes.[89] As to religious freedom, the United Reformed Church in Great Britain declares that 'civil authorities, being always subject to the rule of God, ought to respect the rights of conscience and of religious belief and to serve God's will of justice and peace for all humankind'.[90] The Presbyterian churches also hold to the view that (typically) 'although civil rulers are bound to render obedience to Christ in their own province, yet they ought not to attempt in any way to constrain anyone's religious beliefs, or invade the rights of conscience'.[91] Thus, 'the rights of private judgment in all matters that respect religion are universal and inalienable'.[92]

CONCLUSION

In the Reformed tradition, the triune God rules over all human beings both in the civil kingdom and in the spiritual kingdom. Both kingdoms are regulated by divine

84 United Reformed Church (Great Britain): Manual, Basis of Union A, Sch. D, Version I, 8.

85 Reformed Church in America: The Book of Church Order (2010), Preamble: 'The church shall not exercise authority over the state, nor should the state usurp authority over the church' – Christ is 'the only Head of the Church.'

86 Reformed Church in America: The Book of Church Order (2010), Chapter 1, Part II, Article 14.5: pastors must perform marriages 'subject to state and provincial law'.

87 United Congregational Church of Southern Africa: Constitution (2007), Preamble: the church 'calls all people, society and states . . . to accept and obey Jesus Christ'.

88 United Church of Canada: Manual (2010), Basis of Union 2.20.

89 United Free Church of Scotland: Constitution, V.II.8: 'Application by office-bearers or members to the civil power or Courts for reduction, restraint, review, alteration, or control of the procedure in the . . . Courts of the Church, or of their decisions, is excluded. Parties . . . before the Church Courts, or affected by their decisions, are . . . precluded from recourse to the civil Courts'; United Church of Christ in the Philippines: Constitution, Article VIII.5: 'All questions of state policies and . . . the public justice of the State are beyond the jurisdiction of the Commission [on Discipline and Conflict Resolution]'; Bylaws, Article VI.4: 'No member . . . who is party to any controversy with another member or with the Church may institute any suit or proceeding or apply for remedy before any civil court . . . without . . . exhausting all intra-church remedies.'

90 United Reformed Church (Great Britain): Manual, Basis of Union A, Sch. D, Version I, 8; see also, G: the Equal Opportunities Committee of the General Assembly: Man., I: the Equal Opportunities Policy affirms the commitment to 'the same openness to all people in today's world' and forbids discrimination in the church.

91 Presbyterian Church in Ireland: Code, I.III.13; this cites the Act of the Church of Scotland 1647.

92 Presbyterian Church in America: The Book of Church Order (2005), Preamble II.1.

law. The two kingdoms doctrine has natural law as its 'natural' correlate. It seems as if the natural law/two kingdoms tradition was an integral part of Reformed theology and church polity from John Calvin onward. Whilst it lost its appeal as a result of the debate between Emil Brunner and Karl Barth in the mid-twentieth century, modern Reformed scholars are beginning to develop renewed interest in natural law, not simply to rehabilitate the work of Calvin and others, but also as a valuable concept for contemporary political and ethical issues. In the field of polity too, the early confessions and books of church order recognised the light of reason as a form of general revelation, independent of the special revelation of God in Christ, providing an imperfect image of God, right and wrong. So too the modern regulatory instruments of Reformed, Presbyterian, Congregational and United churches across the world contain what might be styled vestiges of natural law thinking in their use of concepts such as the moral law, conscience, fundamental rights and, to a lesser extent, equity – but the concept of divine law in the Word of God as revealed in Scripture dominates.

8

Natural Law in the Baptist Tradition

Paul Goodliff

It is sometimes claimed that Baptists reject the natural law tradition which has been so central to the development of Western philosophical, ethical and legal thought. Strongly rooted in the Catholic tradition from which Baptists dissented, with Augustine and Aquinas as its two Christian progenitors, it is not surprising that there has been no explicit Baptist theology of natural law. Two contemporary Baptist theologians, John Colwell and James McClendon,[1] echoing this suspicion of an independent natural law, argue that 'we have found no reason to believe in any "natural law", standing outside the law of Christ',[2] and in any case, says Colwell, Aquinas' appeal to a universal 'natural law' must be seen 'within the context of the Christian tradition and, specifically, within the context of the official teaching of the Church'.[3]

Closer inspection, however, reveals that the reasons for their rejection of 'natural law' are not specifically Baptist, but rather a more general suspicion of post-Enlightenment confidence in the power of human reason to discern just what natural law consists in, unaided by any divine revelation or grace, which is the version of natural law at work in a post-Christian context. This is by no means the only conception of natural law, however, and there is an older tradition that closely identifies natural law with divine revelation. Indeed, I will argue that Baptists have adopted a form of natural law from their Calvinistic roots as creatures of the Reformation in England (not the only theological stream from which Baptists sprung in the early seventeenth century, but the most significant at that stage). We will investigate this in the case of three related Baptist convictions: religious liberty; separation of church and state; and the bearing of arms. However, first, a brief introduction to the origins of the Baptists is in order.

[1] John E. Colwell, *Living the Christian Story: The Distinctiveness of Christian Ethics* (Edinburgh: T. & T. Clark, 2001); James Wm. McClendon Jr., *Systematic Theology: Vol. 1. Ethics* (Nashville, TN: Abingdon Press, 1986).

[2] James McClendon, op cit., 235–236.

[3] John Colwell, op cit., 21.

THE ORIGINS OF THE BAPTISTS

While there were certainly some influences from the Radical Reformation on the Continent, and especially in that movement dubbed by its opponents 'Anabaptist', the origins of the first English Baptists lie in the generation that followed the Reformation. The tensions in the Elizabethan Church of England, between those who looked towards Calvinist Geneva (the Puritans) and those who looked towards Rome, remained unresolved at Elizabeth's death – and to a degree remain so even today. Baptists represent one stream of those who wanted the Church of England to be more thoroughly 'reformed' along the lines of the Presbyterian form of government. The English Baptists of the 1640s found the application of the name 'Anabaptist' particularly offensive and damaging, for it implied not just a baptismal polity – with which they had some sympathy – but a political polity with which they most decidedly did not. 'Anabaptist' implied the rejection of a concept of Christendom, believing instead the church should take no responsibility for society whatsoever. Memory of the Anabaptists at Münster in 1534–1535, with its heresies, immorality and disorder, tarred with the same brush all those who held that baptism be reserved for those who had become believers in Christ. Indeed, so pervasive were those 'Münster' allegations that in 1656 a government propaganda pamphlet, 'published to justify some troopers who had roughed up a group gathered in Abingdon for John Pendarves' funeral', was entitled *Münster and Abingdon*![4] (Incidentally, I am the current holder of Pendarves' office as minister of Abingdon Baptist Church.)

The Dissenters, amongst whom the Baptists were a major component, wanted the reformed church to play its part in civil society, and while its disputes with the Church of England lay in sympathy with its Puritan wing, believing reformation had not gone far enough, they were largely ecclesiological in character. Together with the Independents (now we would describe them as Congregationalists), they believed that they had discerned a pattern of church government in the pages of the New Testament that called for the members of a church to comprise those 'committed, convinced and converted',[5] from within a parish, and that those members had the liberty to organise and gather themselves into a church under the guidance of the Risen Christ. Thus, they rejected the oversight of bishops from beyond the local congregation and, indeed, anything that resonated with the apostate Church of Rome whose authority all Reformers had rejected. The Church of England had inherited too much from its Roman predecessor for the Baptists' liking, and the first Baptists (and other Dissenters and Independents) felt they had no choice, therefore, but to form their own church and separate from the 'false' Church of England and its practice of indiscriminate infant baptism and admission to the church those who had not opted into the gathered community. Soon after James I came to the throne

[4] Barrington Raymond White, *The English Baptists of the Seventeenth Century* (Didcot: Baptist Historical Society, 1996), 8–9.

[5] Ibid., 12.

(in 1603), the Hampton Court Conference was convened to decide how far Puritan demands might be allowed. Its minimal reforms proved insufficient, and groups began to separate from the Church of England or else to gather churches within the parish system of the established church. For these 'Separatists', the sign of entry into this reformed church – patterned upon the New Testament, as they believed – was baptism, and the privileges that followed included access to the Lord's Table.

Such a polity threatened the unity not only of the Church of England but also of the state, and so the first half-century or more of Baptist life was one of persecution, albeit not consistently so. The first English Baptist congregation began as John Smyth (c. 1570–1612) and Thomas Helwys (c. 1550–1616) and their associates escaped to exile in Amsterdam in 1608. They were convinced Separatists in their churchmanship and Calvinist in their theology, and while the Mennonites in Amsterdam gave them a welcome, Smyth believed them to be in error on some doctrinal matters, so would not submit to their believers' baptism. Smyth subsequently came to reverse that conviction and reject a Calvinist doctrine of limited atonement, joining with the Mennonites in Amsterdam until his death. The conviction of this group sowed the seeds of that stream of English Baptist life called The General Baptists. Helwys, however, remained aloof from the Mennonites[6] and, with that division, took those in agreement with him back to London in 1612, founding the first Baptist church on English soil. They printed *A Short Declaration of the Mystery of Iniquity*, which for both Baptist and contemporary thinkers is significant in its appeal to King James for religious liberty and toleration of their beliefs and those of other dissenters. For his pains, Helwys was committed to Newgate Prison, where he died in 1616 of tuberculosis. At its conclusion, Helwys wrote that they had returned to England 'to lay down their lives in their own country for Christ and his truth'.[7] For a further twenty-five years this church and others like it had a precarious underground existence in England until in 1646 (after abolition of the episcopacy, towards the end of the civil war, and approaching the demise of monarchy and emergence of the Commonwealth), the old ties between church and state were almost gone. The deep unease that this produced helps to explain how, with the Restoration of monarchy in 1660, a second wave of persecution began, until the Toleration Act of 1689 saw a genuine but limited religious freedom for Baptists.

The story of Baptists in England is only half told with the General Baptists and their theology that was a deviation from classic Calvinism (though not a fundamental break from it). Seven churches subscribed to the London Confession of 1644[8] and provided the theological platform for the more Calvinistic Baptists who

[6] Helwys and his tiny group of followers had drawn up A Declaration of Faith (1611) in Amsterdam, which was followed closely by subsequent General Baptists, including the emphasis that 'God would have all men saved', contradicting Calvinist orthodoxy.

[7] Thomas Helwys, *A Short Declaration of the Mystery of Iniquity*, Richard Groves, ed., *Classics of Religious Liberty*, Vol. 1 (Macon, GA: Mercer University Press, 1998), 154.

[8] The CONFESSION OF FAITH Of those CHURCHES which are commonly (though falsely) called ANABAPTIST (1644).

grew out of the Independent congregation Henry Jacob had founded in London. They wanted a stricter interpretation of church polity, and so were allowed to leave the church in Southwark, that had been led by John Lathrop after Jacob emigrated to Virginia. By 1633 this congregation had become convinced of believers' baptism, while maintaining their Calvinistic doctrine of limited atonement. The London Confession of 1644 repeated with only the smallest modifications much of the Separatist Confession of 1596 and so traces its roots back to the Separatist (termed 'Brownist', after its leader, Robert Browne) controversies under Elizabeth. It differs from that earlier Confession, however, in its understanding of baptism, a lessening of the necessity for ministers to be appointed and administer the sacraments and the severing of church-state links. Not wishing to be mistaken for disloyal subjects, the Confession of 1644 affirms that the state should be obeyed 'in all lawful things commanded by them' and for them this meant being subject to 'the King and Parliament freely chosen by the Kingdome'.[9]

This stream of Baptist life, arising independently of the Smyth-Helwys General Baptists twenty or more years previously, maintained with greater fidelity its roots in Calvinism, and it is here that a doctrine of natural law derived from Calvin, although not expressed explicitly, shapes some of the polity of these early Particular Baptists, whose successors include the present-day Grace Baptists in England and Wales, as well as much Baptist life elsewhere in the world. The Second London Confession (1677), also of the Particular Baptists and adopted in 1689, borrows much from the Westminster Confession of Faith of 1646, adopted by Parliament and the official creed of English Presbyterians. Among the innovations was an article on Scripture (Chapter 1) which affirmed:

> The Holy Scripture is the only sufficient, certain and infallible rule of all saving Knowledge, Faith and Obedience; Although the light of Nature, and the works of Creation and Providence do so far manifest the goodness, wisdom and power of God, as to leave men inexcusable; yet are they not sufficient to give that knowledge of God and His will, which is necessary unto salvation.[10]

THE BAPTIST ADAPTATION OF CALVIN ON NATURAL LAW

This affirmation echoes the Western tradition as seen in Augustine and, later, in John Calvin.[11] In support of its doctrine of 'the light of nature', the Second London

9 William L. Lumpkin, *Baptist Confessions of Faith* (Valley Forge, PA: The Judson Press, 1969), 153–171, at 169; Articles XLVIII and XLIX respectively.

10 William Lumpkin, op cit., 248.

11 Brevity requires this chapter focusses upon Calvin's exposition of natural law, but recent Reformation historiography acknowledges that the development of Reformed theology has multiple sources, and is not solely derived from Calvin. Cf. Richard A. Muller, *Calvin and the Reformed Tradition* (Grand Rapids: Baker, 2012); and 'Diversity in the Reformed Tradition: A Historiographical Introduction', in Michael G. A. Haykin and Mark Jones, eds., *Drawn into Controversie: Reformed Theological Diversity*

Confession cites Romans 2.14–15, which is precisely where Augustine looks to in support of his 'natural law' in his Commentary on the Sermon on the Mount:

> For who but God has written the law of nature in the hearts of men? – that law concerning which the apostle says: 'For when the Gentiles, which have not the law, do by nature the things contained in the law … ' And therefore, as in the case of every rational soul, which thinks and reasons, even though blinded by passion, we attribute whatever in its reasoning is true, not to itself but to the very light of truth by which, however faintly, it is according to its capacity illuminated, so as to perceive some measure of truth by its reasoning.[12]

Calvin, in his discussion of the Ten Commandments in *The Institutes*, writes:

> Now that inward law, which we have above described as written, even engraved upon the hearts of all, in a sense asserts the very same things that are to be learned from the two Tables. For our conscience does not allow us to sleep a perpetual insensible sleep without an inner witness and monitor of what we owe God, without holding before us the difference between good and evil and thus accusing us when we fail in our duty. But man is so shrouded in the darkness of errors that he hardly begins to grasp through this natural law what worship is acceptable to God.[13]

Here, his understanding of *in lege naturali* is associated with conscience, and follows Augustine and Aquinas,[14] and in *The Institutes* he similarly quotes Romans 2.14–15 as evidence that '[t]here is nothing more common than for a man to be sufficiently instructed in a right standard of conduct by natural law (of which the apostle is here speaking)'.[15] Calvin puts severe limitations upon the efficacy of natural law in providing a clear picture of the will of God and ascribes to the Ten Commandments 'a clearer witness of what was too obscure in the natural law'. Nonetheless, there is a natural law written upon the conscience and derived from the created nature of humanity that is independent of specifically Judeo-Christian revelation.[16]

In adopting without much exception the 'natural law' of Calvin, these early Calvinistic Baptists imbibed a natural law ethic in much the same way as he did.

and Debates within Seventeenth-Century British Puritanism (Gottingen: Vandenhoek & Ruprecht, 2011), 17–30.

12 St Augustine, *De Serm. Dom. in Mont.*, 2.9.32 (*Commentary on the Sermon on the Mount*), cited in Jacqueline A. Laing and Russell Wilcox, eds., *The Natural Law Reader* (Chichester: Wiley-Blackwell, 2014), 94. Also in *Commentary on the Sermon on the Mount*, trans. William Findlay, from Philip Schaff, ed., *Nicene and Post-Nicene Fathers*, First Series, Vol. 6 (Buffalo, NY: Christian Literature Publishing Co., 1888).

13 John Calvin, *Institutes of the Christian Religion*, 2.7.1., Vol. 1, John T. McNeill, ed., Ford Lewis Battles, trans., *The Library of Christian Classics*, Vol. XX (Philadelphia, PA: Westminster Press, 1960), 367–368.

14 Thomas Aquinas, *Summa theologiae*, I.II, questions xci. 1–3; xciv; c. 1–5: here, the principles of the Decalogue are identified with those of natural reason.

15 *Institutes*, 2.2.22, Calvin, *Institutes of the Christian Religion*, op cit., 281.

16 cf. *Institutes*, 3.19.15, where Calvin argues for the natural law outworked in the temporal jurisdiction, the political kingdom.

David Little demonstrates how primitive Christians understood Christ as completing the way the world was meant to be.[17] The coming kingdom represented a decisive break with the old and a fulfilment of that for which the whole creation has been longing. However, after the waning of eschatological fervour, the church readily embraced the Stoic doctrine of natural law to help cope with the complications of the everyday world.

To develop a natural law theory, it is necessary to demonstrate that (1) it is possible to establish a set of empirical generalisations about human nature that is constant, both spatially (cross-culturally) and temporally (historically); (2) it is possible to move from a set of generalisations about how people do act to a set of prescriptions regarding how they ought to act; (3) the Christian must also be able to show in what sense human nature, although corrupted by sin, is still a reliable guide independent of Christian obligation; and (4) he must relate his generalisations about natural moral obligation to Christian belief and obligation. Calvin attempted to do just this. As Little puts it:

> If any contemporary 'rehabilitation' of Christian natural law theory is to be accomplished, it is safe to say that the way Calvin tried to solve some of the abiding problems demands careful attention.[18]

Calvin begins with the theological assumption that all things are ordered according to a divine design. Second, right human action is not fully possible without acknowledging from the heart the divine author of the design. What Calvin calls the 'moral law' or 'true and eternal rule of righteousness, prescribed for men of all nations and all times', is simply that God be worshipped by us all and we love one another (*Institutes*, 4.20.15), as we saw in Chapter 7. Moreover, all legal and moral regulations derive from and point towards the 'perpetual rule of love', which is the same as God's eternal law (*Institutes*, 2.8.11):

> For God's will is so much the highest rule of righteousness that whatever he wills, by the fact that he wills it, must be considered righteous ... But the will of God is not only free of all fault, but is the highest rule of perfection, and even the law of all laws.[19]

The second table of the Decalogue is 'engraved upon the hearts of all men' (*Institutes*, 2.8.1). He says that the prohibitions of the law recommend certain positive obligations and that these derive from the perpetual rule of love (*Institutes*, 2.8.9).

On the sixth commandment, 'You shall not kill,' Calvin says: 'The purpose of the commandment is: the Lord has bound mankind together by a certain unity; hence each man ought to concern himself with the safety of all' (*Institutes*, 2.8.39); that is,

[17] David Little, 'Calvin and the Prospects for a Christian Theory of Natural Law', in Gene H. Outka and Paul Ramsey, eds., *Norm and Context in Christian Ethics* (London: SCM Press, 1968), 175–197.

[18] Ibid., 177. [19] *Institutes*, 2.8.13; cf. 1.17.1.

the obligation is not simply to resist murder but to go out of our way to enhance the physical and spiritual well-being of our neighbour. On the eighth commandment, the aim is benevolence and cooperation (*Institutes*, 2.8.46). Neighbour 'includes even the most remote person. It includes the whole human race' (*Institutes*, 2.8.55; cf. 4.12.7). Calvin takes strong exception to the scholastic position on counsels of perfection which limited the more radical precepts of Christian love to monks.

Despite sin, there are certain vestiges, 'crumbs of righteousness', remaining to direct human action towards the good, enabling people to distinguish that good from its opposite. In other words, humanity continues to possess – minimally, to be sure – some conscious awareness of the demands of the law of love. As David Little observes:

> These crumbs or vestiges make up Calvin's explicit doctrine of natural law. Despite all the corruption, God has left His law implanted in man's nature for two reasons: to prod man in the direction of his true end, and, second, to convict and condemn him because he must be prodded and is not voluntarily disposed to act in accord with love of God and man.[20]

Calvin also accepts a qualified place for human reason. In matters of heavenly understanding, reason is 'utterly blind and stupid' (*Institutes*, 2.2.19), but in matters earthly or political, natural reason would appear to stand partly on its own. Men naturally affirm the duties of humankind, which were put into the second table of the Decalogue.

In other words, Calvin has a theory of natural law, but he is not interested in developing a self-contained, independent doctrine. He has

> a derivative theory of natural law, one that has always to be seen in a more inclusive theological and moral design. The theory starts from the notion of love (or mutuality, co-operation, benevolence) as the central ethical principle embodied in revelation, and then works back to make room for those generalisations of human nature considered the conditions or prerequisites for making the realization of love possible.[21]

Andrew Cameron summarises Calvin's approach to natural law by reference to the tradition which Calvin inherited:

> Aquinas had already described how divinely ordered moral reality is experienced by humanity as a 'natural law', which is graciously 'republished' for humanity by God in the Bible. Calvin was sufficiently persuaded by this approach to deploy it in broad outline. 'Moral law' expresses 'natural law'; ceremonial law was a specific instance of the moral law to order worship of God; and civil law was a specific instance of the moral law to order human desires and human society. It follows that the specific instances (the ceremonial law and civil law) are no longer directly relevant to Christians (although there remains much to be learnt in them about Christ and

[20] David Little, op cit., 186. [21] Ibid.

about equity). But those in Christ are regaining access to moral order, so moral law remains relevant to them.[22]

THE APPLICATION OF NATURAL LAW THINKING IN PRACTICE

Baptists, influenced by Calvin and Puritanism, would have agreed. If by 'natural law' we mean an underlying moral order, as revealed in Scripture, and summed up in Christ, that God calls us to utilise in shaping positive law, then Baptists have uncritically absorbed this. Calvin, and even more the Baptists of the seventeenth century, stands on the cusp of the rise of belief in an independent reason, which Aquinas does not recognise, and it is that which begins to undermine the doctrine of natural law as transmitted by Aquinas. By the time of the Enlightenment, this understanding of reason has grown to full flower, and natural law is cut free entirely from the doctrine of general revelation that Calvin still embraces. Baptists disagree today with any notion of a universally present set of moral beliefs embedded in what it means to be human in so far as they may disagree with the contemporary and secular idea that the origins of those beliefs lie in rationality alone. One significant expression of a secular conception would be the idea of universal human rights as secular values for a godless age.[23]

Baptists, in their origins, and still, to some extent, today, would want to tie that morality to the general revelation of God's nature available to all humanity (and thus, the appeal to Romans 1), which revelation is seen most particularly in Jesus Christ, and more generally in Scripture. This, in fact, would be much closer to Aquinas than Baptists would generally acknowledge and provides a way of retaining natural law as a Baptist conviction. It also relativises the universality of natural law, for while there may be some aspects that are widely recognised, cultural and historical particularities serve to colour what natural law prescribes, and for Baptists like Colwell and McClendon, so fatally undermines what natural law, in its contemporary form, asserts, that they dismiss it accordingly. If there is no commonly recognised agreement about the common good, which natural law assumes, then, as MacIntyre argues, all ethics are inherently tradition-dependent. Claims to the position of privileged foundation that Baptists would make for Scripture, and especially the person of Jesus Christ, will be readily dismissed by both secularists and adherents to other religions, yet here is where Baptists would lay claim to natural law: the lesser light – derived from tradition and culture – of the great light of God's will and purpose for humankind revealed in the Old and New Testaments. As the Declaration of Principle of the Baptist Union of

[22] Andrew J.B. Cameron, 'How "Ethics" Works: An Engagement with John Calvin', in Mark D. Thompson, ed., *Engaging with Calvin* (Nottingham: Apollos, 2009), 230–253, at 248.

[23] Cf. David McIlroy, 'Human Rights Theory: Fit for Purpose, Fundamentally Flawed or Reformable?', *Law and Justice: The Christian Law Review* 173 (2014): 129–144, at 133; Francesca Klug, *Values for a Godless Age: The Story of the United Kingdom's New Bill of Rights* (Harmondsworth: Penguin, 2000).

Great Britain puts it: 'Christ is sole and absolute authority . . . As revealed in the Holy Scriptures'; this is a commitment echoed in most other Baptist creedal statements.

What follows offers three case studies on how Baptists have exhibited this commitment to natural law: religious liberty; church-state relations; and the bearing of arms.

Freedom of Religion

While the practice of believers' baptism and congregational independence has come to characterise Baptist polity in the popular mind, a third important strand to Baptist thought is that of religious liberty. In the face of a national state church hegemony, the early Dissenters argued that the king and Parliament had no authority over the individual's conscience or religious convictions. For them, including the Baptists, (perhaps, especially the Baptists) the head of the church was not King James, but Jesus Christ. The church gathered under that lordship, as discerned in Scripture and mediated by the whole church prayerfully meeting together, and demanded freedom from both bishop and magistrate in matters of religious convictions and practice. Such liberty from state intervention was not extended to matters that properly belonged to the temporal realm (although Baptists were sometimes mistakenly believed to hold to such political radical views), and they willingly owed their allegiance to monarch and Parliament in such matters. But when the issue was one of religious practice, freedom of worship and association, church government and doctrinal conviction, Baptists argued for liberty for each congregation and freedom from the state's interference. They wanted to appoint their own 'godly' ministers, for instance, rather than receive the priest appointed by patron or bishop: 'How blessed and comfortable a thing were it, for a holy people so to elect their pastor that should lead them . . . So should a godly people have holy pastors over them, whom they would all love and reverence.'[24]

The *Propositions and Conclusions*, of 1612, is a document that issues from the Baptists who remained with John Smyth in Amsterdam after Thomas Helwys had removed his party back to London (although written after Smyth's death). Article 83 of the document states: '[T]he office of the magistrate, is of a disposition or permissive ordinance of God for the good of mankind . . . that justice and civility, may be preserved among men.'[25] However, this is followed by the statement, in Article 84:

> [T]he magistrate is not by virtue of his office to meddle with religion, or matters of conscience, to force or compel men to this or that form of religion, or doctrine: but to leave Christian religion free to every man's conscience, and to handle only civil transgressions (Rom. xiii), injuries and wrongs of man against man, in murder, adultery, theft etc., for Christ is the only king and lawgiver of the church and conscience (James iv.12).[26]

24 Thomas Helwys, A *Short Declaration of the Mystery of Iniquity*, op cit., 66–67.

25 William Lumpkin, op cit., 139–140. 26 Ibid., 140.

This conviction about the role of the magistrate, and the limits of its authority, is already present in the confession of the Mennonite group in Amsterdam, amongst which the Smyth and Helwys group took refuge upon their arrival from England, and which eventually most of Smyth's contingent joined after his death. The Waterland Confession of 1580 was republished at Smyth's request in 1610.[27] Article XXXVII of this acknowledged that 'it is our duty to reverence magistracy . . . and to show to it honour and obedience in all things not contrary to the word of God'.[28] However, for the Mennonites, they themselves would not seek to exercise this office: '[H]ence we withdraw ourselves from such offices and administrations. And yet we do not wish that just and moderate power should in any manner be despised or condemned.'[29]

So, reverence for the magistracy in all civil matters was always a Baptist principle, but the range of the magistracy's powers did not extend to religious matters. This separation of religious conviction from the authority of the state, presented a direct confrontation with the prevailing principle of *cuius regio eius religio* (the religion of the state follows the religion of the monarch) and thus amounted to treason. In the febrile political atmosphere of the early seventeenth century, and especially following the failed coup by Guy Fawkes and his Catholic co-religionists in 1605, any expression of religious dissent from the prevailing Church of England settlement achieved under Elizabeth (and confirmed under the Hampton Court Conference of 1604) brought only greater curtailment of liberty for Separatists like Smyth and Helwys, as well as for Catholics. To argue that the state had no jurisdiction over the conscience, or in religious questions, rooted in an implicit doctrine of 'natural law' discernable for Christians in Scripture, was a dangerous political act. Hence the flight of the Gainsborough congregation to Amsterdam, and the risks taken by Helwys in bringing his group back to Spitalfields, amounted to political as much as religious actions. In the eyes of the seventeenth-century English state, it was the duty of the king and Parliament to impose religious conformity upon the population.

In writing *The Mystery of Iniquity*, then, Thomas Helwys was taking a huge risk – one that ultimately led to his imprisonment in Newgate. In it he writes very much as a man of his times, polemical in style and vigorous in prose (the work has no great literary merits), and targets those with whom Helwys disagrees:

> It reflects the apocalyptic interest of the time and quotes the Bible in ways that surprise and discomfort most contemporary readers. The theology might not be of the highest quality but it is undoubtedly passionate. These were days when people were prepared to kill and be killed for such matters.[30]

27 A Brief Confession of the Principal Articles of the Christian Faith, prepared by John de Rys and Lubbert Gerrits, Ministers of the Divine Word among the Protestants who, in the Belgian Confederacy, are called Mennonites.

28 William Lumpkin, op cit., 3–4. 29 Ibid., 64.

30 Brian Haymes, 'Thomas Helwys' The Mystery of Iniquity: Is it still Relevant in the Twenty-First Century?', in Anthony R. Cross and Nicholas J. Wood, eds., *Exploring Baptist Origins*, Vol. 1 (Oxford: Centre for Baptist History and Heritage Studies, Regent's Park College, 2010), 60–77, at 65.

However, what is remarkable about this work and why it has continued to draw legal attention is that in the midst of his condemnation of views he considers heretical, Helwys argues that, nonetheless, those holding to them should be afforded liberty:

> For men's religion to God is between God and themselves. The King shall not answer for it. Neither may the King judge between God and man. Let them be heretics, Turks, Jews or whatsoever, it appertains not to the earthly power to punish them in the least measure.[31]

The principle of religious liberty is unmistakably asserted here, to be afforded to even those with whom he so vigorously disagreed, be they Catholic, Jew or Turk (i.e. Muslim). What is so remarkable is not only the assertion itself, but also the fact that it was made when it seems no one else was discussing it. There may have been some influence from a fellow lawyer at Gray's Inn where Helwys had studied (Helwys was an educated layman, and lawyer, rather than churchman and theologian): namely, the Italian Protestant Alberico Gentili (1552–1608), who emigrated to England in 1580, where he later became Regius Professor of Civil Law at Oxford. He was a defender of religious legal liberty and wrote in about 1590 that '[r]eligion is a matter of the mind and will, which is always accompanied by freedom . . . the soul has no master save God only, who alone can destroy the soul . . . Religion ought to be free'.[32]

Helwys may have been familiar with Gentili's work, but he certainly wrote from personal experience of the intolerance of the state towards his own Separatist convictions and the freedom he had known in Amsterdam where toleration was political policy. While we must recognise the debt owed by Helwys to Anabaptist ideas (mediated via the Mennonites), he remains essentially faithful to the Calvinist-Puritan-Separatist tradition from which he came, and not least in his attitude to war. Unlike his Anabaptist or Mennonite hosts in Amsterdam, Helwys will admit magistrates to the body of believers without giving up their rule, and he will allow their use of the sword, especially in defending the religious liberty that is a necessary prerequisite of a social order that allows religious toleration. Ultimately, however, in his appeal for religious liberty, its foundation is his Calvinist commitment to the sovereign rule of Christ – the king over the human conscience, and under whose sway even the earthly King James must submit:

> Then let our lord the king in all happiness and prosperity sit in his princely throne of that mighty kingdom of Great Britain . . . and let all those the king's enemies that would not that he should reign over them be slain before him. And let our Lord Jesus Christ in power and majesty sit upon David's throne . . . and let our lord the king be his subject.[33]

31 Thomas Helwys, *A Short Declaration of the Mystery of Iniquity*, op cit., 53.

32 Gentili, *De iure Belli*, Book 1, Chapter 9, cited by Malcolm D. Evans, *Religious Liberty and International Law in Europe* (Cambridge: Cambridge University Press, 1997), 35–37.

33 Thomas Helwys, *A Short Declaration of the Mystery of Iniquity*, op cit., 39.

It is not derived from an appeal to any notion of universal human rights upon which Helwys builds his argument, but rather from the way in which Helwys encounters Jesus in the Scriptures and, thus, his understanding of God's nature, and the natural law that follows. Since Jesus is not coercive in these matters, neither is God: 'It is the sovereignty of the non-compelling covenant seeking God that guarantees the religious and political freedom of all people. No king may take what God has given.'[34] As the seventeenth century continued, later Baptists came to set limits upon Helwys' radical position on religious liberty. The Particular Baptist Confession of 1677 professes liberty of belief derived from 'the light of nature', so long as it is not contrary to Scripture, 'not prescribed in the Holy Scripture'.[35] However, the General Baptists in 1678 stated, in Article XLVI of their creedal statement, *Of Liberty of Conscience*:

> The Lord Jesus Christ ... is only Lord of Conscience ... he would not have the consciences of men in bondage to, or imposed upon, by any usurpation, tyranny or command whatsoever, contrary to his revealed will in his word ... And therefore the obedience to any command, or decree, that is not revealed in, or consonant to his word, in the holy oracles of scripture, is a betraying of the true liberty of conscience ... an absolute blind obedience, destroys liberty of conscience, and reason also, it being repugnant to both.[36]

This allowed only a limited religious freedom to prevail. This appeal to natural law, or 'the light of nature', served to demonstrate that religious toleration was not a defence of licentious anarchy. However, alongside the appeal to natural law as a foundation for the rule of Christ in matters of conscience, there also came an appeal to the same 'light of nature' from which might be derived the principles by which a Christian society might be ordered, with a resulting tension between competing 'goods'.

This tension remains today: some Baptists privilege a radical religious freedom of conscience, with its concomitant tendency to individualism, while others seek limits upon religious plurality in service of the good ordering of a society that reflects Christian principles. Thus some will support the religious rights of Muslims to worship and build places to do so, while others are fearful of an erosion of 'Christian Britain' and argue against such liberty. John Coffey argues that this radical Separationist view and its absolute religious freedoms, and the other extreme, espoused by a few Baptists caught up in the mid-seventeenth-century Fifth Monarchists, of a complete absence of liberty and pluralism, both reflect minority viewpoints.[37] The majority view, he argues, has been the 'Christian nation' view (Christian Britain or Christian America) with the assumption that Christianity

34 Brian Haymes, op cit., 74.

35 William Lumpkin, op cit., 280, 'Second London Confession, Ch. XXII.1'. 36 Ibid., 331–332.

37 John Coffey, 'From Helwys to Leland: Baptists and Religious Tolerance in England and America, 1612–1791', in D. Bebbington, ed., *Studies in Baptist History and Thought: The Gospel in the World* (Milton Keynes: Paternoster, 2000), 21–22.

should be at the heart of the political nation, discriminating against those who hold another faith or none. In their differing ways, each holds to a variation on the concept of natural law, even if in its origins, Baptist polity held to the radical liberty that has now been adopted by post-Enlightenment secular society as a means of reducing inter-community strife.

Church-State Relations and Human Rights

The separation of church and state finds its contemporary formal expression in, for instance, the constitution of the Baptist Union of South Africa;[38] the Canadian National Baptist Convention also argues for the protection of the churches' liberties by the state;[39] and the moderate American Baptist Churches USA affirms that it is 'committed to religious liberty and to the separation of church and state'.[40] However, the foundation document for the trustee status of the Baptist Union of Great Britain is an Act of Parliament, and it is thus enforceable in the civil courts,[41] which some may consider leads to a blurring of the separation so dearly held by Baptists: British Baptists, then, look to the state and its laws to regulate and protect their legal rights.

Moreover, the separation of church and state does not imply an indifference to wider society. Baptists seek to be 'prophetic' in their public statements, with British Baptists joining the Methodist and United Reformed churches in its Joint Public Issues Team. Yet, the political convictions expressed in such denominational statements cannot be binding upon the churches in membership with the Union. Each member church of the Union retains its liberty of conscience and governmental freedom on the basis of the principle of the autonomy of the local church and its congregation.[42]

What began as a theologically grounded plea for religious freedom has been transformed into a dimension of a much broader field of human rights. Two decades after Helwys, Roger Williams (d. 1684) – at least for some period of his ministry, a Baptist – enlarged the freedoms applied in the settlement of Rhode Island that he founded in 1632 from religious liberty to 'earthly' matters, arguing for the rights of the indigenous Indians to the land upon which the settlement was built. The community he founded was arguably the first place in modern times where religious liberty was assured through separation of citizenship and conscience. In 1640 its leading freemen declared their intention 'still to hold forth liberty of conscience'. To this freedom was added a recognition of the rights of property owed to the natives he encountered, thus recognising their intrinsic humanity at a time when many considered them subhuman.

[38] BUSA: Bylaws. 4.2.7 [39] CNBC: Constitution, 3, Statement of Faith, Article XVII.

[40] ABC-USA: Identity Statement 1998. [41] Baptist and Congregational Trusts Act 1951.

[42] Paul Goodliff, 'Baptist Church Polity and Practice', *Law and Justice: The Christian Law Review* 168 (2012): 5–21.

In particular, it was a Leveller, Richard Overton (d. 1664), with links to the Baptists, who first argued for human rights for all human persons, including religious liberty, economic rights and full participation in society. This came to full expression in his *An Appeal to the Free People* of 1647. In this work he argues for three rights: to religious liberty; to life, including the basic necessities of life; and to dignity in community. Like Helwys, Overton argues that these rights be extended to everyone, including Catholics, Jews and Turks (i.e. Muslims), as well as his own Dissenting community. As one scholar puts it:

> The full concept of human rights was first developed and articulated during the free-church struggle for the right of religious liberty in Puritan England in the 1640s by the Anabaptist/Baptist Richard Overton ... His arguments are based upon Scripture as authoritative ... He also argued from natural law, which had been articulated for centuries prior to the Puritan period.[43]

In other words, Overton argues for freedom from religious coercion, from government-established church and from taxation for religion. He advocates freedom of the press; the right of prisoners not to be tortured, starved or extorted; and various legal rights. In terms of the right to life, he argues for the care of widows, orphans, the aged and handicapped, and the right of the poor to maintain their portion of land. He also maintains that irrespective of belief, there should be rights to petition Parliament and to participate in Parliament irrespective of religious conviction.

Importantly, for natural law thinking, in the earlier *An Arrow Against All Tyrants*, of 12 October 1646, Overton writes:

> For as by nature no man may abuse, beat, torment, or afflict himself, so by nature no man may give that power to another ... For by nature we are the sons of Adam, and from him have derived a natural propriety, right and freedom, which only we require.[44]

Subsequently, Progressive Baptists in the southern United States, such as David Barrow and William H. Brisbane, called for the emancipation of slaves in the early nineteenth century, while in the northern states in the 1830s, Freewill Baptists and Regular Baptists advocated the abolition of slavery on the grounds of moral law (natural law) and human rights. The English Baptist William Knibb decried slavery in Jamaica on similar grounds.[45]

In 1939 all three major US Baptist groups jointly issued *The American Baptist Bill of Rights*, which upheld basic human rights to freedom of religion and personal spirituality, regardless of faith commitment. The Baptist World Alliance, the umbrella body for Baptists worldwide, was granted NGO status at the United Nations, and this

43 Glen H. Stassen, 'Human Rights', in William A. Dyrness and Veli-Matti Karkkainen, eds., *Global Dictionary of Theology: A Resource for the Worldwide Church* (Downers Grove, IL: Inter Varsity Press, 2008), 405–413, at 406.

44 Richard Overton, *An Arrow Against All Tyrants*, 1646: www.constitution.org/lev/eng_lev_05.htm.

45 cf. William H. Brackney, *Historical Dictionary of Baptists* (Lanham, ML: Scarecrow Press, 2009).

has facilitated a steady flow of information about human rights, and their violation, and given a forum to express concerns to various governments around the world. The alliance identifies as one of its prime purposes to recognise fundamental human rights, especially those of religious liberty.[46] Baptist Conventions and Unions around the world also carry human rights as a major concern, and this is often derived from both theological convictions about human dignity and the image of God in humankind, and Enlightenment convictions about the just society. Thus, the Baptist Union of South Africa affirms 'the principle of religious liberty' and respect for 'Private conscience'.[47] In the mix is often an implicit natural law ethic.

If it can be admitted that one fountainhead of human rights, at least, lies with these early Baptist advocates of religious liberty and that they derived those convictions from an implicit natural law ethic, mediated through Scripture, then we might argue that natural law continues to influence profoundly this important and contentious area of international relations and public life.

John Finnis, a proponent of natural law in relation to natural rights, delineates four meanings of 'natural' in natural law:

> (a) that the relevant standards (principles and norms) are not 'positive', that is, are directive prior to any positing by individual decision or group choice or convention; (b) that the relevant standards are 'higher' than positive laws, conventions, and practices, that is, provide the premises for critical evaluation and endorsement or justified rejection of or disobedience to such laws, conventions, or practices; (c) that the relevant standards conform to the most demanding requirements of critical reason and are objective, in the sense that a person who fails to accept them as standards for judgement is in error; (d) that adherence to the relevant standards tends systematically to promote human flourishing, the fulfilment of human individuals and communities.[48]

The origin of such 'natural' laws is not found in some relation to 'the laws of nature', meaning the scientific laws that govern the operation of the physical world, nor is it concerned with some original state of grace, some golden age that must be recovered. Rather, it means that such is the character of human well-being and flourishing, that these norms and principles from which 'positive' laws are derived are inherently fitting to that end. Baptists would have situated the origin in a divine and created source of human existence: that human flourishing is precisely as it is because of the gracious good will of a benevolent God, revealed in Jesus Christ and recorded in Holy Scripture. However, Finnis argues that natural law does not explicitly rely upon such transcendent origins.

We can see some of the basic human goods that constitute human flourishing, and so elements of natural law thinking – knowledge, life, liberty of thought and

[46] BWA: Constitution, Article II. [47] BUSA: Bylaws, 4.2.7.

[48] John Finnis, 'Natural Law', in *Reason in Action: Collected Essays*, Vol. 1 (Oxford: Oxford University Press, 2011), 199–211; also cited in Laing and Wilcox, op. cit., 239.

freedom from unwarranted restrictions on the part of the state, friendship and family life – already enshrined in the early Baptist confessions. Liberty of thought we have recounted above, but note also how in the Propositions and Conclusions of 1612, Article 90 provides: 'That in the necessities of the church, and poor brethren, all things are to be had in common (Acts iv.32), yea and that one church is to administer to another in time of need.'[49] This reflects a notion that there should be a basic right to sufficient goods for survival, albeit derived from the example of the church in the Book of Acts in the New Testament. Similarly, derived theologically from their understanding of human nature, the Amsterdam congregation confessed to every human being created equally in God's image (thus in a primitive way anticipating *universal* and so *equal* human rights), and that 'as there is in all creatures a natural inclination to their young ones, to do them good, so there is in the Lord toward man; for every spark of goodness in the creature is infinitely good in God'.[50] This 'natural' inclination to care for our offspring reflects something of the natural promotion of human flourishing, whether we understand its origins to lie in divine will, or evolutionary biology.

Given this conception of natural law that is 'above' positive laws that hold sway in any human society, it comes as no surprise to see one of the most famous and influential Baptists of the twentieth century, Martin Luther King Jr., arguing for obedience to positive laws that cohere with a 'moral law or the law of God', and disobedience to laws that breach that moral or natural law. Writing from Birmingham City jail on 16 April 1963, where he has been incarcerated for civil disobedience, he states:

> [T]here are two types of laws: There are just laws and there are unjust laws. I would be the first to advocate obeying just laws. One has not only a legal but moral responsibility to obey just laws. Conversely, one has a moral responsibility to disobey unjust laws. I would agree with Saint Augustine that 'An unjust law is no law at all'.

Moreover:

> How does one determine when a law is just or unjust? A just law is a man-made code that squares with the moral law or the law of God. An unjust law is a code that is out of harmony with the moral law. To put it in the terms of Saint Thomas Aquinas, an unjust law is a human law that is not rooted in eternal and natural law. Any law that uplifts human personality is just. Any law that degrades human personality is unjust. All segregation statutes are unjust because segregation distorts the soul and damages the personality ... I can urge men to obey the 1954 decision of the Supreme Court because it is morally right, and I can urge them to disobey segregation ordinances because they are morally wrong.[51]

[49] William Lumpkin, op cit., 141. [50] Ibid., 127–128, proposition 24.

[51] Text taken from the public domain publication listed at: www.afsc.org/ht/d/ContentDetails/i/4019, cited in Laing and Wilcox, op cit., 237.

Whether Baptist ethicists and theologians have been entirely happy or not with natural law playing any part in their schemata, it would appear that at a more vernacular level, Baptists have appealed to a notion of some 'higher law', taking precedence over positive laws, when it comes to religious freedom, moral conduct and civil liberties.

The Bearing of Arms

We move now to a third sphere of concern in which to test Baptist convictions about natural law: their attitude to bearing arms. Unlike the continental Anabaptists, English Baptists were not uniformly, or even predominantly, pacifist, although they began sharing their Mennonite hosts' convictions. The Waterland Confession (1580), in common with other Anabaptist believers, rejects the role of magistrate as befitting a believer. On the one hand, 'Government or the civil Magistrate is a necessary ordinance of God [citing Romans 13.1,3,4,6] instituted for the government of common human society and the preservation of natural life and civil good' and is so worthy of prayerful support. On the other hand:

> This civil government the Lord Jesus did not institute in his spiritual kingdom, the church of the New Testament, nor did he join it to the offices of his church [citing 1 Corinthians 12.28; Ephesians 4.11]: nor did he call his disciples or followers to royal, ducal or other power; nor did he teach they should seize it and rule in a lordly manner; much less did he give to the members of his church the law [citing Matthew 20.25–28; Luke 22.25–27] agreeable to such office or dominion: but everywhere they are called away from it (which voice heard from heaven [citing Matthew 17.5] ought to be heeded) to the imitation of his harmless life [citing John 8.12; 10.27] and his footsteps bearing the cross [citing Hebrews 12.2, 3; 1 Peter 2.21–23], and in which nothing is less in evidence than an earthly kingdom, power and sword. When all these things are carefully weighed . . . they agree either badly or plainly not at all, hence we withdraw ourselves from such offices and administrations. And yet we do not wish that just and moderate power should in any manner be despised or condemned.[52]

This echoed the influential Mennonite Dordrecht Confession of 1632, which was representative of a great many Anabaptists. The confession confirmed the benefits of the magistracy (Article XIII) and provided that they should be prayed for, and that those who exercise it should find earthly and eternal reward for their just work. However, it also provided that those adhering to this confession were 'not to "return evil for evil, nor railing for railing", but to "put up the sword into the sheath", or, as the prophet foretold, "beat them into ploughshares"'. It continues: 'From this we see that, according to the example, life and doctrine of Christ, we are not to do wrong, or

[52] The Waterland Confession, Article XXXVII: William Lumpkin, op cit., 63–64.

cause offence or vexation to anyone'; and 'if we are struck in our "right cheek, rather to turn the other also", than revenge ourselves, or return the blow' (Article XIV).[53]

The Short Confession of 1610 was written by Thomas Helwys to distinguish his church from the group under Smyth that remained in Amsterdam, and which was seeking to join the Mennonites (unlike Helwys' group that intended to remain now in London). It argues that Christ in his kingly office

> governeth the hearts of the faithful by his Holy Spirit and Word; he taketh them into his protection, he covereth them under the shadow of his wings, he armeth them with spiritual weapons for the spiritual warfare against all their enemies ... And ... do change their fleshly weapons, namely their swords into shares, and their spears into scythes, do lift up no sword, neither hath nor consent to fleshly battle.[54]

With regard to the Magistracy, the Short Confession rejects disciples being

> worldly kings, princes, potentates or magistrates ... rather they are called of him ... to the following of his unarmed and unweaponed life, and of his cross-bearing footsteps ... It beseemeth not Christians to administer these offices; therefore we avoid such offices and administrations, notwithstanding by no means thereby willing to despise or condemn reasonable discreet magistrates, nor to place him in less estimation than he is described by the Holy Ghost, of Paul.'[55]

The Propositions and Conclusions produced by the followers of Smyth, those who remained in Amsterdam in 1612, say much the same (Proposition 85).

However, the Somerset Confession of 1656 is a document belonging to the second-generation Baptists. This is a Particular Baptist confession that arose from meetings of the Somerset Association between 1653 and 1657. It is in part a response to the many Baptists attracted by a new movement which threatened the stability of their churches and reduction in their numbers – namely, that of the Quakers, with George Fox himself on a tour of the South West in 1655. In the Somerset Confession, we find that the prohibition on bearing the sword is missing. Article XLIV repeats the earlier belief that the 'ministry of civil justice (being for the praise of them that do well, and punishment of evildoers) is an ordinance of God, and that it is the duty of the saints to be subject thereunto not only for fear but for conscience sake'. But there is no corresponding condemnation of the sword. Presumably, after so many Baptists had found themselves in leading positions in Cromwell's New Model Army, such a prohibition would have seemed hypocritical if insisted upon once the Civil War was won. The flurry of church planting in the 1640s was in part a result of the ministry of Baptists acting as officers in the parliamentary forces.

By the time of the Standard Confession of 1660, the concern is to dismiss those rumours of armed insurrection and threats to the magistracy which were being falsely circulated:

[53] The Dordrecht Confession 1632: William Lumpkin, op cit., 75.

[54] A Short Confession, 1610, Article 18: William Lumpkin, op cit., 107.

[55] Ibid., 112.

> We do utterly, and from our very hearts, in the Lord's fear, declare against all those wicked, and devilish reports, and reproaches, falsely cast upon us, as though some of us (in and about the City of London) had lately gotten knives, hooked knives and the like, & great store of Arms besides what was given forth by order of Parliament, intending to cut the throats of such as were contrary minded to us in matters of Religion.[56]

After the Restoration of the monarchy and the accession of Charles II, and during the early years of the suppression of Baptists, 1662–1689, the Second London Confession was reaffirmed in 1689. This document, in the guise of the Keach Confession, found its way also into North America, where it became the basis of the dominant early Calvinist Confession in the New World, the Philadelphia Confession. This provides that it is 'lawful for Christians to Accept, and Execute the Office of a *Magistrate*, when called thereunto; in the management whereof, as they ought especially to maintain Justice, and Peace, according to the wholesome Laws of each Kingdome, and Commonwealth: so for that end they may lawfully now under the New Testament wage war upon just and necessary occasions.'[57]

The permission to bear arms has now been granted, and the pacifist tradition of the early Baptists, connected to their Mennonite fellow-believers, is redundant. The same is found in the Orthodox Creed of the General Baptists in Buckinghamshire, Hertfordshire, Bedfordshire and Oxford, which met on 30 January 1678. It was published in 1679. Article XLV allows Christians to hold the office of magistrate and provides:

> God hath given the power of the sword, into the hands of all lawful magistrates, for the defence and encouragement of them that do well, and for the punishment of evildoers, and for the maintenance of justice, and peace, according to the wholesome laws of each kingdom, and commonwealth, and that they may wage war upon just and necessary occasions.[58]

There is implicit here the idea of there being just laws, which allow war. The 'natural law', upon which positive laws should rely, produces 'wholesome' legislation, and there are just occasions when war is allowable – there also being by implication, unjust wars that are contrary to natural law.

The pacifist convictions were never entirely absent. Baptists were amongst the many conscientious objectors who refused to bear arms in the First World War, and a significant if minority pacifist viewpoint is held today by the Baptist Peace Fellowship. Similarly, British Baptists were vociferous in denouncing the invasion of Iraq under Tony Blair, and hold as policy that the independent nuclear deterrent represented by the Trident missile system should not be renewed. However, these convictions reflect broader social changes and mores rather than specifically Baptist

56 The General Baptist Standard Confession 1660: William Lumpkin, op cit., 234.
57 The London Confession of 1677 and 1688: William Lumpkin, op cit., 284.
58 The Orthodox Creed, 1679: William Lumpkin, op cit., 331.

doctrines, for, at the same time, the Baptist Union of Great Britain is unequivocally supportive of those forty or so Baptist ministers who serve as commissioned military chaplains. Indeed, in the southern United States, the Southern Baptist Convention (SBC) has become almost synonymous with the Republican Party and fully supportive of the right to bear arms. In these southern states, the SBC has almost the reach, if by no means the status, of a national church, and reflects the full identity of the church with both magistracy and the execution of warfare.

All this seems to reflect a natural law conviction that what constitutes my good is the common good. As Alisdair MacIntyre suggests:

> The life that expresses our shared human nature is a life of practical enquiry and practical reasoning, and we cannot but presuppose the precepts of natural law in asking and answering those fundamental questions through our everyday activities and practices. Generally and characteristically, the social relationships through which we are able to learn how to identify our individual and common goods correctly and adequately are those relationships governed and defined by the precepts of natural law.[59]

MacIntyre argues that in place of general adherence to natural law, with its identity between individual and common goods, the culture of the United States, in its late modernist expression, has developed a culture of individualism and mere self-regard when it comes to choices. Hence, the readiness to be litigious: 'It is notorious that ours has become a society of incessant litigation, in which plain persons can all too rarely hope to resolve matters of dispute by appeal among themselves to evident and agreed moral principles.'[60] Such readiness to resort to law was forbidden by the early Baptist confessions. The first General Baptist confession to reflect the views of more than one congregation is *The Faith and Practice of Thirty Congregations, Gathered According to the Primitive Pattern*, of 1651. It states:

> [S]ome men amongst the brotherhood, who are able to judge in causes of difference that may arise betwixt them in the Church, may be approved or appointed to put an end thereto without partiality, that there may be no unnecessary strivings in the Law to vex one another; 1 Cor. 6:5,6,7.[61]

This at least implies that there is a moral law, though 'natural law' is not specified as expressing it, discernible to ordinary men and women. This moral law allows them to act justly without resort to litigation, but rather in accordance with the prohibition on Christians litigating amongst themselves, a prohibition derived from Paul's writings.

In point of fact, the associated ideas of divine law and morality also surface in the regulatory instruments of Baptist churches. For example, Christ is 'the sole and

59 Alasdair MacIntyre, 'Theories of Natural Law in the Culture of Advanced Modernity', in E.B. McLean, ed., *Common Truths: New Perspectives on Natural Law* (Wilmington, DE: ISI Books, 2004), 123–128, cited in Laing and Wilcox, op cit., 364.

60 Ibid., 366.

61 Thirty Congregations, Article 67: William Lumpkin, op cit., 186.

absolute authority in all matters pertaining to faith and practice'; and '[e]ach Church has liberty, under the guidance of the Holy Spirit, to interpret and administer His Laws'.[62] Again, as a revelation of God, the Holy Bible is part of 'the constitutions and laws' of a Convention, or 'the rule of church law'.[63] Finally, the 'one another passages' from Scripture are a key foundation for the rights and duties of Baptists living under a church covenant; these include the Golden Rule of historical natural law thinking.[64]

CONCLUSION

Unlike the Catholic tradition, which holds to an unbroken link with Augustine and Aquinas, and in which natural law remains an explicit foundation for ethics and the philosophy of law, Baptists have not expressed their understanding of a 'natural light' in so clear a way in their founding confessions. They are more likely to find support from Scripture, and in common with the times, use it as a reservoir of 'proof texts'. However, natural law is implicit, both in what the confessions affirm and from their communities' commitment to Calvin's theology, which includes a natural law foundation to morality. Broadly supportive of the state, except where its policies impose matters of religious observance and conscience upon its citizens, Baptists have found in both their appeal for universal human rights (albeit accompanied by an equal appeal to universal human obligations, under God, to seek the common good, rather than simply to assert individual rights) and in the defence of them by war, a natural law foundation for this area of the common life that particularly concerns them.

The continuing force of this implicit natural law can be seen in the legal instruments that some Baptists apply, or in their stated concerns and aims. So, for instance, the Baptist World Alliance, the body that represents 232 Conventions and Unions globally, is committed to 'defending human rights and justice',[65] and the

62 Baptist Union of Great Britain: Constitution, 1.3.1; and the Baptist Model Trusts for Churches 2003, 2.8.1.

63 National Baptist Convention USA: Constitution, Article X.5. See also American Baptist Churches in the USA: Bylaw, Prologue: the Bible is 'the inspired Word of God [and] final written authority'; each body is 'to order its life in accordance with the Scriptures'; Canadian National Baptist Convention: Constitution, 3: Statement of Faith: the Bible 'reveals the principles by which God judges us' and is 'the supreme standard by which all human conduct, creeds, and religious opinions should be tried'.

64 R. Stanton Norman, *The Baptist Way: Distinctiveness of a Baptist Church* (Nashville, TN: Broadman and Holman, 2005), 118: the 'one another' passages from Scripture express the New Testament characteristics of Christian relationships; they include: to love one another, as Christ loves us (John 13.34); to submit one to another (Ephesians 5.21); to exhort one another (Hebrews 3.13; 10.25); to comfort one another (2 Corinthians 1.4); to consider others as more important than ourselves (Philippians 2.3); to suffer when one suffers and rejoice when another is honoured (1 Corinthians 12.25–26); to instruct one another (Romans 15.14); to admonish one another (Colossians 3.16); to nurture one another toward spiritual maturity measured by the life and ministry of Jesus (Ephesians 4.13); and to restore gently those who sin (Galatians 6.1).

65 Baptist World Alliance website: 2010–2015 Quinquennial Ministry Initiatives, 6.

Australian Baptist Union of Victoria would be typical in affirming: 'Baptists . . . have opposed all forms of religious coercion . . . we seek to affirm diversity even among our own churches.'[66]

That such policies are now widely affirmed in Western democracies, for instance, is in a significant way a result of Baptists' early appeals for religious liberty. That such rights and liberties are still not universally practised, however, or even advocated, demonstrates what both Aristotle and Aquinas understood: the prerequisites for the adoption of the 'good', including adequate moral development and appropriate education, are not always present. Moreover, miseducation and an infantile preference to promote only what meets the individual's immediate needs combine to obscure what natural law demands. At its worst, this amounts to little more than a Nietzschean will-to-power.

All the while, secular society views religion as 'a private consumer product that some people seem to need. Its former social role was poisonous. Its present privatization is harmless enough to wish it well from a civilized distance'.[67] As a result, the natural law thinking offered by Baptists will not be met by wider society uncontested. If every account is historically contingent, however, then, Baptist claims to liberty of conscience become both an important outworking of natural law and an expression of it.

66 Baptist Union of Victoria: *Baptist Distinctives*, July 2012: buv.com.au. *We are Victoria Baptists*, 6.

67 David Tracy, *The Analogical Imagination* (London: SCM Press, 1981), 13.

9

Natural Law in the Ecumenical Movement

Leo J. Koffeman

Most stipulations in the canon law of the Roman Catholic Church have the quality of 'mere ecclesiastical law' (*ius mere ecclesiasticum*). As a result, in principle, they can be changed with a view to contextual circumstances. Some stipulations, however, are based on divine law and claim universality, although they can be reformulated and refined. These stipulations are of two types: *ius divinum positivum* and *ius divinum naturale*. The former entity, often referred to simply as *ius divinum*, regards institutional aspects of the church, such as the fundamental distinction between clerics and lay persons, the pope as 'bishop of the Roman Church', and the role of bishops in general.[1] The latter is often referred to simply as *ius naturale*, natural law. It deals with moral or ethical issues, such as marriage and ecclesiastical goods. Following a short opening on divine law, this chapter examines how natural law surfaces in the ecumenical movement globally – the movement towards greater visible unity between the separated institutional churches of Christianity – including in the work of the World Council of Churches (WCC).[2]

DIVINE LAW IN THE ECUMENICAL ENTERPRISE

Divine law, in the sense of *ius divinum positivum*, is among the central subjects discussed in ecumenical dialogues. It is particularly the ongoing disagreement on the divine law character of historic episcopal succession that has so far made ecclesiological consensus impossible, that is, between those traditions that cherish

[1] It is unclear whether issues such as the exclusive ordination of male persons belong to the area of mere ecclesiastical law: see Leo J. Koffeman, 'The Ecumenical Potential of Church Polity', *Ecclesiastical Law Journal* 17 (2015): 182–193, at 191.

[2] This chapter, with its focus on ecumenical dialogues, does not deal directly with the many ecumenical links forged by theologians and philosophers who treat natural law from different Christian perspectives (such as Matthew Levering, *Biblical Natural Law* (Oxford: Oxford University Press, 2012), and the ecumenical aspects of other works cited elsewhere in this book). As a matter of ecclesiastical practice, theologians and philosophers also participate directly in the dialogues themselves through their appointment to the bodies engaged in such dialogues.

that phenomenon and those that have not maintained it but rather understand apostolic continuity as primarily a matter of faithfulness to the Gospel.

An important recent report of the Faith and Order Commission of the World Council of Churches, *The Church: Towards a Common Vision* (2013),[3] clearly states:

> Almost all Christian communities today have a formal structure of ministry. Frequently this structure is diversified and reflects, more or less explicitly, the threefold pattern of *episcopos-presbyteros-diaconos*. Churches remain divided, however, as to whether or not the 'historic episcopate' (meaning bishops ordained in apostolic succession back to the earliest generations of the Church), or the apostolic succession of ordained ministry more generally, is something intended by Christ for his community. Some believe that the threefold ministry of bishop, presbyter and deacon is a sign of continuing faithfulness to the gospel and is vital to the apostolic continuity of the Church as a whole. In contrast, others do not view faithfulness to the gospel as closely bound to succession in ministry, and some are wary of the historic episcopate because they see it as vulnerable to abuse and thus potentially harmful to the wellbeing of the community. *Baptism, Eucharist and Ministry* [1982], for its part, only affirmed that it 'may serve today as an expression of the unity we seek and also as a means for achieving it' (§ 47).

There are examples of ecumenical agreements that were able to bridge that divide, particularly due to the way the Anglican tradition interprets its heritage of historic episcopate. For instance, the birth of the United Church of South India was in this respect a landmark in the ecumenical movement. In 1947, churches of the Anglican, Methodist, Congregational, Presbyterian and Reformed traditions united into this single institutional church. The union was based on a full mutual recognition of ministries, independent of the question as to whether they were based on historic episcopate, but since the formation of the union all priests and bishops have been ordained by bishops in this tradition of historic episcopate. A similar scheme was used when in 1970 Anglicans, Methodists, Baptists, Brethren and Disciples united together in the Church of North India.

Ecumenical agreements like the *Meissen Agreement* (1988),[4] and the *Porvoo Common Statement* (1992),[5] were also possible because of a less strict interpretation of historic episcopacy in contemporary Anglicanism. The *Meissen Agreement* confirms the full mutual acknowledgement of ordained ministry and oversight between the Church of England and the German Evangelical Churches. The *Porvoo Common Statement* provides a framework for communion and practical unity among, on the one hand, the Anglican churches in England, Ireland, Scotland and Wales and, on the other hand, the Lutheran churches in Scandinavia and the

3 *The Church: Towards a Common Vision*, Faith and Order Paper 214 (Geneva: World Council of Churches, 2013). Cf. *Baptism, Eucharist, Ministry*, Faith and Order Paper 111 (Geneva: World Council of Churches, 1982), § M/22.

4 See www.ekd.de/english/download/meissen_engl_.pdf, § 17.A.iii–iv.

5 See www.anglicancommunion.org/media/102178/porvoo_common_statement.pdf.

Baltic States; it has a similar objective and, therefore, deals with the issue of historic episcopate in this way:

> [T]he time has come when all our churches can affirm together the value and use of the sign of the historic episcopal succession . . . This means that those churches in which the sign has at some time not been used are free to recognise the value of the sign and should embrace it without denying their own apostolic continuity. This also means that those churches in which the sign has been used are free to recognise the reality of the episcopal office and should affirm the apostolic continuity of those churches in which the sign of episcopal succession has at some time not been used (§ 57).

THE UNDERCURRENT OF NATURAL LAW IN ECUMENICAL AGREEMENTS

The concept of natural law – the *ius divinum naturale* – has been used in ecumenical agreement both expressly and implicitly. Sometimes it is an undercurrent in such agreements, one which does not prove to be problematic. However, it might also be a deeply complicating factor. Two case studies illustrate these facts: one involves interchurch marriage, the other, homosexuality.

Interchurch Marriage and Natural Law

Ecumenical agreements on interchurch marriages exist in many countries. For instance, in the Netherlands in 1971 three Protestant churches – that is, the Netherlands Reformed Church, the Reformed Churches in the Netherlands and the Evangelical Lutheran Church in the Kingdom of the Netherlands – signed an agreement with the Roman Catholic Conference of Bishops in the Netherlands in order to facilitate the solemnisation of Protestant-Roman Catholic marriages between the faithful of these traditions. The agreement opens with the statement:

> [T]he churches recognize marriage as an institution of God who created humankind as man and woman, and brought them together in order to build a union in love and faithfulness, and to maintain humankind in so doing (cf. Gen 2, 18–25). According to its origin and intention, marriage is a bond between one man and one woman, binding them for life (cf. Math 19, 3–9).[6]

From a Roman Catholic perspective, as we saw in Chapter 2, marriage is understood in part to be an institution of natural law. However, this concept was never a matter for discussion in this instance, and the Protestant churches involved saw no reason to raise the issue and question it. It would be a fruitful topic for further research as to whether natural law has been the focus of discussion in comparable agreements elsewhere on

[6] See: www.protestantsekerk.nl/Lists/PKN-Bibliotheek/Gemeenschappelijke-Verklaring-PKN-met-RKK-kerkelijk-gemengd-huwelijk.pdf (trans. from the Dutch by Leo Koffeman).

interchurch marriages involving Roman Catholics. However, in 2004, when these three Protestant churches united in the Protestant Church in the Netherlands, the issue of marriage as a 'divine institution' was a major issue for discussion, particularly because of what some saw as an implicit rejection of same-sex marriage.[7]

Natural Law and Homosexuality

Homosexuality is an issue which divides several church families worldwide, such as the Anglican Communion, as well as individual churches within them. It seems evident that interpretations of the concept of natural law play a major role in ways in which church families and churches react to this issue. Indeed, the rejection of the option of accepting homosexuality – dominant in, for instance, the official position of the Roman Catholic Church and Orthodox churches – is often based on an understanding of this sexual preference as 'unnatural'.

In 1995, the Joint Working Group set up by the Roman Catholic Church and the WCC (of which the Roman Catholic Church is not a member) recognised the difficulties in this area in a report on *The Ecumenical Dialogue on Moral Issues*.[8] The report states:

> One Christian vision of the integrity of sexual life links sexual relationship with procreation by an interpretation of natural law and of the biblical accounts of creation. Some churches, such as the Roman Catholic Church, hold this position. Other churches judge it most difficult, even impossible to affirm such a link. Those which find the appeal to natural law inconclusive accept the possible separation of the good of procreation from the good of sexual relationship, and use this argument to approve contraceptive means in marriage (§ III/4).

Moreover (as we have seen in Chapter 2):

> In the Roman Catholic Church, bishops, according to the gift received from the Holy Spirit, and under his guidance, in their ministry of oversight (*episkope*), are the authoritative guardians and interpreters of the whole moral law, that is, both the law of the gospel and the natural law (§ IV.1).

These two brief examples of how natural law may prove either to be uncontroversial (as in the Dutch case of interchurch marriages) or to be problematic (as in the case of homosexuality), are designed to suggest how the theme of natural law may appear in the ecumenical initiatives. The latter example also serves to show how important it is for clarity in understandings of natural law, as these understandings impinge on particular developments in the ecumenical enterprise.

7 Cf. Leo J. Koffeman, 'How the Protestant Church in the Netherlands was born', in Arjan Plaisier and Leo J. Koffeman, eds., *The Protestant Church in the Netherlands: Church Unity in the 21st Century. Stories and Reflections*, Church Polity and Ecumenism – Global Perspectives IV (Zürich: LIT Verlag, 2014), 11–37, 24, 26.

8 See *Ecumenical Review* 48(1996): 143–154. Also: www.wcc-coe.org/wcc/who/crete-08-e.html.

BILATERAL DIALOGUES AND THE CREATIVE USE OF NATURAL LAW

Ecumenical methodology usually distinguishes two kinds of interchurch theological dialogue: multilateral and bilateral. Multilateral dialogue includes participants from many if not most of the Christian communities. On a global level it is particularly the Commission on Faith and Order (in which the Roman Catholic Church is a full member) of the WCC which facilitates such dialogue – as we will see below. But similar dialogues can take place on regional levels and in national contexts. It is self-evident that the reports of such dialogues have to take into account viewpoints and sensitivities from many different sides: therefore, such reports tend not to be very specific in the way they present theological issues. Bilateral dialogue offers better opportunities for a more thorough and detailed theological debate and report, because in this framework it is two Christian traditions that explore commonalities and differences between their respective theological heritages; trilateral dialogue is rare. Reports of bilateral dialogue as practised on a global level – including representatives of two of the main Christian families – have been collected and published under the auspices of the WCC, in four volumes of the series *Growth in Agreement*,[9] which also include some multilateral reports.

It is particularly the Roman Catholic Church that has stimulated bilateral dialogue, and it has done so for decades. Usually, its dialogues with other church families have produced lengthy reports. The Orthodox churches have entered into ecumenical dialogue too; by way of contrast, these dialogues have generally led to shorter statements rather than to expanded reports.

We await a comprehensive study of the part played by natural law in all bilateral ecumenical dialogues. What follows, therefore, examines natural law as it has featured in a selection of bilateral dialogues – and in all of them the Roman Catholic Church is one of the conversation partners. To give a reliable impression of the way our theme is being dealt with and of the ubiquity of natural law thinking in ecumenical discourse (either in the foreground or in the background), five bilateral dialogues have been selected here, in which the Roman Catholic Church is in conversation with Anglicans, Evangelicals, Mennonites, Reformed and Old Catholics, respectively. As we have seen in the other chapters of this volume, interest in natural law has fluctuated as the theological and juristic postures of the Anglican and Reformed traditions have developed in the course of their histories, though this is less so the case within the Roman Catholic Church.

[9] Harding Meyer and Lukas Vischer, eds., *Growth in Agreement: Reports and Agreed Statements of Ecumenical Conversations on a World Level*, Faith and Order Paper 108 (New York/Geneva: Paulist Press/World Council of Churches, 1984); Jeffrey Gros FSC, Harding Meyer and William G. Rusch, eds., *Growth in Agreement II: Reports and Agreed Statements of Ecumenical Conversations on a World Level*, Faith and Order Paper 187 (Geneva: World Council of Churches, 2000); Jeffrey Gros FSC, Thomas F. Best and Lorelei Fuchs SA, eds., *Growth in Agreement III: International Dialogue Texts and Agreed Statements*, Faith and Order Paper 204 (Geneva: World Council of Churches, 2007). Volume IV is due early in 2017. In this chapter, I refer to the Vatican website as the easiest resource but all documents presented here are also available in the aforementioned volumes.

Anglican-Roman Catholic Dialogue

In 1994, the Second Anglican-Roman Catholic International Commission (ARCIC II) produced a report on *Life in Christ: Morals, Communion and the Church.*[10] This report seems to present the most extensive discussion of natural law in ecumenical documents so far. The mandate was

> [t]o examine, especially in the light of our respective judgments on the Final Report [of ARCIC I, 1982], the outstanding doctrinal differences which still separate us, with a view to their eventual resolution; to study all that hinders the mutual recognition of the ministries of our Communions, and to recommend what practical steps will be necessary when, on the basis of our unity in faith, we are able to proceed to the restoration of full communion (Preface).

The Preface also notes that Anglicans and Roman Catholics are as much, if not more, divided on questions of morals as they are in matters of doctrine. However, the report then says: 'Even on those particular issues where disagreement exists, Anglicans and Roman Catholics, we shall argue, share a common perspective and acknowledge the same underlying values' (§ 1).

The structure of *Life in Christ* is characteristic of most reports of ecumenical dialogue. After an Introduction, it starts in its first part from a description of what both traditions have in common (§ 4–35). It then presents a historical overview of how their paths started to diverge (§ 36–53). The next part describes agreement and disagreement on a number of specific issues, including sexuality, marriage after divorce and contraception (§ 54–88). The report concludes with a section entitled 'toward shared witness' (§ 89–105). It is interesting to see that 'natural law', that is, as an implicit concept, surfaces initially in the context of a shared vision of creation:

> In seeking the common good ... the Church listens and speaks, not only to the faithful, but also to women and men of good will everywhere. Despite the ambiguities and evils in the world, and despite the sin that has distorted human life, the Church affirms the original goodness of creation and discerns signs and contours of an order that continues to reflect the wisdom and goodness of the Creator (§ 9).

However, a few lines later in the report, familiar natural law categories are explicitly named:

> Reflection on experience of what makes human beings, singly and together, truly human gives rise to a natural morality, *sometimes interpreted in terms of natural justice or natural law*, to which a general appeal for guidance can be made. In Jesus Christ this natural morality is not denied. Rather, it is renewed, transfigured and perfected, since Christ is the true and perfect image of God (§ 9; emphasis added).

10 See www.vatican.va/roman_curia/pontifical_councils/chrstuni/angl-comm-docs/rc_pc_chrstuni_doc_19930906_life-in-christ_en.html.

Nevertheless, post-Reformation history has stimulated both continuity and change:

> After the breakdown in communion, Anglicans and Roman Catholics continued to develop, in related but distinctive ways, their common tradition of moral theology and its application by a process of casuistry to specific moral problems (§ 43).

Moreover, moralism, rigour and laxity have all, variously, played their part in both traditions – but these characteristics were never decisive. As to the Roman Catholic Church:

> In the second half of the present century the Roman Catholic Church, in its desire to set the moral life within a comprehensive vision of life in the Spirit, has witnessed a renewal of moral theology. There has been a return to the Scriptures as the central source of moral insight. Older discussions, based on the natural law, with the Scriptures cited solely for confirmation, have been integrated into a more personalistic account of the moral life, which itself has been grounded in the vocation of all human persons to participate in the life of God. An emphasis on the community of persons has led to significant developments, not only in the church's teaching on personal relationships, but also in its teaching on the economic and social implications of the common good (§ 44).

The Anglican tradition of moral theology shows a comparable development. It is one which focusses on personal holiness and on an integral spirit of genuine repentance and renewal, so as to prepare Christians for making their own (moral and conscientious) decisions (see § 45).

The report then identifies the differences that remain, though these differences exist around what both traditions share in the umbrella category of 'moral law'; Roman Catholics emphasise what is absolute in the moral law, whereas Anglicans give weight to both its absolute and relative aspects; the report states:

> For example, a notable feature of established Roman Catholic moral teaching is its emphasis on the absoluteness of some demands of the moral law and the existence of certain prohibitions to which there are no exceptions. In these instances, what is prohibited is intrinsically disordered and therefore objectively wrong. Anglicans, on the other hand, while acknowledging the same ultimate values, are not persuaded that the laws as we apprehend them are necessarily absolute. In certain circumstances, they would argue, it might be right to incorporate contextual and pastoral considerations in the formulation of a moral law, on the grounds that fundamental moral values are better served if the law sometimes takes into account certain contingencies of nature and history and certain disorders of the human condition (§ 52).

The report then places this difference in the juridical context of positive law:

> In so doing, [Anglicans] do not make the clear-cut distinction, which Roman Catholics make, between canon law, with its incorporation of contingent and

> prudential considerations, and the moral law, which in its principles is absolute and universal (§ 52).[11]

That said, however:

> In both our Communions . . . there are now signs of a shift away from a reliance on the concept of law as the central category for providing moral teaching. Its place is being taken by the concept of persons-in-community. An ethic of response is preferred to an ethic of obedience. In the desire to respond as fully as possible to the new law of Christ, the primacy of persons is emphasized above the impersonalism of a system of law, thus avoiding the distortions of both individualism and utilitarianism. The full significance of this shift of emphasis is not yet clear, and its detailed implications have still to be worked out. It should be emphasized, however, that whatever differences there may be in the way in which they express the moral law, both our traditions respect the consciences of persons in good faith (§ 52).

This difference in approach to the formulation of law is referred to again in the context of agreement and disagreement with regard to homosexuality:

> Roman Catholic teaching holds that homosexual activity is intrinsically disordered, and concludes that it is always objectively wrong. This affects the kind of pastoral advice that is given to homosexual persons. Anglicans could agree that such activity is disordered; but there may well be differences among them in the consequent moral and pastoral advice they would think it right to offer to those seeking their counsel and direction (§ 87).

Trying to find a way towards shared witness on moral issues, *Life in Christ* starts from the concept of 'communion' – a key concept in present-day ecumenism:

> The theme of communion illumines, we believe, not only the reality of the Church as a worshiping community, but also the form and fullness of Christian life in the world. Indeed, since the Church is called in Christ to be a sign and sacrament of a renewed humanity, it also illumines the nature and destiny of human life as such (§ 90).

Communion is characterised as 'a constitutive characteristic of a fully human life, signifying a relationship based on participation in a shared reality' (§ 91); therefore, 'the moral dimension of human life is itself perceived to be fundamentally relational'. It is this approach (actually recognisable in the document's title, *Life in Christ*) that shapes the final chapter of this report. From this perspective, human life can be valued in its ambiguity: the call to holiness or perfection 'does not ignore human fragility, failure and sin; but it does lay bare the full dimensions of a response

[11] This understanding may itself be open to question, from the Anglican point of view, in light of the insights provided by Chapter 4 of this volume: Anglicans do, broadly, distinguish the moral law and positive law.

that reflects the height and breadth and depth of the divine righteousness and love' (§ 92). And, importantly:

> Human beings are not purely spiritual beings; they are fashioned out of the dust (cf. Gen 2:7). Created in the image of God, they are shaped by nature and culture, and participate in both the glory and the shame of the human story (§ 93).

Life in Christ recognises the challenges of a fast-changing world, in terms of science and technology, including the threats it may imply for our natural environment. In so doing, the report also reflects a meeting of minds between the traditions on nature itself:

> However, there are ultimate limits to what is possible. Nature is not infinitely malleable. Moreover, not everything that is humanly possible is humanly desirable, or morally right . . . The moral task is to discern how fundamental and eternal values may be expressed and embodied in a world that is subject to continuing change (§ 94).

It seems that this tends to reduce the possibility of referring to natural law: 'nature', including the moral guidelines to be derived from it, is less self-evident than it seemed to be the case in earlier times. We live in a broken and imperfect world, subject to futility and sin:

> Its human structures are distorted by violence and greed. Inevitably, conflicts of value and clashes of interest arise, *and situations occur in which the requirements of the moral order are uncertain* (§ 95, emphasis added).

Natural law does not provide final answers to the challenges of our times. As is usual in such ecumenical reports, the final paragraphs point to the kind of issues suitable for further dialogue, and these include the very idea of 'law', its relationship with morals, and the place of 'reason' within moral discourse:

> Continuing study is needed of the differences between us, real or apparent, especially in our understanding and use of the notion of law. A clearer understanding is required of the relation of the concept of law to the concepts of moral order and the common good, and the relation of all these concepts to the vision of human happiness and fulfilment as persons-in-community that we have been given in and through Jesus Christ. However, Anglicans and Roman Catholics do not talk to each other as moral strangers. They both appeal to a shared tradition, and they recognize the same Scriptures as normative of that tradition. They both respect the role of reason in moral discernment. They both give due place to the classic virtue of prudence. We are convinced, therefore, that further exchange between our two traditions on moral questions will serve both the cause of Christian unity and the good of that larger society of which we are all part (§ 102).

However, no further steps seem to have been made to-date in this respect. In 2007, on the occasion of the celebration of forty years of Anglican-Roman Catholic Dialogue, the International Anglican-Roman Catholic Commission for Unity and

Mission published an Agreed Statement, *Growing Together in Unity and Mission*.[12] The statement in fact summarises the positive fruits of four decades of dialogue, including the following paragraph, without any reference to existing differences:

> Anglicans and Roman Catholics share similar ways of moral reasoning. We recognise the normative authority of Scripture and rely on a shared tradition which appeals to natural law and pays attention to the wisdom in the order of creation (§ 83, referring to *Life in Christ*, § 9).

In sum, the concept of natural law has played a part in recent dialogue between Anglicans and Roman Catholics. The concept is presented as part of a common heritage. The natural order reflects the wisdom and goodness of God its creator. Being truly human gives rise to a 'natural morality' which may be interpreted in terms of natural law which is renewed and perfected in Christ. Whilst Roman Catholics emphasise the absolute in the moral law, Anglicans stress both its absolute and its relative aspects. Positive law is not the only medium of instruction in the moral law – reason plays an important role. And there should be greater clarity in the respective understanding of each tradition about the nature of law and its relationship with morality.

Dialogue between the Roman Catholic Church and the World Evangelical Alliance

In 2002, a dialogue between the Roman Catholic Church and the World Evangelical Alliance (WEA) resulted in the report *Church, Evangelization, and the Bonds of Koinonia*.[13] The WEA includes not only recent so-called evangelical communities, but also partners from more traditional and mainstream churches, such as Reformed churches and Methodist churches. The report first explores differences in ecclesiology between both traditions and then focusses on the mutual understanding of evangelisation. Under the headings 'repentance' and 'conversion' respectively, it deals with improper forms of evangelisation and thereafter with possible ways of cooperation and common learning. It is in this latter context that the issue of religious liberty is addressed (§ 74–78). The report identifies common ground on this matter:

> Evangelicals can concur with the position of the Second Vatican Council on religious freedom, namely that all 'are to be immune from coercion on the part of individuals or of social groups and of any human power, in such wise that in matters religious no one is to be forced to act in a manner contrary to his own beliefs. Nor is anyone to be restrained from acting in accordance with his own beliefs, whether

12 See www.vatican.va/roman_curia/pontifical_councils/chrstuni/angl-comm-docs/rc_pc_chrstuni_doc_20070914_growing-together_en.html.

13 See www.vatican.va/roman_curia/pontifical_councils/chrstuni/evangelicals-docs/rc_pc_chrstuni_doc_20111220_report-1993–2002_en.html.

> privately or publicly, whether alone or in association with others, within due limits' (§ 74).[14]

However, the report then notes that 'Evangelicals and Roman Catholics differ somewhat in the theological and anthropological rationale for this position'. On the one hand:

> Catholic social thought bases rights' theory on natural law. It sees human rights as legitimate moral claims that are God-given; free moral agents have a corresponding responsibility to act in the light of those claims. Revelation is seen to complement this understanding of rights (§ 78).

On the other hand:

> In Evangelical teaching, primacy belongs to the divine right over conscience, the Lord's immediate claim on each individual; human rights, then, are viewed not only in creational light but also against the backdrop of the human fall into sin. The history of sin makes the mandate for rights all the more important. God continues to pursue fallen creatures in the unfolding history of grace (§ 78).

Nevertheless:

> Catholics and Evangelicals agree that human rights should be interpreted and exercised within the framework of Scripture teaching and of rigorous moral reasoning. Due regard must be had for the needs of others, for duties towards other parties, and for the common good. Human rights language, also, must guard against being turned into narcissism, self-assertiveness and ideology (§ 78).

It is interesting to see that in this dialogue the Roman Catholic delegation finds common ground with its Evangelical counterpart in a shared plea for 'rigorous moral reasoning'.

Roman Catholic-Mennonite Dialogue

1998 saw the first dialogue of the Roman Catholic Church with the Mennonites, one of the 'historical peace churches' that reject all violence. In 2003, the dialogue resulted in the report *Called to be Peacemakers*. The issue of natural law is lightly touched upon in the context of the different views of political authority:

> While Catholics and Mennonites regard political authority as part of the God-given moral order of the universe, they tend to diverge on the question of participation in government. Catholics understand the social nature of humanity to be blessed by Christ's life and teaching. Participation in government is honoured and encouraged as a contribution to the common good, and military service is respected. At the same time, nonviolent action, conscientious objection, and resistance to immoral orders

[14] The text refers to the Declaration on Religious Freedom of the Second Vatican Council, *Dignitatis Humanae*, § 2.

are strongly endorsed. Because of their long history of persecution and discrimination, Mennonites have tended to mistrust the state. They still tend to be critical of Christian involvement in government because of the use of violence involved and the possible corruption of power (§ 186).

Dialogue between the Roman Catholic Church and the Reformed Churches

I had the privilege to participate in the third round of dialogue between the Roman Catholic Church and the World Alliance of Reformed Churches, 1998–2005.[15] This dialogue generated the extensive report *The Church as Community of Common Witness to the Kingdom of God*. From the beginning, this dialogue intended to bring together the (Roman Catholic) desire to focus on ecclesiology and the (Reformed) intention to speak to issues of justice in the modern world. It transpired that the category of the 'kingdom of God' could serve to link the two.

Therefore, the report first of all deals with 'The Kingdom of God in Scripture and Tradition' (Chapter 1) and then presents three 'narratives' (case studies), dealing with burning justice issues in Canada, South Africa and Northern Ireland, respectively, in 'Witnessing to the Kingdom: Three Narratives from Different Contexts' (Chapter 2). The final chapters, on 'The Kingdom of God and the Church' (Chapter 4) and 'Dialogue and Common Witness' (Chapter 5) formulate common views as well as differences which remain in terms of ecclesiology and witness. But it is Chapter 3, 'Discerning God's Will in the Service of the Kingdom', which provides some interesting views on the evaluation of natural law. It deals with 'discernment' as its key focus. What does 'discernment' mean? How is it related to the Holy Spirit? What sources of discernment are common to both traditions, and where do we see differences between Reformed Christians and Roman Catholics in the use of these sources and in the patterns of discernment?

It is self-evident that natural law might be relevant to the topic of discernment. Can natural law play a role in this respect? The report recognises historical differences in the way both communities deal with normative sources, such as Holy Scripture and inherited tradition, as well as the voice of the poor and the testimony of those people of good will who are not Christians:

> The Reformed tradition is well known for its insistence that, in the last analysis, it is only Scripture, read and understood in specific times and places, by people and church assemblies marked by those times and places, that can be the final authority in the communal discernment process. This is not to say that Scripture is the only authority, but it is the ultimate authority. The pattern of discernment regularly emerges from the dialogue between Scripture and life (§ 135).

New insights, enrichment by the witness of other traditions within the Christian faith and beyond, authorities from the past (such as the creeds and the confessions of

[15] The alliance has since been renamed the World Communion of Reformed Churches.

the Reformed churches themselves) can be regarded only as 'subordinate standards'. For Roman Catholics, Scripture is 'transmitted in an integral way' (§ 137) by the Tradition, which is thus indispensable for its interpretation. Further, Catholics refer to the discernment of the church, especially as it is expressed in official teachings. However, '[t]he process of discernment involves the whole prophetic people of God ... who, along with the gift of faith, are endowed with that "sense of the faith" (*sensus fidei*), which enables them to recognize the Word of God for what it is, to grow in deeper knowledge of it and to apply it to their daily lives' (§ 138). In turn, '[f]inally, the decisive role in the process of discernment is exercised by the bishops, whose unity in faith and love is confirmed by their communion with the successor of Peter, the bishop of Rome' (§ 139). It is against this background that the following statement is made about natural law:

> Reformed and Roman Catholics agree that discipleship to Jesus Christ entails the discernment of God's will regarding ethical issues and moral behaviour. Both of our communities are aware of the complexities involved in moral discernment. The revelation of God's Word remains for us a lasting source of inspiration in this area, while we acknowledge that one cannot expect to find in Scripture a ready-made solution to the moral situations which human beings face today. Both communities acknowledge the contribution of human reasoning to moral and ethical discernment, although theologians and ethicists within our communities have at times evaluated in differing or even contrasting ways that philosophical understanding of good and evil usually called the 'theory of natural law'. As is well known, Catholic teaching affirms the possibility of knowing right and wrong actions on the basis of natural law (§ 140).[16]

Only implicitly does the report seem to suggest that Reformed Christians deny that possibility.

Dialogue between Roman Catholics and the Old Catholics

In 2009, a dialogue between the Roman Catholic Church and the Old Catholic churches produced a report, *The Church and Ecclesial Communion*. The report is

[16] The Roman Catholic view of the relation of nature and grace is also well reflected in the Roman Catholic-Pentecostal dialogue report, *On Becoming a Christian* (2006); see § 177:

> The theological virtues of faith, hope and love enable ongoing communion with God and can be exercised in prayer and service to the Lord and love for one's neighbor. The moral life is also enabled by the development and practice of what are known as the four cardinal virtues – prudence, justice, temperance and fortitude. The principle of grace perfecting nature is very important in Catholic understanding. God takes us where we are with our own temperaments and talents and perfects them at a supernatural level by both healing the effects of sin in one's life and elevating one to participate in the divine life such that Christian virtue exceeds what is possible at the natural level alone – for example, not only to love one's friends but one's enemies as well. See www.vatican.va/roman_curia/pontifical_councils/chrstuni/eccl-comm-docs/rc_pc_chrstuni_doc_20060101_becoming-a-christian_en.html.

very clear about the method of dialogue, in a paragraph on the principles of a 'differentiated consensus'. Such consensus 'consists of two components which are to be differentiated from one another'. They include on the one hand '[a] clear statement on the consensus reached in the fundamental and essential content of a previously controversial doctrine' and on the other hand '[a] declaration that and why the remaining doctrinal differences, which are also to be clearly named, can be considered admissible and thus do not call into question the consensus in the fundamentals and essentials' (§ 34). The latter category includes four issues, characterised as 'open questions': they concern ecclesiology, the Marian dogmas, the ordination of women and some canon law issues. It is in the context of an Old Catholic view with regard to the ordination of women (a contentious issue within this community as well) that natural law thinking is touched upon, at least implicitly, in the approach of those who do not accept the ordination of women – namely, that the requirement that the celebrant of the Eucharist be male reflects what is 'natural':

> [T]here is the argumentation based on a spousal metaphor in the light of which the spiritual relationship between Jesus Christ and his church ought to be seen and represented. The dynamics of the love between Christ and his church, most profoundly comparable to that of a bridegroom and bride, husband and wife, would thus require a *natural representational* depiction in the central act of the celebration of the Eucharist, according to which the male priest refers to Christ and the concelebrating congregation is to understand itself in a metaphorical sense as female, receiving grace (and thus 'Marian') (§ 67, emphasis added).

A brief survey of these five selected case studies indicates that bilateral dialogues represent a rich source for the exploration of natural law thinking in the ecumenical context. The same might be said for formal ecumenical agreements entered by separate churches following successful dialogue. These too commonly contain norms mutually agreed which are designed to enable collaboration in the promotion of justice.[17] Indeed, this is not surprising. The regulatory instruments of individual institutional churches, which may be party to such dialogues, may also address ecumenical matters unilaterally. These norms display some evidence of natural law thinking, in terms of ideas associated historically with the concept of natural law, such as the promotion with the faithful of other churches of human dignity, justice and equity. For example, under the canon law of the Oriental Catholic churches 'it is desirable that the Catholic faithful, undertake any project in which they could cooperate with other Christians, not alone but together, such as works for charity and social justice, defence of the dignity and the fundamental rights of the human person, [and] promotion of peace'.[18] As we have seen elsewhere in this volume,

[17] Norman Doe, *Christian Law: Contemporary Principles* (Cambridge: Cambridge University Press, 2013), 304–308.

[18] Code of Canons of the Oriental Churches (1990), canon 908; cf. canon 930.

the regulatory systems of churches also use similar ideas linked to historical natural law thinking in norms applicable to the members of these churches in their promotion of, for example, human rights, the inherent equality and dignity of all humans and justice.[19]

THE WORLD COUNCIL OF CHURCHES AND NATURAL LAW

Natural law thinking is also present, beyond bilateral dialogues, in the work of the WCC, in relation to human rights and homosexuality, and in the work of its Commission on Faith and Order.

The WCC and Human Rights

The Eighth Assembly of the World Council of Churches met in December 1998, in Harare. On the occasion of the fiftieth anniversary of the *Universal Declaration of Human Rights*, as adopted by the General Assembly of the United Nations in 1948, the WCC Assembly agreed on a Declaration as well as a Statement.[20] It is well known that the United Nations Declaration explicitly refers to natural law thinking in its Preamble: 'Whereas recognition of the *inherent* dignity and of the equal and *inalienable* rights of all members of the human family is the foundation of freedom, justice and peace in the world, . . . now, therefore, the General Assembly, proclaims this Universal Declaration of Human Rights' (emphasis added).

The Harare Declaration states, in turn, 'As Christians, we believe that God created every person infinitely precious and endowed with equal dignity and rights.' Therefore, the WCC recommits itself to the principles of the Universal Declaration of Human Rights and to promote and defend these in a way which takes into account 'the values and insights into human rights and dignity derived from the rich heritage of peoples' religions, cultures and traditions'. Although an explicit reference to 'natural law' is lacking here, we might recognise that this reference to a (supposed) common view on human dignity, shared by Christians and non-Christians, made it possible for the United Nations to issue the 1948 Declaration. Similar expressions may be found in the Harare Statement, as it speaks, for instance, about 'shared or complementary spiritual values and traditions that transcend religious and cultural boundaries in the interests of justice and peace in society' (Statement, § 3.29). So, the Harare Assembly seems to presuppose that human dignity, theologically understood within the Christian tradition from the perspective of 'the human person created in God's image', might serve at the same time as a connecting category

19 Norman Doe, *Christian Law*, op cit., 362–377.

20 See Diana Kessler, ed., *Together on the Way: Official Report of the Eighth Assembly of the World Council of Churches* (Geneva: World Council of Churches, 1999), 192–194 (Declaration) and 195–206 (Statement).

which transcends all religious and philosophical traditions. As we will see below, this approach seems to be questioned in the Faith and Order Paper *Costly Obedience*.

Indeed, this mode of thinking has recently been applied by the Faith and Order Commission of the WCC to the particular issue of freedom of religion; it sees 'religious freedom as one of the fundamental dimensions of human dignity' (paragraph 60).[21] In any event, there is no doubt, that the concept of human dignity provides a solid basis for an ecumenical Christian mutual understanding. However, what about its value in terms of an inter-religious and philosophical exchange (a subject treated more fully in Chapter 10)?[22] There is no question that ecumenical cooperation (the enterprise for greater unity between Christians) has contributed to giving the concept of 'human dignity' a place in the inter-religious and philosophical debate on human rights.[23] Indeed, specific cultural and religious contexts cannot be neglected in this debate. The very dignity of the human person is known through the revealed word of God and by reason itself. This view corresponds with a 'universalist' approach in legal philosophy, as well as with an approach of the essence of law in terms of 'natural law'.

WCC and Homosexuality

As already seen in this chapter, homosexuality is a divisive issue for ecumenism. Up until the end of the twentieth century, it was in fact hardly ever possible to raise this issue in ecumenical circles. The process leading up to the Ninth Assembly of the World Council of Churches (held in Porto Alegre in 2006) included the presentation of a background document, which was designed to prepare the participants for the agenda of the Assembly. The document provides a survey of the way in which issues of human sexuality had been addressed in the WCC since 1961.[24] It mentions several occasions on which such issues were raised – but in reality these were every now and then and only in lists of issues that should be studied.

For example, in the run-up to the Eighth Assembly of the World Council of Churches (Harare, 1998), human sexuality was raised at a meeting of the Central Committee held in Johannesburg in 1994. The matters addressed included the way the government of Zimbabwe (the host country for the upcoming assembly) attacked homosexuals. This led to critical questions about the choice to assemble in Harare. One outcome of this was publication by the WCC of *Facing Our*

21 *Common Vision*, op cit., paragraph 25.

22 See, e.g., ibid., paragraph 60: Christians should consider how 'to appreciate whatever elements of truth and goodness are present in other religions' by means, e.g., of 'interreligious dialogue'; and 'religious pluralism challenges Christians to deepen their reflection about the relation between the proclamation that Jesus is the one and only Saviour . . . and the claims of other faiths'.

23 Cf. Leo J. Koffeman, 'Human Dignity – An Ecumenical Understanding?', *Scriptura* 96 (2008): 288–298.

24 See www.oikoumene.org/en/resources/documents/assembly/2006-porto-alegre/3-preparatory-and-background-documents/churches-response-to-human-sexuality.

Differences (1995), about the churches and their gay and lesbian members.[25] At the Harare Assembly itself,[26] there were workshops on homosexuality: each workshop was styled a *padare* (a Shona word meaning meeting place) for those wishing to bring an issue for discussion amongst Assembly delegates. However, the official Assembly report indicates only that the issue was raised several times in discussion, but without being mentioned explicitly in any of the official documents.[27] The Programme Guidelines Committee also referred to these discussions somewhat cautiously: 'In plenary sessions, Padare streams and the hearings the issue of human sexuality has emerged as an important issue which faces the churches. It is clear that issues surrounding the understanding of human sexuality have divided and continue to divide some churches.'[28] Homosexuality is subsumed under 'human sexuality', and this theme again is only alluded to, by way of example, in the following recommendation:

> As we stand at the dawn of a new millennium, one of the most significant tasks for the churches will be to address the contemporary ethical issues growing out of the enormous advances in fields such as genetic engineering and electronic communication. Issues of personal and interpersonal ethics must also be addressed. The WCC should offer space and direction for conversation and consultation enabling member churches to discuss these difficult issues – including human sexuality – which cause division within and among its member churches. This conversation must build on the shared theological and hermeneutical reflection that has informed earlier ecumenical ethical discussions on issues such as racism.[29]

This may be regarded a rather general and non-committing statement. However, it led to an interesting Faith and Order study on Christian anthropology (see below).[30]

By way of contrast, the document prepared for the Ninth Assembly of the World Council of Churches at Porto Alegre in 2006 suggests that further steps would be possible:

> The Reference Group hopes that from the work done, the churches will be helped to realize that the issues of human sexuality that members are wrestling with are not only about homosexuality. There are diversities in human sexual experience that should be celebrated and addressed through open spaces for discussion.

[25] Alan A. Brash, *Facing Our Differences: The Churches and Their Gay and Lesbian Members* (Geneva: World Council of Churches, 1995). See also Robin Smith, *Living in Covenant with God and One Another* (Geneva: World Council of Churches, 1992).

[26] Birgitta Larsson, 'A Quest for Clarity: The World Council of Churches and Human Sexuality', *Ecumenical Review* 50 (1998): 30–40.

[27] Cf. Diana Kessler, ed., *Together on the Way*, 150, 205, 250, 270.

[28] Ibid., 145.

[29] Diana Kessler, op cit., 137.

[30] *Christian Perspectives on Theological Anthropology: A Faith and Order Study Document*, Faith and Order Paper 199 (Geneva: World Council of Churches, 2005). See www.oikoumene.org/en/resources/documents/commissions/faith-and-order/v-theological-anthropology/christian-perspectives-on-theological-anthropology.

However, the Report of the Programme Guidelines Committee, as adopted by the Assembly, again limits itself to a rather general statement:

> Ecumenical formation also includes the role of the WCC in creating 'safe spaces' for cross-cultural and cross-theological encounter as to engage in honest encounter around issues that divide our churches and our communities, in particular, to continue the dialogue on issues such as family life and human sexuality.[31]

This suggestion, however, was one of the main reasons for the Faith and Order Commission to embark upon a study on 'moral discernment' (see below).

At the most recent, Tenth Assembly of the World Council of Churches, in Busan (Korea), November 2013, the Russian Orthodox Metropolitan Hilarion of Volokolamsk shocked the more liberal delegates in an address in which he attacked what he called 'militant secularism', which would include 'the straightforward destruction of traditional notions of marriage and the family':

> This is witnessed by the new phenomenon of equating homosexual unions with marriage and allowing single-sex couples to adopt children. From the point of view of biblical teaching and traditional Christian moral values, this testifies to a profound spiritual crisis. The religious understanding of sin has been conclusively eroded in societies that until recently thought of themselves as Christian.[32]

Although several delegates would later on express their dismay at this intervention, none of the adopted documents and statements of the assembly refers to the issue of homosexuality.[33]

Faith and Order

World Council of Churches Assemblies do not offer the best podium for thorough discussions on homosexuality (as we have seen above), nor do they provide opportunities for reflective discussion of issues such as natural law. However, the account above does not tell the whole story of the WCC involvement in such issues. It is particularly the Faith and Order Commission of the WCC that has paved the way for a broader ecumenical process in this respect.

In the 1990s, the Faith and Order Commission, together with the WCC department of Justice, Peace and the Integrity of Creation, organised three conferences on the relationship between ecclesiology and the ethical and political challenges facing Christians as the twentieth century came to a close. Each conference resulted in

[31] See www.oikoumene.org/en/resources/documents/assembly/2006-porto-alegre/1-statements-documents-adopted/institutional-issues/report-of-the-programme-guidelines-committee/report-of-the-programme-guidelines-committee-as-adopted, § 20.

[32] See www.oikoumene.org/en/resources/documents/assembly/2013-busan/plenary-presentations/address-by-metropolitan-hilarion-of-volokolamsk.

[33] See www.oikoumene.org/en/resources/documents/assembly/2013-busan/adopted-documents-statements.

a report: *Costly Unity* (Rønde, Denmark 1993); *Costly Commitment* (Tantur, Israel 1994); and *Costly Obedience* (Johannesburg, 1996).[34] Although the first two reports deal extensively with the issue of the Church as a moral community and its role in moral formation, they are completely silent with regard to theological questions arising with regard to the concept of natural law. The third report, however, contains some interesting paragraphs on the issue, without using that particular vocabulary.

Costly Obedience (1996) refers to the fact that many scholars in the field of ethics today search for principles which can help us deal with the hard questions that arise for human beings as such, whatever their communal loyalties or backgrounds (cf. § 12–14). In many cases it seems impossible to build public policy on the moral reasoning offered by any one particular faith community or on a supposed 'overlapping consensus' representing many of them. Ethicists, therefore, sometimes seek to establish principles for 'post-conventional', and therefore potentially universal, forms of moral discourse. Some Christian ethicists today also

> work mainly in this frame of reference, understanding it as a Christian duty to participate fully in humanity's search for the meaning of goodness, or principles for living together in peace on this planet with respect for the dignity of all persons. Yet it is clear that this quest for some sort of universal secular moral discourse – despite agreement on many practical matters such as the defence of human rights – has thus far failed to find common philosophical ground (§ 13).

Subsequently, in 2005, the Faith and Order Commission published a 'study document' on anthropology, *Christian Perspectives on Theological Anthropology*.[35] A 'study document' is not a consensus text: 'It seeks rather ... for the sake of unity of the church, and in an accessible way, to reflect on complex and sensitive issues related to a Christian understanding of human nature' (§ 3). As such it specifies, among others things, differences in the churches' understandings of human nature which impair these churches' common confession, witness and service. Once more, the document does not explicitly deal with natural law, but its deep reflections on what it means to be created in the image of God, and on the place of humanity within creation as a whole, paved the way for a process of reflection which quite recently bore fruit in another study document which does explicitly address natural law: *Moral Discernment in the Churches*.[36]

This study document tests and develops a methodology for ecclesial and ecumenical discussion of ethical issues. It carefully lists a number of sources for moral

[34] See www.oikoumene.org/en/resources/documents/commissions/faith-and-order/vi-church-and-world/ecclesiology-and-ethics. Also published in: Thomas F. Best and Martin Robra, *Ecclesiology and Ethics: Ecumenical Ethical Engagement, Moral Formation and the Nature of the Church* (Geneva: World Council of Churches, 1997).

[35] *Christian Perspectives on Theological Anthropology*, Faith and Order Paper 199.

[36] *Moral Discernment* in *the Churches: A Study Document*, Faith and Order Paper 215 (Geneva: WCC, 2013). See www.oikoumene.org/en/resources/documents/commissions/faith-and-order/i-unity-the-church-and-its-mission/moral-discernment-in-the-churches-a-study-document.

discernment. It distinguishes 'faith sources' – that is, the guidance of the Holy Spirit, Scripture, tradition, teaching authority, spirituality and church culture – from 'human reason and other sapiential sources'. In the latter category it lists: (a) reason, (b) natural law, (c) moral reasoning, (d) natural, social, and human sciences, (e) conscience, (f) experience, (g) civil law and human rights, and (h) culture and cultural artefacts (and language). A paragraph on natural law is worth quoting at length:

> A specific instance of the appeal to the authority of reason is found in the theory of natural law. Natural law draws its moral authority from the claim that human beings, endowed with reason and free choice, can participate in the eternal law that constitutes God's rational plan for creation. It is called 'law', precisely, to denote the claimed authority of the moral precepts derived from the application by reason of the principles of practical rationality, insofar as these precepts are seen to participate in the eternal law.

Moreover:

> These precepts are further held to be knowable and binding for all human beings because all human beings have both a natural inclination to the good and particular goods, and the faculty of practical rationality. This fundamental inclination and the faculty of human reason enable human beings, first, to recognize, and, secondly, to articulate as normative that which is good for human flourishing. There has been, and continues to be, a great deal of debate about how and whether the natural law should be applied in concrete moral issues. Often these differences on how the natural law should be applied are heavily influenced by different styles of moral reasoning (§ 41).

Finally, natural law thinking also surfaces in the latest document produced by the Faith and Order Commission: *The Church: Towards a Common Vision* (2013), which was alluded to in the first section of this chapter. In this document, the commission proposes that the first attitude of God to the world is love, for all creation. Thus, as God intends the Church to serve the divine plan for transformation of the world, so 'service (*diakonia*) belongs to the very being of the Church' (§ 58). In turn, 'a constitutive aspect of evangelization is the promotion of justice and peace' (§ 59). Thus, 'It is on the basis of faith and grace that moral engagement and common action are possible and should be affirmed as intrinsic to the life of being the Church' (§ 61). Moreover, 'The ethics of Christians as disciples are rooted in God, the creator and revealer, and take shape as the community seeks to understand God's will within the various circumstances of time and place'; importantly, 'The Church does not stand in isolation from the moral struggles of humankind as a whole'; rather, 'Together with the adherents of other religions as well as all persons of good will, Christians must promote not only those individual moral values which are essential to the authentic realization of the human person but also the social values of justice, peace and the protection of the environment, since the message of the Gospel extends to the personal and the communal aspects of human existence'; in this churches should discern together moral values which unite them as they become increasingly aware of 'the need to be accountable to each other with respect to their ethical reflections and decisions' (§ 62), and as they address together the world's 'rethinking of many moral norms' and conflicts over 'moral principles' (§ 63). Therefore, the Church should help those without power to be heard, 'work for a just social order, in which the goods of this earth may be shared equitably, the suffering of the poor eased and absolute destitution' eliminated, and advocate peace, seeking to overcome causes of war. Christians must 'acknowledge their responsibility to defend human life and dignity', 'obligations on churches as much as on individual believers'; Christians who have 'acted jointly' to foster human dignity, and who may work with other religions in this, set a good example (§ 64).

CONCLUSION

It is clear from the dialogue reports surveyed here, that the concept of natural law can be a difficult one to agree on within the ecumenical movement. This is particularly true with regard to the position of the Roman Catholic Church on the one hand, and most of the Protestant churches on the other. However, it also seems to be clear that this is a rather recent divisive issue, in contrast to the time of the Reformation when the Western church became divided institutionally, a time when there was broadly far less theological division on the matter of natural law. At that time, as other Chapters in this volume indicate, the appeal to natural law in moral issues was a common feature of theology and legal thought. It is only in the twentieth century that some Christian traditions started seriously to challenge the concept of natural law. It would, therefore, be too easy to label 'natural law' as a typical Roman Catholic concept and to reject it for that reason: the concept itself is very much rooted in the theological history of all major denominations.

Moreover, natural law has the potential to divide churches today, as the issue of homosexuality shows. The cautious way which the WCC tries to keep the debate going, without putting too much pressure on participants in ecumenical dialogue, witnesses to this.

However, Anglican-Roman Catholic dialogue in particular might play an important role in the future of the ecumenical dialogues. As we have seen, the ARCIC II report *Life in Christ* at least suggests the possibility of finding common ground in a shared view of the normative authority of Scripture as well as the significance of natural law and wisdom in the order of creation. This might, in the longer term, lead to a less rigid interpretation of natural law than it is often supposed to be part and parcel of the Roman Catholic tradition. Therefore, in conclusion, it is worth repeating some key sentences from that particular report, sentences which express a challenge which may be appropriate to the whole of the ecumenical movement worldwide:

> A clearer understanding is required of the relation of the concept of law to the concepts of moral order and the common good, and the relation of all these concepts to the vision of human happiness and fulfilment as persons-in-community that we have been given in and through Jesus Christ ... We are convinced, therefore, that further exchange between our two traditions on moral questions will serve both the cause of Christian unity and the good of that larger society of which we are all part (*Life in Christ*, § 102).

10

Natural Law in an Interfaith Context: The Abrahamic Religions

Norman Doe

The term 'natural law' is used for a variety of doctrines which are often contested and differ in detail. They propose the existence of universal principles derived from nature, particularly human nature, which are normative, providing moral standards, or ethical constraints on human behaviour, which determine what actions are right and wrong. These standards are applicable to all humans, discoverable through the use of reason, and should be used as a source of and criterion to assess the legitimacy of actions, and laws. Discovery of natural law is similar to investigation of the physical laws of nature; its principles are ascertained: from determining innate notions (found naturally) in our minds about what is right or wrong; and from enquiry into our nature or the world in general and/or the rules that govern these. Views of what natural law contains vary widely and often depend on prior ideas about 'nature', e.g. the original state of affairs, and the laws of nature, e.g. physical laws of cause and effect – natural law is its order or the sphere of rationality, and so natural law is rational law deducible from rational principles. It proceeds from facts to normativity and so may not necessarily be rooted within a religious understanding of God's creative activity.

Natural law has played an important part historically in Christian theology, ethics and jurisprudence. By way of contrast, traditionally, it has played only a small part in Judaism and Islam. However, today Jewish and Muslim scholars are beginning to develop their own natural law theory in both their world view and their philosophy of law drawing upon what many of them see as explicit or implicit natural law thinking in the classical sources of Jewish and Islamic law. What follows seeks to describe, explain and compare natural law theories and their equivalents historically for Jews, Christians and Muslims, as a source of religious law, as a resource in legal reasoning and as a potential focus in inter-religious ethical dialogue; the latter has recently made its mark in academic debate on natural law doctrine in the three Abrahamic faiths.[1]

[1] E.g. the Global Ethics Network for Applied Ethics has published research on Inter-Religious Ethics. See also Anver M. Emon, Matthew Levering and David Novak, *Natural Law: A Jewish, Christian and*

NATURAL LAW IN JEWISH THOUGHT

There are three basic approaches to natural law in Judaism. The traditional view is that natural law is not a category known to Jewish law; another view is that natural law *doctrine* is present, but of marginal importance, in the historical rabbinic tradition and a minority of scholars propose that historical but marginal natural law thinking should have greater prominence in contemporary Jewish thought.[2]

The traditional assertion is that '[i]n Judaism there is no natural law doctrine, and in principle, there cannot be',[3] and so 'natural law' does not appear in standard contemporary texts on the sources of Jewish law.[4] The assertion is justified on various grounds. The idea of 'a natural order and natural laws is unknown in the [Hebrew] Bible' – the 'nearest reference to nature in the Rabbinic literature is the expression: "The world follows its own habit"'.[5] Only the Torah, the revealed law of God,[6] is acceptable to *halakha* (the whole system of Jewish law by which a Jew 'walks' through life); there is no room in this monist system for a parallel authority – as the Torah is the fullest version of the revealed law of God available to humans, so it is sufficient for every question arising in life. Some Torah commands may in any event be 'rationally justified', and whilst others may have a 'non-evident rationality', 'fulfilling [them] puts us in a position ... to understand their justifications', so that 'understanding and ethically virtuous activity interact in ... mutual reinforcement'.[7]

Moreover, natural law theory does not fit with: the character of *halakha*, 'the complex of norms incumbent on Jews' which are 'commanded by God, and the rest reflect basic values God considers desirable, even if He did not actually command them'; the subject matter of *halakha*, worship of God; the fact that all norms are

Islamic Trialogue (Oxford: Oxford University Press, 2014). Novak proposes 'a Judeo-Christian-Islamic natural law theory'.

2 J. Macy, 'Natural law', in A.A. Cohen and P. Mends-Flohr, eds., *20th Century Jewish Religious Thought* (Philadelphia, PA: The Jewish Publication Society, 2009), 663–672.

3 Marvin Fox, 'Maimonides and Aquinas and Natural Law', *Dinei* 3 (1971): 5. See also Aharon Lichtenstein, 'Does Jewish Tradition recognize an Ethic Independent of Halakha?', in M. Fox, ed., *Modern Jewish Ethics: Theory and Practice* (Columbus, OH: Ohio State University Press, 1975), 62; and Bernard S. Jackson, 'The Jewish View of Natural Law', *Journal of Jewish Studies* (2001): 136–145.

4 See, typically, N.S. Schecht, B.S. Jackson, S.M. Passamaneck, D. Piatelli and A.M. Rabello, eds., *An Introduction to the History and Sources of Jewish Law* (Oxford: Oxford University Press, 1996).

5 Louis Jacobs, ed., *Concise Companion to the Jewish Religion* (Oxford: Oxford University Press, 1999), 167.

6 The Torah (lit. teaching) is the will of God revealed to the people of Israel: it is a revealed divine law found in the Written Torah (the Pentateuch) and the Oral Torah (given verbally to Moses, and which in rabbinical tradition embraces the teachings of the sages of Israel transmitted down the generations, and in the depositories of the Oral Torah – the Mishnah and Talmud), with its 613 commands (*mitzvot*).

7 Jonathan A. Jacob, 'The Reasons of the Commandments: Rational Tradition without Natural Law', in J.A. Jacobs, ed., *Reason, Religion and Natural Law* (Oxford: Oxford University Press, 2012), 106ff.

ultimately grounded on revelation; the power of God to operate with absolute freedom; and the absence of a need to seek theoretical justification for the obvious.[8] Also, as there is no basic distinction between law and morals, no moral code independent of divine law, so there is no universal law discoverable by and justified through reason without appeal to God;[9] rather, *halakha* already contains 'moral rights and duties': 'Jewish law . . . is bound to advert to the ethical or higher aspect oftener and with greater emphasis than purely secular legal systems' as to what is 'intrinsically right or wrong'; 'the ruling of the higher law . . . although not invested with the ordinary legal sanctions, is none the less binding from the ethical standpoint'.[10] In short, natural law jars with the legal monism of Judaism: the source of all halakhic norms is the written and oral law, not natural law – no valid norms exist outside the revealed law of God.

However, some scholars recognise the presence (albeit marginal) of natural law theory in the historical development of Judaism. They suggest that the pre-revelation Noahide laws imply that 'all human beings know either instinctively or by tradition what constitutes justice and righteousness'; i.e. the 'basic rules which all humans are expected to follow' which 'constitute the Torah for the Gentile world' – a 'son of Noah' (*ben Noah*), i.e. a Gentile, must keep the laws to belong among 'the righteous of the nations of the world' who may share in the world to come.[11] The seven commandments Noah reiterated after the Flood are the precept to set up courts of law for justice; and six norms against blasphemy, idolatry, adultery and incest, homicide, robbery, and eating flesh from a living animal. For Maimonides (see below), these (except the last, from Scripture) are known by 'rational compulsion' or else 'reason inclines towards them' and were 'commanded to the first humans'. Moreover, the Jewish thinker Philo of Alexandria (c.25 BCE–c.50 CE), influenced by Hellenistic ideas, sees the law revealed to Moses as based on principles of nature: '[T]he world and the law are in mutual accord'; and 'a man who is law-abiding is thereby immediately constituted a world citizen [*cosmopolites*] guiding his actions correctly according to nature's intent, in conformity with which the entire universe is administered.'[12]

Several medieval scholars recognise universal norms in 'the reasons for the commandments' of the Torah discoverable by reason, including norms which may not appear in the Torah and thus may not be totally dependent on divine command. For

8 Avi Sagi, 'Natural Law and *Halakha*: A Critical Analysis', *The Jewish Law Annual* 13 (2000): 149–196.

9 Stephen Nadler, 'Baruch Spinoza and the Naturalization of Judaism', M.L. Morgan and P.E. Gordon, eds., *The Cambridge Companion to Modern Jewish Philosophy* (Cambridge: Cambridge University Press, 2007), 14–34.

10 Rabbi Isaac Herzog, *The Main Institutions of Jewish Law*, 2 Vols. (London and New York: The Soncino Press Limited, 1st edn 1936, 2nd edn 1965), Vol. 1, 381: 'Moral Rights and Duties in Jewish Law'.

11 Louis Jacobs, op cit., 169.

12 See generally Henry A. Wolfson, *Philo: Foundations of Religious Philosophy in Judaism, Christianity and Islam*, Vol. 2 (Cambridge, MA: Harvard University Press, 1947).

Saadia Gaon (882/892–942), Jewish law consists of 'rational laws' and 'revealed laws'; 'wisdom, which is identical with reason', requires acceptance of rational laws with regard to submission to and worship of God, the duty not to blaspheme God or swear falsely in His name, the enforcement of the practice of justice, proper social relations and ethical actions:

> As human beings require a prophet, besides their own reason, to explain to them the revealed commandments, so they require other commands, besides the revealed ones. The goodness of these other commandments is rooted in human reason and understood through it, since it is only through words that they learn what is moral. How would they understand [the obligation to heed the prophet] without logic and rational discernment?

Similarly, for Rabbi Nissim Gaon (990–1062), 'As for the commandments that depend upon reason and understanding, all are binding from the day that God created human beings, on them and on their children after them, forever and ever'; and for Judah Halevi (c. 1075–1141), 'For the divine law cannot become complete till the social and rational laws are perfected'; 'a society failing to abide by norms so fundamental to human life is unworthy of receiving the Torah'; and 'There are the rational laws, being the basis and the preamble of the divine law, preceding it in character and time. There are, however, the ordinations especially given to Israel as a corollary to the rational laws.'[13]

Whether Maimonides (1135/38–1204) also used natural law theory is debatable.[14] For some, he was perhaps 'the most systematic rationalist theorist in the history of Jewish law', but would not be drawn into natural law discourse or integrate it into his jurisprudence, though elements of this are compatible with natural law thinking.[15] The law revealed to Moses at Mount Sinai is not universal but for Israel only:

> Moses, our teacher, bequeathed the Law and commandments to Israel, as it is said an inheritance of the congregation of Jacob [Deuteronomy 33:4], and to those of other nations who are willing to be converted, as it is said: One law and one ordinance shall be both for you, and for the resident alien [Numbers 15:16]. But no coercion to accept the Law and commandments is practiced on those who are unwilling to do so.

However, 'Moses ... was commanded by God to compel all human beings to accept the commandment enjoined upon the descendants of Noah ... *even before the Law was given*' (emphasis added), and 'if his observance thereof is based upon a reasoned conclusion he is not deemed a resident alien, or one of the pious of the gentiles, but one of their wise men'.[16]

[13] Avi Sagi, op cit., at 167–171 and 181.

[14] Supra n. 3, and Oliver Leaman, 'Maimonides and Natural Law', *Jewish Law Annual* 6 (1987): 78–93.

[15] See Joseph David, 'Maimonides, Nature and Natural Law', *Journal of Law, Philosophy and Culture*, V (2010): 67–82, at 67–69.

[16] Ibid. These passages are from Maimonides' Code, the Mishneh Torah.

Maimonides also proposes that the stimulus for and object of divine law is human nature, and he links human society to nature itself: humans are political by nature; it is the nature of humans to live in society, and society needs government. Moreover, diversity amongst humans is a natural necessity: '[Y]ou may find among us two individuals who seem, with regard to every moral habit, to belong to two different species'; this is 'accidental'. Yet, 'natural diversity is hidden through the multiple points of conventional accord' so that 'the community becomes well ordered'; order is needed to counter natural diversity – the revealed law provides this: 'Therefore, I say that the Law, although it is not natural, enters into what is natural. It is part of the wisdom of the deity with regard to the permanence of this species of which He has willed the existence, that He put it into its nature that individuals belonging to it should have the faculty of ruling.'[17] Maimonides, then, relates divine law, which is supernatural, to the nature of humanity and its rule, and the revealed law itself is rational for to attribute to God non-rational laws would be blasphemous.[18]

The first Jewish thinker to use the term 'natural law' (*dat tiv'it*) was Yosef Albo (c.1380–1444), using Christian and Islamic sources. There are three kinds of law: 'Natural law is the same among all peoples, at all times, and in all places'; '[p]ositive or conventional law is a law ordered by a wise man or men to suit the place and time and nature of the persons ... controlled by it', like laws for 'those who worship God as human reason dictates without any divine revelation'; and '[d]ivine law ... is ordered by God through a prophet, like Adam or Noah, or like the custom or law which Abraham taught men', e.g. to worship God and circumcise by divine command, or 'through a messenger whom He sends and through whom He gives a law, like the Law of Moses'. Each has its own purposes: (1) natural law is 'to repress wrong [and] to promote right, in order that men may keep away from theft, robbery and murder, that society may be able to exist'; (2) positive law is 'to suppress what is unbecoming and to promote what is becoming, that men may keep away from indecent [things] according to human opinion'; it cannot exist unless a ruler or judge, placed at the head of the group, compels the people to observe the law for 'the welfare of the group'; and (3) divine law is the product of revelation and its end is spiritual: 'to guide men to obtain true happiness, which is spiritual happiness and immortality', showing them the way to obtain it, and laying down rules so that the community may be ordered in a proper manner and so that 'the bad order of their social life may not prevent them from attaining true happiness, which is the ultimate end ... to which they are destined by God. Divine law is therefore superior to conventional or positive [law]'.[19]

[17] Ibid. These passages are from Maimonides' *The Guide of the Perplexed*.

[18] Tamar Rudavsky, 'Natural Law in Judaism: A Reconsideration', in J.A. Jacobs, ed., *Reason, Religion and Natural Law: From Plato to Spinoza* (Oxford: Oxford University Press, 2012), 83, at 93.

[19] Joseph David, op cit., 78–90.

For one modern scholar, therefore, 'a fully-fledged natural law theory in the modern sense is absent in the medieval Jewish tradition' but it has 'natural law sentiments'; medieval thinkers were 'moving toward a natural law theory, according to which moral truths are universally binding, reflective of our human nature, and accessible to human reasoning'.[20] A similar trend emerges from the centuries that followed. For example, Rabbi Shimon Shkop (1860–1939) proposed that worshipping God is 'an obligation and a need according to the norms of reason and knowledge'; and Rabbi Samuel Glasner (1856–1924):

> As for things that human beings find revolting and loathsome, even had the Torah not forbidden them, all those who would transgress are even more abominable than one violating an explicit biblical prohibition. Because trespassing on a matter that enlightened people find abominable, even if not explicitly forbidden in the Torah, is worse than breaching the laws of the Torah . . . since these [transgressions] can no longer be considered to have been created in his image.[21]

The contemporary Jewish scholar David Novak advocates a robust reappraisal and articulation of natural law theory in Judaism.[22] He bases his propositions on a multitude of texts cited from Scripture and the classical rabbinic tradition:

(1) *Natural law originates in God*: Natural law is created by God, exists as God-given law or commandment (*mitzvah*) and represents what God has wisely willed for all humans. But it is not in itself divine – like all creation: it is made in time; it stems from the eternal nature of God; and it is 'natural' as it is discovered by humans (made in His image) when reasoning about the indispensable requirements of their (divinely) created human nature (which is unique), and their authentically natural (or essential) condition, i.e. according to the way or plan which God creates humans to be.[23]

(2) *Natural law is discoverable through the free use of practical reason*: The 'discovery of authentic human nature and its requirements comes when practical or moral reason is properly exercised' through 'philosophical reflection [on] what their nature is and how to act in accordance with it'. Unlike other creatures which have 'their own nature', humans have 'the choice whether to act according to their nature', but 'not inasmuch as they are subjects of law *qua* commandments'; other creatures are subjects of God's directives with no capacity to accept or reject these. However, humans share with other animals 'certain sub-rational appetites or inclinations'.[24]

20 Tamar Rudavsky, op cit., at 105. 21 Avi Sagi, op cit., 172–174.

22 David Novak, 'Natural Law and Judaism', in A.M. Emon, M. Levering and D. Novak, op cit., Chapter 1.

23 Noahide law represents natural law precepts which God demands all humans to follow.

24 He cites (n. 17), e.g., Rashi (*Ra*bbi *Sh*lomo *Yi*tzhaki, 1040–1105): human beings became human persons when God gave them the capacity for intelligent speech enabling them to relate to each other.

(3) *Natural law is different from the laws of nature*: Sub-rational impulses and inclinations may be governed by the 'laws of nature', but these are not really laws because laws are commands one free rational person addresses to another free rational person; sub-rational impulses only become the concern of natural law as 'moral law' when they are involved in interpersonal relationships between humans – and some moral norms may be known by instinct before being revealed in the Torah.[25]

(4) *Natural law governs the realm of inter-human relations*: 'Natural law is about specific interpersonal commands ... accepted by rational persons' as having good and beneficial ends. Its precepts are universally addressed to all humans, unlike the revealed law of God which is addressed 'to a particular human society'.[26] Moreover, '[w]hen the reason of the commands is universal and thus immediately evident to all *a priori*, the command can be considered a natural law precept'; when the command is not universal and not evident to all, it may be known through revelation *a posteriori*.[27]

(5) *Natural law is the normative aspect of human nature*: Human nature means that to be adequately human we must be actively and intelligently involved with other humans (as 'naturally political animals') and God (whose image we bear); religion is the medium by which we are related to God and is 'endemic to human nature'. We 'act naturally when we make legitimate claims upon one another ... consistent with the reasonable needs' of all the parties involved. That is what makes human nature 'an essentially normative idea'. So, '[n]atural law is law because it is what God the Creator has commanded His human creatures to [be] actively and authentically'.

(6) *Natural law and divine law*: 'Natural law is divine law', but 'unlike divine law that is revealed, natural law is not immediately received as God's commandment'. Instead, we learn natural law 'when we methodically discover (i.e. by the mediation of human reason) ... the authentic requirements of our created nature (i.e. what we naturally need) and by our rational formulation of these ... into ... norms'. These norms are recognised as God's commandments 'during the course of subsequent human experience' – we need not recognise *ab initio* 'a general divine command of which natural law precepts are its subsequent specifications'. Revelation is 'the maximal manifestation of God's law'; natural law is 'the minimal manifestation of God's law'.

(7) *Natural law aids interpretation of divine law*: Natural law allows 'the normative claim of revealed law to be intelligible'. Therefore, 'the Sages have the right, even the duty, to devise answers [which] cannot be found in Scripture'. Natural

25 He cites Mishnah: Avot 3.18 (and Gen. 9.6).

26 He cites J. David Bleich, 'Judaism and Natural Law', *Jewish Law Annual* 7 (1988):5ff.

27 The terms for this 'universalizable reasoned practice' are *derekh erets* ('the way of the earth': he cites (n. 104) Midrash Rabbah: Leviticus 3.9 as to Gen. 3.24); and *tiqqun ha'olam* ('the mending of the world' see Mishnah: Gittin 4.5 as to Isa. 45.18).

law thinking provides the reasons for some scriptural commandments. However, a norm of revealed law should be kept irrespective of whether we know God's reason for it: keeping it does not depend on knowing the reason for it; doubt may lead to not keeping it; God may have no other reason for it than to test whether we will obey it out of faith; and it might insult God to attribute no reason to Him. So, we may never know all of the reasons for God's commands. Yet, He may relate reasons to us through revelation; and for some commands we may surmise the reasons. In other words, 'the fact is that even though we have to keep the commandments of the Torah with the reasons for them being affirmed only *a posteriori*, those commandments that have already been manifest in natural law have reasons that can be found *a priori*'.

(8) *Natural law provides criteria for legislating human-made Jewish law*: Most scholars who consider natural law thinking not genuinely Jewish neglect Jewish laws for which '[t]here is little from scripture, but much from traditions (*halakhot merubbot*)'. As laws may fall out of Jewish usage or later sages think the reasons for making them are no longer valid or their ends are better attained by other means, so 'the preponderance of evidence from the Talmud and related sources is that rabbinic legislation had to be rationally and politically justified in order to be accepted by a people who even asked God for reasons to accept His law in good faith'.[28]

For Novak, then, there has been within Judaism 'a deliberate attempt to avoid a theistic formulation of natural law as a universal law promulgated by God even when Jewish theology may distinguish between divine law which is revealed in history to a particular people and divine law which all people may discover . . . through their use of reason'. However, 'Jewish thinkers who have seen the idea of natural law operating within the Jewish tradition, especially the Jewish legal tradition, are in a minority – albeit not a miniscule or marginal minority.' Today, 'most scholars of Jewish law . . . are legal positivists, looking to Jewish law as they would at the constitution of a modern nation state'. Nevertheless, 'there is enough of a tradition of natural law thinking in Judaism for any contemporary Jewish thinker to continue it and even develop it. Critical thinking within a normative tradition like Judaism is itself a normative pursuit'; and this tradition enables its interpreters 'to rely on minority opinions if [they provide] the more appropriate answer to the normative question that the situation . . . calls for than does the majority opinion'. Therefore, 'natural law thinking is an authentic Jewish form of thought, influencing how Jews look upon their morally significant relations with the non-Jewish world, and how Jews are to continually interpret and re-interpret morally significant relations among ourselves'.[29]

28 He cites David W. Halivini, *Mishnah, Midrash and Gemara* (Cambridge, MA: Harvard University Press, 1986).

29 See also Avi Sagi, op cit., at 180: assuming 'divine command reveals rather than determines . . . natural law, and if the perception of *halakha* as a pluralistic system is feasible, we have no reason to reject the

NATURAL LAW IN ISLAMIC THOUGHT

The classical view is that Islamic law (*sharia*) is created by God whom the devout must obey. Reason alone cannot oblige obedience – at most it corroborates what is established by texts endowed with divine authority.[30] Therefore, there is no natural law tradition in Islam or Islamic jurisprudence.[31] Rather, the dominant thesis is that of 'scriptural positivism', the supremacy of the Quran, which rejects a role for reason in law (*fiqh*), theology (*kalam*) and philosophy (*falsafa*); and, traditionally, for legal theory (*usul al-fiqh*), if there is no Scripture on a matter, there is a state of legal suspension (*tawaqquf*) and no coherent way to determine divine law on the matter, so it is not possible to attribute to God a ruling with normative force; all determinations of divine law must find expression, either directly or indirectly, from Scripture.[32]

However, some scholars consider that human beings may speak authoritatively on the basis of reason without recourse to the revealed divine law and Scripture.[33] Moreover, whilst the Quran is the revealed word of God and the foundation of sharia, 'claiming that God is the sole legislator and that human-made law has no legitimacy cannot be sustained'; humans have no direct access to God's will following the revelation, which ceased at the death of the Prophet, but, as humans 'do not have perfect access to the will of God, they are not able to be the executor of the Divine Will without involving their subjectivity in the process'.[34] Thus, other sources of law recognised in Islam imply the use of human reason and experience: the consensus of jurists (*ijma*); reasoning by analogy (*qiyas*); jurisprudence (*fiqh*); and custom (*urf*). As a *mujtahid* is one 'who exercises independent reasoning (*ijtihad*) in the interpretation of Islamic law' (*fiqh* is doctrines derived from jurists' interpretive effort [*ijtihad*]), so *aql* is intelligence or natural human knowledge (in Ismaili thought, the intellect as divine emanation), and in jurisprudence it is reason as a source for sharia.[35]

Scholars today propose that pre-modern Sunni jurists recognised the authority of reason – whether and how reason alone may require good and prohibit bad, and so justify norms under sharia. For these jurists, nature links the divine will and human reason. God created nature for the benefit of humanity. Since nature reflects His

doctrine' on 'logical grounds'; also, 'God would not hand down commands to a society that did not comply with elementary norms of rationality'; it is 'a precondition' to implement God's commands.

30 Anver M. Emon, *Islamic Natural Law Theories* (Oxford: Oxford University Press, 2010).

31 George Makdisi, *Ibn 'Aqil: Religion and Culture in Classical Islam* (Edinburgh: Edinburgh University Press, 1997), 130; Patricia Crone, *God's Rule – Government and Islam: Six Centuries of Medieval Islamic Political Thought* (New York: Columbia University Press, 2004), 263–264.

32 Anver M. Emon, 'Natural Law and Natural Rights in Islamic Law', *Journal of Law and Religion* 20 (2004–2005): 351–395, at 351.

33 Frank Griffel, 'The Harmony of Natural Law and Shari'a in Islamist Theology', in A. Amanat and F. Griffel, eds., *Islamic Law in the Contemporary Context* (Palo Alto, CA: Stanford University Press, 2007), 38–61.

34 A. Black, H. Esmaeili and N. Hosen, *Modern Perspectives on Islamic Law* (Cheltenham: Edward Elgar Publishing, 2014), 9.

35 John L. Esposito, *The Oxford Dictionary of Islam* (Oxford: Oxford University Press, 2003), 22, 214.

goodness, it fuses both fact (what is) and value (what ought to be). Consequently, as a divinely created good, nature can be investigated to reach both empirical and normative conclusions about right and wrong. Within these broad categories, however, scholars adopted a variety of different positions on human nature.[36] Their starting point is the Quran 30:30: 'So [prophet] as a man of pure faith [*hanif*], stand firm and true in your devotion to religion. This is a natural disposition [*fitra*] God instilled in mankind – there is no altering God's creation – and this is the right religion, though most people do not know it'.[37] So, *fitra* is the original state in which humans were created by God, and being a *hanif* is to follow this disposition towards God: 'Every child is born according to the *fitra*', and it is only the parents who make their child Jewish or Christian or Zoroastrian; but due to the temptations of evil, the revelation is intended by God to ensure the return of humans to the right path.[38]

Three pre-modern schools of thought are relevant here: the Mutazilites proposed that human reason may discover the will of God independently of revelation; the Asharites rejected this idea – the revealed law of God is the sole moral criterion for humans; and the later Asharites accepted a limited scope for reason under divine law and sharia.

The Mutazilites are those (notably Wasil Ibn Ata (d. 131/748) who withdrew (*i'tazala* is 'to withdraw') from the school of Hasan of Basra (Hasan al-Basri). They considered the created order (of nature) (*fitra*) to contain the same norms as revealed in the Quran (which was created not eternal); there is harmony between reason and revelation and God's command may not be the sole criterion to determine the correctness of an action – the command by itself may be insufficient as an agent for action. For example, for the Hanafi jurist Abu Bakr al-Jassas (d. 370/981), when Scripture is silent, discretion must be used to determine a relevant norm, and reason could provide a sufficient basis to assert divine law – God does not act unjustly without purpose.[39] Moreover, on the basis of the concepts of goodness (*husn*) and badness (*qubh*), certain inherent characteristics of acts render those acts good (*hasan*) or bad (*qubih*). These are discoverable by the rational evaluation of an act because God created nature with the express purpose (*gharad*) of benefiting humans. Therefore, that which is not prohibited either by Scripture or a rational universal obligation (*wajib*) is permitted.[40]

The Asharite school considered that rational deduction from the empirical observation of nature devalues revelation, undermines the omnipotence of God, and erroneously suggests that the created order is sufficient to disclose the will of God.[41] This Sunni school, founded by Abu al-Hasan al-Ashari (d. 935), and

[36] See generally Anver M. Emon, *Islamic Natural Law Theories*, op cit.
[37] Translated by M.A.S. Abdel Haleem, *The Qur'an* (Oxford: Oxford University Press, 2004).
[38] See U. Rubin, 'Hanafi', in J.D. McAuliffe, ed., *Encyclopedia of the Qur'an* (Leiden: Brill, 2001–2006).
[39] Qadi 'Abd al-Jabbar (d. 414–415/1025); and Abu al-Husayn al-Basri (d.436/1044) also proposed this.
[40] Anver Emon, 'Natural Law', op cit., at 355; he labels this the 'hard natural law' theory.
[41] Richard M. Frank, 'Moral Obligations in Classical Muslim Theology', *Journal of Religious Ethics* 11 (1983): 205–223, at 207–210.

associated with Hanbali, Shafi'ite, and Maliki jurisprudence, offered a voluntarist critique of the Mutazilites and was later understood to express Islamic orthodoxy. That God cannot do evil and must reward or punish humans because of their own reasoned determinations, undermines God's omnipotence: morality is willed by God; it does not exist objectively; nor is it discoverable independently by unaided human reason. The view that humans have the capacity to judge right and wrong assumes that God can or cannot prescribe for them and so implies limits on His power. Moreover, conclusions from reason alone are arbitrary, shaped by circumstance, socialisation, subjectivity, human will, desire and intuition, and should not be confused with identifying a ruling of God; to hold otherwise means that revelation would be irrelevant. Rather, the role of reason is to prove the truth of revelation, interpret it and perhaps extend it to uncovered areas according to approved methods.[42] As the Shafi'ite jurist Al-Juwayni (d. 478/1085) puts it: 'It is not prohibited [for humans] to investigate these two characteristics [i.e. good and bad] where harm may arise or where benefit is possible, on condition that [the determination] not be attributed to God, or obligate God to punish or reward'; thus, assessing good (*husn*) and bad (*qubh*), but not obligation (*taklif*), was possible without reliance on Scripture.[43]

The Asharite Al-Ghazali (d. 1111), drawing on Muslim and Aristotelian thought,[44] adopts a more nuanced position: 'Every human is originally created with the belief in the one God', a belief rooted in the soul, though some people turn away from God. However, God is a legitimate subject of human understanding. Thus, independent of revelation, norms may be deduced from self-evident principles and observations of nature; indeed, rational arguments lead to the conclusion that there is only one God. Therefore, revelation and the conclusions of reason may be identical but this does not apply to normative judgments on human conduct and sharia. Laws to determine which actions are good or bad cannot be drawn from nature or the human mind,[45] but must be based on revealed texts.[46] Moreover, the object of law may be nature itself; the purposes or benefits (*maslaha*) of law are to protect: religion (*din*), life (*nafs*), reason (*aql*) and property (*mal*); in turn, law exists to prohibit disbelief, murder, fornication and adultery, theft and consuming intoxicating substances: 'It is impossible that any society or any legal system, which aims to benefit creation (*islah al-khalq*) would not include prohibitions against neglect and restraint from these five values.' Indeed, 'it is not farfetched that the interpretation of a jurist would lead to such a rule although no specific source of law exists as evidence for it'. Importantly, therefore:

42 Anver Emon, *Islamic Natural Law Theories*, op cit., Chapter 3: he labels this the voluntarist school.
43 George F. Hourani, *Reason and Tradition in Islamic Ethics* (Cambridge: Cambridge University Press, 1985), 124–134.
44 He was countered later by Ibn Rushd (Averroes, d. 1198).
45 George Hourani, op cit., 135–166.
46 Frank Griffel, op cit., at n. 42: he cites M. Kerr, *Islamic Reform: The Political and Legal Theories of Muhammad Abduh and Rashid Rida* (Berkeley, CA: University of California Press, 1966), 58–66.

> Reason indicates them [the *maslaha*] and decides upon them whether or not there is law. [They] are those for which no law can be without according to those who speak of the good and the bad as rational matters ... [But] we do not deny the power of rational capacities to indicate the beneficial and the corrupt, and their ability to warn against harm and to desire obtaining bounties and fulfilment.[47]

Later Asharite scholars, therefore, developed the idea that reason may be used, as a matter of God's grace (*fadl; tafaddul*), when definitive revelatory Scripture is silent.[48] Sayf al-Din al-Amidi (d. 631/1233) wrote that before we can be obligated under the law, we must have rational capacity (*aql*); for Abd al-Jabbar:

> The individual needs reason because by it he knows much of what he is obligated to do, such as the obligation of returning bailment and thanking the benefactor, as well as the evil of oppression, and the goodness of kindness. He reaches knowledge of all that he is obligated to do through the method of investigation into the scriptural and rational [bases for the obligation].

And according to Ibn Qayyim al-Jawziyya (a traditional Hanbalite), who seeks to harmonise reason and revelation: 'Sharia is ... justice, mercy, goodness and wisdom'; however, 'Anything which forsakes justice for injustice ... is not part of the Sharia even if it is included in it on the basis of interpretation.'[49]

This later Asharite approach surfaces in the work of modern scholars. It is summed up by Al-Bajuri (1783–1860): 'According to Sunnis, good (*hasan*) is what revelation (*al-shar*) calls good, and bad (*qubih*) is what revelation calls bad ... The Asharites hold that all normative judgments are determined by revelation, but in a way that does not violate reason'.[50] Therefore, for Muhammad Abduh (1849–1905), all normative judgments on human conduct need not be based on revelation – universal laws may be known through reason. However, this faculty of reason (*quwwat al-aql*) is not exercisable by everyone – only those 'trained in the use of reason' (*uqala*) who know right from wrong through their rational capacity (*quwwat al-aql*) are able to lay down 'rules of justice' (*qawaid al-adl*). But, as experience shows that people simply do not listen to those trained in the use of reason or obey their deductions from it, society is more prepared to submit to a higher authority than reason, namely prophecy. Consequently, only revealed law adequately prescribes actions in this life and rewards and punishments in the next – and thus gives a clearer incentive to do right than is given by reason. That is, 'the unequal distribution of the faculty of reason among humans required human societies to accept divine law rather than natural law'.[51]

47 Anver Emon, 'Natural Law', op cit., at 372–378.

48 Scholars include: Fakhr al-Din al-Razi (d. 606/1209); Shihab al-Din al-Qarafi (d. 684/11285); Najm al-Din al-Tufi (d. 716/1316); and Abu Ishaq al-Shatibi (d. 790/1388). Anver Emon, *Islamic Natural Law*, op cit., Chapter 4: he labels this the 'soft natural law' position.

49 Ibid. This is associated with Hanbali scholar Ibn Taymiyya (d. 1328).

50 Frank Griffel, op cit., at n. 47.

51 Ibid., at nn. 53–55.

Sayyid Qutb (1906–1966) also synthesises revelation and reason: as principles can be deduced from God's creation and God confirms these in revelation, moral guidance has three sources all of which are in harmony: the signs of nature; the faculty of moral awareness (which God breathes into us); and divine revelation – and so sharia is part of the universal law which governs and mirrors nature.[52] First, God created 'the *fitra* of [the] human soul together with the nature (*tabi'a*) of his religion (*din*)'; 'both are in agreement with the law that governs existence (*namus al-wujud*)', and 'with one another'; and the capacity to distinguish good from bad is concealed within the 'dual nature' of humans – namely, two 'dispositions are created according to the *fitra*, formed according to nature, and concealed as inspiration', or instinct (*ilham*).[53]

Secondly, this instinct is 'the faculty of moral awareness' (*al-quwava al-waiyya*); '[t]here is within the human essence alongside these innate and concealed capacities a faculty that is heedful, perceptive, and refining ... Whoever employs this faculty for the refinement of his soul, for its purification and the further advancement of the disposition to do good that is within the soul ... he will be prosperous'; those who suppress this faculty will not. Distortions (*shiqaq*) of 'the natural way of things appear when mankind – under the influence of his whims and desires (*ahwa*) – sways from the truth that is hidden in the depths of his *fitra* ... when he accepts a moral law for his life that is based on his whims and desires rather than on God's Sharia'.[54]

Thirdly, with this faculty comes a responsibility (*tabia*) which exists from the moment of creation. Revelation assists humans with this responsibility: 'God did not make [humans] to rely entirely on the dual disposition of man's instinctive *fitra*' or on 'the faculty of moral awareness that enables them to turn [toward good]'. Rather, 'He helps them through revelations that lay down the scales [of morality] in a firm and precise manner'. Through revelation God discloses to humans: what their instincts had told them; 'the signs of right-guidance that were [already] in the human soul'; and by it 'the right becomes clear'. Therefore, 'Sharia is nothing else than one section (*quita*) of the divine general law that governs human *fitra* and the general *fitra* of existence, and all parts are well coordinated with one another'.[55] As the 'Sharia that God has ordained for ... humanity is a universal Sharia in the sense that it is connected to and in harmony with the general law of the universe', so

[52] He was Egyptian, a Minister, and member of the Muslim Brotherhood; for the influences on him, see William E. Shepard, *Sayyid Qutb and Islamic Activism* (Leiden: Brill, 1996). He broadly follows Taymiyya.

[53] Frank Griffel, op cit., nn. 56 and 60. See also Esposito, 252: *Qalb* (or *fuad*) is heart, a central concept in Sufi theology based on frequent references in the Quran as 'an intuitive faculty by which the inner reality of things is perceived. Sufis consider *qalb* superior to logical reasoning in grasping the divine mysteries'.

[54] Frank Griffel, op cit., nn. 61–62, 88.

[55] Ibid., n. 64: Fizilal al-Quran 6:3917–3918; Y. Mohamed, *Fitra: The Islamic Concept of Human Nature* (London: Ta-Ha Publishers, 1996), 57.

obedience to sharia is necessary to 'harmonize human life to the life of the universe and to harmonize the law (*namus*) that governs the human *fitra* [with] that [which] governs the universe'.[56]

By way of contrast, Abu al-Ala Mawdudi (1904–1979) tends to the Hanbali position.[57] Moral values of human action are absolute and laid down in sharia as allowed actions (*marufat*) and disallowed actions (*munkarat*): *marufat* 'have always been accepted as "good" by human conscience', and *munkarat* 'have always been condemned by human nature as "evil"'; and so, *marufat* are in harmony with human nature and *munkarat* against it. Sharia defines precisely *marufat* and *mankurat*, clearly indicating the standards to which individuals and society should aspire.[58] However, '[t]he Quran leaves no room for the impression that the divine law may mean merely the law of nature and nothing more'. Instead, 'humankind should order the affairs of its ethical and social life in accordance with the law i.e. Sharia, that God has communicated through His Prophets ... It denies in the clearest terms the right of humans to exercise any discretion in such matters as have been decided by God and His Prophet'. Further, '[e]ven if this world and its natural laws (*qawanin tabi'iyya*) are sufficient and adequate for what is within the human essence of mineral, organic and animal elements, they cease to be sufficient for his creational element' which 'needs a different order for the universe, an order in which the only governing law is the creational law and in which the natural law is only auxiliary to it'.[59]

From these ideas, therefore, it is possible to speak of Islamic natural law thinking in very broad terms and in a number of ways. The Mutazilites advocate a naturalist thesis to ground their use of reason with objectivity and normative authority. The Asharites are positivist in the sense that they look to the scriptural text for authority and clarity on divine obligations, although resort may be had to reason when Scripture is silent. For the modern thinkers Abduh, Qutb and Mawdudi, humans have always been able to distinguish right from wrong in accordance with the universal law which pre-dates the revelation. However, their use is subject to the post-revelation sharia, for it is in obedience to sharia that humans are able to realise their natural disposition towards God and thus their harmony with the created universe.[60]

56 Frank Griffel, op cit., nn. 57–58, 60, 92: on the relationship between reason and revelation in Sayyid Qutb, see Ibrahim M. Abu-Rabi, *Intellectual Origins of Islamic Resurgence in the Modern Arab World* (Albany, NY: State University of New York Press, 1996), 191–192.

57 See his *Islam ka nizam i hayat: The Islamic Way of Life*, K. Ahmad and K. Murad, ed. and trans. (Leicester: Islamic Foundation, 1986); and: *The Islamic Law and Constitution*, 2nd edn (Lahore: Islamic Publications, 1960); see also Seyyed Vali Reza Nasr, *Mawdudi and the Making of Islamic Revivalism* (Oxford: Oxford University Press, 1996), 57–63.

58 *The Islamic Way of Life*, 17–21.

59 *The Islamic Law and Constitution*, 75. See Frank Griffel, op cit., at nn. 85, 89–90.

60 See also A. Kevin Reinhart, *Before Revelation: The Boundaries of Muslim Moral Thought* (Albany, NY: State University of New York Press, 1995), 4–5: jurists used hypothetical cases to deal with novel and difficult situations.

NATURAL LAW IN CHRISTIAN THOUGHT

Natural law doctrine historically has enjoyed a prominent place in Christian thought.[61] Many scholars see Paul's Letter to the Romans as containing a germ of the doctrine: 'When Gentiles who have not the law do by nature what the law requires, they are a law to themselves, even though they do not have the law. They show that what the law requires is written in their hearts' (Romans 2.14–15).[62] The doctrine was developed by the early Fathers of the Church (though some today think its role in Patristic writing was minimal).[63] For example, according to Origen of Alexandria (185–254), natural law is the physical law governing the cosmos and the law of reason binding humans as universal ethical norms and following from the Golden Rule (do to others as you would have them do to you [Luke 6.31]); moreover, all humans are able to obey natural law, but need Christ the redeemer who teaches a morality going beyond natural law, otherwise our sin would not be expiated and we could not have a share in God's righteousness.[64] Similarly, for Augustine (354–430), there is a 'law which is called supreme reason, which must always be obeyed, by which the evil deserve an unhappy life and the good a blessed life'; this law is the eternal law: 'the divine reason or will of God which commands that the natural order be preserved and forbids that it be disturbed'. However, unless humans are united to the salvation won by Christ with the grace of the Holy Spirit, they cannot sufficiently obey natural law.[65]

In the medieval period, Aquinas famously argues (along Aristotelian lines): humans are rational creatures, with the capacity to reason; by using reason to reflect on human nature, we may discover the specific ends towards which we naturally tend (e.g. to live, reproduce, have an ordered society and worship God), and the general end for which God created us, i.e. salvation in eternal communion with God. When we have discovered these ends, it is then possible for us to determine the means required to achieve them. This understanding of God's plan for humans, implanted in us by His act of creation, is natural law – it is a participation in the eternal law of God – and from natural law precepts may be induced moral duties (and rights).[66] Some elements of the theory were retained at the Reformation; e.g. for Calvin, humans have a 'sense of divinity' or 'sense of God', 'the seed of religion', corrupted but not obliterated by sin, but for certain knowledge of God humans need to turn to the Word of God.[67]

61 Matthew Levering, 'Natural Law and Christianity', in Emon, Levering and Novak, op cit., Chapter 2.

62 See, e.g., Francisco J. Contreras, ed., *The Threads of Natural Law: Unravelling a Philosophical Tradition* (New York: Springer, 2013).

63 See, e.g., Robert Louis Wilken, *The Spirit of Early Christian Thought: Seeking the Face of God* (New Haven, CT: Yale University Press, 2003), 320.

64 B.L. Dunkle, 'A Development of Origen's View of the Natural Law', *Pro Ecclesia* 13 (2004): 337–351.

65 Matthew Levering, op cit., Augustine's *On Free Will.*

66 See, e.g., John Finnis, *Natural Law and Natural Rights* (Oxford: Clarendon Press, 1980).

67 Institutes, I.ii.4.

However, partly on the basis of the doctrine of original sin, later Reformation theology generally rejected the competence of fallen human reason to engage in natural theology, a view asserted by Karl Barth (1886–1968): 'What is pleasing to God comes into being when all human righteousness is gone, irretrievably gone, when men are uncertain and lost, and when they have abandoned all ethical and religious illusions, and when they have renounced every hope in this world and in this heaven'; indeed, when gentiles 'show that what the law requires is written on their hearts' (Romans 2.15), they show precisely that they no longer cling to any human resources, including "natural law"'.[68] Generally, therefore, arguments against natural law theory typically include the propositions that (1) natural law theory is flawed because it moves from observable facts to moral principles; it attempts to base ethics (ought) on a non-moral account of what human beings are like (is) – what humans are like does not tell us what they ought to be like morally; (2) the picture of human nature is likely to be as controversial as the moral conclusions at which it arrives – that picture is itself the product of a moral outlook rather than an independently established basis by which a moral outlook can be supported; (3) that human reason alone (and fallen human reason at that), reflecting on human nature, can understand God's will for us, undermines the need for God's grace, devalues the revelation in Christ – if humans can know what is good in God's eyes, this unacceptably exalts human reason; and (4) natural law theory plays down or denies specifically Christian ethics – whereas Christianity actually requires a radically new set of imperatives instituted by Christ.[69]

Nevertheless, as we have seen in earlier chapters, there are today Catholic,[70] Orthodox,[71] Lutheran,[72] Reformed[73] and other scholars,[74] who propose natural law

68 Karl Barth, *The Epistle of Paul to the Romans* (Oxford: Oxford University Press, 1933), 68.

69 Gerard J. Hughes, 'Natural Law', in J.F. Childress and J. Macquarrie, eds., *A New Dictionary of Christian Ethics* (London: SCM Press, 1986), 412–414; Stanley Hauerwas, *The Peaceable Kingdom: A Primer in Christian Ethics* (Notre Dame, IN: University of Note Dame Press, 1983); Paul Ramsey, *Basic Christian Ethics* (Louisville, KY: Westminster-John Knox Press, 1993), 84–85.

70 Germain Grisez, 'The First Principles of Practical Reason: A Commentary on the *Summa Theologiae*, 1–2, Question 94, Article 2', *Natural Law Forum* 10 (1965): 168–201; Javier Hervada, *Critical Introduction to Natural Law*, M. Emmons, trans. (Quebec: Wilson and Lafleur, 2006).

71 See, e.g., Vigen Guroian, *Incarnate Love: Essays in Orthodox Ethics* (Notre Dame, IN: University of Notre Dame Press, 1987), 31.

72 C.E. Braaten, 'A Lutheran Affirmation of the Natural Law', in R.C. Baker and R.C. Ehlke, eds., *Natural Law: A Lutheran Reappraisal* (St Louis, MO: Concordia Publishing House, 2011), 3–16.

73 See, e.g., David VanDrunen, *Natural Law and the Two Kingdoms: A Study in the Development of Reformed Social Thought* (Grand Rapids, MI: William B. Eerdmans, 2010), 95, and his *A Biblical Case for Natural Law* (Grand Rapids, MI: Acton Institute, 2006) and Stephen J. Grabill, *Rediscovering the Natural Law in Reformed Theological Ethic* (Grand Rapids, MI: William B. Eerdmans, 2006).

74 J. Daryl Charles, *Retrieving the Natural Law: A Return to Moral First Things* (Grand Rapids, MI: William B. Eerdmans, 2008); Ralph P. George, ed., *Natural Law Theory: Contemporary Essays* (Oxford: Clarendon Press, 1992); Jean Porter, *Natural Law and Divine Law: Reclaiming the Tradition for Christian Ethics* (Grand Rapids, MI: William B. Eerdmans, 1999), Chapter 3.

theory, rooted in the idea that God imprints upon all a capacity to discern through our natural inclination the ordering which God has given us,[75] whether the discoverability of universal ethical principles is affected by sin,[76] or not.[77] For example, the Anglican theologian Nigel Biggar proposes that to 'affirm natural law' means that there is a form of flourishing given in and with the nature of human being; reflection on human nature can achieve an understanding of that flourishing and its basic goods; reflection on our experience can produce a grasp of kinds of disposition and action that respect and promote those goods; all humans are, despite their sinfulness, *somewhat* capable of an accurate grasp of basic goods and their practical requirements, and, therefore, there are sometimes areas of ethical agreement between Christians and others. However, 'None of this . . . makes the Christian theological salvation narrative ethically irrelevant. It does not say that sinful humans have the motivation to do sufficiently what they know to be right, apart from penitence, faith, gratitude, and hope that the story of God's salvific initiative inspires', nor 'that they have the power, unaided by biblical tradition, to know completely what is good, what is virtuous, or what is right.'[78]

Similarly, for Matthew Levering the principles of natural law are capable of specific articulation and should function as the basis for any just legal system which seeks to recognise the dignity of the human person and to maintain justice. He proposes:

(1) Natural law does not obviate the need for the grace of the Holy Spirit and the work of Jesus Christ. Knowing its precepts does not mean that we will observe them, or that our outward observance of them will be matched by our interior attitude (which should be that of love). As human sinfulness obscures natural law and makes it impossible to know its precepts adequately and observe them rightly, so we need to be transformed by the grace of the Holy Spirit and the redeemer Christ in order to be reconciled to God and become the righteous people God intended us to be.

(2) In following conscience and striving to act justly to God and neighbour, humans may be moved by grace that unites them to the salvation won by Christ, even without knowing God explicitly. This explains the presence in the Bible of righteous gentiles. Grace is not limited to the time after Christ. God cares for all humans not just the people of God. The visible people of God

[75] E.g. Catholic thinkers, see Russell Hittinger, *A Critique of the Natural Law Theory* (Notre Dame, IN: University of Notre Dame Press, 1987); and S.A. Long, 'Natural Law or Autonomous Practical Reason: Problems for the New Natural Law Theory', in R.P. George (above, n. 74).

[76] Russell Hittinger, *The First Grace: Rediscovering the Natural Law in a Post-Christian World* (Wilmington, DE: ISI Books, 2003), 3–37, 63–91 and 93–112.

[77] Jean Porter, 'Does the Natural Law provide a Universally Binding Morality?', in L.S. Cunningham, ed., *Intractable Disputes about Natural Law: Alisdair MacIntyre and Critics* (Notre Dame, IN: University Press of Notre Dame, 2009), 53–95.

[78] Nigel Biggar, *Behaving in Public: How to Do Christian Ethics* (Grand Rapids, MI: William B. Eerdmans, 2011), 41–42.

(e.g. Israel/Church) are cared for by God in various ways, including natural law that enables them to distinguish right from wrong.

(3) Like all humans, Christians possess natural law and are required to live by its precepts. Imitating Christ would not suffice, indeed it would not be possible, if Christians lacked natural law. That is, 'the cruciform moral path of Christians should not be set at odds with the natural law precepts one finds in the Golden Rule and Decalogue, as Jesus affirmed. Part of the task of Christian [approaches to] natural law, then, is to remind Christians of what Christians should be doing, rather than solely to call upon others to value the dignity of all human persons.'

(4) Natural law doctrine helps to affirm God's universal providence and His desire to save all humans (I Timothy 2.4), affirms the worth of each human, and shows that there are certain things that no human being or institution can rightly do to other humans. It also upholds the value of free choice: 'Since God will render to every man according to his works (Romans 20.6), natural law doctrine supports the obvious point that knowledge and good works are by no means limited to Christians.'[79]

(5) Natural law is our participation in God's eternal law, and it is constituted and promulgated by the Creator God, who imprints it on our hearts. Natural law requires recognition of a divine lawgiver.[80] As a rational sharing in God's providence, natural law is ordered towards human fulfilment and flourishing, which involves hierarchically ordered ends or goods. Its teleological character, and its rootedness in human inclinations (shaped by human rationality), follows from the fact that God creates humans in his image for the good of communion with God and with fellow humans.

(6) Human positive law is properly grounded upon natural law. Murder would still be wrong even if the positive law of a society approved it.[81] People know by natural law, e.g., that preservation of human life is good and murder is evil. Law is not a solely historical and cultural constraint, according to which some actions are right or wrong depending on time and place. Some actions are simply wrong because they violate God's law which we know however imperfectly by natural law.

(7) Human sinfulness obscures but does not eliminate our ability to perceive the precepts of natural law. One of the common rebuttals to natural law doctrine is that humans have not been able to agree on its content. With the exception of certain basic precepts (e.g. the prohibition against murder), people often

[79] Matthew Levering, *Jewish-Christian Dialogue in the Life of Wisdom: Engagement with the Theology of David Novak* (London: Continuum, 2010), Chapters 3 and 4.

[80] Levering cites J. Budziszewski, *The Line Through the Heart: Natural Law as Fact, Theory, and Sign of Contradiction* (Wilmington, DE: ISI Books, 2009), 23–40.

[81] He cites Hadley Arkes, *Constitutional Illusions and Anchoring Truths: The Touchstone of the Natural Law* (Cambridge: Cambridge University Press, 2010).

> disagree about what natural law entails. Even with regard to murder, people differ as to what is 'murder'. People also have different ideas as to what human flourishing involves. The fact that sin obscures but does not obliterate the perception of natural law makes sense of what would otherwise be a strange paradox i.e. that both the Torah and Jesus Christ reveal precepts that belong to natural law. The obscuring of natural law also helps to explain the historical variance with respect to what has counted as the content of natural law. Over the course of history, and for all sorts of historical reasons, different individuals and societies will perceive the precepts of natural law more or less clearly.

In Christianity, then, natural law has a wide variety of meanings, but it is generally seen as the law implanted in nature by God which rational creatures can discern through the use of natural reason; it is thus contrasted with the revealed law, though aspects of divine law may also be precepts of natural law. However, there are differences of opinion about the content of natural law beyond broad agreement that good is to be done and evil avoided; this suggests that natural law 'underwrites morality as such, rather than any particular moral code'.[82] The theory also appears in 'natural theology', knowledge about God obtained by human reason without the aid of revelation; the objects of natural theology include God (known through His works), the human soul (its freedom) and natural law.[83] Moreover, natural law goes not generally appear explicitly in the modern juridical texts of churches worldwide, though they do invoke concepts of divine law, the revealed law of God, as well as large moral ideas rooted in ethical standards perhaps conceivable as universal.[84]

CONCLUSION

There are several fundamental similarities and differences in the approaches of Judaism, Christianity and Islam to natural law doctrine, not only as between these faiths, but also within each faith. Whereas natural law doctrine has historically played a prominent part for the majority of Christian traditions, though some contest its potential to devalue revelation in Christ, in Judaism and Islam it is a minority position: the revealed law is sufficient of itself and reason is not a free-standing normative category independent of revelation and Scripture – though reason has a place, for example, as an aid to interpret revelation and Scripture, but some modern scholars argue that it should have a greater part in Judaism and Islam today. Yet, it is possible to identify profound areas of commonality between both the majority and minority positions across and within these faiths if we are prepared to abandon the term 'natural law' and focus instead on the single category divine law communicated

82 See generally Roger Ruston, *Human Rights and the Image of God* (London: SCM Press, 2004).

83 F.L. Cross and E.A. Livingstone, eds., *Oxford Dictionary of the Christian Church* (Oxford: Oxford University Press, 2005), 1139.

84 For concepts of divine law, moral law, conscience, and equity, see Norman Doe, *Christian Law: Contemporary Principles* (Cambridge: Cambridge University Press, 2013).

to humans as a universal law at their creation by God, the imperfect apprehension of which is perfected by the subsequent revelation of God in the form of revealed law.

First, all three faiths agree that God created the natural order, made humankind in His own image, designed these to function in accord with a universal law, communicated this law by implanting in humans the capacity for moral awareness, and enabled humans the use of reason in order to judge right from wrong. In turn, this divine universal law is accessible to the human reason and the authority of reason may be articulated in the form of (moral) requirements. However, our use of reason to identify the norms of this universal law is not infallible but subject to the vicissitudes of human nature, the circumstances of time and place, and the capacity of humans not to act as God intended. For this reason and for the benefit of humans to enjoy the right relationship with God which He intended, God graciously willed revelation.

Secondly, the revelation of God reiterates the divine law (previously communicated in the universal law), for the better understanding of humans, as the revealed law (of God). Revelation assists humans to overcome their imperfect apprehension of the universal law hitherto discoverable only by means of the fallible use of human reason. This revealed law is deposited in Scripture, and its object is the authentic exercise of human nature as God originally intended in the form of right moral judgment shaped by that revealed law. Scripture and the faith it envisions is sufficient for humans and their moral judgments in harmonising these with God's will as expressed in the universal law the apprehension of which is perfected through the revealed law.

Thirdly, though, the human capacity to use reason to judge what is right and wrong is not destroyed or made redundant by revelation and by Scripture. As the universal law pre-dates revelation, and reason was available as a means to apprehend it, so reason should be used to understand the revealed law, to interpret Scripture when Scripture is silent on a matter and, therefore, to formulate moral principles latent within the divine law in its original form (universal law) and reiterated form (revealed law).

Reason and revelation, then, are modes by which God communicated the divine law for the flourishing of humankind: both are creatures of the divine will and wisdom; the light of revelation clarifies what human reason imperfectly apprehends as the will of God. It may therefore be possible to elucidate by means of reason, but imperfectly, the reasons for which God made the pre-revelation universal law applicable to all humans and the reasons for the norms which God reiterated in revelation. However, reason is the servant of revelation and it should not be used outwith revelation. To elevate reason as a free-standing law (rational law) may indeed devalue revelation, Scripture and faith based upon them, and reason should not attribute to God a norm not found in revelation. Nevertheless, humanly created norms, including religious laws and those operative in the interstices of revealed law, and interpretations of Scripture, should themselves be rational. The universal pre-revelation law is perfect, but the human apprehension of it is not. Revealed law seeks to perfect this apprehension of the divine universal law – and reason must be used in this quest.

Finally, debate about a shared concept of divine law, communicated at creation to all humans as a universal law, but whose imperfect human apprehension is perfected by a knowledge of the revealed law (to which reason is a servant) is clearly worthwhile as a means of identifying common ground in dialogue between the Abrahamic faiths, perhaps to counteract what seems to be the problematic use of the term 'natural law'.

11

Natural Law and Philosophical Presuppositions

Owen Anderson

This chapter studies the role of general revelation in natural law theory. General revelation, what all persons can know about God and the good, provides the foundation of natural law thinking. However, special revelation (revealed religion) is often invoked before basic questions about the reality of God and the good have been answered. This chapter studies the claim that all persons ought to know God and that knowing God is the highest good.

One way to understand natural law is as the study of the moral law from general revelation. By way of contrast, Christianity relies on special revelation to make claims about the need for redemption through the atoning work of Christ. Nevertheless, they share important presuppositions about knowledge, reality and what is good. The following chapter will look at the philosophical foundation presupposed by natural law and by Christianity and the ways that these reinforce each other. One way this will be achieved is by considering the influential contemporary work of John Finnis and how he has explained natural law. The chapter will explain the argument that there must be a clear natural moral law to make sense of the Christian claims about the reality of sin and the need for redemption. It will become clear that it is impossible to avoid philosophical foundations about God and the good and this means the case must be made that humans ought to know God. This law is presupposed by special revelation although the Scriptures affirm that there is a clear general revelation of God's nature and the moral law.

Before considering specific thinkers like Finnis or Aristotle it is worth considering a few important presuppositions of Christianity. Specifically, special revelation (revealed religion related through testimony) as redemptive revelation presupposes that there is a clear general revelation of God's nature and the moral law (Romans 1). It is the failure to know God and keep this law that puts humans in the condition of needing redemption. Special revelation affirms both God and the moral law but cannot be a proof for either without becoming circular (I believe the Bible because it is God's word, and I know God exists because the Bible says so).

Scripture uses the terms 'life' and 'death' to refer not simply to physical life but to spiritual life and humanity's highest goal (John 17:3). Natural law has used the general revelation term 'the good' to refer to the end in itself, that at which all things aim. The good, as opposed to a good, refers to the highest goal or chief end. Presupposed by both natural law and Christianity is that the good is knowable by all persons. Redemption is a restoration to the good, or eternal life, which was lost due to sin. Therefore, any study of both Christianity and natural law must begin with the good, how it is known and how it relates to human nature.

Since *the good* is a general revelation concept it is not surprising that thinkers like Plato and Aristotle made contributions to its articulation. This means that *the* good as the highest goal is an idea that all persons, even those without access to special revelation, can think about. Aristotle is especially linked to the history of natural law due to the influence of Aquinas. One of the observations to be made is in how a thinker's beliefs about what is real (sometimes called metaphysics) shapes how that thinker understands the good. Consequently, Plato and Aristotle, although having differences, were metaphysical dualists who denied that there was a creation. Aquinas, as a theist, believed in creation *ex nihilo*. So while all three might use the term *God* in their respective languages, and even claim that the knowledge of God is the highest good, the difference in how *God* is defined means that there is also significant difference in the content of the good. If there is no God, or all is God, or God is the former but not creator (demiurge/unmoved mover), a very different conception of the good comes out in contrast to God as the Creator.

Natural law has often been dismissed by modern thinkers because of its association with Aquinas and Aristotelian teleology. As a consequence contemporary thinkers who want to revive natural law thinking have often looked for ways to do so without reference to metaphysics or teleology. Yet because natural law is the study of the nature of things and what is good for the nature of a thing, it is impossible, in an important sense, to avoid making claims about what is real in order to justify beliefs about what is good. In order to see how contemporary natural law theorists attempt to avoid metaphysics we will look at John Finnis.

Does natural law theory require a philosophical foundation? John Finnis and others working on the New Natural Law Theory have argued that there are goods which are self-evident as the objects of practical rationality. This has been called 'new natural law' to distinguish it from 'old natural law' which often relied heavily on Aristotelian and Thomistic metaphysical theory. Knowing these as goods does not require a foundation of speculative, or theoretical, rationality about the nature of being. Finnis and Grisez reject the idea attributed to the classical natural law theory that nature is normative.[1] 'One cannot derive the moral "ought", according to Grisez and Finnis, from the "is" of human nature.'[2] Instead, we can know about human flourishing by understanding how practical rationality aims at goods that are ends in themselves. Practical rationality assumes a goal and is a matter of figuring out how best to achieve that goal.

[1] Robert George, ed., *In Defense of Natural Law* (Oxford: Clarendon Press, 1999), 60. [2] Ibid., 60.

And yet Ralph McInerny tells us that the theoretical use of the mind is primary, presupposed by the practical use.[3] Indeed, he states that the practical and speculative uses of reason are not separate faculties but different uses of the same faculty. To judge that something is good presupposes some knowledge of the thing judged to be good and the being for which it is good.[4] McInerny tells us this is all but true by definition. 'It is difficult to imagine Finnis and friends dissenting from this. It is because, at the least, they seem to dissent from it, that they have been the object of so much criticism.'[5] Do Finnis and friends dissent from what McInerny argues is true by definition or is something else going on?

The is/ought problem is a standard feature of modern ethical thought. Have Grisez and Finnis found a way around it or is McInerny correct that the problem is itself a mistake? In the following I will present the view of Finnis about human goods and some of the best known objections to his view. Then I will argue that any form of natural law requires philosophical foundations that begin with understanding the role of God the Creator and the knowledge of God as the highest good for humans. Just as the Decalogue begins with affirming God, so too does the natural law and any consistent thought about the highest good. Robert George tells us that 'the whole of creation is, for Aquinas, suffused with meaning and value by divine intelligence and free choice'.[6] Should humans know this meaning and what it reveals about the Creator? If so this seems to indicate that some truths about being and human nature in relation to the nature of God are clear and should be known by all persons.

EPISTEMOLOGY AND SELF-EVIDENCE

John Finnis tells us that it is simply not true that any form of natural law requires deriving propositions about man's duties and obligations from propositions about human nature or the nature of things.[7] 'On the contrary, Aquinas asserts as plainly as possible that the first principles of natural law, which specify the basic forms of good and evil and which can be adequately grasped by anyone of the age of reason (and not just by metaphysicians), are *per se nota* (self-evident) and indemonstrable'.[8] In order to avoid deriving the moral 'ought' from the factual 'is', John Finnis argues that there are first principles of practical rationality that are self-evident.[9] These are foundational to moral arguments. Since they are self-evident they are not argued to as one might argue towards a conclusion. They can be illustrated or defended by dialectical arguments that refute arguments against them but since they are self-evident they cannot be argued for directly.[10]

3 Ralph McInerny, *Aquinas on Human Action: A Theory of Practice* (Washington, DC: Catholic University of America Press, 1992), 191.

4 Ibid., 192. 5 Ibid., 193. 6 George, 41.

7 John Finnis, *Natural Law and Natural Rights*, 2nd edn (Oxford: Clarendon Press, 2011), 33.

8 Ibid., 33. 9 Ibid., 63, and George, 44. 10 George, 45.

Finnis does tell us that Aquinas would concede that if man's nature were different so too would be man's duties.[11] But the way to understand these duties, according to how Finnis reads Aquinas, is not by an external study of psychology, anthropology or metaphysics, but by experiencing one's nature 'from the inside'.[12] McInerny considers this a movement from our experienced abilities to the ends or goals of these abilities and puts it in contrast to the Aristotelian move from our nature to the goal and hence our abilities.[13] Christopher Tollefsen phrases it as a matter of grasping reason directed at action through which we understand self-evidently desirable goods.[14] These goods are incommensurable and are the basis for making moral laws although the grasping of them as self-evident is not itself moral.[15]

These foundational principles are about what Grisez-Finnis call 'basic human goods'. Their self-evidence can be illustrated by reflecting on the nature of choice and action. When we make a choice we are acting towards some end. Many of these ends are themselves steps towards further ends. The goal of ordering lunch is to eat. And the goal of eating is health. We can use this idea of an end in itself to see that not every goal of choice is an end in itself. But it is, according to Finnis, self-evident that some things are ends in themselves. The basic goods of life, knowledge, friendship, play, aesthetic experience, practical reasonableness and religion are understood to be self-evidently ends in themselves. If a person gives as an explanation that he is acting to achieve knowledge this is a comprehensible goal and no further explanation is needed.

The first principles of practical reasoning are not themselves moral laws. Instead they state the condition of any coherent practical thinking about means/ends.[16] In this sense the first principles are weak and require only coherence and not actual moral correctness.[17] A morally evil choice is intelligible precisely because it is aimed at an intelligible goal. The goal of treating another person unfairly is intelligible even if morally wrong.

CRITICISMS AND RESPONSES

One criticism about these self-evident goods is that Finnis is relying not so much on self-evidence as on his own intuition. Russell Hittinger makes this argument in *A Critique of the New Natural Law Theory*.[18] He argues that the Grisez-Finnis approach is a kind of intuitionism that leaves their basic human goods open to doubt.[19] As proof of this Hittinger points out that Finnis often relies on arguments to support his claims about these goods as self-evident. However, George responds

[11] Finnis, 34. [12] Ibid., 34. [13] McInerny, 185.

[14] Christopher Tollefsen, 'Reasons for Action and Reasons for Belief', *Social Epistemology* 20 (2006): 56.

[15] Ibid., 57. [16] George, 37. [17] Ibid., 37.

[18] Russell Hittinger, *A Critique of the New Natural Law Theory* (Notre Dame, IN: University of Notre Dame Press, 1987).

[19] George, 61.

by arguing that 'dialectical argumentation focusses on the relationships between propositions (including putatively self-evident propositions) to be defended and other knowledge'.[20] The goal of this kind of argument is to show that if what is self-evident is denied it leads to other unacceptable problems such as self-referential absurdity.

Notice that this kind of argument presupposes the law of non-contradiction. It illustrates that by denying supposedly self-evident goods one runs into unacceptable contradictions. In this sense it is the law of non-contradiction that is self-evident and this is an application, perhaps a foundational application, of that law to human choice and action. This law is presupposed by any knowledge claim and is therefore presupposed by any moral assertion.

This means that these goods of human action are self-evidently grasped not immediately but upon understanding the concepts involved. This begins to suggest that some knowledge of the nature of being is required. McInerny tells us that 'under pressure from Henry Veatch,[21] Finnis now agrees that first principles are derived from experience which includes "not only the stirrings of desire and aversion, but also an awareness of possibilities, likelihoods, *ut in pluribus* outcomes, and so forth"'.[22] We can add to this some knowledge of human nature since these are called basic *human* goods.

Does this mean that Finnis and others are wrong about the self-evidence of these basic human goods? There are two ways to consider this. One is that as explanations of human action they might be acceptable 'conversation stoppers' but it does not follow that they are ends in themselves. For instance, it might be true that it is intelligible to say that I work to get money to buy medicine for my health. Not much more explanation is needed in an ordinary discussion. However, people stay healthy, or want health, in order to be better able to achieve other goals. What a person considers to be an acceptable level of health will depend on how that person understands their goals in life. A marathon runner might think of this differently than a philosophy instructor.

Second, McInerny considers the direction proposed by Finnis for arriving at moral knowledge. 'Finnis has often said that we do not have to know metaphysics and anthropology before doing ethics, but a similar, obviously true point is made by saying that we do not have to have studied moral philosophy in order to engage in moral activity.'[23] Finnis says that our grasp of the self-evident human goods is independent of our knowledge of other speculative truths. However, McInerny points out that the speculative and practical intellects are not two distinct faculties but are instead two different ways of using the same faculty, 'and since being is the first

[20] Ibid., 62.

[21] Henry Veatch, *Swimming Against the Current in Contemporary Philosophy: Occasional Essays and Papers*, Vol. 20 (Washington, DC: Catholic University of American Press, 1990).

[22] McInerny, 189. [23] Ibid., 190.

thing the mind grasps, knowledge of being is presupposed by all human knowledge, whether speculative or practical.'[24]

Exactly how an individual person arrives at some belief about human goods is a distinct matter from what is logically presupposed by judgments about the good. An individual might not reason from the nature of things to a belief about what is good. However, the belief about what is good presupposes claims about being and about the nature of the being for which it is good. These in turn presuppose claims about the nature of reality and God.

How these goods are understood, or interpreted, will depend on the larger world view in which they are nested including metaphysical and epistemological presuppositions. This makes their 'self-evidence' unhelpful since how to interpret them is not self-evident.

This leads some scholars of Thomas Aquinas to argue that the Grisez-Finnis formulation of Aquinas is not accurate. Edward Feser, in his book *Aquinas*, makes the case that the is/ought problem is a modern formulation that Aquinas did not accept.[25] He says that the Grisez-Finnis approach to natural law begins with the fact/value distinction and that this is a disastrous assumption of modern ethical theory. Feser understands the point of new natural law 'from its inception has been to provide an alternative philosophical foundation for Catholic moral teaching'.[26] He argues that 'the attempt of the "new natural lawyers" to square this circle – to smuggle in a bit of disguised Aristotelianism after all, under the Humean radar – results in obscurantism and incoherence'.[27]

Since this is not a chapter about the true reading of Aquinas that aspect of Feser's criticism may not be fully answered here. Earlier Finnis was quoted as arguing that Aquinas would indeed say that if human nature were different so too would be human duty. At other times new natural law theory sounds like Grotius in asserting that the law would be what it is even if there were no God. For our present interest it is true that Finnis and others in the new natural law school accept the is/ought distinction as a real problem for any moral theory.

I believe we can make some progress in untangling these disagreements by considering how the different theorists are arriving at their conclusions. Perhaps there is not so much a conflict between them as a difference in perspective. It might indeed be true that there are self-evident ends of action or choice that I can grasp by reflecting on choice. These are grasped without also reflecting on human nature and are therefore not derived from nature.

However, it is also true that human choice and human goods presuppose truths about human nature and God as the creator of human nature. So if Grotius meant that humans can agree on laws without first agreeing on theology then this appears to be true (at least in the short run). But if he meant that if God, as a necessary being,

[24] Ibid., 190. [25] Edward Feser, *Aquinas* (London: OneWorld Publications, 2009). [26] Ibid.
[27] Ibid.

might not exist and that this has no influence on any other truths then this cannot be true by definition of 'necessary being'. At best Grotius was making a rhetorical point but he could not have been making a modal or ontological point.

In a similar way Finnis can be understood as arguing with those who reject God's role in law. Finnis can still point out to such persons that there are ends which are sought in practical rationality. These can largely be agreed upon by persons who disagree about theology and metaphysics. And yet it is also true that these goods presuppose God and human nature when understood correctly. In fact, I believe Finnis relies upon a proof for God's existence that uses this kind of thinking and which I will detail later in this chapter. First, I want to look at what it means for truth claims to have presuppositions about the nature of things. To do this I turn to Aristotle.

ARISTOTLE AND PRESUPPOSITIONS

Aristotle begins the study of metaphysics by noting that all humans desire to know. His statement seems to affirm that it is self-evident that humans desire to know; knowledge is a self-evident human good. We find delight in knowing. This is directly related to the good or meaningful life.

When Anaxagoras was asked 'What is the meaning of life? Why would somebody choose to come into the world and live?' he is said to have answered, 'to observe the heavens, and the stars and moon and sun in them,' everything else being unimportant. A successful life is either a life of understanding, or a life of pleasure, or a life of moral virtue; whichever it is, the most important contribution we can make to it is to take up the study of philosophy.[28]

Finnis also uses 'knowledge' as the example of a human good in Chapter 3 of *Natural Law and Natural Rights*. This provides us with common ground in thinking about what it means for knowledge to be a good. There is an important sense in which we do not want to know in order to achieve some other end but simply for its own sake. We can distinguish between what is sought as a means to something else, what is sought for its own sake and what is an effect of possessing that which is sought for its own sake. Sometimes these are described as virtue, the good and happiness. Knowledge is something that can be sought for its own sake. Indeed, of the basic goods that Finnis lists, it seems that knowledge is inherent and essential to each such that what we enjoy in them is the knowing and understanding. 'This state of knowing is a virtue in itself and brings its own rewards, since we naturally enjoy understanding things.'[29]

In order to identify the human good Aristotle explains that we must identify human nature. It is here that modern thinkers begin to get nervous that metaphysics is making

[28] D.S. Hutchinson, 'Ethics', in Jonathan Barnes, ed., *The Cambridge Companion to Aristotle* (Cambridge: Cambridge University Press, 1995), 197.

[29] Ibid.

an unnecessary infusion into law. However, all legal theories presuppose beliefs about human nature. This is not unique to Aristotle. What Aristotle helps us do is realise that we have such presuppositions. There is a direct relationship between our beliefs about human nature and our beliefs about what is a good life because in realty there is a direct relationship between human nature and the good life.

> What then is the most successful way for us to live? Like every other creature in the world, man has a particular nature, and the best way for a man to live is to live up to his nature, which is to be a creature directed by a rational soul. The proper function of rational human souls is to make men live well – in other words, in a rational way. Living a well-lived life is the best possible good for man, and this is what it is to succeed as a human being.[30]

The Grisez-Finnis system affirms this by beginning with the claim that humans have practical rationality that is aimed at ends. This is a claim about what it means to be a human and therefore it is, as Ralph McInerny reminded us, impossible to avoid making some comment on human nature when talking about the human good.

Aristotle's *Organon* is a study of knowledge and thinking. When we consider the modern rejection of Aristotle we will see how modern epistemology was responding to Aristotle's *Organon*, sometimes explicitly as in Francis Bacon's *Novum Organon*. Aristotle begins with ideas and the words we attach to them and from there provides a study of judgments and the logical relationship between judgments. Judgments are either true or false; any combination of words that is not either true or false has not yet attained the status of a judgment.

Much of his time is spent on the relationship between judgments and how judgments can be formed into syllogisms and deductive reasoning. But for our purposes we can notice that we have ideas and we form them into judgments about reality either by combining two ideas or denying their combination. Formally this is symbolised as 'S is P' or 'S is not P'. To say of S that it is P tells us something about the nature of S. This is obvious and is why McInerny said that it seems difficult to believe anyone would deny it. However, what Aristotle also shows us is that when we begin making judgments about the nature of a thing this involves further presuppositions about the nature of reality.[31] For instance, judgments about what is changing or potential involve presuppositions about what is unchanging and eternal.

Now, relating this to our considerations about metaphysics we can understand that we have beliefs about reality. Specifically, we have beliefs about eternal existence – about what has existed from eternity without a beginning. This is the most basic belief presupposed by any system of beliefs about what is real. Whatever has started to exist presupposes its beginning to exist from what has always existed. In Aristotle's case we are offered a form of dualism that explains change in the world through potentiality and actuality. There was no creation *ex nihilo* but instead all being has always existed. We want knowledge of what is eternal for its own sake:

30 Ibid. 31 Arist. *Post An.* 1.2, 72, trans. G.R.G. Mure.

> And understanding and knowledge pursued for their own sake are found most in the knowledge of that which is most knowable (for he who chooses to know for the sake of knowing will choose most readily that which is most truly knowledge, and such is the knowledge of that which is most knowable); and the first principles and the causes are most knowable; for by reason of these, and from these, all other things come to be known... and the science which knows to what end each thing must be done is the most authoritative of the sciences, and more authoritative than any ancillary science; and this end is the good of that thing, and in general the supreme good in the whole of nature... this must be a science that investigates the first principles and causes; for the good, i.e. the end, is one of the causes.[32]

In this sense, Aristotle says, human nature can participate in divine nature. 'The only way for us to realize our human nature is to realize our divine nature, and the mind is the divine element in us; by virtue of possessing reason, we can approach the happy state of the gods.'[33] This can be very ambiguous. For Aristotle the divine nature is in eternal contemplation of what is perfect, itself. And so, too, the best human life is one spent in contemplation of the divine. 'But the highest possible way of life is that which expresses the highest element in us, the divine element of reason. This is the life devoted to the appreciation of truth, the activity that Aristotle calls intellectual contemplation.'[34] Aristotle denies that God is the Creator and is active in human history.

In Aristotelian dualism the divine or unmoved mover is co-eternal with the material world. Both have always existed. The role of the unmoved mover is as a cause in the sense of what is potential striving to become actual. So here we see (1) this is a rejection of the idea of God the Creator; (2) the Unmoved Mover has no interest in the rest of existence; and (3) the highest good, therefore, involves a similar kind of detachment and contemplative life. These are in stark contrast to Christian theism. Therefore, while it is formally true that all legal theories will presuppose beliefs about what is real (metaphysics), it is also true that we need not uncritically accept Aristotle's beliefs about reality.

It is this kind of knowledge that is sought for its own sake. This is knowledge about the world and what the world reveals about what is eternal. Aristotle describes the good in this way:

> If, then, there is some end of the things we do, which we desire for its own sake (everything else being desired for the sake of this), and if we do not choose everything for the sake of something else (for at that rate the process would go on to infinity, so that our desire would be empty and vain), clearly this must be the good and the chief good. Will not the knowledge of it, then, have a great influence on life?[35]

He distinguishes the good from the many things that are called goods and argues that the human good is happiness.

[32] Arist. *Met.* 1.2, 30, trans. W.D. Ross. [33] Hutchinson, 196. [34] Ibid., 205.
[35] Arist. *EN.* 1.2, trans. W.D. Ross.

> Now such a thing is happiness, above all else, is held to be; for this we choose always for itself and never for the sake of something else, but honor, pleasure, reason, and every virtue we choose indeed for themselves (for if nothing resulted from them we should still choose each of them), but we choose them also for the sake of happiness, judging that by means of them we shall be happy. Happiness, on the other hand, no one chooses for the sake of these, nor, in general, for anything other than itself.[36]

We can replace 'happiness' with 'flourishing' in the Grisez-Finnis system in order to make the point that the goods identified by the new natural law theory are only understood to be goods insofar as they produce human flourishing. This means that they are a means to a further end. Notice that Aristotle does concede that we choose other things besides happiness for their own sake while also choosing them for the sake of happiness. A problem arises here. In noting that we choose these for the sake of happiness, Aristotle is helping illustrate that happiness is not sought directly. Happiness is the effect of achieving some other goal. And this happiness can be lasting or not lasting depending on whether the other goal was actually good or only appeared to be good. In this sense happiness is not the good but is instead the effect of possessing what we think is good. We can see this when he says:

> If happiness is activity in accordance with virtue, it is reasonable that it should be in accordance with the highest virtue; and this will be that of the best thing in us. Whether it be reason or something else that is this element which is thought to be our natural ruler and guide and to take thought of things noble and divine, whether it be itself also divine or only the most divine element in us, the activity of this in accordance with its proper virtue will be perfect happiness. That this activity is contemplative we have already said.[37]

We can take from this consideration of Aristotle (1) formally, it is impossible to avoid beliefs about reality presupposed in law (metaphysics); (2) Aristotle's own beliefs are a kind of dualism in which matter and the Unmoved Mover have both existed from eternity; and (3) the highest good according to Aristotle is contemplation of the Unmoved Mover which is detached from the material world (coming down as the beatific vision). These insights contribute to the purpose of this chapter which is to highlight the impossibility of avoiding philosophical foundations in thinking about human goods and natural law. Now we can contrast Aristotle's view of the eternal with the argument given by Finnis in *Natural Law and Natural Rights* about God. We will then be able to make the case that not only is God foundational to thinking about human goods but that humans ought to know God.

Although modernity rejected the metaphysics of teleology, it did so on an epistemological basis. It replaced teleology with another kind of metaphysical speculation, but this also faced epistemological challenges. The problem facing natural law is both its metaphysical grounding and the epistemology needed to know that grounding. While it might be true that from a first person account an individual thinker

[36] Arist. *EN*. 1.7, trans. W.D. Ross. [37] Arist. *EN*. 10.7, trans. W.D. Ross.

arrives at conclusions about human goods without first studying metaphysical foundations, these truths nonetheless have metaphysical presuppositions.

Although Finnis presents us with many different and irreducible goods, he does suggest that perhaps these can be unified in a highest good. This comes out of the consideration about personal sacrifice. A person might need to sacrifice one irreducible good for another or might need to sacrifice for the larger community. Friendship with God is a good that all have access to and that is greater than any sacrifice or loss of other goods. But in order to explain this good, Finnis must explain why we should think there is a God.

A TRANSCENDENTAL ARGUMENT

Finnis approaches the existence of God in two ways. First, he suggests what we can call a transcendental argument: God is the prerequisite or necessary explanation of the existing state of affairs in the universe. Second, he says this argument is not sufficient and that for greater certainty and more information about the nature of God humans need special revelation. He states both of these:

> In short, direct speculative questions about the significance, implications, or source of the orderliness of things yield, by themselves, no clear or certain answers. But this is not the end of the matter. As well as the orderliness of the order(s) of things, there is their sheer existence – the fact that propositions picking out states of affairs are sometimes true. Philosophical analysis has gradually refined our undifferentiated wonder (Why?) about the origin of things, by differentiating the fact that entities and states of affairs are what they are from the fact that they are. There thus remains an alternative route for investigation, starting with the sort of which we start in the investigations by which we our knowledge of order, viz. the fact that this or that state of affairs exists (or existed, or will exist).[38]

There must be some such explanation of the state of affairs which itself does not need a similar explanation. To ask of God 'what are the prerequisites of God's existence?' is to misunderstand God.

> How D (or God) thus is the explanation of all this is not known; what is considered to be known is simply that D (or God) is whatever is required to explain them. Already, therefore, it should be clear that to ask for an explanation of D (or God) is to miss the sense and reference of claims made about D (or God).[39]

God is the necessary explanation of contingent states of affairs, but God is not contingent and so is not in need of a similar explanation. He explains it this way:

> The only available explanation of the whole causing state of affairs is that there is some state of affairs causing that whole causing set of prerequisites or conditions of the first-mentioned state of affairs, but which is not itself included in that causing set

[38] Finnis, 382. [39] Ibid., 404.

> of conditions precisely because, unlike all the members of that set, its existing does not require some prerequisite condition (not included in itself) to be satisfied. This newly postulated state of affairs can (and should, given the sense we are giving to 'cause') be called an uncaused causing.[40]

This leads him to ask: 'What conditions or prerequisites will have (had) to be fulfilled for that state of affairs to exist?... All these prerequisite states of affairs may or may not exist (might or might not have existed). And they in their turn exist only if further prerequisites not included in themselves are satisfied.'[41] God, or the explanation of these states of affairs (Finnis calls *D*), is presupposed by the existence of contingent beings.

In one way Finnis uses this observation as a response to the problem of evil. The problem of evil is often used to support the claim that there is no God. However, Finnis argues that as humans we are not in a position to make that kind of claim about the universe.

> The norms in terms of which we judge states of affairs to be evil, in any of the four orders, are not applicable to D as creator. Thus, we have no ground to judge that D's creative causality is defective. In short, if there is an Eternal Law, we do not know enough of it to be able to judge D's creative performance defective in terms of it.[42]

This can be phrased as saying that for all we know God is working out a greater good from what we perceive to be the evils of this world.

In another way Finnis also uses this observation to support his claim that we cannot ultimately know whether or not God exists apart from special revelation. Finnis notes that Plato and Aristotle did not acknowledge this distinction (general and special revelation).[43] Augustine tried to account for Plato's knowledge of God by suggesting that the latter had access to the prophets of Israel.[44] Plato certainly acknowledged the distinction between divine oracles, such as the one that said Socrates is the wisest, and what can be known by human inquiry. But Plato also rejected the idea of God the Creator; if he did have access to the prophets of Israel, he rejected the God they proclaimed.

Plato, and specifically Aristotle, could not affirm that humans can have friendship with God.[45] For Aristotle, God is involved in eternal self-contemplation and takes no notice of humanity. This is not the God of Judaism and Christianity. What we see is that Plato and Aristotle are not theists but instead propose a competing metaphysical foundation called dualism. Finnis says:

> Still, there is deep uncertainty in their knowledge of God's nature and relation to this world and this uncertainty could be illustrated in many ways. Suffice it here to take a representative instance. Aristotle quite often speaks of the friendship (*philia*) of God or the gods for and of men for God or the gods; but in his fundamental

40 Ibid., 386. 41 Ibid., 383. 42 Ibid., 391. 43 Ibid., 393. 44 Ibid., 393. 45 Ibid., 397.

> analysis of friendship he expresses his considered opinion: God is so remote from man that there can be no friendship between God and man.[46]

His conclusion from this is that:

> Without some revelation more revealing than any that Plato or Aristotle may have experienced, it is impossible to have sufficient assurance that the uncaused cause of all the good things of this world (including our ability to understand them) is itself a good that one could love, personal in a way that one might imitate, a guide that one should follow, or a guarantor of anyone's practical reasonableness.[47]

Thus, special revelation is needed to confirm that God is personal and that God provides the connection between our choices and their consequences.

Finally, this friendship with God cumulates in contemplation of the divine nature.[48] This is a direct, immediate, experience of God. There are problems in the idea of being able to directly experience God as opposed to attaining the knowledge of God mediated through the works of God in creation and providence. One can 'contemplate' these truths known by the works of God, but this is in a different sense than the one meant by advocates of the *beatific vision*. One important difference is that God is knowable now through his works not merely in the afterlife, that this knowledge is mediated through God's works and not immediate, and that there is a moral obligation to know God in this life because the works of God clearly reveal the divine nature and eternal power of God.

This is set in contrast to the claim that special revelation is needed to know God. The first problem is that special revelation is not self-attesting. Why believe the assertions of special revelation? And which supposed special revelation? Any answer must go beyond appealing to special revelation and is, therefore, an appeal to the human ability to understand through reason. That is to say, special revelation presupposes general revelation.

Secondly, special revelation itself (the Bible) asserts that God can be known through the works of creation. The eternal power and divine nature of God are clearly seen in the works of creation so that unbelief is without excuse.[49] This includes the unbelief of Plato and Aristotle who denied God the creator. Thus, according to Scripture, the problem for Plato and Aristotle was not that they did not have Scripture but that they denied what is clear from the creation around them.

It has been common for Christian thinkers to encounter non-theistic world views and look for the 'highest power' in that world view and then claim this is synonymous to 'God' in theism. However, in many cases these world views are monist or dualist and deny that there was a creation. The analogous relationship then between the 'highest power' in monism and dualism and God in theism is simply that in each world view they are appealed to as what is eternal. They are the metaphysical foundation. However, in both monism and dualism all being is eternal (has always

[46] Ibid., 397. [47] Ibid., 398. [48] George, *In Defense of Natural Law.* [49] Romans 1:20.

existed) because there was no creation – only forming what already was there. This conflict cannot be resolved by appealing to special revelation since theistic Scriptures presuppose God the creator and Plato and Aristotle will say 'why should we believe that?'

CONCLUSION

We began with the insight from Ralph McInerny that it is hard to imagine anyone denying that judgments about what is good for a human presuppose at least some beliefs about human nature. Natural law is well known for constructing arguments from the nature of things to what ought to be done. In an important way all ethical and legal theories do this. To overlook that reality is to miss the essential and dividing differences between ethical theories. McInerny doubted that Finnis and friends deny this but that their appearance of denying this has led to challenges about new natural law theory.

Therefore, the question facing anyone working on legal theory is not whether to accept metaphysics or not but rather which metaphysics to use as the logical foundation for ethical and legal assertions. Although it is true that a person's individual practical reasoning might not rely on conscious beliefs about human nature to reach conclusions about self-evident goods, these same conclusions nevertheless do have presuppositions. We have called these the philosophical foundation of law. The most basic of these have to do with our beliefs about the nature of God (what is eternal).

There are important ways that this understanding can affect positive law. This chapter has not addressed positive law in much detail. However, positive law is understood to be the application of natural law to a particular time and circumstance. Positive law is not relative in the absolute sense although it is a relative application of the natural law to specific circumstances. A 'good' positive law helps direct the society towards the good. Thus, positive law cannot contradict natural law. This has significant applications for what are called 'hot button topics' like abortion and marriage.

Finnis deals with the epistemological question by looking for self-evident goods. However, these goods do have presuppositions about human nature and this is seen in Finnis quoting Aquinas to say that if human nature were different so too would be human obligation. Since our beliefs about human nature presuppose truths about the nature of God we are forced to think about both God and how God is known. If humans are culpable for keeping a law that presupposes truths about God then these truths must be knowable and humans are also culpable for denying these truths about God.

We saw that Finnis offers a kind of transcendental argument for God's existence. We studied this not to offer criticisms of the argument but in order to highlight the need for this kind of work. More needs to be done in his formulation of a solution to the problem of evil and his ultimate reliance on special revelation. The Thomistic idea that special revelation is needed because it is more clear, and most people do not have time to think about these things, removes human culpability for knowing God through his works of creation and providence.

The study of natural law quickly involves us in the study of the most basic and important questions that humans can ask. What is good, what is real and how do we know? Modern legal theory has denied that truths about human obligation are derivable from truths about human nature. One of the important insights that Finnis and others in the new natural law theory have provided is that there are goods or ends of practical rationality that persons can agree on without initially agreeing on a metaphysical foundation. Nevertheless, these truths do indeed make presuppositions about what is real – about the nature of God and humanity. Therefore, the initial agreement about the ends of practical rationality leads us into discussions about the nature and existence of God and the highest good.

Instead, the solution must reside in the use of reason to know what is clear about God and the good. If the eternal power and divine nature of God can be known from what has been created, then humans as rational beings are responsible to know this. This forms both the epistemological and metaphysical basis for any further claims about human nature and the human good. It is a necessary presupposition to the use of practical rationality to achieve the human good and lead a flourishing life.

12

Towards a Jurisprudence of Christian Law

Russell Sandberg

At the end of one battle, another began. It is often said that the horrors of the Second World War led to the renaissance of natural law theory. The story goes that determination to avoid another war on such a scale and with such devastating consequences led to the development of international standards seeking to protect such basic rights as the right to be free from torture, the right to a fair trial and so on. The articulation of these natural law-like rights within an embryonic system of international law was seen as reawakening a sleeping quarrel that runs to the very heart of legal theory: that between natural law and legal positivism.[1]

These two labels can be used to describe a plethora of positions whose advocates have very different theoretical mindsets. The basic conceptual difference lies in the way that positivist theories see the status of law and obedience to it as depending upon the fact that it has been laid down in a certain way recognised by a particular legal system, while natural law theorists, to varying extents, reject the notion that norms have the quality of law and must be obeyed simply because they have been created through the mechanisms of a particular legal system. For positivists, the two questions of 'is it law?' and 'is it good law?' are essentially different. Positivist legal theory contends that whether something is law simply depends upon whether it is the product of certain processes of governance. By way of contrast, natural law theory suggests that there are universal standards associated with human nature which are discoverable in a similar manner to the physical laws of nature.[2] These standards are normative and are often reflected in 'positive law' – in the context of secular law, the legal rules and regulatory instruments of national

[1] I am grateful for the research assistance of Kelly Stant and Scarlet Thomas-Perry in preparing this chapter.

[2] For Robert Alexy, the difference is that positivist theories defend the 'separation thesis', that 'there is no conceptually necessary connection between law and morality, between what the law commands and what justice requires, or between the law as it is and the law as it ought to be', while natural law theories support the 'connection thesis', that 'the concept of law is to be defined such that moral elements are included': *The Argument from Injustice: A Reply to Legal Pluralism* (Oxford: Oxford University Press, 2002), 3–4.

and sub-national bodies. The development of universal human rights standards, within the international community, may therefore be seen as being underwritten with natural law assumptions. Natural law theories often directly oppose positivist ideas: whether something is law also depends upon whether it is good law, adopting the maxim *lex injusta non est lex*: '[A]n unjust law is not law.'[3] This conflict of ideas, therefore, forms part of a wider debate as to the relationship between law and morality.

The clash between these two positions has dominated 'secular' legal theory and jurisprudence historically, and it continues to do so today. This concluding chapter falls into two parts. It will begin by outlining the main skirmishes between the natural law and positivist camps, exploring the resulting impasse and identifying five propositions about natural law theory. The second part, drawing on earlier chapters, will then examine whether these five propositions can be found within Christian jurisprudence, theology and to an extent church polity, and indicates a number of points of convergence. The purpose of the chapter is to place the previous chapters within the context of the natural law-positivist debate, identifying propositions about natural law before examining whether and how these are articulated (and can be further articulated) in the ecumenical context. Two tentative conclusions are reached. First, it will be suggested that the use of natural law by Christians in their legal systems should enable a much wider recognition of the role of natural law in legal systems generally, and this could allow resolution of the stand-off between natural law and legal positivism. This conclusion will underscore how the findings of the previous chapters in this volume are of great value for the understanding of natural law in 'secular' legal theory and jurisprudence. Second, it will be suggested that the study of the use of natural law by Christians in their church legal systems should also stimulate a much richer jurisprudence of Christian law itself.[4] This will also emphasise how the works of 'secular' legal theory and jurisprudence are of significance to those who practise and/or study Christian legal orders.[5] Both conclusions, therefore, point to a need for greater dialogue between experts in religious law and theorists who specialise in jurisprudence and to the desirability of developing a jurisprudence of Christian law.

3 Margaret Davies, *Asking the Law Question* (London: Sweet & Maxwell, 1994), 59, 66.

4 The term 'Christian law' is used to describe the regulatory systems of Christian churches and traditions including their laws, rules, norms and policies expressed formally and informally, in sacred texts and functional instruments: see Norman Doe, *Christian Law: Contemporary Principles* (Cambridge: Cambridge University Press, 2013). For a discussion of how far the term 'Christian law' may be extended, see Frank Cranmer, 'Ecclesiastical Regulation and Secular Law: A Comparative Exploration', in C. Kenny, R. Sandberg, M. Hill and F. Cranmer, eds., *The Confluence of Law and Religion* (Cambridge: Cambridge University Press, 2016), 112.

5 A legal order can be said to exist wherever there is a community sharing a system of rules and a mechanism, however informal, to resolve disputes about validity, interpretation and enforcement: Russell Sandberg, 'The Impossible Compromise', in R. Sandberg, ed., *Religion and Legal Pluralism* (Aldershot: Ashgate, 2015), 1.

THE UNWINNABLE WAR

For generations of law students, the terms 'natural law' and 'legal positivism' conjure up memories from books and courses dedicated to jurisprudence, however labelled,[6] that invariably began with a similar, if not identical, military roll-call presenting theorists from each of the natural law or positivist camps.[7] Numerous classical authors are typically cited as early proponents of natural law, including Plato, Aristotle and Cicero.[8] For Cicero, 'true law' is 'right reason in agreement with nature; it is of universal application, unchanging and everlasting', while Aristotle distinguished between 'natural justice', which was the same everywhere, and 'legal justice', which varied from place to place.[9] However, as Chapter 1 points out, most accounts of natural law begin with Christian writers such as Augustine and Aquinas. Augustine is attributed with originating the maxim *lex injusta non est lex*, while Aquinas distinguished four types of law, the eternal, the natural, the human and the divine: eternal law is God's plan for the universe; natural law is that part of eternal law discoverable by reason; human law consists of rules made by humans on the basis of natural reason; while divine law is God's law revealed in Scripture.[10] This meant that 'every human law has just so much of the law of nature as it is derived from the law of nature. But at any point it deflects from the law of nature, it is no longer a law but a perversion of the law.'[11] As Davies points out, early natural law accounts adopted the maxim *lex injusta non est lex* and, following Aquinas, positive law was 'justified in some sense by its connection with natural law'.[12] It was this maxim that prompted the development of a contrary school of thought: positivism.

Positivism as a school of legal thought needs to be differentiated from the general positivist philosophy of Auguste Comte (1798–1857), who has a claim to be the founder of sociology.[13] While there are many potential founders of positivism in the context of jurisprudence, John Austin (1790–1859) is usually taken as the greatest early influence. Developing the work of Jeremy Bentham (1748–1832), but being far

6 The term 'jurisprudence' here is used as an umbrella term to describe all forms of legal philosophy. For discussion of the different ways in which the subject is seen by experts in the field, see the essays collected in Morton E.J. Neilson, ed., *Legal Philosophy: 5 Questions* (New York: Automatic Press-VIP, 2007).

7 For some, all jurisprudential theories are either natural law or positivist, even if they differ significantly in their approach: Richard Nobles and David Schiff, 'The Evolution of Natural Law', in J. Penner, D. Schiff and R. Nobles, eds., *Jurisprudence and Legal Theory: Commentary and Materials* (London: Butterworth, 2002), 35, 36.

8 See, e.g., Brian Tierney, 'Natural Law and Natural Rights', in John Witte Jr. and Frank S. Alexander, eds., *Christianity and Law: An Introduction* (Cambridge: Cambridge University Press, 2008), 89–103.

9 Aristotle, *The Ethics*, Bk. 5, VII, 1134b–1135b; Cicero, *De re publica*, Bk. IIII, xxi: both cited by Margaret Davies, op cit., Chapter 3.

10 Margaret Davies, op cit., 64.

11 *Summa theologiae*, II, excerpted in Dino Bigongiari, ed., *The Political Ideas of St Thomas Aquinas* (New York: Free Press, 1997), 58–59.

12 Margaret Davies, op cit., 59, 66.

13 See, e.g., Mike Gane, *Auguste Comte* (London: Routledge, 2006).

less concerned in questioning how the law ought to be, Austin distinguished positive law from other forms of law, such as the laws of morality, social norms and the law of God ('natural law'), on the basis that law 'properly so called' consisted solely of general commands made by a sovereign.[14] For Austin, positive law did not depend upon morality for its validity. This deep demarcation of positive from other forms of law was also found in the work of the Austrian jurist Hans Kelsen (1881–1973) who pointed out that law can be distinguished from other social or moral rules in that laws are compulsory and result in sanctions if they are broken. For Kelsen, law was to be sharply contrasted with 'other social orders which pursue in part the same purposes as the law, but by different means'. He gave the example that while moral restraints are limited to 'requiring', legal restraint 'consists of coercion enacted by the order and socially organized'; he reasoned that legal norms can therefore be distinguished from religious norms in that although religious norms are often accompanied by a sanction, that sanction is not socially recognised but is an act of 'superhuman authority'.[15] For Kelsen (as for Austin), it is the source, procedure and status of law within a system of law that renders it law. He was insistent that '[t]he validity of a legal system cannot be questioned on the ground that its contents are incompatible with some moral or political value. A norm is a valid legal norm by virtue of the fact that it has been created according to a definite rule and by virtue thereof only'.[16]

These positivist ideas were developed in the work of H.L.A. Hart (1907–1992) who rejected Austin's notion of the sovereign to formulate instead the idea that developed legal systems were formed of both 'primary' and 'secondary' rules; that is, duty-imposing rules of substantive law (primary rules) and rules about rules which specify how primary rules are to be 'conclusively ascertained, introduced, eliminated, varied, and the fact of their violation conclusively determined' (secondary rules).[17] For Hart, it is the meeting of the primary and secondary rules that create the core of the legal system. The basic source of legal authority is the overarching 'rule of recognition'. A law is simply law because it has been made in accordance with the rule of recognition. He noted that, in the context of England, the rule of recognition is 'what the Queen in Parliament enacts as law'.[18] These positivist ideas have become prevalent. As Michael Freeman points out, 'the nineteenth century, the century of materialism and sovereignty, belonged to positivism'.[19] And these ideas were

[14] 'The matter of jurisprudence is positive law: law, simply and strictly so called: or law set by political superiors to political inferiors': *The Province of Jurisprudence Determined* (London: John Murray, 1832), 9.

[15] Hans Kelsen, 'The Law as a Specific Social Technique', *University of Chicago Law Review* 9 (1941): 75–97, at 79–80. This, of course, ignores the phenomenon of religious law.

[16] Hans Kelsen, *General Theory of Law and State*, Anders Wedberg, trans. (Clark, NJ: The Law Book Exchange Ltd., 2009, originally Cambridge, MA: Harvard University Press, 1945), 113.

[17] H.L.A. Hart, *The Concept of Law*, 2nd edn (Oxford: Oxford University Press, 1984), 94.

[18] Ibid., 107.

[19] Michael Freeman, *Lloyd's Introduction to Jurisprudence*, 9th edn (London: Sweet & Maxwell, 2014), 107.

articulated and accepted by English law far before the Victorian age.[20] The brief flirtation of the common law with natural law,[21] which reached its height in the suggestion in *Dr Bonham's Case* (1610), that the 'common law will control Acts of Parliament, and sometimes judge them to be utterly void [when] an Act of Parliament is against common right and reason',[22] has long been replaced by the wedlock of common law to the principle of parliamentary sovereignty;[23] nevertheless, the common law today uses the fiction that abhorrent 'foreign law' is void.[24]

However, although following the Enlightenment, it would be fair to say that positivism has been winning the battle of ideas, it has not won an outright victory – and since the end of the Second World War natural law theories have achieved something of a comeback. As Freeman puts it, '[I]n the twentieth century, there was a revival of interest in natural law.'[25] Yet, such talk of a comeback is also a simplification. A number of natural law theories were developed long before the defeat of Nazism. McLeod, for instance, has argued that the works of Grotius, Hobbes and Locke are all examples of what he terms the 'secularisation of natural law'.[26] This terminology is suspect, however, given that such writings typically returned to Plato, Aristotle and Cicero, seeing natural law as a sociological phenomenon and not necessarily the result of divine creation. It is clear that natural law theories continued to be articulated and debated during the age in which positivism dominated. The major change that occurred following the Second World War was not that natural law theories were being articulated or even that they were being articulated without reference to Christianity. The step-change was that such theories were being listened to and seen as being not necessarily incompatible with positivist ideas. As Davies proposes, incompatibility between the two schools is perceived but does not necessarily exist: '[I]t all depends on what view of natural and positive law is taken.'[27] In particular, it is not the case that all natural law theorists have adopted the maxim *lex injusta non est lex*. This is especially true of the modern natural law

20 See Norman Doe, *Fundamental Authority in Late Medieval English Law* (Cambridge: Cambridge University Press, 1990): this explores the tension between natural law thinking and the emergence of ideas associated with legal positivism in the work of the common law practitioners and the theorists of the fifteenth century.

21 See, however, Richard H. Helmholz, *Natural Law in Court* (Cambridge, MA: Harvard University Press, 2015), 94–126, at 124: 'evidence from the English reports demonstrates that in litigation the law of nature had a status commensurate with its place in the treatises written by common lawyers'.

22 (1610) 8 Co. Rep. 114; see also *Day v Savadge* (1614) Hob. 85.

23 See, e.g., *British Railway Board v Pickin* [1974] 1 All ER 609. However, notions of natural justice continued to exist, most notably today in English administrative law, albeit now presented in modernised legal guises. It is also worth noting the influence of the work of Sir William Blackstone (1723–1780): his *Commentaries on the Laws of England* (1765–1769) placed great emphasis upon natural law.

24 Norman Doe, 'The Problem of Abhorrent Legislation and the Judicial Idea of Legislative Supremacy', *Liverpool Law Review* 10 (1988): 113–127.

25 Michael Freeman, op cit., 107.

26 Ian McLeod, *Legal Theory*, 2nd edn (London: Palgrave, 2003), 54 et seq.

27 Margaret Davies, op cit., 64.

theorists, such as John Finnis and his 'major restatement of classical natural law theory'.[28]

For Finnis, principles of natural law 'justify the exercise of authority in community', and they require 'that authority be exercised, in most circumstances, according to the manner conveniently labelled the Rule of Law, and with due respect for the human rights which embody the requirements of justice, and for the purpose of promoting a common good in which such respect for rights is a component'; moreover, importantly:

> There is a (i) a set of basic practical principles which indicate the basic forms of human flourishing as goods to be pursued or realized, and which are in one way or another used by everyone who considers what to do, however unsound his conclusions; and (ii) a set of basic methodological requirements of practical reasonableness (itself one of the basic forms of human flourishing) which distinguish sound from unsound practical thinking and which, when all brought to bear, provide the criteria for distinguishing between acts that (always or in particular circumstances) are reasonable-all-things-considered (and not merely relative-to-a-particular purpose) and acts that are unreasonable-all-things-considered, i.e. between ways of acting that are morally right or morally wrong – thus enabling one to formulate (iii) a set of general moral standards.[29]

Therefore, for Finnis, the principles of natural law are not derived from anything but are, rather, self-evident.[30] Natural law is the product of 'practical reason'. However, as Davies has argued, this raises the question of '*whose* idea of reason it represents and whose ideas it excludes'.[31] For Finnis, however, 'the standards of natural law that are developed through the process of applying practical reason provide criteria for deriving and evaluating the laws of a legal system'.[32] This is a complex process based on practical reasoning: 'The central principle of the law of murder, of theft, of marriage, of contract ... may be a straightforward application of universally valid requirements of reasonableness, but the effort to integrate these subject matters into the Rule of Law will require of judge and legislator countless elaborations.'[33] This does not mean that law is invalid if it contradicts natural reasoning. Rather, 'the principles of natural law explain the obligatory force (in the full sense of "obligation") of positive laws, even when those laws cannot be deduced from those principles'.[34] In Finnis' account, instead of providing a moral justification for every positive law, natural law is 'concerned to elaborate on the requirements of

[28] Raymond Wacks, *Understanding Jurisprudence*, 3rd edn (Oxford: Oxford University Press, 2012), 23.

[29] John Finnis, *Natural Law and Natural Rights* (Oxford: Clarendon Press, 1980), 23.

[30] Margaret Davies, op cit., 67.

[31] A similar critique could be made of Finnis' identification of six self-evident 'goods' grasped through life, knowledge, play, aesthetic experience, sociality, practical reasonableness and religion. Davies mocks Finnis' broad definition of religion, 'an order of things "beyond" each and every man', on the basis that there is indeed an order of things 'beyond' each and every man, namely, 'billions of women': ibid., 68, 69.

[32] Ibid., 70. [33] John Finnis, op cit., 289. [34] Ibid., 23–24.

practical reasonableness in relation to law'.[35] Thus, the natural law tradition is concerned with showing 'that the act of "positing" law (whether judicially or legislatively or otherwise) is an act which can and should be guided by "moral" principles and rules; that these moral norms are a matter of objective reasonableness, not of whim, convention or mere "decision"'. Natural law theory 'is not content to observe the historical or sociological fact that "morality" thus affects "law", but instead seems to determine that the requirements of practical reasonableness really are, so as to afford a rational basis for the activities of legislators, judges and citizens'.[36]

This new role of natural law can also be seen in the work of Lon Fuller (1902–1978). Drawing on Aristotle, Fuller developed an understanding of natural law that had 'nothing to do with any brooding omnipresence in the skies' – it was, rather, 'entirely terrestrial in origin and application' and represented a 'lower' instead of a 'higher' law. This is because, for Fuller, natural law relates to 'the enterprise of subjecting human conduct to the governance of rules', and these exist 'like the natural laws of carpentry, or at least those laws respected by a carpenter who wants the house he builds to remain standing and serve the purpose of those who live in it'.[37] Fuller developed an understanding of the 'internal morality of law' – internal in that the requirements are implicit in the concept of law and a form of morality in that they provide standards for evaluating conduct.[38] Fuller identified eight such requirements: that the law must be general, promulgated, non-retroactive, clear, coherent, capable of being complied with and constant – and there must be congruence between the declared rule and official action. For Fuller, 'a total failure in any one of those eight directions does not simply result in a bad system of law; it results in something that is not properly called a legal system at all' and where the internal morality of law is breached 'there can be no rational ground for asserting that a man can have a moral obligation to obey a legal rule'.[39] Similar ideas appear in the work of Joseph Raz, a positivist, in his instrumental conception of the rule of law.[40] As to his eight requirements,[41] Raz argues that legal systems that embody the rule of law can aim at morally bad purposes provided that they respect the freedom and dignity of an individual as a rational chooser.[42] He concludes that moral reasoning is not relevant to the question of 'what the law is' but that it may be relevant to how judges decide cases according to law.[43]

35 Margaret Davies, op cit., 70. 36 John Finnis, op cit., 290.

37 Lon L. Fuller, *The Morality of Law* (New Haven, CT: Yale University Press, rev. ed., 1969), 9.

38 Michael Freeman, op cit., 111. 39 Lon L. Fuller, op cit., 39.

40 Joseph Raz, *The Authority of Law* (Oxford: Clarendon Press, 1979).

41 Namely, that laws must be prospective, relatively stable, made in conformity with clear secondary rules, applied by an independent judiciary, applied in open and fair hearings, susceptible to judicial review by higher courts, applied in a timely manner and free from arbitrary discretion.

42 For a useful summary, see David Ingram, *Law: Key Concepts in Philosophy* (London: Continuum, 2006), 32–33.

43 Joseph Raz, 'Postema on Law's Autonomy and Practical Reasons: a Critical Comment', *Legal Theory* 4 (1998): 1. See also Brian Bix, *Jurisprudence: Theory and Context*, 6th edn (London: Sweet & Maxwell, 2012), 50 et seq.

This causes a certain blurring of the line between the two sets of combatants. It is generally the case that 'positivists today are less positivistic than they were a few years ago'.[44] Even Hart developed a 'minimum theory of natural law': given the existence of universal human frailties, to survive as a community, certain fundamental rules need to exist – such as those which protect persons and property.[45] However, this does not mean that the battle lines are no longer drawn. Hart himself entered into debate with natural law theorists such as Fuller.[46] Yet, perhaps the most famous English battle in the twentieth century was that between Hart and Devlin following the publication of the Wolfenden Report in 1957, which concerned the role, if any, that morality should have in determining what conduct is classified as criminal.[47]

Sir John Wolfenden's report on the law relating to homosexual offences and prostitution recommended reform of the law on prostitution and that consensual homosexual acts between adult males should no longer be unlawful.[48] The report reasoned that, although the function of the criminal law is, among other things, 'to preserve public order and decency' and 'to protect the citizen from what is offensive or injurious', there nevertheless 'must remain a realm of private morality and immorality which is, in brief and crude terms, not the law's business'.[49] This conclusion was attacked by Sir Patrick Devlin, a High Court judge and later a law lord, who took the view that the legislature was entitled to outlaw behaviour that is generally condemned as immoral because such conduct (likened to treason) threatens the continued existence of social cohesion.[50] Devlin was then criticised by Hart, for whom immorality alone was not sufficient – only acts that cause harm to others should be criminalised.[51]

The influence (or infamy) of the Hart-Devlin debate has overshadowed the developments in natural law theory, and it has perpetuated the impression that the battle lines between natural law and positivist thinkers are firmly entrenched around disagreement about the maxim of *lex injusta non est lex*. This is unfortunate since, as we have seen, by delving a little deeper it is clear that a more nuanced picture emerges. Both natural law and positivist ideas have long informed, and been expressed both explicitly and implicitly, by judges in court rooms. Historical

44 Michael Freeman, op cit., 113.

45 Namely human vulnerability, approximate equality, limited altruism, limited resources and limited understanding of strength and will: H.L.A. Hart, *The Concept of Law*, 193, et seq.

46 H.L.A. Hart, 'Positivism and the Separation of Law and Morals', *Harvard Law Review* 71(4) (1958): 593–629; Lon L. Fuller, 'Positivism and Fidelity to Law – A Reply to Professor Hart', ibid., 630–672.

47 It was not the first such conflict, however. See, notably the famous debate in the second half of the nineteenth century between John Stuart Mill and Sir James Fitzjames Stephen: J.S. Mill, *On Liberty* (London: Collins, 1962) and J.F. Stephen, *Liberty, Equality, Fraternity* (Cambridge: Cambridge University Press, 1967).

48 Lesbianism had not been illegal.

49 Wolfenden Report (Command Paper 247, 1957), paragraphs 13 and 61.

50 Patrick Devlin, *The Enforcement of Morals* (Oxford: Oxford University Press, 1965), 13.

51 This followed the approach taken by John Stuart Mill. See H.L.A. Hart, *Law, Liberty and Morality* (Oxford: Oxford University Press, 1963).

research has shown that positivist ideas have long existed alongside natural law ideas and associated concepts, such as that of reason, conscience and equity, in the early common law.[52] Indeed, even those accounts which place most stress on the autonomy of law, such as the 'systems theory' of Niklas Luhmann (1927–1998),[53] nevertheless accept that law is influenced by wider societal factors. Many authors, most notably Ronald Dworkin (1931–2013),[54] have written about the way in which morality infuses law as it is applied and interpreted.[55] Lawmakers and other law-deciders can never be neutral. They are shaped by the society in which they live, by their experiences and by the relationships they form. It is inevitable, therefore, that this socialising influence will shape their decisions, especially since the application and interpretation of law is not akin to a game of chess;[56] rather, legal decisions and reasoning are constantly performed within a social context. The legal issues present can never be fully detached from their social, political and cultural context and the way in which they are argued and determined always owes at least something to the social make-up of the court personnel who despite their titles and official garb are still people.

This notion, that an element relating to natural law is a necessary feature of all legal systems in terms of the resolution of disputes, is well expressed in the writings of the German theorist Robert Alexy. His work recognises a tripartite distinction of three elements that are to be found in legal communications.[57] The first, 'authoritative issuance', defines a statement as law if certain procedural or status-based requirements are met. This includes and is epitomised by Austin's command theory of law and the theories of Kelsen and Hart, discussed above. The second, 'social efficiency', defines a statement as law by reference to how it is observed to function in society.[58] This includes 'external aspects' such as the Weberian understanding that law exists as law where there is a possibility of it being applied by 'coercion though action aimed at enforcing compliance or punishing violation'.[59] It also includes 'internal aspects' which embrace subjective approaches, whereby law is law if people recognise it as such.[60] The third, 'correctness of content', defines a statement as law if it is 'rationally

52 See Norman Doe, *Fundamental Authority in Late Medieval English Law* and David J. Seipp, 'Trust and Conscience in Early Common Law', in F. Cranmer et al., eds., *The Confluence of Law and Religion* (Cambridge: Cambridge University Press, 2016), 48.

53 Niklas Luhmann, *Law as a Social System* (Oxford: Oxford University Press, 2004); and his *A Sociological Theory of Law*, 2nd edn (London: Routledge, 2014).

54 Ronald Dworkin, *Taking Rights Seriously* (Cambridge, MA: Harvard University Press, 1978); Ronald Dworkin, *Law's Empire* (Cambridge, MA: Harvard University Press, 1986).

55 Also Tony Honoré, 'The Dependence of Morality on Law', *Oxford Journal of Legal Studies* 13 (1993): 1–17.

56 Cf. David J. Ibbetson, *A Historical Introduction to the Law of Obligations* (Oxford: Oxford University Press, 1999), 11.

57 Alexy, *The Argument from Injustice*, 13. 58 Ibid., 14–16.

59 Max Weber, *Economy and Society* (Berkeley, CA: University of California Press, 1978), 34.

60 Interestingly, Alexy groups Luhmann under this heading (see Alexy, *The Argument from Injustice*, 16). Luhmann understood law as being defined by the social system of law itself. For a discussion which

justifiable' within the context of the legal system.[61] Alexy considers that positivist approaches to law are based solely on 'authoritative issuance' and/or 'social efficiency', while natural law accounts are those which attach significance only to 'correctness of content'.[62] His work concludes that all three of these requirements are needed. And so he arrives at a definition of law which not only includes all three elements but which places 'correctness of content' in prime place.[63] This is because, as Bertea suggests, Alexy sees law 'mainly as a reasonable enterprise shaped by legal conflicts, disputes, clashes of opinions and conflicting values: it can be profitably understood as a set of practices'; such '[p]ractices, which although may be distinguished in a number of disparate and specific sub-practices (legislation, adjudication, legal advice, legal doctrine), are all forms of deliberative reasoning'.[64] This practical focus – based on argumentation – regards law as 'a dynamic ordering rich in potentialities, an order constantly in process and open to external influences, a set of premises to be developed by argumentation'.[65]

The common depiction of natural lawyers and positivists as two warring tribes is therefore a simplification. Ideas and assumptions from both camps are found in the day-to-day life of all legal systems. To use Alexy's terminology, although at times emphasis will be placed more upon 'authoritative issuance' or 'social efficiency' or 'correctness of content' – all three are important and present within the legal system as a whole. Reference to the treatment of natural law in mainstream legal theory reveals that first impressions about natural law are invariably misleading. In consequence, five general propositions can be drawn at this point.

First, natural law theories are more persistent than is commonly assumed: talk of the decline and rise of such theories is too simplistic. Second, natural law theories

distinguishes and prefers Luhmann's approach to subjective theories, see Russell Sandberg, 'The Failure of Legal Pluralism', *Ecclesiastical Law Journal* 18 (2016): 137–157.

61 Robert Alexy, *A Theory of Legal Argumentation* (Oxford: Oxford University Press, 1989), 16. 'There is no claim that the normative statement asserted, proposed, or pronounced in judgments is absolutely rational, but only a claim that it can be rationally justified within the framework of the prevailing legal order': ibid., 214.

62 Alexy, *The Argument from Injustice*, 13.

63 Alexy arrives at a definition of law as: 'a system of norms that (1) lays claim to correctness, (2) consists of the totality of norms that belong to a constitution by and large socially efficacious and that are not themselves unjust in the extreme, as well as the totality of norms that are issued in accordance with this constitution, norms that manifest a minimum social efficacy or prospect of social efficacy and that are not themselves unjust in the extreme, and, finally, (3) comprises the principles and other normative arguments on which the process or procedure of law application is and/or must be based in order to satisfy the claim to correctness': ibid., 125.

64 Stefano Bertea, 'Legal Argumentation Theory and the Concept of Law', in F.H. van Eemeren et al., eds., *Anyone Who Has a View: Theoretical Contributions to the Study of Argumentation* (The Hague: Kluwer, 2003), 213–226.

65 This necessarily excludes the perceptions of law common in traditional jurisprudence such as the understanding of law 'as a stable order grounded on the existence of an impartial, neutral, authority' and the 'conception of law as an objective entity, a finite set of social facts that can be identified and brought back to unity without resorting to complex, deliberative, and evaluative forms of reasoning': ibid.

are varied in their content and in the claims they make but are based on a common understanding that there are universal standards found in nature which are normative. The most controversial aspect of natural law relates to its effect on the validity of unjust positive law – the maxim *lex injusta non est lex*. However, this is not a necessary requirement of natural law theories and the discussion concerning whether a law has to be moral in order to be valid is largely a theoretical one that has little bearing on the existence and application of natural law thinking on a day-to-day basis as part of legal interpretation and adjudication. Third, there exist both Christian and non-Christian versions of natural law theory (and some non-Christian versions pre-date Christian ones). However, the differences between Christian and non-Christian theories relate primarily to the origins of the natural order: Christian theories assert that the natural order is God-made, while non-Christian theories do not include this precursor. Fourth, natural law ideas exist implicitly rather than explicitly. Principles derived from and articulations of natural law are often vague, imprecise and difficult to extrapolate. This may owe to the fact that they are foundational and that their existence and content is often assumed and inherited rather than created. Fifth, the label 'natural law' is contaminated. Many of the ideas associated with natural law theory become much less controversial if they are presented without naming the theory. The next section will suggest that these problems and characteristics of natural law are also reflected in legal systems of Christian traditions.

NATURAL LAW AND CHRISTIAN JURISPRUDENCE

Given that Chapter 10 has already summarised some key elements of natural law thinking in Christianity – in the context of comparing the similarities and differences in the approaches to natural law within Judaism, Islam and Christianity – it will not be necessary here to draw out in detail the commonalities and divergences in the approaches of Christian traditions to natural law. Nevertheless, reference to the previous chapters, shows that within Christianity, as with 'secular' jurisprudence, first impressions about natural law are misleading. Support for the five propositions described above can be found by looking at Christian systems of church law, order and polity, and doing so sheds further light on each proposition.

The first proposition, that natural law theories are more persistent than is commonly assumed, is reflected throughout the contributions from the various traditions, and even Chapter 1 concludes that natural law was so important to Christians historically that the apparent marginalization of it today is a radical change. As Chapter 10 maintains, natural law doctrine has historically enjoyed a prominent place in Christian thought dating back for some to biblical texts such as Paul's Letter to the Romans (as containing a germ of the doctrine). However, over the centuries, natural law fell out of favour with some Christian traditions. As several chapters point out, the turning point was the Reformation, though the Reformers themselves still invoked the concept in their theological and juridical discussions. Later Reformation theology generally rejected the competence of fallen human reason to engage in natural theology, and this view (asserted, for example, by Karl Barth) meant that some traditions would no longer cling to any human resources including natural law. Yet, today, support for natural law approaches is not divided upon denominational lines. A number of contemporary scholars across the traditions – from Matthew Levering (Roman Catholic), Stanley Harakas (Orthodox) to Nigel Biggar (Anglican) and Stephen Grabill (Reformed) – advocate natural law theory. Natural law ideas are not exclusive to the Roman Catholic Church. Indeed, as Chapter 2 shows, although there is a rich tradition of natural law within Roman Catholic thought, and crucially a rich tradition of natural law teaching through the magisterium, a plurality of perspectives on natural law continues to exist even within that tradition as shown by a revisionist perspective. It is also the case that natural law ideas continue to be influential in those traditions where natural law historically has been less dominant. Chapter 3 points to the less prevalent role of natural law in the Orthodox world as compared with the Christian West to the extent that many Orthodox Christians are not obvious advocates of natural law. Nonetheless, it was argued that the absence of explicit reference to natural law cannot be taken as evidence that it does not exist and that it is possible to arrive at a tentative outline of a natural law approach by excavation of Patristic sources and reference to modern scholarship. Similar conclusions were reached in the chapters that followed. Chapter 6, for instance, describes how while the notion of natural law is not widely used in the Methodist tradition, which has not developed a sophisticated theory of natural law, nevertheless the idea is widely presupposed. And Chapter 8 discusses how there is no explicit Baptist theology of natural law but that Baptists have adopted a form of natural law thinking from their Calvinistic roots as creatures of the Protestant Reformation. Indeed, Chapter 11 suggests that natural law is inevitably part of the philosophical foundations of law. Even if we do not consciously rely upon beliefs about human nature to reach conclusions about goods then those conclusions are nevertheless based on such propositions.

It is also clear from the chapters that the place of natural law within Christian traditions is shaped by external factors. Chapter 5, amongst others, underlines the importance of the effect of the medieval natural law inheritance on the Lutheran Reformation. By way of contrast, Chapter 4 on Anglicanism suggests that the common law tradition had meant that a dominant legal culture of positivism had come to shape the practice of ecclesiastical law in the Church of England and beyond.[66] The influences of religious leaders and teachers have also had an impact. This can be seen in Chapter 7, which proposes that Reformed, Presbyterian, Congregational and United churches have no single understanding of natural law or of its implications for church polity – and this may reflect the diverse modern

66 Chapter 10 described how the same was true of Judaism.

interpretations of John Calvin himself. Moreover, the Barth-Brunner debate of the 1930s meant that natural law lost its appeal in the Reformed tradition but that there has been renewed interest in natural law, including its relevance for contemporary political and ethical issues. This is an identifiable trend throughout this volume: although the focus and prestige of natural law tends to ebb and flow, it never truly disappears – and the current era seems to be one of flow. Chapter 10 indicates that this is even true of the other Abrahamic faiths. Although some deny the existence of natural law within Judaism and Islam, and although a fully fledged, majoritarian theory of natural law is missing, natural law sentiments exist. This is likely to be the case since, as Chapter 11 reminds us, talk of natural law involves study of the most basic and important questions we can ask: what is good, what is real and how do we know?

The chapters also provide ample evidence for the second proposition that natural law theories are varied in their content and in the claims they have made but are based on a common understanding that there are universal standards found in nature which are normative. As Chapter 10 suggests, natural law is generally seen as the law implanted in humans by God, a law that rational creatures can discern though the use of natural reason; and one that may be contrasted with revealed law. It is also the case that there are different approaches to natural law even within the same tradition. This was shown in Chapter 5. This contrasts within Lutheran thought the approach of Luther, that natural law is not based on human nature but on divine love, with that of Melanchthon, that natural law consists of those aspects of divine law discoverable and understood through the use of divine reason. Chapter 7 too proposes that in the Reformed tradition some focus on a 'general revelation' as the source of our understanding of right and wrong (implanted in humankind at creation), and others do not.

Moreover, although there are differences between the Christian traditions, relating mostly to the doctrinal differences that exist following the Reformation, there are points of convergence. Chapter 8 explores how a natural law theory could only be developed where it is possible to establish a set of empirical generalisations about human nature that is constant both spatially (cross-culturally) and temporally (historically) and then to move from a set of generalisations about how people do act to a set of prescriptions regarding how they ought to act. It is clear that such natural law theories exist in the Christian traditions studied in this book: though the content and precision with which they are articulated differ significantly.

The third proposition, that there exist both Christian and non-Christian versions of natural law theory, and that the differences between Christian and non-Christian theories relate primarily to the origins of the natural order, can also be found articulated in the chapters. As Chapter 1 underscores, there was never a perfect match between the teachings of the Christian religion and the tenets of natural law, but there did exist a decided factual link. Chapter 2 accepts that there was no Christian let alone Roman Catholic monopoly on natural law; this is one thrust of the International Theological Commission in 2009, which recognised that the search for common ethical language concerns all 'persons of good will, whatever their religious convictions'. Christian natural law theories are clearly different to 'secular' theories, in that they regard the creation of the natural order as being divine in origin. Also in several traditions there is the question of the extent to which 'fallen' humankind is able to use reason to understand natural law.[67] However, the basic content of natural law ideas and principles does not tend to differ in Christian as opposed to 'secular' natural law theories. Indeed, Chapter 11 shows how the 'new' natural law theories can be used within a Christian context. The contrast between religious and 'secular' theories of natural law is greater in relation to religions that adopt a revealed understanding of religious law. Chapter 2 quotes Pope Benedict XVI: 'unlike other great religions, Christianity has never proposed a revealed law to the State and to society, that is to say a juridical order derived from revelation' and has pointed instead 'to nature and reason as the true sources of law'; and elements of the Lutheran and Reformed traditions too tend to regard natural law as applicable to the kingdom of the world rather than the spiritual kingdom of the church. Chapter 10 explains that, beyond Christianity, this has meant that natural law is a minority position in Judaism and Islam because for those faiths the revealed law is sufficient of itself and reason is not a freestanding normative category. There is no mainstream natural law tradition since the classical view is that of 'scriptural positivism', the idea that law created by God is recorded in sacred texts. This suggests that differences between religious and secular legal systems are more pronounced with respect to the divine law than to the natural law.

There is ample evidence of the fourth proposition that natural law ideas exist implicitly rather than explicitly. On the one hand, in the Roman Catholic tradition, as Chapter 2 explains the Code of Canon Law includes many norms which are representations of, or else implement, the negative precepts of natural law. On the other hand, for most of the traditions studied here, natural law does not generally appear explicitly in the modern juridical texts of churches.[68] However, as Chapter 4 puts it, echoes of natural law may be identified in the law but often under different guises. The regulatory instruments of Anglican churches, for example, sometimes employ a number of categories historically associated with the natural law tradition, like 'reason', 'natural justice', 'equity' and 'conscience'. The same is true of other Christian traditions.[69] Chapter 7 discusses how Calvin's Ecclesiastical Ordinances 1541 made no explicit reference to natural law but invoked its broad thinking, while

[67] Chapter 8 proposes that a natural law theory needs to demonstrate that the Christian must also be able to show in what sense human nature, although corrupted by sin, is still a reliable guide independent of Christian obligation and relate his generalisations about natural moral obligation to Christian belief and obligation.

[68] Positive precepts of natural law are generally absent in the juridical instruments across the traditions studied.

[69] Chapter 7 similarly suggests that Reformed norms associate law with abstract normative entities like equity.

Chapter 8 explores how natural law is implicit both in what Baptist Confessions affirm and from the communities' commitment to Calvin's theology, which includes a natural law foundation to morality and polity. The exception to this trend seems to be ecumenical instruments.

As Chapter 9 teaches us, the concept of natural law has been used in ecumenical dialogues and agreements both expressly and implicitly, and it is also present in the work of the World Council of Churches in relation to human rights, homosexuality and faith and order. Yet, that chapter concludes by stating that the concept of natural law can be a difficult one to agree upon within the ecumenical movement. This may suggest why the traditions have preferred implicit or euphemistic references to natural law. This was underlined in Chapter 6, in its treatment of natural law thinking in the Methodist tradition: we struggle to find the right language about natural law which means that natural law claims are accepted, presupposed, contested, ignored and developed. That chapter underscores once again the importance of digging deeper to overcome superficial conclusions about the absence of natural law. With Methodism, although we look in vain for any explicit discussion or use of 'natural law', a closer look reveals much in Wesley's theology which is 'open' to natural law approaches. This is a critical point to make for the quest for a Christian understanding of natural law. Chapter 8 made a similar point in relation to Baptists, suggesting that Baptists had a theory of natural law but were not interested in developing a self-contained independent doctrine. The chapter also maintains that the recognition of basic human goods that constitute human flourishing means that elements of natural law thinking were already enshrined in early Baptist confessions. This is developed in Chapter 7: systems of church order in the Reformed tradition are forms of applied ecclesiology; natural law thinking is part and parcel of this.

The fifth proposition, that the label 'natural law' is a contaminated one, is less prevalent in this volume than might be suspected. Several contributors express the initial expectation of themselves or their co-religionists about the apparent foolhardiness of their endeavour – but these initial doubts seem to evaporate as they go about their quest. Even contributors from those traditions which have not placed a great weight historically on natural law conclude that there is something to be said and there is a need for further research. Chapter 3, on the Orthodox position, for instance, concludes that there are a number of unresolved disputes surrounding the existence, definition, structure and contemporary relevance of natural law which requires further research. Not one of the contributors concludes that discussion of natural law is irrelevant or that the quest should be aborted. There is, however, a suggestion in Chapter 10 that the use of the term 'natural law' is problematic in developing an interfaith understanding. It is argued that there would be commonality between the Abrahamic religions if we abandon the term 'natural law' and focus instead on the single category of 'divine law' communicated to humans as a universal law at their creation by God, the imperfect apprehension of which is perfected by the subsequent revelation of God (in the form of specially revealed law). This suggestion, however, requires further work. There is a need to explore in greater depth how divine law is regarded within the Christian traditions, and another category perhaps more palatable to both interfaith and ecumenical discourse, that of the 'moral law'. The focus of this volume on natural law has meant that its contributors have concentrated on divine law only within that context. It is clear that a number of different understandings exist of the relationship between divine law and natural law. The complicated nature of the relationship was stressed in Chapter 1 where it was said that divine law was separate from natural law but they overlapped. This is a point also made in Chapter 3 which asserts, from an Orthodox perspective, that natural law is not synonymous with divine law but rather forms part of divine law and is sufficient to order human relationships.

Chapter 10 proposes that debate about a shared concept of divine law is worthwhile as a means of identifying common ground between Judaism, Islam and Christianity.[70] The same might apply within Christianity itself. Indeed, the chapters of this volume have underscored the need for a greater dialogue between traditions about how they understand their respective legal systems, the role of natural and divine law and the influence of natural law and positivist thinking not only in the creation of their church rules but also in the way in which their legal systems operate, law is practised and justice is achieved. The aim of such dialogue is not convergence of thought or practice, but the sharing of ideas and recognition of similarities and differences. This volume has shown what can happen when it is asked whether a concept thought to be prevalent in some traditions is actually also of influence (in divergent forms and ways and to different extents) in traditions where it is commonly thought that there is no tradition of that concept or even that the concept does not exist there. Such an analysis, such a quest, often sheds a new light upon materials uncovering existing but forgotten links and connections and suggesting new forms of analysis and ways of thinking that do not undermine the distinctiveness or uniqueness of the particular tradition in question.

A PHILOSOPHY OF LAW AND RELIGION

One final point may be made. The content and method of this book underscores the need for greater dialogue between those who practice and study particular religious legal systems. There is a need for Baptists to talk to Catholics, for instance, and a need for the Abrahamic religions to talk to one another.[71] However, the dialogue needs to extend further than that. The conversation also needs to take in experts in

[70] It may identify less common ground, however, between 'religious' and 'secular' natural law theories.

[71] And, indeed to other faiths, upon which we know significantly less about their relationship with law and their legal orders, particularly within Western societies. See, further, Amina Hussain, 'Legal Pluralism, Religious Conservatism', in R. Sandberg, ed., *Religion and Legal Pluralism* (Aldershot: Ashgate, 2015), 151.

'secular' jurisprudence. The fact that the five propositions outlined above can be found in both 'secular' jurisprudence and the Christian traditions studied in this book suggests that such a dialogue would be useful. It is possible to go further and suggest that a conversation of this sort is necessary given that writers in both spheres have much to learn from one another. There is a need to discuss further the differences between Christian and 'secular' natural law theories and whether the prevalence, persistence and implicitness of natural law ideas are features of all legal systems. Such discussion would have the advantage for 'secular' jurisprudence of banishing superficial notions that natural lawyers and positivists are two warring tribes. Such dialogue would be useful for religious traditions to show the universal nature of the issues that they grapple with. Developing a jurisprudence of Christian law would build upon the work done in recent years on the similarities and differences between traditions and the identification of principles of Christian law.[72] It would encourage asking deeper questions about the nature of Christian law, whether it can be properly designated law, what its relationship with morality is, and how the need and role for law can be reconciled with the nature of Christian faith.

A jurisprudence of Christian law – or indeed, more generally of religious law – would contribute to taking religious legal systems seriously rather than regarding them as medieval throw-backs, a perception that has dominated much of the discourse on religious courts over recent years where a fear of Sharia has been prevalent. This was epitomised by the way in which discussion of Archbishop Rowan Williams' erudite lecture on the way in which religious laws were already recognised under English law were accompanied by images of stoning during television news broadcasts.[73] However, it will be important in opening up the debate that the religious nature of religious legal systems is not forgotten. This may be achieved by developing an insight developed in another context.[74] There is a need to craft a 'philosophy of law and religion' bringing together three, not two, different communities. The first community comprises those who practice or study religious law: we can say for convenience that their focus is the relations between religion and law. The second community comprises those who specialise in 'secular' jurisprudence: we can say that their focus is on the relations between philosophy and law.

72 Doe, *Christian Law*; and Christian Law Panel of Experts: 'Response to the World Council of Churches Faith and Order Commission Paper *The Church: Towards a Common Vision* (2013)', December 2015.

73 Rowan Williams, 'Civil and Religious Law in England – A Religious Perspective', *Ecclesiastical Law Journal* 10 (2008): 262–282. For an analysis of the media reaction to the Archbishop's lecture, see Chapter 7 of Nahid A. Kabir, *Young British Muslims* (Edinburgh: Edinburgh University Press, 2010). For discussion of the resulting moral panic, see Ralph Grillo, *Muslim Families, Politics and the Law* (Aldershot: Ashgate, 2015).

74 Namely in the call for a 'sociology of law and religion', on which see Norman Doe, 'A Sociology of Law on Religion – Towards a New Discipline: Legal Responses to Religious Pluralism in Europe', *Law and Justice: A Christian Law Review* 152 (2004): 68–92; and Russell Sandberg, *Religion, Law and Society* (Cambridge: Cambridge University Press, 2014), Chapter 6.

Bringing together insights from these two groups would be valuable in that they both have a focus in common on law. However, the conversation may at times be one-sided since the first group consists of those who are not expert in philosophy (though the studies in this volume make a first step in that direction) and the second group does not generally consist of experts in religion. There is, therefore, a need to introduce a third group to the discussion: those who specialise in the philosophy of religion, that is, those with an interest in philosophy and religion. None of these groupings (or sub-disciplines) can in isolation understand the relations between religion, law and philosophy. Each is missing one element. Law and religion omits the study of philosophy; legal philosophy misses the study of religion; and the philosophy of religion neglects the study of law. If the focus of the study is the relationship between all three entities – philosophy, religion, and law – then a single sub-disciplinary approach will not suffice and a synthesis of all three sub-disciplines is needed: a 'philosophy of law and religion'.

This is not to say that such a fusion of approaches would be risk-free. Indeed, much of what has been written elsewhere about the risks of a 'sociology of law and religion' would also apply here. Two points in particular are worth making again. First, it would be important that the interdisciplinary synthesis builds upon the contributions of each sub-discipline rather than replacing them. All too often interdisciplinary approaches to law become law-lite. This should be avoided. So, too, should the dominance of legal approaches: too legalistic an approach misses what is religious about religious law. Second, an alternative and perhaps preferable conception of interdisciplinary work is to regard interdisciplinary approaches to law not as separate sub-disciplines but rather as methods that should be an integral part of the study of law (and therefore every legal sub-discipline) alongside the doctrinal study of the current legal position. This understanding rejects the current position of philosophy of law, the sociology of law, and the history of law, as separate sub-disciplines within law on the basis that this position has led such scholarship to become ghettoised. The notion that there are experts on the philosophy/sociology/history of law and that they operate in a self-contained sub-discipline has meant that their publications, methods and approaches have not become part of the toolkit of law as a whole. A preferable but radical approach would be to regard a doctrinal research method (the elucidation, explanation and evaluation of legal sources) as one method alongside philosophical, sociological and historical approaches and to see these methods as complementing and building upon each other. Such a re-conceptualisation would, of course, require further thought and research. This in itself is the main purpose of this book. It demonstrates that the study of Christianity and natural law provokes new research questions, debunks simplified assumptions, and questions old orthodoxies. Much more can be achieved if a different call to arms is issued and we abandon a conflict between the two supposedly rival armies of legal positivism and natural law.

Bibliography

Abu-Rabi, Ibrahim M., *Intellectual Origins of Islamic Resurgence in the Modern Arab World* (Albany: State University of New York Press, 1996).

Alexy, Robert, *A Theory of Legal Argumentation* (Oxford: Oxford University Press, 1989).

Alexy, Robert, *The Argument from Injustice: A Reply to Legal Pluralism* (Oxford: Oxford University Press, 2002).

Allan, Trevor R.S., *Constitutional Justice* (Oxford: Oxford University Press, 2001).

Alonso-Lasheras, Diego, *Luis de Molina's 'De Iustitia et Iure': Justice as Virtue in an Economic Context* (Leiden and Boston, MA: Brill, 2011).

Anglican Communion Network of Legal Advisers, *Principles of Canon Law Common the Churches of the Anglican Communion* (London: Anglican Communion Office, 2008).

Anglican-Roman Catholic International Commission (ARCIC II), *Life in Christ: Morals, Communion and the Church* (London: Church House, Catholic Truth Society, 1994).

Arkes, Hadley, *Constitutional Illusions and Anchoring Truths: The Touchstone of the Natural Law* (Cambridge: Cambridge University Press, 2010).

Arthur, William, *Religion without God and God without Religion* (London: Bemrose and Sons, 1885–1888).

Austin, John, *The Province of Jurisprudence Determined* (London: John Murray, 1832).

Avineri, Shlomo, *Hegel's Theory of the Modern State* (Cambridge: Cambridge University Press, 1972).

Ayer, Alfred Jules, *Language Truth and Logic*, 2nd edn (London: Gollancz, 1946).

Babie, Paul, 'Looking East to the Concept of Property: A Review Essay of Witte and Alexander (eds), *Christianity and Law: An Introduction*', *Adelaide Law Review* 30 (2009): 175–184.

Badcock, Gary, 'Hegel, Lutheranism and Contemporary Theology', *Animus* 5 (2000): 144–158.

Bangs, Nathan, *Predestination Examined* (New York: J.C. Totten, 1817).

Baptism, Eucharist, Ministry, Faith and Order Paper 111 (Geneva: World Council of Churches, 1982).

Barth, Karl, *Church Dogmatics*, G.W. Bromiley and T.F. Torrance, eds. (Edinburgh: T. & T. Clark, 1956).

Barth, Karl, *The Epistle of Paul to the Romans* (Oxford: Oxford University Press, 1933).

Barth, Karl and Emil Brunner, *Natural Theology*, Peter Fraenkel, trans. (London: Geoffrey Bles, 1946).

Bauer, Clemens, 'Melanchthon: Naturrechtslehre', *Archiv für Reformationsgeschichte* 42 (1951): 64–100.

Beal, J.P., J.A. Coriden and T.J. Green, eds., *New Commentary on the Code of Canon Law* (New York: Paulist Press, 2000).

Bergier, J.F. and R.M. Kingdon, *Registres de la Compagnie des pasteurs de Geneve au temps de Calvin*, 2 Vols. (1962–1964), G.R. Potter and M. Greengrass, trans., *Jean Calvin* (London: Edward Arnold, 1983).

Berkman, John and William C. Mattison III, eds., *Searching for a Universal Ethic: Multidisciplinary, Ecumenical, and Interfaith Responses to the Catholic Natural Law Tradition* (Grand Rapids, MI: William B. Eerdmans, 2014).

Berkowitz, Roger, *The Gift of Science: Leibniz and the Modern Legal Tradition* (Cambridge, MA: Harvard University Press, 2005).

Berman, Harold J., *Law and Revolution II: The Impact of the Protestant Reformations on the Western Legal Tradition* (Cambridge, MA: Harvard University Press, 2003).

Bertea, Stefano, 'Legal Argumentation Theory and the Concept of Law', in F.H. van Eemeren, J.A. Blair, C.A. Willard and F.A. Snoeck Henkeman, eds., *Anyone Who Has a View: Theoretical Contributions to the Study of Argumentation* (The Hague: Kluwer, 2003), 213–226.

Best, Thomas F. and Martin Robra, *Ecclesiology and Ethics: Ecumenical Ethical Engagement, Moral Formation and the Nature of the Church* (Geneva: World Council of Churches, 1997).

Bibbings, Lois S., 'The Hetero-State: Hegemonic Heterosexuality and State Power', in R. Coleman, J. Sim, S. Tombs and D. Whyte, eds., *State, Power, Crime* (London: Sage, 2009), 35–48.

Biggar, Nigel, *Behaving in Public: How to do Christian Ethics* (Grand Rapids, MI: William B. Eerdmans, 2011).

Bigongiari, Dino, ed., *The Political Ideas of St. Thomas Aquinas* (New York: Free Press, 1997).

Bix, Brian, *Dictionary of Legal Theory* (Oxford: Oxford University Press, 2004).

Bix, Brian, *Jurisprudence: Theory and Context*, 6th edn (London: Sweet & Maxwell, 2012).

Black, A., H. Esmaeili and N. Hosen, *Modern Perspectives on Islamic Law* (Cheltenham: Edward Elgar Publishing, 2014).

Blackburn, Simon, *Being Good: An Introduction to Ethics* (Oxford: Oxford University Press, 2001).

Bleich, J. David, 'Judaism and Natural Law', *Jewish Law Annual* 7 (1988): 5–42.

Bolt, John, 'Herman Bavinck on Natural Law and Two Kingdoms: Some Further Reflections', *The Bavinck Review* 4 (2013): 64–93.

Bowne, Borden P., *The Principles of Ethics* (New York: Harper, 1892).

Braaten, C.E., 'A Lutheran Affirmation of the Natural Law', in R.C. Baker and R.C. Ehlke, eds., *Natural Law: A Lutheran Reappraisal* (St. Louis, MO: Concordia Publishing House, 2011), 3–16.

Brackney, William H., *Historical Dictionary of Baptists* (Lanham, ML: Scarecrow Press, 2009).

Brash, Alan A., *Facing Our Differences: The Churches and Their Gay and Lesbian Members* (Geneva: World Council of Churches, 1995).

Braybrooke, David, *Natural Law Modernized* [Toronto Studies in Philosophy] (Toronto: University of Toronto Press, 2001).

Bretzke, James, *A Morally Complex World: Engaging Contemporary Moral Theology* (Collegeville, MN: Liturgical Press, 2004).

Brightman, Edgar Sheffield, *The Moral Laws* (New York: Abingdon, 1943).

Brock, Stephen, *Action and Conduct: Thomas Aquinas and the Theory of Action* (Edinburgh: T. & T. Clark, 1998).

Brundage, James A., *Medieval Canon Law* (Harlow: Longman, 1995).

Budziszewski, J., *The Line Through the Heart: Natural Law as Fact, Theory, and Sign of Contradiction* (Wilmington, DE: ISI Books, 2009).

Buitenbag, Johan, 'Die wêreld as gelykenis: 'n Trajek om die middelterm van die "teologie" te vind', *HTS Theological Studies* 59(4) (2003): 1063–1064.

Burns, Tony, 'Hegel and Natural Law Theory', *Politics* 15 (1995): 27–32.

Butler, Michael, 'Orthodoxy and Natural Law' (Lecture delivered at Acton University, 21 June 2013): www.ancientfaith.com/specials/episode/orthodoxy_and_natural_law.

Calvin, John, *Commentary on the Sermon on the Mount*, W. Findlay, trans., from P. Schaff, ed., *Nicene and Post-Nicene Fathers*, First Series, Vol. 6 (Buffalo, NY: Christian Literature Publishing Co., 1888).

Calvin, John, *Institutes of the Christian Religion*, 2.7.1., Vol. 1, John T. McNeill, ed., Ford Lewis Battles, trans., *The Library of Christian Classics*, Vol. XX (Philadelphia, PA: The Westminster Press, 1960).

Cameron, Andrew J.B., 'How "Ethics" Works: An Engagement with John Calvin', in M.D. Thompson ed., *Engaging with Calvin* (Nottingham: Apollos, 2009), 230–253.

Caparros, E., H. Aube, M. Theriault and J. Thorn, eds., *Code of Canon Law Annotated*, 2nd edn (Montreal: Wilson & Lafleur, 2004).

Casiday, Augustine, ed., *The Orthodox Christian World* (London: Routledge, 2012).

Charles, J. Daryl, *Retrieving the Natural Law: A Return to Moral First Things* (Grand Rapids, MI: William B. Eerdmans, 2008).

Christian Law Panel of Experts, 'Response to the World Council of Churches Faith and Order Commission Paper, *The Church: Towards a Common Vision* (2013)', December 2015.

Christian Perspectives on Theological Anthropology: A Faith and Order Study Document, Faith and Order Paper 199 (Geneva: World Council of Churches, 2005): www.oikoumene.org/en/resources/documents/commissions/faith-and-order/v-theological-anthropology/christian-perspectives-on-theological-anthropology.

Church, Evangelization, and the Bonds of Koinonia (2002), Report of the International Consultation between the Catholic Church and the World Evangelical Alliance (1993–2002).

Cobb, John B., *A Christian Natural Theology* (London: Lutterworth, 1965).

Coertzen, Pieter, *Church and Order: A Reformed Perspective* (Leuven: Peeters, 1998).

Coffey, John, 'From Helwys to Leland: Baptists and Religious Tolerance in England and America, 1612–1791', in D. Bebbington, ed., *Studies in Baptist History and Thought: The Gospel in the World* (Milton Keynes: Paternoster, 2000), 21–22.

Colwell, John E., *Living the Christian Story: The Distinctiveness of Christian Ethics* (Edinburgh: T. & T. Clark, 2001).

Conradie, Ernst M., 'All Theology is Natural Theology: The Hermeneutic Necessity of Natural Law?', *Dutch Reformed Theological Journal* 52 (2011): 58–65.

Contreras, Francisco J., ed., *The Threads of Natural Law: Unravelling a Philosophical Tradition* (New York: Springer, 2013).

Corzine, Jacob, 'Friedrich Julius Stahl: A Lutheran's Rejection of Natural Law', in R.C. Baker and R.C. Ehlke, eds., *Natural Law: A Lutheran Reappraisal* (St. Louis, MO: Concordia Publishing House, 2011), 99–115.

Costigane, Helen, 'Catholic Adoption Agencies and "Gay Adopters"', *Law and Justice: The Christian Law Review* 161 (2008): 98–110.

Costigane, Helen, 'Catholic Education in England – What is to be Taught?', *Law and Justice: The Christian Law Review* 163 (2009): 103–109.

Costigane, Helen, 'A Protected Rite?', *America* (30 July 2013).

Covell, Charles, *The Defense of Natural Law: A Study of the Ideas of Law and Justice in the Writings of Lon L. Fuller, Michael Oakeshot, F.A. Hayek, Ronald Dworkin, and John Finnis* (New York: St. Martin's Press, 1992).
Cranmer, Frank, 'Ecclesiastical Regulation and Secular Law: A Comparative Exploration', in C. Kenny, R. Sandberg, M. Hill and F. Cranmer, eds., *The Confluence of Law and Religion* (Cambridge: Cambridge University Press, 2016), 112.
Craske, Jane, *Being Human* (London: Peterborough Epworth, 2007).
Crone, Patricia, *God's Rule – Government and Islam: Six Centuries of Medieval Islamic Political Thought* (New York: Columbia University Press, 2004).
Cronin, Kieran, *Rights and Christian Ethics* (Cambridge: Cambridge University Press, 1992).
Cross, F.L. and E.A. Livingstone, eds., *Oxford Dictionary of the Christian Church*, 3rd rev. edn (Oxford: Oxford University Press, 2005).
Cunliffe, Christopher, ed., *Joseph Butler's Moral and Religious Thought: Tercentenary Essays* (Oxford: Oxford University Press, 1992).
Curran, Charles E., *The Catholic Moral Tradition Today: A Synthesis* (Washington, DC: Georgetown University Press, 1999).
Dallinger, William, *The Creator and What We May Know of the Methods of Creation* (London: T. Woomer, 1887).
David, Joseph, 'Maimonides, Nature and Natural Law', *Journal of Law, Philosophy and Culture* V (2010): 67–82.
Davies, Margaret, *Asking the Law Question* (London: Sweet & Maxwell, 1994).
Davies, Oliver and Thomas O'Loughlin, eds., *Celtic Spirituality* (Mahwah, NJ: Paulist Press, 2000).
Davis, James, *Medieval Market Morality* (Cambridge: Cambridge University Press, 2012).
Dawkins, Richard, *The God Delusion* (London: Bantam Press, 2006).
Demmer, Klaus M.S.C., 'Ius caritatis: Zur christologischen Grundlegung der augustinischen Naturrechtslehre', *Analecta Gregoriana*, Vol. 118, Series Facultatis Theologicae: sectio B, n. 40 (Liberia Editrice dell'Università Gregoriana: Roma, 1961), 141–143.
Devlin, Patrick, *The Enforcement of Morals* (Oxford: Oxford University Press, 1965).
Doe, Norman, 'The Problem of Abhorrent Legislation and the Judicial Idea of Legislative Supremacy', *Liverpool Law Review* 10 (1988): 113–127.
Doe, Norman, *Fundamental Authority in Late Medieval English Law* (Cambridge: Cambridge University Press, 1990).
Doe, Norman, *The Legal Framework of the Church of England* (Oxford: Clarendon Press, 1996).
Doe, Norman, *Canon Law in the Anglican Communion* (Oxford: Clarendon Press, 1998).
Doe, Norman, 'Canonical Approaches to Human Rights', in Mark Hill, ed., *Religious Liberty and Human Rights* (Cardiff: University of Wales Press, 2002), 185–206.
Doe, Norman, 'A Sociology of Law on Religion – Towards a New Discipline: Legal Responses to Religious Pluralism in Europe', *Law and Justice: A Christian Law Review* 152 (2004): 68–92.
Doe, Norman, *An Anglican Covenant: Theological and Legal Considerations for a Global Debate* (Norwich: Canterbury Press, 2008).
Doe, Norman, *Christian Law: Contemporary Principles* (Cambridge: Cambridge University Press, 2013).
Doherty, Sean, '"Love Does Not Delight in Evil, but Rejoices With the Truth". A Theological and Pastoral Reflection on My Journey Away From A Homosexual Identity', *Anvil* 30(1) (2014): 5–16.
Domingo, Rafael, 'The Metalegal God', *Ecclesiastical Law Journal* 16 (2014): 147–167.
Duchrow, Ulrich, *Christenheit und Weltverantwortung: Traditionsgeschichte und systematische Struktur der Zweireichelehre* (Stuttgart: Klett-Cotta, 1980).

Dulles, Avery, *Models of the Church* (Dublin: Gill and MacMillan, 1988).
Dunkle, B.L., 'A Development of Origen's View of the Natural Law', *Pro Ecclesia* 13 (2004): 337–351.
Dworkin, Ronald, *Taking Rights Seriously* (Cambridge, MA: Harvard University Press, 1978).
Dworkin, Ronald, *Law's Empire* (Cambridge, MA: Harvard University Press, 1986).
Emon, Anver M., 'Natural Law and Natural Rights in Islamic Law', *Journal of Law and Religion* 20 (2004–2005): 351–395.
Emon, Anver M., *Islamic Natural Law Theories* (Oxford: Oxford University Press, 2010).
Emon, Anver M., Matthew Levering and David Novak, *Natural Law: A Jewish, Christian and Islamic Trialogue* (Oxford: Oxford University Press, 2014).
Engelhardt, H. Tristram, *The Foundations of Christian Bioethics*, 2nd edn (Oxford: Oxford University Press, 1996).
Eschmann, Ignatius Theodore, *Ethics of St. Thomas Aquinas*, Edward A. Synan, ed. (Toronto: Pontifical Institute of Medieval Studies, 1997).
Esposito, John L., *The Oxford Dictionary of Islam* (Oxford: Oxford University Press, 2003).
Evans, Malcolm D., *Religious Liberty and International Law in Europe* (Cambridge: Cambridge University Press, 1997).
Faith and Order Commission, *Moral Discernment in the Churches: A Study Document*, Faith and Order Paper 215 (Geneva: World Council of Churches, 2013).
Feser, Edward, *Aquinas* (London: OneWorld Publications, 2009).
Finnis, John, *Natural Law and Natural Rights*, 2nd edn (Oxford: Clarendon Press, 2011)
Finnis, John, 'Natural Law', in *Reason in Action: Collected Essays*, Vol. 1 (Oxford: Oxford University Press, 2011), 199–211.
Finnis, John, 'Natural Law Theories', in Edward N. Zalta, ed., *The Stanford Encyclopaedia of Philosophy* (Fall 2014 Edition): http://plato.stanford.edu/archives/fall2014/entries/natural-law-theories/.
Foot, Philippa, *Virtues and Vices* (Oxford: Blackwell, 1978).
Foot, Philippa, *Natural Goodness* (Oxford: Clarendon Press, 2001).
Fox, Marvin, 'Maimonides and Aquinas and Natural Law', *Dinei* 3 (1971): 5–36.
Fraher, Richard, 'Preventing Crime in the High Middle Ages: The Medieval Lawyers' Search for Deterrence', in Stanley Chodorow and James Sweeney, eds., *Popes, Teachers and the Canon Law in the Middle Ages: Festschrift for Brian Tierney* (Ithaca, NY: Cornell University Press, 1989), 212–233.
Frank, Richard M., 'Moral Obligations in Classical Muslim Theology', *Journal of Religious Ethics* 11 (1983): 205–223.
Franke, Reiner, *Die Entwicklung des (Darlehens-)Zinses in Frankreich* (Berlin: Duncker and Humblot, 1996).
Freeman, Michael, *Lloyd's Introduction to Jurisprudence*, 9th edn (London: Sweet & Maxwell, 2014).
Freppert, Lucas, *The Basis of Morality According to William Ockham* (Chicago, IL: Franciscan Herald Press, 1988).
Friedrich, Carl Joachim, *The Philosophy of Law in Historical Perspective*, 2nd edn, 5th impr. (Chicago and London: The University of Chicago Press, 1963).
Fuller, Lon L., 'Positivism and Fidelity to Law – A Reply to Professor Hart', *Harvard Law Review* 71(4) (1958): 630–672.
Fuller, Lon L., *The Morality of Law*, rev. edn (New Haven, CT: Yale University Press, 1969).
Gane, Mike, *Auguste Comte* (London: Routledge, 2006).
García, José Barrientos, *Un Siglo de moral económica en Salamanca, 1526–1629 Francisco de Vitoria y Domingo de Soto* (Salamanca: Ediciones Universidad Salamanca, 1985).

George, R.P., ed., *Natural Law Theory: Contemporary Essays* (Oxford: Clarendon Press, 1992).

George, R.P, *In Defense of Natural Law* (Oxford: Clarendon Press, 1999).

Gomez-Lobo, Alfonso, *Morality and the Human Goods: An Introduction to Natural Law Ethics* (Washington, DC: Georgetown University Press, 2002).

Goodliff, Paul, 'Baptist Church Polity and Practice', *Law and Justice: The Christian Law Review* 168 (2012): 5–21.

Gore, Charles, *Lambeth on Contraceptives* (London: Mowbray, 1930).

Goyette, John, Mark Latkovic and Richard S. Myers, *St. Thomas Aquinas and the Natural Law Tradition: Contemporary Perspectives* (Washington, DC: Catholic University of America Press, 2004).

Grabill, Stephen, *Rediscovering the Natural Law in Reformed Theological Ethics* (Atlanta, GA: Emory University Studies in Law and Religion, 2006).

Gray, John Chipman, *The Nature and Sources of the Law*, 2nd edn (Cambridge, MA: Harvard University Press, 1921).

Grayling, Anthony C., *The God Argument* (London: Bloomsbury, 2013).

Grayling, Anthony C., *What is Good?* (London: Weidenfeld and Nicolson, 2003).

Griffel, Frank, 'The Harmony of Natural Law and Shari'a in Islamist Theology', in A. Amanat and F. Griffel, eds., *Islamic Law in the Contemporary Context* (Palo Alto, CA: Stanford University Press, 2007), 38–61.

Grillo, Ralph, *Muslim Families, Politics and the Law* (Aldershot: Ashgate, 2015).

Grisez, Germain, 'Revelation versus Dissent', in John Wilkins, ed., *Understanding Veritatis Splendor* (London: SPCK, 1994), 1–8.

Grisez, Germain, 'The First Principle of Practical Reason: A Commentary on the *Summa Theologiae*, 1–2, Question 94, Article 2', *Natural Law Forum* 10 (1965): 168–201.

Gros, Jeffrey, Harding Meyer and William G. Rusch, eds., *Growth in Agreement II: Reports and Agreed Statements of Ecumenical Conversations on a World Level*, Faith and Order Paper 187 (Geneva: World Council of Churches, 2000).

Gros, Jeffrey, Thomas F. Best and Lorelei Fuchs, eds., *Growth in Agreement III: International Dialogue Texts and Agreed Statements*, Faith and Order Paper 204 (Geneva: World Council of Churches, 2007).

Growing Together in Unity and Mission, International Anglican-Roman Catholic Commission for Unity and Mission (2007): www.vatican.va/roman_curia/pontifical_councils/chrstuni/angl-comm-docs/rc_pc_chrstuni_doc_20070914_growing-together_en.html.

Gunter, W. Stephen, *Wesley and the Quadrilateral: Renewing the Conversation* (Nashville, TN: Abingdon Press, 1997).

Guroian, Vigen, *Incarnate Love: Essays in Orthodox Ethics* (Notre Dame, IN: University of Notre Dame Press, 1987).

Haakonssen, Knud, *Natural Law and Moral Philosophy: From Grotius to the Scottish Enlightenment* (Cambridge: Cambridge University Press, 1996).

Haakonssen, Knud, *Grotius, Pufendorf, and Modern Natural Law: The International Library of Critical Essays in the History of Philosophy* (Aldershot, England: Dartmouth, 1999).

Haara, Heikki, 'Pufendorf, Samuel', *Logos-ensyklopedia* (2014): http://filosofia.fi/node/6580/.

Halivini, David W., *Mishnah, Midrash and Gemara* (Cambridge, MA: Harvard University Press, 1986).

Harakas, Stanley S., 'Eastern Orthodox Perspectives on Natural Law', *American Journal of Jurisprudence* 24 (1979): 86–113.

Harakas, Stanley S., 'The Natural Law Teaching of the Eastern Orthodox Church', *Greek Orthodox Theological Review* IX (1964): 215–224.

Harakas, Stanley S., *For the Health of Body and Soul: An Eastern Orthodox Introduction to Bioethics* (Greek Orthodox Archdiocese of America, Brookline, MA: Holy Cross Orthodox Press, 1980): www.goarch.org/ourfaith/ourfaith8076.

Harrod, John A., *Weaving the Tapestry of Moral Judgement: Christian Ethics in a Plural World* (London: Epworth, 2007).

Hart, H.L.A., 'Positivism and the Separation of Law and Morals', *Harvard Law Review* 71(4) (1958): 593–629.

Hart, H.L.A., *Law, Liberty and Morality* (Oxford: Oxford University Press, 1963).

Hart, H.L.A., *The Concept of Law*, 2nd edn (Oxford: Oxford University Press, 1984).

Hart, Trevor, 'A Capacity for Ambiguity: The Barth-Brunner Debate Revisited', *Tyndale Bulletin* 44(2) (1993): 289–305.

Hartmann, Wilfried and Kenneth Pennington, eds., *The History of Medieval Canon Law in the Classical Period, 1140–1234* (Washington, DC: Catholic University of America Press, 2008).

Hauerwas, Stanley, *A Community of Character* (Notre Dame, IN: University of Notre Dame Press, 1981).

Hauerwas, Stanley, *A Peaceable Kingdom: A Primer in Christian Ethics* (Notre Dame, IN: University of Notre Dame Press, 1983).

Hauerwas, Stanley and William Williman, *Resident Aliens* (Nashville, TN: Abingdon Press, 1993).

Haymes, Brian, 'Thomas Helwys' *The Mystery of Iniquity*: Is it still Relevant in the Twenty-First Century?', in A.R. Cross and N.J. Wood, eds., *Exploring Baptist Origins*, Vol. 1 (Oxford: Centre for Baptist History and Heritage Studies, Regent's Park College, 2010), 60–77.

Heckel, Johannes, *Lex Caritatis: Eine juristische Untersuchung über das Recht in der Theologie Martin Luthers* (München: Abhandlungen der bayerischen Akademie der Wissenschaften, 1953).

Helm, Paul, *John Calvin's Ideas* (Oxford: Oxford University Press, 2004).

Helmholz, Richard H., 'Natural Law and Human Rights in English Law: From Bracton to Blackstone', *Ave Maria Law Review* 3 (2005): 1–22.

Helmholz, Richard H., *Natural Law in Court: A History of Legal Theory in Practice* (Cambridge, MA: Harvard University Press, 2015).

Helwys, Thomas, *A Short Declaration of the Mystery of Iniquity*, in Richard Groves, ed., *Classics of Religious Liberty*, Vol. 1 (Macon, GA: Mercer University Press, 1998), 53.

Hervada, Javier, *Critical Introduction to Natural Law*, Mindy Emmons, trans. (Quebec: Wilson & Lafleur, 2006).

Herzog, Rabbi Isaac, *The Main Institutions of Jewish Law*, 2 Vols. (London and New York: The Soncino Press Limited, 1st edn, 1936, 2nd edn, 1965).

Hettche, Matt, 'Christian Wolff', *Stanford Encyclopedia of Philosophy* (2014): http://plato.stanford.edu/entries/wolff-christian/.

Hill, Mark, 'Gospel and Order', *Ecclesiastical Law Journal* 4 (1996): 659–663.

Hittinger, Russell, *A Critique of the Natural Law Theory* (Notre Dame, IN: University of Notre Dame Press, 1987).

Hittinger, Russell, *The First Grace: Rediscovering the Natural Law in a Post-Christian World* (Wilmington, DE: ISI Books, 2003).

Hogan, Linda, *Confronting the Truth: Conscience in the Catholic Tradition* (New York: Paulist Press, 2000).

Holmes, Oliver Wendell, 'Natural Law', in *Collected Legal Papers* (New York: Harcourt, Brace and Howe, 1920, repr. 1952), 312.

Honderich, Ted, ed., *The Oxford Companion to Philosophy*, 2nd edn (Oxford: Oxford University Press, 2005).

Honoré, Tony, 'The Dependence of Morality on Law', *Oxford Journal of Legal Studies* 13 (1993): 1–17.

Hopkins, John, *A Scriptural, Ecclesiastical and Historical View of Slavery* (New York: Pooley and Co., 1861).

Hourani, George F., *Reason and Tradition in Islamic Ethics* (Cambridge: Cambridge University Press, 1985).

Hughes, Gerard J., 'Natural Law', in J.F. Childress and J. Macquarrie, eds., *A New Dictionary of Christian Ethics* (London: SCM Press, 1986), 412–414.

Hume, David, *Treatise of Human Nature*, L.A. Selby-Bigge, ed. (Oxford: Oxford University Press, 1888).

Hussain, Amina, 'Legal Pluralism, Religious Conservatism', in R. Sandberg, ed., *Religion and Legal Pluralism* (Aldershot: Ashgate, 2015), 151.

Hutchinson, D.S., 'Ethics', in Jonathan Barnes, ed., *The Cambridge Companion to Aristotle* (Cambridge: Cambridge University Press, 1995).

Hutchinson, D.S., *The First Grace: Rediscovering the Natural Law in a Post -Christian World* (Wilmington, DE: ISI Books, 2003).

Ibbetson, David J., *A Historical Introduction to the Law of Obligations* (Oxford: Oxford University Press, 1999).

Ingram, David, *Law: Key Concepts in Philosophy* (London: Continuum, 2006).

Jackson, Bernard S., 'The Jewish View of Natural Law', *Journal of Jewish Studies* 52.1 (2001): 136–145.

Jacob, Jonathan A., 'The Reasons of the Commandments: Rational Tradition without Natural Law', in J.A. Jacobs, ed., *Reason, Religion and Natural Law* (Oxford: Oxford University Press, 2012), 106.

Jacobs, Louis, ed., *Concise Companion to the Jewish Religion* (Oxford: Oxford University Press, 1999).

Jensen, Gregory, *Criticizing the Critics* (29 February 2009): http://palamas.info/criticizing-the-critics/.

Jensen, Gregory, *Orthodox Criticism of Natural Law* (23 February 2009): http://palamas.info/orthodox-criticism-of-natural-law/.

Joint Working Group, Roman Catholic Church and the World Council of Churches, 'The Ecumenical Dialogue on Moral Issues' (1995), *Ecumenical Review* 48 (1996): 143–154: www.wcc-coe.org/wcc/who/crete-08-e.html.

Jones, Richard G., *Groundwork of Christian Ethics* (London: Epworth, 1984).

Josefson, Ruben, *Guds och Sveriges lag: Studier i den lutherska socialetikens historia* (Uppsala: A.-B. Lundequistiska bokhandeln; Leipzig: Otto Harrassowitz, 1950), 19–22.

Joyce, Alison J., *Richard Hooker and Anglican Moral Theology* (Oxford: Oxford University Press, 2015).

Juntunen, Hannu, *Oikeuden idean teologiset perusteet* (Helsinki: Kauppakaari Lakimiesliiton Kustannus, 2000).

Kabir, Nahid A., *Young British Muslims* (Edinburgh: Edinburgh University Press, 2010).

Kalaitzidis, Pantelis, 'From the "Return of the Fathers" to the Need for a Modern Orthodox Theology', *St. Vladimir's Theological Quarterly* 54(1) (2010): 5–36.

Kant, Emmanuel, *Lectures on Ethics*, L. Enfield, ed. (London: Methuen, 1930).

Keenan, James F., 'The Open Debate: Moral Theology and the Lives of Gay and Lesbian Persons', *Theological Studies* 64 (2003): 127–151.

Keenan, James F., *A History of Catholic Moral Theology in the Twentieth Century* (London: Continuum, 2010).

Kelsen, Hans, 'The Law as a Specific Social Technique', *University of Chicago Law Review* 9 (1941): 75–97.

Kelsen, Hans, *General Theory of Law and State*, Anders Wedberg, trans. (Clark, NJ: The Law Book Exchange Ltd., 2009, originally Cambridge, MA: Harvard University Press, 1945).

Kerr, M., *Islamic Reform: The Political and Legal Theories of Muhammad Abduh and Rashid Rida* (Berkeley, CA: University of California Press, 1966).

Kessler, Diana, ed., *Together on the Way: Official Report of the Eighth Assembly of the World Council of Churches* (Geneva: World Council of Churches, 1999).

Klempa, William, 'John Calvin on Natural Law', in George Timothy, ed., *John Calvin and the Church: A Prism of Reform* (Westminster: John Knox, 1990), 72–76.

Kloosterman, Nelson D., 'A Response to "The Kingdom Of God Is Twofold": Natural Law and the Two Kingdoms in the Thought of Herman Bavinck by David VanDrunen', *Calvin Theological Journal* 45 (2010): 165–176.

Klug, Francesca, *Values for a Godless Age: The Story of the United Kingdom's New Bill of Rights* (Harmondsworth: Penguin, 2000).

Koffeman, Leo J., 'Human Dignity – An Ecumenical Understanding?', *Scriptura* 96 (2008): 288–298.

Koffeman, Leo J., 'How the Protestant Church in the Netherlands was born', in A. Plaisier and L.J. Koffeman, eds., *The Protestant Church in the Netherlands: Church Unity in the 21st Century: Stories and Reflections, Church Polity and Ecumenism – Global Perspectives*, Vol. IV (Zürich: LIT Verlag, 2014), 11–37.

Koffeman, Leo J., 'The Ecumenical Potential of Church Polity', *Ecclesiastical Law Journal* 17 (2015): 182–193.

Korkman, Petter, 'Valtio ja sen lait modernissa luonnonoikeusperinteessä' (The State and its Laws in the Modern Natural Rights Tradition), in J. Tontti, K. Mäkelä and H. Gylling, eds., *Filosofien oikeus* (Helsinki: Suomalainen Lakimiesyhdistys, 2001), 96–97.

Kulakov, Mikhail, 'Vladimir Nikolaievich Lossky', in John Witte Jr. and Frank S. Alexander, eds., *The Teachings of Modern Christianity: On Law, Politics, and Human Nature*, Vol. 1 (New York: Columbia University Press, 2006), 612.

Kyriazis, K.B., *To Physikon kei to Kanonikon Dikeion ex Epooseos Orthodoxou*, Vol. 1 (Athens: Apostolike Diakonia Press, 1957), 69.

Laing, Jacqueline A. and Russell Wilcox, eds., *The Natural Law Reader* (Chichester: Wiley-Blackwell, 2014).

Larsson, Birgitta, 'A Quest for Clarity: The World Council of Churches and Human Sexuality', *Ecumenical Review* 50 (1998): 30–40.

Leaman, Oliver, 'Maimonides and Natural Law', *Jewish Law Annual* 6 (1987): 78–93.

Leibniz, G.W., *Filosofisia tutkielmia* (Philosophical Studies), trans. into Finnish by T. Aho, K. Jylhämö, S. Kivistö, P. Korkman, M. Oksanen, A. Repo, M. Roinila, J. Siukonen, H. Sivenius and R. Vilkko (Helsinki: Gaudeamus Helsinki University Press, 2011).

Leibniz, G.W., *Frühe Jugendschriften zum Naturrecht*, trans. into German, H. von Hubertus Busche (Hamburg: Felix Meiner Verlag, 2003).

Leith, John H., *Introduction to the Reformed Tradition: A Way of Being the Christian Community*, rev. edn (London: Westminster John Knox Press, 1981).

Lesaffer, Randall, *European Legal History: A Cultural and Political Perspective*, Jan Arriens, trans. (Cambridge: Cambridge University Press, 2009).

Levering, Matthew, *Jewish-Christian Dialogue in the Life of Wisdom: Engagement with the Theology of David Novak* (London: Continuum, 2010).

Levering, Matthew, *Biblical Natural Law* (Oxford: Oxford University Press, 2012).
Levering, Matthew, 'Natural Law and Christianity', in A.M. Emon, M. Levering and D. Novak, *Natural Law: A Jewish, Christian and Islamic Trialogue* (Oxford: Oxford University Press, 2014), Chapter 2.
Lewis, H.D., *Morals and the New Theology* (London: Gollancz, 1947).
Lewis, H.D., *Our Experience of God* (London: GAU, 1959).
Lichtenstein, Aharon, 'Does Jewish Tradition recognize an Ethic Independent of Halakha?', in M. Fox, ed., *Modern Jewish Ethics: Theory and Practice* (Columbus, OH: Ohio State University Press, 1975), 62.
Lidgett, John Scott, *The Christian Religion* (London: Robert Cully, 1907).
Lisska, Anthony J., *Aquinas's Theory of Natural Law: An Analytic Reconstruction* (Oxford: Clarendon Press, 1996).
Little, David, 'Calvin and the Prospects for a Christian Theory of Natural Law', in G.H. Outka and P. Ramsey, eds., *Norm and Context in Christian Ethics* (London: SCM Press, 1968), 175–197.
Livingstone, Elizabeth A., ed., *The Concise Oxford Dictionary of the Christian Church*, 2nd rev. edn (New York: Oxford University Press, 2006).
Long, D. Stephen, *John Wesley's Moral Theology* (Nashville, TN: Abingdon Press, 2005).
Long, S.A., 'Natural Law or Autonomous Practical Reason: Problems for the New Natural Law Theory', in Robert P. George, ed., *Natural Law Theory: Contemporary Essays* (Oxford: Clarendon Press, 1992).
Lossky, Nikolay O., *History of Russian Philosophy* (New York: International Universities Press, 1951).
Louth, Andrew, 'The Greek Tradition', in Augustine Cassiday, ed., *The Orthodox Christian World* (Abingdon: Routledge, 2012), Chapter 1.
Luhmann, Niklas, *Law as a Social System* (Oxford: Oxford University Press, 2004).
Luhmann, Niklas, *A Sociological Theory of Law*, 2nd edn (London: Routledge, 2014).
Lumpkin, William L., *Baptist Confessions of Faith* (Valley Forge, PA: The Judson Press, 1969).
MacIntyre, Alisdair, 'Theories of Natural Law in the Culture of Advanced Modernity', in E.B. McLean, ed., *Common Truths: New Perspectives on Natural Law* (Wilmington, DE: ISI Books, 2004), 123–128.
MacIntyre, Alasdair, *Intractable Disputes about the Natural Law*, Lawrence S. Cunningham, ed. (Notre Dame, IN: University of Notre Dame Press, 2009).
Mackie, John L., *Ethics: Inventing Right and Wrong* (Harmondsworth: Penguin, 1977).
Maclagan, W.G., *The Theological Frontier of Ethics* (London: GAU, 1961).
Macy, J., 'Natural law', in A.A. Cohen and P. Mends-Flohr, eds., *20th Century Jewish Religious Thought* (Philadelphia, PA: The Jewish Publication Society, 2009), 663–672.
Maddox, Randy, 'Wesley's Engagement with the Natural Sciences', in R. Maddox and J. Vickers, eds., *Cambridge Companion to John Wesley* (Cambridge: Cambridge University Press, 2010), 160.
Maddox, Randy, *Responsible Grace* (Nashville, TN: Abingdon, 1994).
Makdisi, George, *Ibn 'Aqil: Religion and Culture in Classical Islam* (Edinburgh: Edinburgh University Press, 1997).
Manninen, Julia and Markus Wahlberg, 'G. W. F. Hegelin oikeusfilosofian synty ja asema' (The Formation and Status of G. W. F. Hegel's Philosophy of Right), in *G.W.F. Hegel, Oikeusfilosofian pääpiirteet eli luonnonoikeuden ja valtiotieteen perusteet*, Suomentanut ja selityksin varustanut Markus Wahlberg (Oulu: Kustannus Pohjoinen, 1994).

Mannion, Gerard and Eduardus Van der Borght, eds., *John Calvin's Ecclesiology: Ecumenical Perspectives* (London: Bloomsbury, 2011).
Marzoa, A., J. Miras, R. Rodriguez-Ocana and I.M. de Azpilcueta, *Exegetical Commentary on the Code of Canon Law*, Vol. III/2 (Montreal: Wilson & Lafleur, 2004).
Mawdudi, Abu al-Ala, *The Islamic Law and Constitution*, 2nd edn (Lahore: Islamic Publications, 1960).
Mawdudi, Abu al-Ala, *Islam ka nizam i hayat: The Islamic Way of Life*, K. Ahmad and K. Murad, trans. and ed. (Leicester: Islamic Foundation, 1986).
McClendon, James William, *Systematic Theology: Vol. 1, Ethics* (Nashville, TN: Abingdon Press, 1986).
McCoubrey, Hilaire, *The Obligation to Obey in Legal Theory* (Aldershot: Ashgate, 1997).
McGovern, John F., 'The Rise of New Economic Attitudes – Economic Humanism, Economic Nationalism – During the Later Middle Ages and the Renaissance', *Traditio* 26 (1970): 217–253.
McIlroy, David, 'Human Rights Theory: Fit for Purpose, Fundamentally Flawed or Reformable?', *Law and Justice: The Christian Law Review* 173 (2014): 129–144.
McInerny, Ralph, *Aquinas on Human Action: A Theory of Practice* (Washington, DC: Catholic University of America Press, 1992).
McLeod, Ian, *Legal Theory*, 2nd edn (London: Palgrave, 2003).
Meyer, Harding and Lukas Vischer, eds., *Growth in Agreement: Reports and Agreed Statements of Ecumenical Conversations on a World Level*, Faith and Order Paper 108 (New York/Geneva: Paulist Press/World Council of Churches, 1984).
Meyerson, Denise, *Understanding Jurisprudence* (London: Routledge, 2007).
Mill, John Stuart, *On Liberty* (London: Collins, 1962).
Mill, John Stuart, *On the Subjection of Women* (1869) (Oxford: Oxford World's Classic, 1912).
Mohamed, Y., *Fitra: The Islamic Concept of Human Nature* (London: Ta-Ha Publishers, 1996).
Moore, George Edward, *Principia Ethica* (Cambridge: Cambridge University Press, 1903).
Morelli, George, *Pastoral Considerations on Current Problems: Sex, Natural Law and Orthodoxy* (Orthodox Research Institute, April 1976): www.orthodoxresearchinstitute.org/articles/ethics/morelli_sex_natural_law.htm.
Muller, Richard A., *Calvin and the Reformed Tradition* (Grand Rapids: Baker, 2012).
Muller, Richard A., 'Diversity in the Reformed Tradition: A Historiographical Introduction', in Michael G. A. Haykin and Mark Jones, eds., *Drawn into Controversie: Reformed Theological Diversity and Debates within Seventeenth-Century British Puritanism* (Gottingen: Vandenhoek & Ruprecht, 2011), 17–30.
Nadler, Stephen, 'Baruch Spinoza and the Naturalization of Judaism', in M.L. Morgan and P.E. Gordon, eds., *The Cambridge Companion to Modern Jewish Philosophy* (Cambridge: Cambridge University Press, 2007), 14–34.
Nasr, Reza and Seyyed Vali, *Mawdudi and the Making of Islamic Revivalism* (Oxford: Oxford University Press, 1996).
Neilson, Morton E.J., ed., *Legal Philosophy: 5 Questions* (New York: Automatic-VIP Press, 2007).
Nobles, Richard, and David Schiff, 'The Evolution of Natural Law', in J. Penner, D. Schiff and R. Nobles, eds., *Jurisprudence and Legal Theory: Commentary and Materials* (London: Butterworth, 2002), 35.
Noonan, John T., *The Scholastic Analysis of Usury* (Cambridge, MA: Harvard University Press, 1957).

Norman, R. Stanton, *The Baptist Way: Distinctiveness of a Baptist Church* (Nashville, TN: Broadman and Holman, 2005).

Novak, David, 'Natural Law and Judaism', in A.M. Emon, M. Levering and D. Novak, eds., *Natural Law: A Jewish, Christian and Islamic Trialogue* (Oxford: Oxford University Press, 2014), Chapter 1.

Nussbaum, Martha, *Love's Knowledge* (Oxford: Oxford University Press, 1990).

O'Connor, Daniel John, *Aquinas and Natural Law* (London: Macmillan, 1967).

O'Donovan, Joan Lockwood, *Theology of Law and Authority in the English Reformation* (Grand Rapids, MI: William B. Eerdmans, 1991).

O'Donovan, Oliver, 'The Natural Ethic', in David F. Wright, ed., *Essays in Evangelical Social Ethics* (Exeter: Paternoster Press, 1979), Chapter 1.

O'Donovan, Oliver, *Resurrection and Moral Order: An Outline for Evangelical Ethics*, 2nd edn (Leicester: Apollos, 1994).

O'Donovan, Oliver and Joan Lockwood O'Donovan, eds., *From Irenaeus to Grotius: A Sourcebook in Christian Political Thought* (Grand Rapids, MI: William B. Eerdmans, 1999).

Ombres, Robert, 'Faith, Doctrine and Roman Catholic Canon Law', *Ecclesiastical Law Journal* 1 (1989): 33–41.

On Becoming a Christian: Insights from Scripture and the Patristic Writings (2006), Report of the Fifth Phase of the International Dialogue between Some Classical Pentecostal Church and Leaders and the Catholic Church (1998–2002): www.vatican.va/roman_curia/pontifical_councils/chrstuni/eccl-comm-docs/rc_pc_chrstuni_doc_20060101_becoming-a-christian_en.html.

Pahman, Dylan, 'Fr. Michael Butler: Orthodoxy and Natural Law' (21 June 2013): http://blog.acton.org/archives/56420-fr-michael-butler-orthodoxy-and-natural-law.html.

Pahman, Dylan, 'Orthodoxy and Natural Law: A Reappraisal' (7 March 2013): http://blog.acton.org/archives/51078-orthodoxy-and-natural-law-a-reappraisal.html.

Pailin, David A., *God and the Processes of Reality* (London: Routledge, 1989).

Parsons, Susan F., 'Feminist Ethics', in Bernard Hoose, ed., *Christian Ethics: An Introduction* (London: Cassell, 1998), 135–148.

Pelikan, Jaroslav, *What Has Athens to Do with Jerusalem? Timaeus and Genesis in Counterpoint* (Ann Arbor, MI: University of Michigan Press, 1998).

Perreau-Saussine, Amanda, 'Bentham and the Boot-Strappers of Jurisprudence: The Moral Commitments of a Rationalist Legal Positivist', *Cambridge Law Journal* 63(2) (2004): 346–383.

Peters, E.N., ed., *The Pio-Benedictine Code of Canon Law* (San Francisco, CA: Ignatius Press, 2001).

Pless, John T., 'After Barth: Three Lutheran Appraisals of Natural Law', in Robert C. Baker and R.C. Ehlke, ed., *Natural Law: A Lutheran Reappraisal* (St. Louis, MO: Concordia Publishing House, 2011), 117–134.

Plumb, John H., *England in the Eighteenth Century* (Harmondsworth: Pelican, 1950).

Plaatjies van Huffel, Mary Anne, *Principles of Reformed Church Polity* (Zurich: Lit Verlag, 2014).

Pope, Stephen J., 'Natural Law and Christian Ethics', in R. Gill, ed., *The Cambridge Companion to Christian Ethics* (Cambridge: Cambridge University Press), 77–95.

Pope, William Burt, *Compendium of Christian Theology* (London: Wesleyan Conference Office, 1875).

Porter, Jean, *Natural Law and Divine Law: Reclaiming the Tradition for Christian Ethics* (Grand Rapids, MI: William B. Eerdmans, 1999).

Porter, Jean, *Nature as Reason: A Thomistic Theory of the Natural Law* (Grand Rapids, MI: William B. Eerdmans, 2005).

Porter, Jean, 'Does the Natural Law provide a Universally Binding Morality?', in L.S. Cunningham, ed., *Intractable Disputes about Natural Law: Alisdair MacIntyre and Critics* (Notre Dame, IN: University of Notre Dame Press, 2009), 53–95.

Price, Richard, 'A Review of the Principal Questions in Morals', in L.A. Selby-Bigge, ed., *British Moralists*, Vol. II (Oxford: Oxford University Press, 1897), 151.

Pryor, C. Scott, 'God's Bridle: John Calvin's Application of Natural Law', *Journal of Law and Religion* 22 (2006): 225–254.

Pufendorf, Samuel von, *The Whole Duty of Man According to the Law of Nature*, trans. Andrew Tooke 1691, and by Basil Kennett (London, 1729) (Indianapolis, IN: Liberty Fund, 2003).

Ramsey, Paul, *Basic Christian Ethics* (Louisville, KY: Westminster John Knox Press, 1993).

Raunio, Antti, *Summe des christlichen Lebens: 'Die Goldene Regel' als Gesetz der Liebe in der Theologie Martin Luthers 1510 – 1527*, Veröffentlichungen des Instituts für europäische Geschichte (Mainz: Zabern Verlag, 2001).

Raunio, Antti, 'Divine and Natural Law in Luther and Melanchthon', in V. Mäkinen, ed., *The Lutheran Reformation and the Law* (Leiden, Boston: Brill, 2006), 21–61.

Raunio, Antti, 'Natural Law and Christian Love in Luther's Theology', in K. van Kooten Niekerk and Ulrik Nissen, eds., *Lidenskab & Stringens: Festskrift til Svend Andersen* (København: Forlaget Anis, 2008), 249–261.

Raz, Joseph, *The Authority of Law* (Oxford: Clarendon Press, 1979).

Raz, Joseph, 'Postema on Law's Autonomy and Practical Reasons: A Critical Comment', *Legal Theory* 4 (1998): 1.

Reed, Esther D., *The Genesis of Ethics* (London: Darton, Longman and Todd, 2000).

Reinhart, A. Kevin, *Before Revelation: The Boundaries of Muslim Moral Thought* (Albany, NY: State University of New York Press, 1995).

Report of the House of Bishops' Working Group on Human Sexuality, General Synod 1929 (London: Church House Publishing, 2013).

Reuver, Marc, *Faith and Law: Juridical Perspectives for the Ecumenical Movement* (Geneva: World Council of Churches, 2000).

Rhonheimer, Martin, 'The Secular State, Democracy, and Natural Law', in Marta Cartabia and Andrea Simoncini, eds., *Pope Benedict XVI's Legal Thought: A Dialogue on the Foundation of Law* (New York: Cambridge University Press, 2015), 79–92.

Robinson, O.F., T.D. Fergus and W.M. Gordon, *European Legal History*, 3rd edn (Oxford: Oxford University Press, 2000).

Rodopoulos, Panteleimon, *An Overview of Orthodox Canon Law*, W.J. Lillie, trans. (Rollinsford, NH: Orthodox Research Institute, 2007).

Roinila, Markku, 'Leibnizin oikeusfilosofia' (Leibniz's Philosophy of Right), in J. Tontti, K. Mäkelä and H. Gylling, eds., *Filosofien oikeus* (Helsinki: Suomalainen Lakimiesyhdistys, 2001), 133–152.

Romanides, John S., *Franks, Romans, Feudalism, and Doctrine* (Brookline, MA: Holy Cross Orthodox Press, 1981).

Rommen, Heinrich, *The Natural Law: A Study in Legal and Social History and Philosophy*, T.R. Hanley, trans. (Indianapolis, IN: Liberty Fund, 1999).

Roover, Raymond de, 'Scholastic Economics: Survival and Lasting Influence from the Sixteenth Century to Adam Smith', *Quarterly Journal of Economics* 69 (1955): 161–190.

Rubin, U., 'Hanafi', in Jane Dammen McAuliffe, ed., *Encyclopedia of the Qur'an* (Leiden: Brill, 2001–2006).

Rudavsky, Tamar, 'Natural Law in Judaism: A Reconsideration', in J.A. Jacobs, ed., *Reason, Religion and Natural Law: From Plato to Spinoza* (Oxford: Oxford University Press, 2012), 83.

Runyon, Thomas, *The New Creation: John Wesley's Theology Today* (Nashville, TN: Abingdon Press, 1958).

Ruston, R., *Human Rights and the Image of God* (London: SCM Press, 2004).

Saastamoinen, Kari, 'Morality of the Fallen Man: Samuel Pufendorf on Natural Law', *Studia Historica* (1995): 52.

Sagi, Avi, 'Natural Law and *Halakha*: A Critical Analysis', *The Jewish Law Annual* 13 (2000): 149–196.

Salzman, Todd A. and Michael G. Lawler, *The Sexual Person: Toward a Renewed Catholic Anthropology* (Washington, DC: Georgetown University Press, 2008).

Sandberg, Russell, *Religion, Law and Society* (Cambridge: Cambridge Univeristy Press, 2014).

Sandberg, Russell, 'The Impossible Compromise', in R Sandberg, ed., *Religion and Legal Pluralism* (Aldershot: Ashgate, 2015), 1.

Sandberg, Russell, 'The Failure of Legal Pluralism', *Ecclesiastical Law Journal* 18 (2016): 137–157.

Schecht, N.S., B.S. Jackson, S.M. Passamaneck, D. Piatelli and A.M. Rabello, eds., *An Introduction to the History and Sources of Jewish Law* (Oxford: Oxford University Press, 1996).

Seipp, David J., 'Trust and Conscience in Early Common Law', in C. Kenny, R. Sandberg, M. Hill and F. Cranmer, eds., *The Confluence of Law and Religion* (Cambridge: Cambridge University Press, 2016), 48.

Shepard, William E., *Sayyid Qutb and Islamic Activism* (Leiden: Brill, 1996).

Shier-Jones, Angela, *A Work in Progress: Methodists Doing Theology* (Peterborough: Epworth, 2005).

Sidgwick, Henry, *The Elements of Politics* (London: Macmillan, 1891).

Siewers, Alfred Kentigern, *Secular Privilege and Natural Law* (7 July 2014) Orthodox Christian Network: The Sounding: http://myocn.net/secular-privilege-and-natural-law/.

Simon, Yves R., *The Tradition of Natural Law*, Vukan Kuic, ed. (New York: Fordham University Press, 1965).

Smith, Robin, *Living in Covenant with God and One Another* (Geneva: World Council of Churches, 1992).

Some Issues in Human Sexuality: A Guide to the Debate, General Synod 1519 (London: Church House Publishing, 2003).

St. Adomnán of Iona, *Life of St. Columba*, Richard Sharpe, trans. (London: Penguin, 1995).

St. Adomnán, *Law of the Innocents (Cáin Adomnáin): A Seventh Century Law for the Protection of Non-Combatants*, Gilbert Markus, trans. (Kilmartin: Kilmartin House Trust, 2008).

Stassen, Glen H., 'Human Rights', in W.A. Dyrness and V-M. Karkkainen, eds., *Global Dictionary of Theology: A Resource for the Worldwide Church* (Downers Grove, IL: Inter Varsity Press, 2008), 405–413.

Stephen, James Fitzjames, *Liberty, Equality, Fraternity* (Cambridge: Cambridge University Press, 1967).

Stewart, Cameron, 'The Rule of Law and the Tinkerbell Effect: Theoretical Considerations, Criticisms and Justifications for the Rule of Law', *Maquarie Law Journal* 4 (2004): 135–164.

Stott, John, *New Issues Facing Christians Today* (London: Marshall Pickering, 1990).

Takala, Martti, *Lex Dei – Lex Politica Dei: teos ja Kaarle IX: nlainsäädäntö* (Helsinki: SHS/SKHS, 1993), 34–35.

The Canon Law: Letter and Spirit, The Canon Law Society of Great Britain and Ireland (London: Geoffrey Chapman, 1994).

The Church: Towards a Common Vision, Faith and Order Paper 214 (Geneva: World Council of Churches, 2013).

The Concise Oxford Dictionary of the Christian Church, 2nd rev. edn (New York: Oxford University Press, 2006) 'Orthodoxy'.

The Official Report of the Lambeth Conference 1998 (Harrisburg, PA: Morehouse Publishing, 1999).

The Qur'an, M.A.S. Abdel Haleem, trans. (Oxford: Oxford University Press, 2004).

The Rudder (or Pedalion), D. Cummings, trans. (Chicago, IL: The Orthodox Christian Educational Society, repr. 1957; Luna Printing Co., 1983).

Thorsen, Don, *The Wesleyan Quadrilateral* (Lexington, KY: Emeth Publisher, 2005).

Tierney, Brian, '*Natura id est Deus*: A Case of Juristic Pantheism?', *Journal of the History of Ideas* 24 (1963): 307–322.

Tierney, Brian, 'Natural Law and Natural Rights', in John Witte and Frank S. Alexander, eds., *Christianity and Law: An Introduction* (Cambridge: Cambridge University Press, 2008), 89–103.

Tollefsen, Christopher, 'Reasons for Action and Reasons for Belief', *Social Epistemology* 20 (2006): 55–65.

Torrance, Thomas F., *Calvin's Doctrine of Man* (London: Lutterworth Press, 1949).

Towards the Common Good, Statement on the Future of the Welfare Society by the Bishops of the Evangelical Lutheran Church of Finland (March 1999): http://sakasti.evl.fi/sakasti.nsf/0/AC5B7C3890F48F5AC22577030038D858/$FILE/Towards%20the%20Common%20Good.htm.

Tracy, David, *The Analogical Imagination* (London: SCM Press, 1981).

Troeltsch, Ernst, 'Christian Natural Law', in his *Religion in History*, J.L. Adams and W.F. Bense, trans. (Minneapolis, MN: Fortress Press, 1991), 159–167.

Valliere, Paul, 'Introduction to Modern Orthodoxy', in John Witte Jr and Frank S. Alexander, eds., *The Teachings of Modern Christianity: On Law, Politics, and Human Nature*, Vol. 1 (New York: Columbia University Press, 2006), 505.

Valliere, Paul, 'Vladimir Soloviev', in J. Witte and F.S. Alexander, eds., *The Teachings of Modern Christianity: On Law, Politics, and Human Nature*, Vol. 1 (New York: Columbia University Press, 2006), 533.

VanDrunen, David, *A Biblical Case for Natural Law*, Studies in Christian Social Ethics and Economics, No. 1 (Grand Rapids, MI: Acton Institute, 2006).

VanDrunen, David, *Natural Law and the Two Kingdoms: A Study in the Development of Reformed Social Thought* (Grand Rapids, MI: William B. Eerdmans, 2010).

VanDrunen, David, '"The Kingship of Christ is Twofold": Natural Law and the Two Kingdoms in the Thought of Herman Bavinck', *Calvin Theological Journal* 45 (2010): 147–164.

Van Til, C., 'Common Grace', *Proceedings of the Calvinistic Philosophy Club*, Edward Heerema, ed. (1941): 61.

Veatch, Henry Babcock, *Swimming Against the Current in Contemporary Philosophy: Occasional Essays and Papers*, Vol. 20 (Washington, DC: Catholic University of American Press, 1990).

Verhey, Alan, 'Natural Law in Aquinas and Calvin', in Clifton J. Orlebeke and Lewis B. Smedes, eds., *God and the Good* (Grand Rapids, MI: William B. Eerdmans, 1975), 86.

Wacks, Raymond, *Understanding Jurisprudence*, 3rd edn (Oxford: Oxford University Press, 2012).
Wakefield, Gordon, *Methodist Devotion* (London: Epworth Press, 1966).
Walzer, Michael, *Just and Unjust Wars: A Moral Argument with Historical Illustrations*, 4th edn (New York: Basic Books, 1977).
Ware, Metropolitan Kallistos, 'The "Neo-Patristic Synthesis"' (Lecture delivered at the Cambridge Orthodox Forum Lectures, Cambridge, 1 May 2012): www.ancientfaith.com /podcasts/cambridge/the_neo_patristic_synthesis.
Warnock, Geoffrey, *The Object of Morality* (London: Methuen, 1971).
Weatherhead, James L., ed., *The Constitution and Laws of the Church of Scotland* (Edinburgh: The Board of Practice and Procedure, 1997).
Weber, M., *Economy and Society* (Berkeley, CA: University of California Press, 1978).
Westerman, Pauline C., *The Disintegration of Natural Law Theory: Aquinas to Finnis* (Leiden; New York: Brill, 1998).
Whichcote, Benjamin, 'Several Discourses', reproduced in G.R. Evans and J.R. Wright, eds., *The Anglican Tradition: A Handbook of Sources* (London: SPCK, 1991), 284.
Whitby, Daniel, 'An answer to Sure Footing' (1666), reproduced in G.R. Evans and J.R. Wright, eds., *The Anglican Tradition: A Handbook of Sources* (London: SPCK, 1991), 263.
White, Barrington Raymond, *The English Baptists of the Seventeenth Century* (Didcot: Baptist Historical Society, 1996).
Wilken, Robert Louis, *The Spirit of Early Christian Thought: Seeking the Face of God* (New Haven, CT: Yale University Press, 2003).
Williams, Rowan, 'Richard Hooker: The Laws of Ecclesiastical Polity Revisited', *Ecclesiastical Law Journal* 8 (2006): 382–391.
Williams, Rowan, 'Civil and Religious Law in England – A Religious Perspective', *Ecclesiastical Law Journal* 10 (2008): 262–282.
Witte, John, *Law and Protestantism: The Legal Teachings of the Lutheran Reformation* (Cambridge: Cambridge University Press, 2002).
Witte, John, 'Natural Rights, Popular Sovereignty, and Covenant Politics: Johannes Althusius and the Dutch Revolt and Republic', *Mercy Law Review* 87 (2007): 565–627.
Wogaman, J. Philip, *A Christian Method of Moral Judgment* (London: SCM, 1976).
Wogaman, J. Philip, *Christian Ethics: An Historical Introduction* (London: SPCK, 1994).
Wolfe, Christopher, *Natural Law Liberalism* (New York: Cambridge University Press, 2006).
Wolfson, Harry A., *Philo: Foundations of Religious Philosophy in Judaism, Christianity and Islam*, Vol. 2 (Cambridge, MA: Harvard University Press, 1947).
Ziegler, Robert, 'Natural Law in the Lutheran Confessions', in R.C. Baker and R.C. Ehlke, eds., *Natural Law: A Lutheran Reappraisal* (St. Louis, MO: Concordia Publishing House), 65–78.
Zizioulas, John, *Being as Communion: Studies in Personhood and the Church* (New York: St. Vladimir's Seminary Press, 1997).

Index

For EU product safety concerns, contact us at Calle de José Abascal, 56–1°, 28003 Madrid, Spain or eugpsr@cambridge.org.

www.ingramcontent.com/pod-product-compliance
Lightning Source LLC
LaVergne TN
LVHW011523200926
848484LV00001B/129